RTÉ AND THE GLOBALISATION
OF IRISH TELEVISION

By Farrel Corcoran

intellect™
Bristol, UK
Portland, OR, USA

For Mary

'Farrel Corcoran has enjoyed the unique situation of simultaneously being a university Dean and the Chair of Governors of a national public service broadcaster. Such a privileged position allows the author, for the first time, to offer unique insider insights into the daily operations and pressures of such an institution infused with the dispassionate analytic abilities of a senior media academic. As a result, this fascinating and intellectually engaging book makes a major contribution to the controversial debates surrounding the globalisation of the media in the 21st Century.'

Art & Design

DATE DUE

Demco, Inc. 38-293

First published in UK in 2004 by
Intellect Books, PO Box 862, Bristol BS99 1DE, UK

First published in USA in 2004 by
Intellect Books, ISBS, 920 NE 58th Ave. Suite 300, Portland, Oregon 97213-3786, USA

Copy Editor: Holly Spradling
Cover Design: Gabriel Solomons

A catalogue record of this book is available from the British Library.
ISBN 1-84150-090-9

Printed in Great Britain by Antony Rowe Ltd.

CONTENTS

Progress is a Snail.

Gunther Grass

INTRODUCTION

For three quarters of the last century, RTÉ has dominated the media landscape in Ireland, first as Radio Eireann, the only radio station in the country, operating under the ever-watchful eye of the Government, and since 1961, as a public corporation with responsibility presently for three television and four radio channels. With a wider reach than all newspapers combined, RTÉ provides the dominant pictures of the world by which we make sense of life around us. It has played a major role in dominating the symbolic environment in which Irish people construct their sense of identity and weave the "common sense" that underpins the everyday life of the community. RTÉ's social role has been to find ways of "narrating the social" that make sense of their society for viewers and listeners, by drawing from the available stock of frameworks and narratives and marking the boundaries of what is permissible.

The question now is whether television and radio in the Western world have all but ceased to function as a shared public space. Some would argue that except for occasional media events – major sporting contests, public funerals, catastrophes or celebrations, major conquests in war or the rites of passage of the great, major acts of social excommunication – the nation no longer gathers together in a common symbolic space which commands attention from everyone and offers a gamut of views to feed the great national conversation that takes place in both public and private spaces every day of the year. Is national cohesion and political participation in jeopardy in Ireland? If democracy is practised primarily in the nation state and depends upon national identification to sustain collective solidarity and popular involvement in the democratic process, should we be concerned when changes in the media system brought about by globalisation no longer bring the nation together in one central space constituted by mass media? Is there a growing separation between the increasingly globalised television system and the nation state? Is media globalisation weakening national cultural identities?

The historical relationship between the media, the nation and globalisation is more complex than this. Economic globalisation is a complex, uneven and discontinuous process and the world economy was in some respects more integrated in the early 20th century, before the energy of the world's major empires was sapped away in World War I. The media were highly globalised in that period too, if we take into account the integrated power of the 19th-century news agencies – the French Havas, British Reuters and German Wolff – that divided the entire world market for news production and distribution among themselves. This cartel had the awesome power, without any competition, of defining the world in words and pictures for the European ruling class, supplying Governments with strategic information about far away places to guide war-planning and sustain the imperial system. But at the same time, as Benedict Anderson reminds us, localisation was also at work: newspapers in places like Latin America were redefining readers' sense of time and place so deeply that media audiences, within a generation or two, began to evolve into members of emerging national formations with their own distinct cultural identities, no longer mere colonies

1

of European powers.[1] Globalisation intensified in the period between the two World Wars in the 20th century. Two great American cultural industries were well into the process of achieving world hegemony by then: film and recorded music. But this is also the period when public service broadcasting, deeply indigenous in its ambitions, was established in several countries. The balance in globalising tendencies was tipped yet again when television successfully challenged cinema from 1950 on, restabilising national media systems at least in those places where the state was strong enough to provide resources for nationally originated material.

Even a brief historical overview is enough to caution against an overly deterministic – or pessimistic – view of cultural globalisation and the huge changes that are now taking place in broadcasting. These changes can be ambiguous in their effect and have the potential to take media developments in different directions. This book examines one particular broadcasting system in its present phase of transition, and the wider context in which it operates, European and global. Implicit in the analysis is a tension between the nation, where people find their identity, and the state, which regulates, provides resources and is a major link to globalising processes.

There is an important sense in which television functions as a collective rite of communion that evokes a sense of togetherness, a quickening of hope (the Celtic Tiger!), a sharing of disappointment, a celebration of common values, a renewal of a sense of national purpose. It can counteract, or exacerbate, tendencies towards the privatisation of experience and rampant individualism. When television first arrived in Ireland as a mass medium in 1961 (some people had already purchased sets as early as 1952, to participate in the cult of monarchy and its major rite of passage, the coronation of Elizabeth II), it was often portrayed as a modernising force, dragging society away from its traditional roots, especially what remained of Gaelic and Catholic tradition. Reactions to Gay Byrne's Late Late Show exemplified this. Academic critics of television took on board Frankfurt School beliefs that among the major casualties of the age of mechanical reproduction was a breakdown in the communal experience of a shared past. Yet today we might be inclined to think more positively that indigenous television content can provide a vital communal link with the nation, and to worry more about the ability, or the interest, of the state in maintaining a secure production base for an indigenous film and television culture. This base depends not only on RTÉ but also on how the mandate given to the Broadcasting Commission of Ireland is used. A secure production base for television and film holds out the promise of these popular media being able to maintain a creative connection with popular culture as it is lived in Ireland today, with all the ambiguities that this implies, without enduring the pathology of excessive dependence on a film and television culture produced in California.

In some parts of the world, especially in North America, there is a crisis in the relationship between the state, the nation and the media system, with all the dangers to democracy of the disenfranchisement of the public that this threatens. We have to look no further than CanWest, parent company of Ireland's TV 3, and the tensions created by editorial decisions on content that have inflamed relationships between media professionals, media owners and Canadian politicians. The CanWest controversy, explored later in this book, illustrates the dangers posed to press freedom and democratic governance by corporate centralisation of news editorial control. Quebec Communications Minister Diane Lemieux called the crisis in the Canwest system "an extremely concrete illustration of the dangers inherent in the heart of corporate media concentration." What is remarkable about the rapid accumulation of media power by CanWest in Canada is that it has passed almost unnoticed in Ireland, where the company's influence over Irish television, the regulation of broadcasting and the politics of media funding, is steadily increasing.

In other parts of the world, a combination of a weak television economy and an unregulated commercial television system, can wreak havoc on the public's right to good information and entertainment that connects them with the culture they live in. Ireland undoubtedly has a weak film and television economy, with cinema screens dominated by Hollywood's output and with nine television channels now dipping into a total pot of only 200 million in advertising revenue (RTÉ One, Network Two, TG4, TV3, UTV, Sky One, Sky News, Channel 4 and E4). Ireland also has a weak regulatory regime, with the BCI committed, like so many other European regulators before it influenced by the American *laissez-faire* regulatory model, to what is termed "light touch" regulation, and to continually increasing the number of radio and television channels that must operate within the same weak media economy. Both of these tendencies within the BCI heavily favour the agenda of the advertising industry and the business sector it serves, though the language used to justify this bias speaks of increasing viewer and listener "choice." It remains to be seen how Government will frame new broadcasting due before 2004, so that it will maximise the resourcing of indigenous programming in radio and television. Without this support from the state, television will follow in the footsteps of the cinema, for similar reasons: the cost of imports is a fraction of the cost of filling the same screen or time slot with an original production, and this creates an ever stronger pressure for global market integration in film and television.

A strong public service broadcasting system is clearly the best hope for original Irish production. But in much of the world, public broadcasting is now trying to withstand a combined ideological, political and commercial assault. New hostile lobbies have been formed in several countries, including Ireland: new deregulatory policies have been implemented; and new private broadcasters have been licensed to broadcast. Despite these assaults, RTÉ has just come through the worst period in its history and survived a radical "downsizing" in fairly good shape, with a stronger focus on new programming commitments issued as promises to its audience at the beginning of 2003. Crucial to its future will be its ability to increase its output of engaging indigenous programming, especially documentary and drama, and to sharpen its critical edge through investigative journalism, so that it never gets drawn back into a situation where it is closely identified with the state. To be relevant to the nation, it must maintain its critical distance from the state, even though this is the hand that feeds it.

Despite the importance of RTÉ in Irish life, very few books have been published which take aim at the institutional forces that shape the programme output.[2] But RTÉ needs to be examined as an institution, within the socio-political environment in which it operates. This wider context includes relationships with Government, changes in the competitive environment of Irish broadcasting, EU cultural politics and the rise of global media conglomerates. Very little research has been produced, even in other countries, which examines how decisions are produced within broadcasting organisations. This is because broadcasters generally do not provide easy access to academics who want to do fieldwork inside their organisation and this makes it difficult to gain real insight into other institutional relationships, involving Government or competitors. When the BBC opened its doors to social researchers, the experience only increased its resistance to such scrutiny in the future. Burn's classic study The BBC: Public Institution and Private World (1977) was published 14 years after the initial fieldwork, because of a veto exercised over publication by the Corporation. Schlesinger's study of television news, Putting Reality Together (1978) comes close to being a good insider view, but his fieldwork was completed only after he overcame a great deal of BBC wariness about the uses to which research results would be put. Academics' success in penetrating the BBC has been slower since then, especially after the critical work of the Glasgow Media Group was published, though fascinating aspects of the work of the Corporation can be perused in the work of John Tulloch, Henry Jenkins, Tim Madge, Paddy Scannell, David Cardiff and Manuel Alvarado.

HOW THIS BOOK IS STRUCTURED

When the Government appointed me Chairman of the RTÉ Authority in 1995, it dissolved the insider-outsider threshold for me. The point of view privileged in this book, therefore, is based on both an insider's hands-on engagement with strategic issues at the core of Irish broadcasting, and an outsider's long-term professional interest in broadcasting as an object of analysis in university settings, at different times Irish and American. The sources drawn upon here, apart from those referred to in footnotes, include a large amount of internal RTÉ documentation, reports, memos, minutes and personal diaries. The book necessarily makes a selection of themes to be pursued, omitting some important aspects of Irish broadcasting that certainly deserve examination. Aspects deserving of careful research in the future include RTÉ and its public, how we must understand broadcasters' audiences in the digital age, the effect of cultural globalisation on viewers' interests, and the role of audience research; how television programming takes shape within a broadcasting institution and the compromises that are made between the ideal schedule profile and what emerges after all the pressures have had an impact across Programme Departments; the emergence of the independent production sector in Ireland, major structural adjustments it generated within RTÉ and hopes for RTÉ's role in a rejuvenated film industry; major changes in the radio industry in Ireland since deregulation in the late 1980s and its impact on RTÉ; music policy in Ireland, the marginalisation of art music, the PIANO Report on the orchestras and RTÉ's responsibility as the country's most important patron of music. These are not dealt with here but certainly deserve thorough analysis in the future.

In the structure of what follows, we turn first to RTÉ as an institution and a workplace, at a time when the New Right ideology of deregulation and market liberalisation was gaining a firm foothold in Irish society. Chapter One includes a view from the Boardroom on how RTÉ is governed, an exploration of the crucial relationship between Chairman and Director General and the challenges posed by perceived weaknesses in RTÉ as it set about recruiting a new Director General in 1997. It also includes an examination of how a particularly sensitive programming issue appeared to the Authority, the challenges presented by television's new engagement with the Sinn Fein, energised by the ending of censorship that formed an essential part of the Peace Process then gaining momentum since the early 1990s. Chapter Two moves outside the confines of RTÉ to examine the regulation of broadcasting in Ireland and the political actors who influenced this in the 1990s, beginning with two very different Ministers, Ray Burke and Michael D. Higgins. It traces the evolution of ideas informing the Green Paper on Broadcasting and the response of various groups to this policy document. The debate shaping planned new broadcasting legislation was influenced as much by the increased penetration of non-Irish channels and the launch of indigenous competition for RTÉ, as it was by fascination with alternative models of regulation emerging elsewhere, especially the experience of New Zealand.

Chapter Three takes a closer look at the relationship between RTÉ and the Government in the broadcaster's continuing struggle to consolidate its self-governing independence, formally granted after it had ceased to be embedded in a Government department in the 1960s. Key moments in recent years include the crisis triggered by an RTÉ documentary exposing the identity of "poison pen" letter writer whose anonymous literary efforts amounted to what one Government Minister declared was "a naked attempt to destabilise the Government." Chapter Three also details the Government's role in approving (or refusing) important commercial ventures being pursued by RTÉ, such as the proposed investment in what was soon to become an extremely lucrative mobile phone market, as well as investment in the cable television business. Does Government dictate editorial policy to RTÉ? We analyse how RTÉ relates to Government as it tries to handle competing interests in coverage of referendum campaigns and we revisit the acrimonious debate in the RTÉ Authority about how the organisation should respond to legal challenges to its editorial practices. The account presented here differs sharply from an account of the same debate published in a recent book by another member of this RTÉ Authority.

Without realistic funding, public service broadcasting withers on the vine. Chapter Four tackles the economic forces impinging on the work of RTÉ, particularly the development of competition throughout the 1990s in radio and television, competition for audiences, for advertising revenue and for rights to acquired programming. The continuing struggle to convince politicians of the need for public funding forms a central part of this story. The next chapter examines the emergence of a new technology potentially more significant than colour television. When digital technology emerged from research laboratories in the early 1990s, it was a technology that "worked" in engineering terms but still had to develop a social, business and communicative purpose. Chapter Five analyses RTÉ's role in developing plans for Digital Terrestrial Television in Ireland and the ultimate failure of those plans to deliver an Irish system which could speed up the convergence of the Internet with television for the majority of the people.

The attention of broadcasters to the needs of children, the most vulnerable members of society, is often taken as an indicator of the strength or weakness of public service broadcasting in a particular country. Chapter Six examines RTÉ's relationship with children, against the backdrop of the emergence of children's television in the 1990s as a major global industry, driven initially by changes in the American television regulatory system and pressures within the toy industry. It also details some of the Boardroom battles that have taken place in RTÉ in recent times over the question of advertising directed at children. Chapter Seven explores Irish society's long and painful relationship with its native language and the struggle to establish a separate Irish language television channel, as the ambition to use the mass media to revive the language was supplanted by the notion of respecting minority language rights. In a broader sense, beyond the continuing struggle for funding and legitimacy in the body politic, TG4 is seen here as a creative reaction to the increasing sense of cultural globalisation widely discussed in the late 1990s.

Chapter Eight focuses directly on the theme of globalisation and offers an *entre* to theories of globalisation as a way to understand deep changes taking place in broadcasting. Part of the challenge presented to small countries like Ireland is how to safeguard public interest goals in broadcasting with the arrival of direct foreign investment in the television sector. CanWest's control of TV3 is relevant here, as are the controversies currently embroiling the parent company in Canada as it is seen by many to be reducing diversity of opinion in its widespread news operations and threatening press freedom. Chapter Nine briefly draws some conclusions and focuses on the question of the future of public service broadcasting in Ireland.

NOTES

[1] Benedict Anderson (1983) *Imagined Communities: Reflections on the Origin and Spread of Nationalism*. London: Verso.

[2] Gorham's *Forty Years of Irish Broadcasting* (1967) gives a historical account of radio in Ireland and Dowling, Doolan and Quinn's Sit Down and Be Counted (1969) examines a series of crises that dominated the first six years of RTÉ. Fisher's *Broadcasting in Ireland* (1978) chronicles the progress of RTÉ into its second decade. McLoone and MacMahon's *Television and Irish Society* (1984), Sheehan's *Irish Television Drama* (1987) and Devereux's *Devils and Angels* (1998) examine particular aspects of programming output. Savage's *Irish Television: Political and Social Origins* (1996) investigates the debate about television that flourished in the 1950s before RTÉ was established. Horgan's *Irish Media: A Critical History* (2001) is a history of both press and broadcasting across the eight decades since the foundation of the state. *Maverick* (2001) narrates the personal reminiscences of Bob Quinn, my former colleague on the RTÉ Authority, with a number of whose views I take issue in this book.

ACKNOWLEDGEMENTS

I owe a debt of gratitude to many people. Exchanges with both undergraduate and postgraduate students in Dublin City University have helped me greatly in thinking about the complex interplay that exists between the political economy of the media, how the media represent the world in their output, and how this cultural labour has an impact on society. Colleagues in the School of Communication have consistently provided a stimulating, interdisciplinary environment in which to let ideas about the public interest in media breathe and be refined. Many of them have themselves written about broadcasting, in books, academic journals and newspaper columns, as have former colleagues Luke Gibbons, Desmond Bell and Jeff Chown. I have benefited greatly from this research momentum, as I have from the work of colleagues in the UK, many of them also members of the International Association for Media and Communication Research, especially Richard Collins, James Curran, Nicholas Garnham, Peter Golding, Graham Murdock, Philip Schlesinger, Colin Sparks, Annabelle Sreberny and Brian Winston. In American scholarship, Herbert Schiller and Noam Chomsky have inspired a whole new generation of critical research. I am grateful to Slavko Splichal, Editor of Javnost-The Public in Slovenia, who has published some of the ideas here in slightly different form in his journal. I have benefited considerably from the advice of Manuel Alvarado, who provided at short notice valuable feedback on a first draft of this book, as well as from his detailed knowledge of the vagaries of the publishing business. A Government of Ireland Senior Research Fellowship allowed me to put aside the pleasures and demands of regular university work for a year. I am very grateful to the Irish Research Council for the Humanities and Social Sciences for this freedom to concentrate on writing, and for the support of Dublin City University in granting me sabbatical leave.

My ability to undertake institutional analysis of television in Ireland would have been severely curtailed had I not been given the opportunity to work as Chairman of RTÉ by Michael D. Higgins, Minister with responsibility for Broadcasting in the Rainbow Coalition Government. His passionate belief in the role of public broadcasting in fostering a healthy democracy (and his not infrequent frustrations with impediments to seeing RTÉ's full potential realised) was always inspiring, but especially so against the backdrop of a political environment where persistent Ministerial vision, rather than the tendency to simply arbitrate among competing forces, is a rare commodity. One of the major rewards of working in RTÉ has been the opportunity to meet many colleagues from different parts of the organisation, who generously gave me the benefit of their experience in broadcasting. Colleagues on the RTÉ Authority were liberal with their time and ideas and in helping to solve many of the problems encountered in the very practical work of regulation and policy-making: Garret Fitzgerald, Des Geraghty, Anne Haslam, Betty Purcell, Bob Quinn, Patricia Redlich, Maureen Rennicks and Anne Tannahill. My first major seminar on how RTÉ operated was given by Director General Joe Barry the Saturday morning after my appointment, over a pot of coffee in the Berkeley Court Hotel. Joe's unfailing courtesy and support throughout the early years, and informally since then, is greatly appreciated. Bob Collins, his successor, steered RTÉ through one of the darkest periods of its history, as the dreaded issue of "downsizing" had to be tackled, a time when it was also appropriate to face down the pessimists and plan for the future, including the launch of both Lyric FM and Teilifís na Gaeilge. His sharp wit, intellectual integrity and persistent sense of what public broadcasting was all about inspired everyone who worked with him and was a constant source of insight for me. My work as Chairman was greatly assisted by the keen professionalism and dedication to bridging the gap between the Authority and the organisation itself, embodied in Tom Quinn, Secretary to the Authority, ably supported by Carmel O'Reilly. Daphne O'Donnell operated a highly efficient office and gave many a good piece of advice on incoming or outgoing correspondence. Since leaving RTÉ, she also contributed a great deal to the preparation of this book for publication. A special word of appreciation is due to my predecessors in the Chairman's office and former Director Generals, men and women who served RTÉ very well in the past, always generous with their advice to me on the RTÉ of the present.

I have learned a great deal about broadcasting from those in senior management who worked closely with the Director General: Peter Branagan, , Niall Doyle, Claire Duignan, Cathal Goan, Kevin Healy, Liam Miller, Ed Mulhall, Joe Mulholland, Eugene Murray, Adrian Moynes, Gerry O'Brien, Pol O Gallchoir, Helen Shaw. I am grateful to many more people in RTÉ who shared their insights with me at various times: Vincent Browne, Con Bushe, Charles Byrne, Laurie Cearr, Seamus Crimmins, David Davin-Power, Pat Feeley, Peter Feeney, Marion Finucane, Michael Garvey, Paddy Glackin, Tommie Gorman, Tom Gormley, Dermot Horan, Tim Lehane, Brian Lynch, Mick McCarthy, Philip McGovern, John McMahon, Mike Milotte, Padhraig O Ciardha, Tony O'Connor, Margaret O'Farrell, Geraldine O'Leary, John O'Regan, Dominic O'Reilly, Mary O'Riordan, Colman Pearce, Richard Pine, Mary Rafferty, Gerry Reynolds, Alan Smale, Noel Smyth, Simon Taylor, Alan Walsh, Martyn Westerman. Critiques of my performance as Chairman from former broadcasters Muris Mac Conghail and Nollaig O Gadhra were always welcome, notwithstanding the robustness and certitude of their style.

Vitally important creative moments for meditating on the themes explored in this book were provided on many occasions during concerts by the National Symphony Orchestra and the RTÉ Concert Orchestra. I am grateful to the players and to the inspiring energy of their conductors, Alexander Anissimov, Gerhard Markson and Proinnsias O Duinn, for these wonderful acoustic spaces that signify, and stand in for, the full actualisation of the great potential of the total public service broadcasting system. These creative occasions forced on me again and again the amazing realisation that this system, despite its many financial crises over the years, has been able to sustain, against all the odds, an oasis of inspired musical performance for so long in what would otherwise be an empty desert.

Above all of these, if I single out my family for special thanks, it is because they have been a constant source of encouragement in my work. My children, John, Medb and Oisin, have lived with the obsession of this book for longer than we all should have. My most intensely felt debt is to Mary O'Connell, the best media critic I know, who has been more than generous in sharing her own insights, advice and finely honed sense of how the media should perform. I have benefited enormously from her ever-alert sense of right and wrong in public life and I have drawn energy from her fierce indignation at how power is so frequently abused. Her supportive patience in the face of my long preoccupation with this project, with all the bouts of isolation involved in writing and revision, was the secure foundation for the whole undertaking.

1 RTÉ UNSETTLED

A combination of technological innovation and grand vision has characterised key moments in the development of mass communication since its inception. If we look at the history of the steady stream of communications technologies that have been introduced into Western societies over the last 150 years, we find some are developed successfully from prototype to invention and into the marketplace, while others are rejected by the market and become historical redundancies. Despite the brilliance of their prototypes, some technologies are constrained by social forces that coalesce to limit the threat of disruption to the status quo that can be caused by the new technologies. A working telegraph was demonstrated as early as 1816 but the British Navy refused to acknowledge the superiority of electromagnetic over semaphore technology in long-distance signalling, until changes in naval battle formation demanded a better than line-of-sight system. The difference between success and failure is frequently related to the presence or absence of utopian discourse that grabs a hold of the public imagination and influences whether and how the new technology is adapted for social use.

In the dismal year of 1947, many people in Ireland grew disenchanted with the Fianna Fail Party for not producing rapid improvements in living standards at the end of the Second World War and prepared to vote the party out after 16 years in office, at the General Election of February 1948. At the same time, Radio Eireann was going through a new phase of expansion and development. Plans were drawn up to launch a short-wave radio station, so that listeners in America, India and South Africa would be able to hear programmes from Ireland, what the Minister P. J. Little referred to as the best that is to be found in Ireland, "the everyday story of the new Ireland, spoken with its own voice."[1] The station would have an output of 100 kilowatts, using a transmitter of the latest type available, just out of the laboratory stage, which would dwarf in power even Vatican Radio's powerful reach across the globe. Production too would be boosted, through the addition of Outside Broadcasting officers who would travel up and down the country, recording local singers, seanchais (storytellers) and local events. The goal of putting Ireland worthily before the world also entailed expanding the Radio Eireann Orchestra and establishing a second or salon orchestra "for the higher kinds of music."

Big technology, big vision. An early moment of globalisation. The short wave station failed to materialise but the two orchestras survived the change of Government and went on to become the National Symphony Orchestra and the RTÉ Concert Orchestra of today, that play such a large role in the musical life of contemporary Ireland, in concert halls of varying degrees of comfort across the country. P. J. Little's vision is belatedly fulfilled as the two orchestras now reach overseas audiences directly through tours and by technological mediation via satellite and the Internet.

In the middle of 1995, when the RTÉ Authority I was to chair for five years took office, new technologies were again coming onto the agenda of public debate. The concept of digital compression had just recently moved out of the electronic engineering laboratories into the boardrooms of large communications corporations. The British Government was moving quietly to ignore digital television's potential for providing a new high definition 1000+ line standard, which would give viewers an image crispness to match that developed by NASA for observing space explorations. It was licensing the technology to the established television companies in Britain so that they could expand the number of channels they controlled and lever themselves into stronger market positions by exploiting the potential of digital compression. If accurate public information on digital compression and its possibilities was hard to come by in 1995, there was no shortage of visionary rhetoric.

The Clinton-Gore Administration took an early lead in the Western world in creating a political project out of the emerging popularity of the Internet and the new opportunities it opened up for global communication. George Bush's attempt to define the post-Communist world in the early 1990s as moving towards a New International Order led by the US, retained a distinctly Old Order feel to it when his ad hoc alliance of Western and Arab forces locked horns with Iraq in the Gulf War to protect oil supplies to the West. But Clinton's notion of a Global Information Infrastructure, promoted vigorously at high-level international venues – G7, OECD, World Bank and IMF meetings – recaptured some of the Kennedy-era style of driving a political project with the force of a vision tied to new communication technologies.

Kennedy's New Frontier vision both fed off and reinforced the utopian imagination that infused discussion of television in the early 1960s, at a time when sales of television sets escalated dramatically in the US and foreign earnings from television programme syndication came to match domestic American revenues. Marshall McLuhan gave academic respectability to the Cold War rhetoric of global television which, diffused by American satellite technology, would sweep scattered populations worldwide into a single Enlightenment embrace: school children receiving space-based educational programmes in the classrooms of India, African farmers learning modern agricultural techniques that would defeat poverty, citizens of the Global Village who would espouse democratic values and strengthen the Free World against the perils of Communism. As a popular medium, television would shore up Third World unrest and win hearts and minds for the steady spread of US multinational corporations and military bases around the world. American New Frontier global television rhetoric integrated into a single utopian project the economic interests of the largest corporations and the government's foreign policy, in all its Cold War polarisation of Western freedom against Soviet totalitarianism. The dominant discourse of the time brought together into one seamless ideological whole the dream of enhanced global community and co-operation, with the imperial ambitions of the superpower struggle. It promised a better quality of life for all, at the same time as it locked in US hegemony. It offered the free exchange of ideas worldwide while also consolidating corporate goals. It was actually called the doctrine of Free Flow for many years by American diplomats, until a Third World revolt in UNESCO began to relabel it Cultural Imperialism.

MARKET LIBERALISATION

Thirty years later, the Clinton-Gore project offered a new discursive framework within which to think about the future, but it was based on an older ideological structure, adjusted for the fall of Communism. The idealised "global society" now about to emerge, with the worldwide spread of the Internet, would caringly, even passionately, address public purposes, but the means to pursue these would be private enterprise rather than state intervention. It would entail the global application of some key concepts: free trade, industrial development, modernisation, technological progress, and, above all, competition. The term "globalisation" began to gain currency. The very big corporate players were already in a frenzy of conglomeration, as media giants consolidated joint ventures, strategic alliances and cross-ownership deals: Time Warner (now merged with AOL), News Corporation, Viacom, Bertelsmann, TCI, CLT, Kirch and others. In the wake of developments in the Reagan-Thatcher era, the post-Cold War revival of the ideology of market liberalisation was on a roll, sweeping through policy-making and media spaces alike, accusing its critics on the left of being out of date and out of step with the times. Only "dinosaurs" opposed the inherent goodness of competition. Giant media corporations would now be the main players in the Global Information Infrastructure and individual states would settle into their new role as brokers of agreements, law takers rather than law makers, no longer devising policy but more often acting on Information Society issues originating in corporate headquarters, framed and articulated in the World Trade Organisation, the International Telecommunications Union, the World Intellectual Property Organisation and other global institutions. Unprecedented levels of political power were quietly slipping away from national control to a handful of supranational agencies devoid of democratic accountability. The Global Information Infrastructure was advancing on the basis of the decline of Soviet-style totalitarian social models but at the expense of public service social models, as deregulatory frameworks gave ever more autonomy to private capital in the communication sector.

The European Commission followed the American lead and took up the cause of the market liberalisation of information with ever more fervour in the 1990s, with Commissioner Martin Bangemann leading the ideological charge. The Information Society would enhance democratic principles, add huge new capacities to human intelligence and build a more equal and balanced society. The French Government had secured a little breathing space in its GATT battle with White House trade negotiator Mickey Cantor, ably advised by Hollywood's seasoned veteran lobbyist Jack Valenti, in gaining a temporary "cultural exception" for transnational audiovisual trade. This inserted a vital non-economic recognition into the meaning of communication in trade negotiations, mostly film and television, though American negotiators seemed genuinely surprised that Information Sector issues should have any higher claim on public policy than does clothing, or soap powder or food and drink. Non-discriminatory access to all domestic markets, regardless of its cultural impact or the destruction of domestic media industries, was to them the highest principle of international law.

But the French victory in 1993 was a temporary aberration in the drive by multinational corporations to restore competition to what liberal marketeers regarded as its "natural state" and to press back the power of the state to what they saw as the twin pillars of its proper minimal terrain: to guarantee law and order and to uphold the primacy of property rights. Pushed to its logical limits, this policy thrust would provide no space for public interest criteria, such as content diversity in radio, television or cinema, or the right of universal access to high quality, affordable information and entertainment. Cultural policies to enforce obligations of media pluralism within national territories, still a core value in Europe but not recognised in the US, would be recast as barriers to international trade in information services. Policies to limit concentration in media ownership, so that competition could emerge, were to be seen, paradoxically, as unacceptably interventionist distortions of trade. And public subsidies in Europe to protect universal service or diversity in media output, were increasingly being redefined in complaints to the Commission as a form of "state aid" that interfered with the "level playing field" of free trade and thus threatened proprietary freedoms within the cultural sector. Regulatory force was being applied on the media supply-side only, to protect the freedom to make profits by media companies, but it was not being applied to the demand-side, to protect citizens' rights to a universal service that offered a genuine plurality of content in a healthy public sphere. The accelerating trend towards the market liberalisation of information recognised no inherent relationship whatsoever between information conditions in society and democratic conditions. This relationship is as old as the earliest thinking in civic republicanism that originated in Greece. It emphasised that, freed from the rule of tyrants, self-government can be given a quality check by examining the social conditions that either encourage or exclude space for an enlightened citizenry, or in today's jargon, a healthy public sphere.

The Global Information Infrastructure of the Clinton-Gore years must therefore be seen as deeply ideological and two-edged in its thrust. True, it offered liberation for all, like Kennedy's New Frontier before it, via a wired, digital, interconnected world. But this promised liberation would take place against a backdrop of dramatically redistributing power from the public to the private sector, a movement which represented what many academic commentators saw as a concentration of public communication under proprietary governance on a scale not encountered since the passing of feudal society. There is a glaring paradox in this shift of power. It was being facilitated by Government action in a growing number of countries, enacting public policy which conferred enormous new powers of regulation on a handful of supranational agencies that have no democratic accountability mechanisms designed into their structures, in the way the United Nations does. We now turn to an examination of broadcasting in Ireland, to see how it functions against this international backdrop.

ROLE OF MEDIA

This book is about Irish broadcasting, mostly television, in the 1990s. When the Global Information Infrastructure vision was being outlined by American press agents at the G7 meeting in Brussels in 1995, Michael D. Higgins had just published a Green Paper on Broadcasting, to which I had contributed. It was intended to initiate a public debate by pointing up some of these global trends and their relevance for Ireland. There was little information on offer on how to tackle the issues that would emerge from digital convergence, but there was plenty on the vulnerability of public service broadcasting in a world where the ideology of deregulation and market liberalisation was sweeping all before it. Later that year, I was asked to take on the job of Chairman of the RTÉ Authority, the governing body that is entrusted with representing the public interest in the running of the national public service broadcasting system. Working within an organisation doesn't automatically provide a ladder for climbing to insightful vantage points, especially when local interests and anxieties interfere with realistic interpretation of contemporary trends in broadcasting. All vantage points produce partial views, of course, and the perspective of the Chairman is not the same as that of a programme producer or a news editorial manager. The point of view in my case is based on a combination of an insider's hands-on engagement with strategic issues at the core of the public broadcasting organisation, and an outsider's long-term professional interest in media as important objects of research and university teaching. This was inflected by thirty years of experience in Ireland and the US of academic involvement with the sociology of culture and the role of media in society.

During the five years between 1995 and 2000, the gap between theory and practice had to be bridged quickly on the RTÉ Authority. And it was a fascinating experience. I found myself directly engaged with some of the most profound changes that have ever taken place in Irish broadcasting. These changes included the establishment of the Irish-language television channel Teilifis na Gaeilge (now TG4); the arrival of the Canadian-based multinational television company CanWest in Ireland as a major force in the launch of TV3 (to be followed by Granada as co-owner); the opening up of the radio sector to increased competition in the form of private radio, led by the national station Radio Ireland (now Today FM); the launch by RTÉ of the classical music station Lyric FM; and the development of a national strategy for digital television.

Ireland's geographical position in the northwest European archipelago close to Britain, and its sharing of a common language with its more densely populated neighbour, are important historical factors in its very stressful and complicated relationship with England. They are also important factors in the relationship between broadcasters and audiences in Ireland. Broadcasting overspill into Ireland from transmitters in Northern Ireland and the west of England has been part of the Irish experience of radio and television from the very beginning. As new technologies of distribution arrived, cable, microwave, deflectors (legal and illegal) and satellite, British television channels reached ever deeper into Irish villages and valleys. More than 80 percent of the population today has access to British channels and this percentage is already increasing with the current deployment of the Sky and Freesat satellite systems.

Since overspill could not be prevented, Government response initially was to launch first a national radio station, then a national television channel, in the hope that the availability of an Irish perspective, rooted in Irish popular culture, would counteract any feared negative cultural influence from the old imperial centre. Government and ecclesiastical censors were active in the early development of both radio and television and were even more ferocious in their condemnation of most forms of sexual representation in films, novels and occasionally stage plays. But a pragmatic approach was adopted towards British television. Since it couldn't be stopped, it was ignored. And in any case, British television reception did not extend into the rural Irish heartland until the 1980s, and even then did not succeed in capturing a significant share of the available audience. A ministerial proposal in the mid-1970s to set up a second national television channel, which would in effect retransmit a selection of BBC programmes, was roundly defeated by an adroit public campaign by RTÉ and overwhelming survey evidence that most Irish people wanted a second RTÉ channel in preference to an increase in the availability of British television, however worthy the selection of content might be.

In contemporary Ireland, not only has the Church lost its credibility as a censor, due largely to the sexual conduct of some of its clerics, but the format, production values and styles of Irish-made television have converged steadily with those driving British television (which themselves have converged with other European and American television systems). During my term as Chairman, I received only a single complaint from a bishop about RTÉ output, and this was an accusation from the Bishop of Meath that a Prime Time documentary on a proposed sex education course for school children wasn't critical enough of the course. Fears that access to British television would allow Sinn Fein to reach Irish audiences were allayed when Margaret Thatcher put in place television censorship that paralleled what was known as Section 31 censorship in Ireland. Both states withdrew these controls in the early 1990s as a "confidence-building" measure to draw Sinn Fein into the politics of the fledgling peace process in Northern Ireland. The period from 1995 to the present reveals Irish broadcasting's deeper engagement with processes that have come to be labelled "globalisation" and that have had a profoundly unsettling impact on the national public broadcasting system, an impact greater than anything it has ever experienced since its inception. This book examines these developments with a view to being able to peer into the near future and see what kind of broadcasting we may have in Ireland over the next decade.

For about 40 years, RTÉ's radio and television channels have played an enormous role in shaping Irish social and cultural life. As the national publicly owned and funded broadcaster, RTÉ is probably the biggest cinema, school, sports stadium, market square, performance stage, town crier and concert hall in Ireland. In its news, current affairs, sports, serial drama and documentary output especially, it sets the agenda for the national conversation that drives modern Ireland. With a reach wider than all newspapers combined, it provides the dominant pictures of the world that underpin economic and political life and it is the most influential source of explanations in private as well as public spheres. It is the dominant creator of the imagery by which we make sense of our lives and society around us. RTÉ may not quite be able to tell the nation what to think, but it certainly tells the nation what to think about. In its work of interpreting Ireland to itself, it necessarily selects certain aspects of the world and frames them in particular ways so that they dominate citizens' worldviews for significant periods of time. It has the power to magnify or shrink issues of potential public importance. Sometimes it succeeds in making issues command the attention of Governments as matters of urgent public policy.

Radio and television play a historically unprecedented role in dominating the symbolic environment of modern life from early childhood. They begin to socialise children almost at the same time as family influences are activated, taking over much of that basic master narrative role once occupied by other cultural institutions and sources of identity – religion, class, nationality, family, workplace, locality – that have declined in influence in proportion to the growing power of the media and the leisure industry – and the consumer lifestyles in which both are bound up in this period of late capitalism. Powerful flows of messages and images in both fiction and non-fiction genres now tell most of the stories, most of the time. Through these dense networks of narrative, Irish people create their own sense of identity, their awareness of unity and feelings of difference, and create their place in an increasingly globalised world. Through the media-driven streams of discourse surrounding us daily, rooted in our lifeworld, we shape our conceptions of reality and spin out the collective "common sense" which underpins everyday life. This forms the basic tissue of the prevailing sense of communality in every part of Ireland. This may be the electronic media's most powerful and important effect.

Contentious public argument is part of this national conversation, as representatives of different ideological carrier groups, situated in their own particular spaces in the social structure, contest entrenched positions on the airwaves, polarise what might have been sets of mundane truths and draw on the accents and conventions of Irish talk to articulate their positions. This is how democracy is supposed to function, of course, drawing on a public sphere that is nurtured by a healthy media system sensitive to the need for pluralism and diversity in the market place of ideas. In its ideal existence, against which actual performance can be measured – the normatively perfect model of public broadcasting that should inspire it – RTÉ nurtures this public sphere, by facilitating the articulation of different discourses from different parts of society. When it is at its best, RTÉ also performs a kind of due diligence on the public sphere on behalf of its stakeholders – individual citizens and licence fee payers – by fulfilling its role as a public watchdog, revealing abuses in the exercise of power and generating debate on the functioning of Government.

RTÉ plays a role across the dimension of time too, as it controls the most powerful technology of memory in modern Ireland. Through its archive of radio and television programmes, now being digitised, an archive that is significantly expanded just as soon as yesterday's broadcasting day is ended, RTÉ is the most important producer and custodian of collective memory in the country. Important symbolic residues of events that occurred in the twentieth century (and of historical representations of events before that) are deposited on contemporary recollection and appear in public life through the creation of literature and other arts, but especially through the popular media of radio and television. Memory feeds identity, which acts as a powerful motive force of history.[2] Cultural memory creates the bonds that attach people together through the collective consciousness that undergirds the contemporary sense of the self in this media-saturated phase of late modernity. All of our individual identities require a cultural grounding. We find it in the patterned meanings of the dominant culture, Irish society's sense of itself that is particularised in the experience of each individual within it. Whether these structures of public meaning remain sturdy, or become destabilised or even traumatised, is an outcome of the representational processes of the media, what Walter Lippmann long before the arrival of television called the "pictures in our heads." These are subtly enmeshed with the output of the cultural industries, particularly radio and television. In an increasingly media-driven society, representation is all: social crises and social triumphs are mediated to us through a complex semiotic of representation that transforms the social into the cultural, the event into its public meaning. The complexity of the SARS crisis is all contained in the endlessly reproduced close-up of a surgically masked face in a Hong Kong street.

Several forces shape RTÉ as an organisation of highly skilled media workers. Some of these developed over time inside the organisation; some are perpetually pressing against it from the outside. Legislation, public policy debates and Government decisions have a profound, though often subtle, influence, as does the tradition of interpreting what is expected of public service broadcasting accumulated over the years by successive RTÉ Authorities, Directors-General, Executive Boards, Producer groups and so on. The institution of RTÉ is shaped by the accumulation, in its organisational memory, in its various explicit and implicit codes of work, of standards regarding best practice in the production of radio and television programmes. Professional norms, ideologies and work practices, rarely foregrounded for inspection but exerting a powerful influence on new recruits, shape the output of every Division and Department. This ranges from the news values that underpin the work of the RTÉ Newsroom, to international music programming norms applied to the appointment of a new Principal Conductor and the design of a new concert season for the National Symphony Orchestra, to notions of "public service" infusing Authority decisions. Resources, or lack of them, influence everything, much more than is acknowledged in popular or academic critiques.

Institutional structures function within a wider economic and political context. RTÉ Television was launched in the early 1960s but had little time to enjoy its monopoly position, as first terrestrial overspill from Wales and Northern Ireland, then cable and satellite technologies, and recently MMDS and digital satellite signals, brought into the country channels originating in the UK and beyond, most of them resourced to levels that dwarf RTÉ's comparatively puny revenue streams. Today, viewers in less than 25 percent of Irish households are restricted to the Irish national channels. In the late 1980s, the wave of deregulation that surged across the European political system on the heels of the ideological wash of neo-liberalism out of Reagan's Washington and Thatcher's London, finally lapped on Irish shores. RTÉ Radio now competes for listeners' attention with a robust, privately owned local radio sector as well as a national, private, commercial station and a growing number of community stations. After a decade of false starts, private television finally appeared at the end of the decade in the form of TV3, now consolidating its position with a shrewdness in fighting its corner with regulators learned from its sister stations in Canada, Australia and New Zealand. With the arrival of very lightly regulated private broadcasting, democratic capitalism in Ireland took on board more stridently than ever before the ideology of market liberalisation and perhaps a certain structure of feeling going with it that coincided with the arrival of the cultural manifestations of the Celtic Tiger.

While the aims and operating ethos of public and private broadcasters are fundamentally different, they compete for audiences, advertising revenue and programme rights in ever tightening spirals of rivalry that neo-liberal ideologists would have us believe are designed for the sole benefit of viewers and listeners. Recent moves to establish digital television and facilitate its convergence with the Internet underscore the relevance of the global context in which RTÉ operates. In a real sense its competitors include not only Canwest, Canadian parent company of TV3 and the world's largest buyer of American film and television material outside of the US itself, and its TV3 partner Granada Television, but also the large British broadcasters, now available in over 75 percent of Irish homes, eating inexorably into what used to be RTÉ's audience share. More ominous competitive pressures can be discerned in recent shifts in the broader political economy of the media, in the huge global conglomerates emerging over the last ten years, their appetites for profit in overseas markets whetted by the prospect of implementing new "windowing" strategies with the arrival of digital convergence. These strategies aim to create more and more opportunities to show the same media content, extracting added value each time from subscriptions or advertising or both. Chief among these conglomerates is Rupert Murdoch's News Corporation, often regarded as the prototype of the twenty-first-century media corporation, because of the zeal with which it pursues vertical and horizontal integration within a vast transcontinental media system.

RTÉ AND THE NEW RIGHT

This book is an examination of RTÉ's present state of health and an investigation of its future. It is aimed at a relative vacuum that exists in public knowledge of what happens behind the cameras and the microphones in Montrose, behind the production of the endless output of radio and television that is scatter-beamed from transmitters every day and consumed in large amounts by Irish people. For all the rhetorical support of Government Ministers for public service broadcasting and its vaunted value to the democratic functioning of Irish social life, there is little real understanding of RTÉ as a cultural institution outside of those who work there. Even among staff, particular positions within the organisational structure can sometimes create significant blind spots in understanding the deep changes that are taking place in broadcasting worldwide. Politicians grudgingly recognise the symbiotic relationship they enjoy with broadcast journalists and prominent presenters and warm to public condemnation of broadcasters' mistakes and failures. But in my dealings with the political representatives of the people, the most common scenario I encountered was an immediate quickening of interest among them in such weighty matters as the income of star television presenters, such as Gay Byrne (who just managed to slip into retirement without his salary becoming public knowledge) but stifled yawns at the mere mention of the need to develop a long-term policy for broadcasting in Ireland.

The situation is not very different when the press turns its attention to broadcasting. The glamorisation of television stars, inherited from the Hollywood system, dominates tabloid newspaper coverage of RTÉ. Elsewhere in the press, entrenched news values dictate that almost any story about RTÉ is newsworthy, however much massaging must be applied to it before it gains some substance, and that "RTÉ" in a front-page headline will sell papers (as "BBC" will in Britain). Yet much of the press coverage of RTÉ is trivial, gossipy, disjointed, ill-informed or lazy. Frequently it is biased by a dominant newspaper editorial demand for a negative angle, emanating not just from general news values rooted in old journalistic traditions, but also from an over-developed sense of cross-media competition, between television and newspapers, for advertising support. RTÉ stories are not infrequently biased by journalists' unacknowledged personal grudges or still sensitive emotional wounds inflicted at one time or another in some part of the RTÉ organisation. But despite all of this, the series of public meetings in towns all across Ireland, arranged over the last eight years by the Director-General and his senior management team, has demonstrated a surprising level of public interest in engaging in serious discussion about broadcasting and in knowing more about how the national public service broadcaster does its work. This book intends to contribute to this curiosity so that debate about broadcasting can be more informed.

Because Ireland is a relatively small, homogeneous country that has depended entirely on a public service broadcasting system for so long, the monopoly position of RTÉ has meant that it has influenced probably every individual and group in the country in some way, directly or indirectly. But it also means that so many people have wanted to influence its output. Small country, many agendas. Engagement with RTÉ, positive and negative, runs very deep in Ireland. It is argued over every night in kitchens and pubs. There is intense interest in how it does its work, fuelled by the recently enacted Freedom of Information law and the increase in the number of newspaper stories that can now more easily line up RTÉ in their sights. Entrenched news values dictate that this range-finding exercise is driven by a thirst for bad news – and this may have social implications for future public support for it. Like many media companies, RTÉ's work is frequently shrouded in secrecy and mystique, which in turn often translates into an ideology of glamorisation that stands in the way of understanding. In the absence of transparency and a real effort to demystify this national institution, conspiracy theories abound.

Philip Elliott once pointed out the importance of institutional metaphors deployed by the leadership of the BBC at different stages in its development, in setting out a vision for all its staff and stakeholders.[3] John Reith favoured nautical metaphors, others used the "mirror of society," still others the notion of the BBC as the "register" of different voices on the "great stage." I favour Jurgen Habermas's concept of the "Public

Sphere" and have used it within RTÉ for defining the mission of public broadcasting. It is also at the core of this book, as is the notion of "globalisation," as a way of referring to the broader world context in which Irish broadcasting takes place. The work of mediating and re-presenting the world through radio and television takes place within specific institutional structures, and it is these that form the central focus of what follows, rather than programme output and the way the world is represented in it. The concern here is for policy, strategy and institutional interaction with the political-economic environment of the late 1990s. That environment is Irish, European and global.

The language of the new right was having a quiet impact on Ireland in this period, in particular on the set of principles – social, political, economic and cultural – through which the idea of public service broadcasting is articulated. One began to hear more frequently the notion that paying for television from the public purse will become obsolete, that it will be replaced by direct subscription and commercial funding. A market model began to emerge in public discussion, attacking the concept of a citizenry needing a public sphere with universal access, in which human experience is that is enriched by the media. The language of "increased choice" for the individual was being elevated as the bedrock of a new culture constructed around the market. Ways of talking about radio and television showed signs of changing too, especially in the output of the new radio stations, as they increasingly interpreted their relations with their audiences not in terms of maintaining a common culture in a rapidly changing Ireland but in terms of the demographic needs of advertising. Challenges posed to the very idea of public culture became widespread and strident, as they had done a decade earlier in Britain. These originated in the proposition that social good flows, not so much from collective activity organised from the top down, but from millions of individual decisions organised from the bottom up. What matters is consumer sovereignty, the principle that brings together into a single ideological belief the notion of the individual person as both economic actor and also the possessor of basic democratic rights, but now democracy is thought of as exercised more in the shopping mall than in the polling both. Indeed, the idea was gaining ground during the Celtic Tiger period, that markets, with their blind mechanisms of supply and demand, and their reliance on market survey and focus group, manage to express the popular will more articulately and more meaningfully than do mere elections. Since markets express the will of the people, any criticism of market distortions of popular culture and broadcasting, or any suggestion that society can be organised in any way other than the market way, could be described as elitist. By their very nature, new right ideology was insisting, markets confer democratic legitimacy and give us what we want. One had to struggle harder now to be heard above the public muzak with an argument that people are not only consumers in the market economy but also citizens within the democratic system, and that they have the right to be adequately informed about matters relating to the common good. If earlier periods in Irish life were marked by a more collectivist concept of public culture and a shared experience of a continuous past, the 1990s were being marked by market populism as a new secular religion, the promised liberation of the individual as consumer, encouraged daily to think from within the self and its wants, rather than with any developed sense of community able to offset the gravitational pull towards possessive individualism.

My own hope in the mid-1990s was that the idea of the public sphere – that is, a media space accessible to everyone in society, where a diversity of viewpoints on life could thrive in a broad range of fiction and non-fiction broadcasting genres – could nudge broadcasters and policy-makers alike to bestow a central place in the policy agenda to the further development, rather than the abandonment, of the benefits of public service broadcasting. Between this ideal, in all its hopefulness, and the reality of an under-resourced RTÉ, many a shadow would fall. These shadows include inadequate funding, poor organisation of resources, low staff morale, the clamorous clobbering of an emerging breed of new right commentators in the newspapers and so on. And, in fairness to the best critics, who go to some effort to point out how RTÉ could be better, an attempt is sometimes made by broadcasters to use "public service broadcasting" as a shibboleth behind which to protect shoddy programmes from well-deserved criticism. The result of this is to create cynicism rather than support for public broadcasting. But with more of an effort to articulate clearly what public radio and television should and could achieve, we could both avoid the shibboleth syndrome and work to maintain in Ireland, despite our small population base and economy, a broadcasting system at least as good as what we have had in the past, or as good as best practice in broadcasting economies of comparable size.

My personal and professional experience of American media has convinced me that the dominant US model of a market system for producing media culture is deeply flawed. Yet many commentators and politicians in Ireland have been tilting admiringly towards the American model, although most of them have had no direct experience of the output they produce. The operation of the market across the Atlantic produces a media culture (sometimes referred to as "the world of the media") whose dominant tendency is shallow, trivial, voyeuristic, exploitative and deeply frustrating of the human desire for better narratives (since all forms of broadcasting is based on story-telling) that would enrich the human experience. Its news culture keeps the citizenry in a state of deep, parochial ignorance of what its Government gets up to in its foreign adventures. Michael Tracey, an English academic working in an American university, is correct when he argues that the greater use of the market principle in broadcasting beyond the US will inevitably have a negative impact of the prevailing character of culture in every country. The dilemma that many societies now face is that the felt need to be modern and economically successful "will force the rejection of those values and sentiments that are felt in the heart. The social, psychological and emotional consequences will be substantial and disturbing. In short, in importing the US economic model, they will also import the social neuroses which lurk in that deeply troubled society. That, I think, is sad."[4] The precedent set for new post-Soviet states by changes in US media policy was formally raised in the middle of 2003 by the Organisation for Security and Co-operation in Europe (OSCE). Of particular concern to the OSCE was the proposed FCC change that would allow big broadcasters and newspapers to own more radio and television stations, even in the same city, and how the culture of press freedom would be impacted by allowing a further concentration of information in the hands of major media owners, such as News Corp., General Electric, Disney, Viacom and AOL Time Warner.[5]

VIEW FROM THE BOARDROOM

When the new RTÉ Authority that took up office in the middle of 1995, our first task was to come to grips with the mix of personalities and talents at senior management level, so that together we could fashion the necessary consensus behind a programme of work for the development of RTÉ. Since this aspect of Board behaviour is generally assumed to be unproblematic, it is not analysed very often. Yet one hears from time to time of communication difficulties and serious breakdowns in Board functioning, that can have a major impact on how an organisations functions. Little of this is ever analysed, because conventions of privacy and confidentiality surround the workings of Boards, and maybe there is also more than a little macho posturing that denies the existence of Boardroom tensions. Therefore some insight into the operation of the RTÉ Authority is in order here: how we "gelled," how consensus was reached and missed, how the Authority related to staff and senior management.

At the beginning, there was a heightened awareness of the party political affiliations of colleagues on the Authority, but this rapidly receded as we began the process of deep immersion in the issues facing RTÉ. Party affiliations were very strong among some colleagues and practically non-existent among others, but it was always surprising that they played no role in our deliberations for the next five years. Members' professional backgrounds had a much greater influence on debates: academia, trade union movement, private business, media production, politics, journalism and publishing. Party affiliation was discussed only once, when we appointed a recruitment sub-committee in 1996 to find a replacement for Joe Barry, when he announced his retirement from the role of Director-General. Mindful of the controversial refusal of Government to approve the appointment of John Sorohan to the same job in 1985, and the subsequent decision to appoint Vincent Finn, and motivated by this to forefend against possible accusations of political party influence in the choice of next Director-General, I explicitly took account of our links with the three-party Rainbow coalition when assembling the recruitment sub-committee. In most cases, these links were very informal. But it was a concern of mine rather than something that derived from contention within the Authority, where some members even urged that we ignore party links. When I invited Garret Fitzgerald to join the sub-committee in place of Bob Quinn, the only objection came from then Fianna Fail Opposition spokesperson on Broadcasting, Sile De Valera, who called on the RTÉ Authority and the Minister to clarify Dr Fitzgerald's position as matter of urgency, arguing that it was wrong to have a former Leader of a political party sitting on an interview panel in a highly sensitive state board. No objection came from any other quarter and we proceeded with our search.

Access to the media was one of the first issues we had to confront and it continued to dog us for much of our term of office. It has also presented problems on other state boards, especially where individual members disagree with the majority view on important issues and want to use the media to be seen to be distanced from a Board decision. Press access is part of the wider issue of how information flows within and between institutions. Should Board members be able to access information directly from any part of the organisation that they govern, or would such direct Boardroom requests unsettle staff unnecessarily and undermine senior management? How should a balance be struck between the need for Board members to have access to certain information in order to facilitate policy-making, and the possibility of maverick or even mischievous requests for information which bypass the rest of the Board and senior management? How should Boards develop a code of conduct among members about areas of discretion and confidentiality? How should information about Boardroom decisions and debates be shared with staff generally?

The organisational culture that had evolved in RTÉ up to the mid-1990s did not encourage high levels of information flow between Authority and staff, despite growing pressure from staff, especially in television production, to know what was happening at Authority and Executive Board levels. Pressure to change this was mounting under the influence of a new model of Industrial Relations emerging in other public companies, shaping the work of the RTÉ Trade Union Group Forum that was established in the wake of the major strike in RTÉ earlier in the decade. This new model played a significant role later in the formation of the Partnership structures in 1998 that underpinned the Transformation Agreement. Openness was also encouraged by the debate on the enactment of the Freedom of Information Bill, which was starting to gain momentum. Surveys of staff morale pointed to various levels of frustration with information deficit, particularly regarding the transparency of the Authority's own deliberations and alienation between staff at Department level and middle management. Betty Purcell, Editor of the very successful television current affairs programme *Questions and Answers*, had been elected onto the Authority by staff, as a result of an innovative decision by Michael D. Higgins to fill one of the nine seats. It was intended that this would open up staff-Authority communication and build stronger links, though it was emphasised that this was not a Worker Director position. Betty had campaigned for staff support on the issue of transparency and promised to produce a monthly Newsletter and provide feedback to staff on Authority decisions.

This proved to be an extremely difficult thing on which to find agreement. We spent a lot of time debating the merits of a Newsletter authored by an individual Authority member, versus one generated by and seen to represent the Authority as a whole. Senior management felt uneasy about what it saw as an undermining of its primary role in the flow of information to staff. We eventually agree that the Newsletter should be seen to come from the whole Authority, that Betty Purcell would draft the text in consultation with me, and that it would be published in the staff magazine *Access*. It took a surprising amount of debate to arrive at this consensus, such was the culture of information control in which we were all immersed, with all its anxieties about the possible effects of releasing information. This was an organisational culture built up over many years in RTÉ, but it was also part of the wider Irish culture, which had not yet been exposed to the intense public debate that was generated by Eithne Fitzgerald's plan to radicalise access to information in a FOI Bill. Greater openness in decision-making was being encouraged by a growing public awareness of how decisions are made outside of Ireland, especially in Sweden. Publishing the Newsletter probably went some way to dissolving the mystique surrounding Authority meetings, and it certainly did not cause any discernible problems for management. Pent-up curiosity among staff quickly dissipated and the Newsletter very soon lost its "must read" status.

A much more intractable problem for the new Authority was the question of how it would relate to the media. This was pitched onto our agenda in October 1995 when our debate on children and advertising was suddenly opened up to scrutiny by Bob Quinn on the Pat Kenny Show on radio. He blandly declared that both European law and RTÉ's own Guidelines were being transgressed every day in the programme schedules and lambasted RTÉ for being " damn near a pure commercial station ... drowning in commercials." This intervention raised an interesting question. While Bob Quinn insisted he was speaking personally and not representing the Authority, for how long could this distinction be maintained in the public mind? Surely there would be some association established with a general Authority position, since he would be deemed to be reflecting at least some element of discussion at Authority meetings? An Authority member's presence on such a programme would make it impossible to have a management representative on the same programme, possibly disagreeing in public on major issues and causing confusion about which is the corporate voice of RTÉ.

There were some crucial issues of civil rights to be disentangled here, as well as issues of solidarity and group responsibility in corporate governance. As citizens of a democracy, individual Authority members obviously have the usual rights of free speech, yet there are occasions when these rights have to be tempered by duties imposed by membership of a corporate body such as RTÉ. There are certain occasions when engagement with the media in public debate is not only inappropriate but actually damaging to the credibility of the Authority and therefore to its effectiveness as trustee of the public interest in broadcasting. Some form of self-discipline must be adopted whereby a collective process, co-ordinated by the Chairman, must regulate what, how and when the Authority communicates with the media. After considerable debate, we adopted a policy which would allow us to speak with one voice and avoid carrying our internal debates into the media before we had arrived at some closure on decisions. This meant being able to recognise issues that are "live," either in the sense that they are on the rolling agenda for further discussion pending closure, or that they could arrive on that agenda precipitously, such as the simmering issue of how RTÉ was reporting on difficulties being experienced in the Catholic Church relating to child abuse. The tension between the individual's urge to speak out and the group's need for solidarity, was submerged rather than resolved. It was to appear once more during the recruitment of a new Director-General and again during discussions about how referendum campaigns should be reported on RTÉ and how RTÉ should respond to legal interventions by Anthony Coughlan.

Anonymous leaks cause no less difficulty for any Board, as we found in the middle of the process of deciding among four internal candidates – Bob Collins, Liam Miller, Joe Mulholland and Eugene Murray – on the shortlist for appointment to the position of Director-General at the end of 1996. Working in RTÉ often feels like operating in a giant fish bowl, with journalists of all types peering hungrily through the glass in search of some morsels of gossip. Choosing a new CEO is one of the most important events in the life of an organisation and generates high levels of curiosity. Search Committee meetings took place away from Montrose, in order to minimise the gossip factor. Leaks could hurt any of the contenders in the final stage, all of whom would continue to work in RTÉ, and damage the credibility of the Authority's approach to what was one of the major decisions it would make during its term of office. Despite our precautions, the *Sunday Tribune* carried a report towards the end of our search on the merits of each candidate, built on leaks from our Committee that presented information uncannily close to what we actually shared in an atmosphere of intense confidentiality. The need for secrecy was heightened by our desire to be able to present a decision to the first Cabinet meeting of 1997 and our anxiety about receiving prompt Government approval for that decision, so that a smooth transition in leadership could be achieved. We did not want a repetition of the political rocking of the boat that took place in 1985 or any possibility that our decision would be tainted with suggestions that it was party-politically loaded in any way.

AUTHORITY – DIRECTOR-GENERAL RELATIONSHIP

If appointing a new Director-General is one of the most important decisions an Authority can make, the efficacy of that decision is greatly reduced unless the Authority, and in particular the Chairman, can work with the Director-General in an atmosphere of mutual trust. Initially, this means focussing on the fuzzy line between regulation and policy-making on the one hand, and executive functions on the other, and getting a general, often tacit, agreement from colleagues on where that line is to be drawn. In most corporations, public and private, the Board takes the major strategic decisions and retains full, legal control of the organisation, while allowing management sufficient flexibility to run the business efficiently and effectively within a centralised framework of accountability. Board members have access to the advice of the Secretary, the executive responsibility for ensuring Authority procedures are followed and supplying members with information on which decisions can be based. In our case, Tom Quinn played that role with great distinction.

Most Boards reserve certain areas of corporate activity for direct review, including approval of annual financial statements, corporate planning, annual budgets, investment in joint ventures, major acquisitions and disposals, major contracts and capital expenditure, responsibility for overall organisational structure, particularly the reporting relationships of senior executives, and senior management appointments. In many ways, the relationship between RTÉ Chairman and Director-General is crucial to the successful leadership of the whole enterprise. Mutual trust and respect take time to build up to the optimal level. The Chairman must come to know that management is providing needed information in a thoroughly transparent way and acting on Authority decisions. The Director- General must come to knows that the Chairman will give support in the public arena and to Government when needed, hold the Board together during times of contention, keep the whole governance of the organisation intact and strive to reduce the divisiveness that can wreck a Board and stymie the work of the organisation.

This does not mean that a cosy duopoly has to reign, or that the best role for the Chairman is to "go native." The relationship of trust must in fact be tempered in an environment where each can critique the other. Individual personality factors and interpersonal styles will shape the expression of this critique, as will social codes of hierarchy, deference and authority that have their roots deep in Irish culture. Despite its relatively short history, the organisational culture of RTÉ is the result of an organisational memory on which former Chairmen, Chairwomen (there was only one) and Directors-General, their portraits solemnly lining one wall of the Boardroom, have etched their own unique styles.

On taking up office, I was aware of previous tensions in the vitally important and complex Chairman-Director-General relationship, mirrored in other state companies also, which tended to cast a shadow over the way the Authority and the Executive articulated with each other. There are two extreme positions, between which every Board has to find its own ground. One is the chronically weak Board, passive, undermotivated, diffident, underqualified, bringing very little new expertise to the leadership of the organisation, so that it tends not to challenge the Chief Executive, either because it doesn't want to or because it isn't organised to do so. Such Boards mostly rubber stamp the plans of the Chief Executive, who regards the Board as little more than a legitimiser and legal defender of decisions taken elsewhere. The other model is the Board that is overbearing in its style, unrealistic in its expectations, unreflective of its limitations, suspicious of management, led by a Chairman who relishes the egoistic pleasure of usurping Chief Executive power and mounting frequent raids across that blurred line separating policy and executive domains, sometimes even setting up and maintaining a camp on the opposite shore with an open-door policy of receiving every disgruntled employee who wants to gripe, and thus undermining the role of the Chief Executive.

As Joe Barry, former Director-General, pointed out to me, there is a solitary aspect to the job of CEO which often requires very lonely decisions. The management development process tends to place a strong emphasis on team play and many managers' rise to senior ranks is dependent on the encouragement they receive from their bosses. But once they get into the corner office on the top floor of the RTÉ Administration Building marked "DG," there is no one there to give positive feedback. Add to that vacuum Irish cultural codes of deference and reticence, which prevent colleagues from acknowledging achievement and administering praise, plus a style of newspaper comment which creates news values around negative, often very cruel and cynical, depictions of RTÉ. This negativism is also related to the Irish penchant for "slagging," very noticeable to anyone who has worked with the more direct communication style dominant in North American organisations. The result is a powerful need at the top of the organisation for a relationship between Chairman and Director-General where issues can be discussed in total confidence, over a working lunch or a late evening chat in the office. Worries can be shared, new ideas can be tried out away from the glare of scrutiny in the Boardroom, and positive feedback can be given on the achievements of the CEO where appropriate. This is also important after particularly fractious Authority meetings, where the demands of some members may be too unrealistic, as with the issue of children and advertising (see Chapter 6), or members may have difficulty sticking with a decision in a complex legal area, like the dispute over how to handle referendum coverage (see Chapter 3). I was extremely fortunate as Chairman to work with two very able Directors General, Joe Barry and Bob Collins, with whom a good, open, trusting relationship could be built. This trust was to prove vitally important as we moved on to deal with sensitive issues such as political communication, and to make some major decisions on the future of digital television in an intellectual atmosphere where no one, inside or outside the country, could claim to know all the answers and be sure of making the right decisions.

CHOOSING A DIRECTOR-GENERAL

For all its obvious importance, the way the RTÉ Director-General is chosen is little understood because rarely discussed. In many companies, the question of CEO succession remains an obscure area of Board management. The succession process has traditionally unfolded behind locked doors, a little like Papal succession, in an atmosphere of rumour and counter rumour and suspicions of political influence. In the past such secrecy was taken for granted. Today it is not. The relationship between Authority and Director-General has become much more complex than in earlier periods of RTÉ's history, when the overall broadcasting environment was stable: no new competition from either inside or outside the country; no competition from new radio and television channels; no new radio or televisions services to be established within RTÉ; no threats to privatising the transmission network or any other part of the organisation; no challenges presented by digital compression and the convergence of broadcasting, telecommunications and the Internet; no major foreign investors in Irish broadcasting, such as Granada, CanWest or Scottish Media Holdings.

Authorities now need to be active agents shaping the organisational structure of RTÉ and overseeing the entire Director-General succession process in a manner that is careful, rigorous and defensible. Conventional corporate wisdom suggests that the best source of CEO candidates is inside the corporation itself, provided there has been in place an effective management development programme that will enable successors to emerge from within. There is a real risk in many companies that if an outsider is brought in as CEO, most of the top management will bolt for the door and seek their fortunes elsewhere. From this point of view, it is probably better to bring outside talent into the executive pool of candidates well before the CEO departs, so that an abrupt cultural revolution can be avoided. Boards need to have direct contact from time to time with promising candidates, both formally, at Board meetings where presentations are made and interrogated, and informally, in casual conversations on social occasions. It is important that the incumbent does not manipulate the succession process by steering it towards one candidate and thus closing down the options too soon. Yet it is necessary that the incumbent give some thought to creating a pool of potential successors, if necessary by bringing new people from outside the organisation into the top management pool. Many companies now have a formal policy of regularly seeding the management team with outsiders, to prevent its management from becoming in-bred. This implies that the CEO evaluates this team individually and shares evaluations with the Board, which needs to get a strong sense of candidates' managerial skills but also their sturdiness in standing up to the venal temptations of the job. There are no reporting relationships except to the Chairman, and less frequently to the whole Board , and the job carries a number of potentially ego-boosting perquisites that can be abused or can provide opportunities for the CEO to regress into an overly autocratic managerial style that can quickly destroy staff morale.

The Authority appointed in 1995 had just a year before appointing a new Director-General to get a sense of how RTÉ was fulfilling its public service remit, to be confident that we knew where both the strengths and the weaknesses were to be found, as well as the opportunities for growth and the threats to that growth. We concentrated on how we wanted the organisation to develop, in an environment that was becoming radically more competitive than ever before in its history and that must now plan its transition from analogue to digital technology. The most immediate challenge was radical transformation of the organisation, that complex structure of roles, relationships, attitudes, professional norms, ideologies and identities on which the production of radio and television programming depended. Memories of the all-out strike of the early 1990s had left a residue of alienation and suspicion of management right across the organisation. We would need leadership that could move it from a resistance culture to a change culture without losing too much time. Middle management problems needed attention. There was a lack of openness with staff, poor communication style and an inability to involve colleagues in building a strategic vision at Department level. The strike had left a legacy of low morale, anxiety about the future and a sense of defeatism in the face of increasing competition. New talent and new programme ideas were urgently needed. Programme makers had to be more involved in programme decisions. Viable bi-media strategies would have to be explored, so that creative synergies might be unlocked without large extra expenditure, despite well entrenched views that television and radio programme making could never be mixed. Could the staff-management Forum, especially after the strike, play a key role in organisational change, or would a more radical process of transformation be needed? By 1996, it was clear that despite good intentions, one of the major problems with the Forum was its cumbersome structure for meaningfully involving large constituencies of staff in decision-making.

The new Director-General would need to stimulate all levels of the organisation towards radical change, beginning at senior management level. RTÉ had no Policy Research Unit, unlike the better-funded BBC, but intellectual capital would need to be mobilised quickly at senior level to give the Authority and Director-General advice on a range of policy issues. These included the deployment of digital television, managing the slow-moving but profoundly important developments in the politics of broadcasting at European level, and controlling the vagaries of national politics in the context of the Green Paper and impending new legislation. The whole Television Division had to adapt more quickly to the realities of the 1993 Broadcasting Act, which was pushing RTÉ relentlessly towards accepting a new identity as broadcaster –

publisher. The Act specified yearly increases in the proportion of the programme budget to be sliced off for investment in the independent production sector.

The emerging vision in the Director-General recruitment process was to restructure the senior management team so that the Executive Board could be made smaller and more focussed and senior roles could be redesigned to focus on the most pressing needs. Such was the range and depth of organisational change needed that one senior executive would be required to focus on this alone. Public Affairs badly needed a clearer focus too, to reach the public in new ways and to communicate more forcefully with the entire range of the political apparatus of the State. Revenue generation would need the exclusive concentration of a senior executive at Managing Director level. The Editorial Group would need to be enlarged to include a wider spectrum of staff interest. It tended to be too reactive, concentrating on *post hoc* analysis of programmes already transmitted, rather than stimulating and challenging new programme ideas. Overall staff levels would have to be reduced without delay, using early retirement incentives. This was the logical outcome of the broader economic trends shaping broadcasting in Ireland in the 1990s. The SKC Report of 1985 recommended reducing the size of the workforce, but very little actual reduction was achieved. This time, the process, always painful, would need full discussion and consensus within the organisation and the new Director-General would have to tackle this challenge as a matter of priority.

The major area needing attention was revenue enhancement, so that there would be no slippage in the quality and range of RTÉ's programming output. Firmly established trends in the mid-1990s indicated that RTÉ's costs would overtake its revenues unless both could be tackled robustly. Existing revenue would need to be maximised. The Advertising Sales area in particular needed to become more proactive and to escape from reactive modes of work in which staff energies were taken up with processing deals more easily done in less competitive times, rather than selling airtime more aggressively and in new ways to new customers. With the imminent arrival of TV3 and the entry of UTV and British channels into the Irish advertising market for the first time, RTÉ Television had to be blooded for stiff competition. Radio was already leading the way, since indigenous competition in the radio advertising market was already well advanced.

Television Production Facilities was also on the list of targets for immediate attention. The working through of the schedule set out in the 1993 Act meant that more funds were earmarked each year for independent production, building up to a full 20 percent of the television programme budget by 1999. The building out of the independent sector enabled by this legislation, much of it nourished by skilled professionals who had learned the business in RTÉ, had obvious implications for staff reductions within RTÉ. But it also meant that the huge investment in production equipment and studio space would now have to generate revenue in the new production environment in which both independent producers and RTÉ producers were supplying programmes for the schedules of two television channels (and soon TnaG). Production Facilities would have to earn income from both sets of producers, internal and external. We baulked at notion of adopting John Birt's "Producers Choice" system at the BBC, of transferring funds internally between producers and facilities providers, but we had no hesitation in pushing for the readying of RTÉ Facilities for competition with other production houses in Dublin, some of them already acting like cartels. Success in this area would mean that some of the funding being invested by RTÉ in independent production would return to it in the form of fees, to be invested in new technology.

RTÉ would have to generate new streams of revenue in a national and international broadcasting marketplace where huge changes in technology and increasing support for deregulation allowed many new businesses to get involved in television. Could RTÉ compete with some of these new companies in the independent production sector, to make programmes for other broadcasters, including now cable, satellite and terrestrial services to be brought into being once digital compression technology is deployed on a large scale? As new interactive media develop, it is likely they will generate an appetite for archival material also, which can be more easily retrieved and repurposed into new media artefacts once digitised. Could we find the extra funding necessary to digitise the RTÉ archive, so that the value of this national treasure could be enhanced? RTÉ already included in its corporate structure a subsidiary company called Commercial Enterprises Ltd. (CEL), entrusted with the task of generating further revenue for RTÉ beyond its Irish broadcasting services. But were the goals set for CEL in the early 1990s too modest? Could the new Director-General, with a Managing Director of Revenue, stimulate CEL to exploit more fully the huge comparative advantage for RTÉ of operating within the Anglophone world, the world's richest language community, by enhancing its programming catalogue for international markets and by directly entering television broadcasting in the UK and the US?

THE PROGRAMMING CHALLENGE

The most important area needing the invigorated vision of new leadership was radio and television programming. All other organisational functions ultimately exist for one purpose: programming. Press criticism of broadcasting in Ireland, with a few impressive exceptions, is notoriously bad, that is, often ill informed, lazy, egoistic, frivolous, fixated on milking minor RTÉ organisational crises for headline value. What is too often lacking is a build-up of press expertise in broadcasting matters that pursues well researched, sustained analysis of trends in programming, organisational developments, policy choices, use of resources and media politics. Despite the paucity of good criticism, however, a persistent strand of press feedback began to make itself felt in the 1990s in ways that deserved respect, as more Irish people gained access to British channels and formed a wider comparative framework for analysis of RTÉ's performance. More people could now begin tacitly to compare RTÉ with all the other channels available – BBC One and Two, Channel 4, ITV, UTV, Sky – though often forgetting the huge disparity in resources available on each side of the Irish Sea. RTÉ programmes, it was frequently said, were timid and dull, relied too much on small pools of expertise with their very predictable analyses of public events, and were too low-brow and downmarket in taste. Over reliance on advertising was blamed for this slide towards tabloidisation. RTÉ producers themselves agreed that the schedules lacked lustre, that the station had lurched too readily towards the inexpensive, studio-based talk and game show format, that a radical overhaul of prime-time television schedules was needed, that Network Two had long since lost its way since the inspiring fight in the distant past to establish it in the face of Conor Cruise O'Brien's Ministerial resolve in the 1970s to use the channel to re-broadcast BBC programmes into Ireland. Was Current Affairs, the flagship Department of all television companies, the victim of organisational balkanisation in its existence within the Television Programmes Division rather than the News Division? Should News and Current Affairs merge, or at least converge a lot more than heretofore, and if so, would the pressure to report on daily events crowd into the space available for analytical, reflective and investigative journalism? Loud cries came persistently from outside the coastal counties of Leinster that RTÉ was too preoccupied with the world of the capital city. Should a more robust regional programming strategy be implemented and was this affordable? Should the headquarters of the second television channel be relocated to Cork in a genuine move towards regionalisation, or would this be a futile exercise in expensive duplication of resources?

Some very substantial issues in the area of programming would face the incoming Director-General. Huge inflation in some areas of television programming costs was already underway, especially in sports rights. Could new cultural alliances – with the film industry, co-production partners, Section 35 investors, Diaspora groups, even the Abbey Theatre – help to invigorate drama, the most expensive genre of programming, and stretch the possibilities well beyond serial fiction in the form of situation comedy or soap opera? Could documentary be made more central to the schedules, along with arts and books programmes? Could new talent in comedy writing be tested in pilot form more often, so that formative research with audiences could hone writing and production styles and ensure that expensive failures could be avoided? Could the new Director-General regenerate creativity in some areas, retire jaded programme-makers in others and cultivate new talent in all areas? Could digital technology now be scrutinised to see how best a national strategy on platforms and television services could be formulated, create new possibilities for local and regional broadcasting and begin to satisfy the needs of minority audiences?

A major concern focussed on RTÉ's relationship with that relatively quiet but still powerful elite, mostly Dublin-based, the traditional guardians of the vulnerable Reithian ideals of public service broadcasting, whose long-established aspiration for RTÉ was that it would widen popular access to good drama, music, political analysis and the arts. The liberal Enlightenment view of this social group was articulated so ably throughout the 1950s by Leon O Broin, out of his admiration for the spirit of Victorian reformism animating the BBC at that time. This English reformist spirit of the time is best summed up in the Pilkington Report of 1962, which hailed television as a great agency of moral and cultural improvement, a means by which people could gain knowledge of others, develop active leisure pursuits, extend their intellectual horizons and grow as human beings "connected to a whole range of worthwhile, significant activity and experience."[6] O Broin finally won the argument in the Lemass Government that decided to establish RTÉ as a public corporation, rather than commit Ireland to the loving embrace of privately owned commercial television. Many of the views of O Broin were still animating opinion-leaders in the civil service and the professions in the 1990s, mean and women who believed in the value of public broadcasting. They were still supportive of RTÉ in its potential to deliver on its public service remit, but they were increasingly critical of its actual performance in programming. That criticism was far from being coherently expressed, however, even when we put advertisements in the national newspapers inviting criticism and suggestions for improving programming. The question now was whether the quality of both radio and television was alienating this once-powerful opinion-leading establishment that in previous times could be counted upon to defend public service ideals: politicians, senior civil servants, the clergy, teachers, academics, lawyers and other members of the professions.

The cultural power of this social class was undoubtedly being eroded by a new young business class, whose abrasively expressed ideas on market liberalisation and the power of the consumer, were most adroitly articulated by people close to the advertising industry. The ethos and discourse of market populism was increasing in intensity throughout the 1990s, emboldened by the successful wooing of Eastern Europe away from Stalinism and towards consumer capitalism, in newspapers, magazines and the new commercial radio stations rolling off the IRTC's licensing conveyor belts like shiny new cars. The central ideological tenet of market populism is that markets are not just about exchanging money for goods: they generate consent, peace and harmony. Markets give us what we want, express the will of the people, confer democratic legitimacy. They look out for the interests of the ordinary person, the "little guy," or in Irish parlance, the "ordinary punter." Any criticisms of the excesses of market-based thinking, therefore, could be described as "elitist" and flying in the face of common sense. Any proposals to organise human affairs outside the power of markets, or to point out how harmful market-driven models of broadcasting can be, or to argue for ways to control their ravages, would now have to articulated more loudly, in clearer logic. The momentum of market populism, with all the ideological force of a secular religion, could be seen in new ways in the Ireland of the 1990s, in the relentless attacks by the *Sunday Independent*, for instance on Michael D. Higgins as Minster for Culture, whenever he spoke out in favour of public service principles in broadcasting. In fact, his spelling out of a vision for broadcasting was no more radical than what Leon O Broin was saying in the 1950s, pushing for a public ownership model against the sneaking regard for commercial television that was driving Sean Lemass and his advisers. But now in the 1990s, Ireland wasn't listening so keenly to the message, or at least large swaths of the press weren't in a mood to listen, and they had a new-found power to frame media issues in novel ways that were in harmony with the global ideology of market liberalism.

This tension is relevant here in so far as the new Authority worried that the actual performance of RTÉ in its programming might not be perceived by an influential sector of Irish society, well disposed to public service ideals, as living up to its potential as a national broadcaster owned and funded by the people and therefore expected to cater for all taste communities. The new Director-General would have to be sensitive to these tensions between cultural liberalism and market populism, critically examine programme performance within the realities of financial constraints and take appropriate action as Editor-in-Chief.

But it would not be enough to assume that good programming can speak for itself, especially as competitive broadcasters lobby hard for their interests in both Dublin and Brussels. Such intervention would need to be augmented by the rejuvenation of the corporate commitment to Public Affairs. RTÉ needed to be more proactive in telling the good news of its achievements before hostile press coverage would pull it all into the steady stream of negative criticism. RTÉ had to reconnect with alienated opinion-leaders, inside and outside politics. It had to communicate more clearly with its public in face-to-face meetings where senior management could listen carefully to RTÉ's stakeholders and exchange in clear communication both the achievements, plans and ambitions of programme-makers, as well as honest self-criticism and awareness of the problems and challenges to be tackled. It had to communicate more clearly with politicians in Dublin and in Brussels, who yield enormous economic and legal power over broadcasting and are increasingly listening to the arguments of market populism, that public service models of broadcasting are elitist and historically outdated, and that therefore control of all the visual and aural content that embodies the stories we tell ourselves every day in the most popular media, should be substantially shifted out of public ownership and be given over to private control.

The Holy Grail for all broadcasters, of course, for different reasons, is sustained access to the largest possible number of viewers and listeners. For all broadcasters who depend for revenue on the continued interest of advertising agencies in selling their clients products in breaks between programme segments, the connection is clear. The radio industry had pioneered the move away from generalist stations that attempt to offer something for everyone, towards niche-seeking stations with their sights fixed on specific demographic sectors having clearly identifiable lifestyles, access to disposable income and specific spending habits. The dominant objective is to engage only with people younger than 35. Television in Ireland hasn't yet gone very far in that direction, because of the small size of the population, but it is poised on the verge of a revolution in distribution systems – digital satellite, cable and terrestrial – that will begin to target very specific social groups as potential viewers, once they can be aggregated with niche taste communities in other countries, all addressed by the same global television channels. When this happens, broadcasters will follow newspapers and magazines in worrying more about the demographic composition of their audiences rather than their gross size. For broadcasters who do not depend on advertising revenue (the BBC) or depend only partly on it (RTÉ), the audience imperative is still important, if only to demonstrate to sceptics that public service broadcasting is worth funding because, despite intensifying competition, it still reaches a significant proportion of the population on a regular basis. All public broadcasters face the possibility of hitting a legitimacy barrier if their audience share is radically affected by new competition. Below this barrier, public funding would no longer be defensible. This has already happened in other parts of Europe.

There are more fundamental reasons why one of the major challenges presented to an incoming Director-General of RTÉ is to manage the totality of relationships between the national broadcaster and its many audiences, by leaving himself ample personal and creative space to stimulate excellence and diversity in programming. This would encompass commissioning, purchasing and production of radio and television programmes, as well as ensuring that a creative flair is applied in scheduling them for maximum audience impact. Since public broadcasting is funded by a levy paid by every household in the country, it has a duty to provide a wide range of programmes to satisfy a wide range of tastes – not an easy task in an age when audience fragmentation means not only the weakening of brand loyalty to the oldest broadcaster in the country, but an accelerated splintering of audiences into a wide range of very different taste communities, embodying different patterns of pleasure experienced by different subcultures as they consume radio and television output.

As Editor-in-Chief (as well as CEO of a large organisation), the new Director-General we were recruiting in 1996 would operate in a programming environment none of his predecessors had experience of, except Joe Barry, who managed the early stages of the articulation of RTÉ with the nascent independent production sector, along with Clare Duignan and her staff of Commissioning Editors in the newly established Independent Production Unit. It can be argued that in the fast-changing social and cultural conditions of this period of late modernity, where taste cultures mutate and fragment continuously, one single production organisation, because of the psychosocial dynamics underpinning organisational ethos, norms and perceptions, is no longer able to "know" this changing cultural environment in sufficient breadth and depth to respond to it promptly and fully with engaging programming. Independent production companies had more pragmatic business arguments to make, about needing access to audiences through the editorial gatekeepers in television channels. But it will be some time yet before we can decide whether the range of small companies now providing programmes through the Independent Production Unit, can in fact relate more nimbly to the changing wants and needs of different taste cultures. A new Director-General in RTÉ would need to reflect on the new programme provision regime and guide it to its fullest actualisation. We had serious doubts in 1996 about whether the production skill level in the independent sector was as high as its advocates claimed. Would RTÉ need to become involved in training? Could the sector handle the commissioning needs of the new Irish-language channel about to be launched, as well as absorb the very large chunk of the RTÉ production budget that would be heading its way in the near future? Should RTÉ maintain a distanced, reactive relationship with the production sector or seek to integrate it more into its operations, perhaps even into its schedule planning, or would this stifle the fresh impetus that the sector could possibly bring to RTÉ? Should RTÉ encourage a coherence in the sector, to minimise any squabbling over who was favoured with commissions and who was ostracised by the RTÉ editorial system, though bodies like Film Makers Ireland, or leave it to its own devices? As the independent sector grew, it was clear that it was developing its own coherence through FMI, under the able leadership of its Chairman James Hickey.

I have stressed the recruitment of the Director-General because the series of decisions involved are among the most crucial any Authority has to make. As CEO, he (so far it has always been a man,) leads an organisation of about 1,500 staff (it was

2,000 in 1996) focussed on providing an output of 32,680 hours of radio per annum across four radio channels, and 13,000 hours of television across two television channels, as well as 365 hours to TG4. RTÉ is the biggest employer of musicians and actors in Ireland and is the country's biggest film and video producer. This diversity of activities gives its corporate operation a unique complexity and presents its Director-General with unique demands. Few other companies share this challenge that is peculiar to broadcasting, in as much as what is being managed is creative activity. RTÉ is a complex organisation, with a turnover of over 300 million dedicated to the generation of a very broad range of information and entertainment in an uncertain environment of constantly changing, fickle taste.

In our search for a new corporate leader, we focussed on three objectives: the enhancement of creativity, including the cultivation of new talent and the rejuvenation of programme schedules; secondly, improving RTÉ's financial viability, including radical cost reduction and finding new revenue streams; thirdly, maximising RTÉ's organisational effectiveness, including the management of urgently needed change in every area of the organisation. The question was which candidate had the best strategies for the development of RTÉ, the vision as well as the action plan and the ability to actualise those strategies?

Our search culminated in the choice of Bob Collins, who took up office in April 1997. He had worked in RTÉ since 1975 in a variety of roles, including Director of Corporate Affairs and Secretary to the Authority, Director of Television Programmes and Assistant Director-General. At the same time, we worked with the new Director-General to make changes in the top management team that would bring about renewal at several levels. Liam Miller was appointed Managing Director: Organisation and Change. Joe Mulholland became Managing Director: Television and Conor Sexton Managing Director: Revenue. Adrian Moynes became Special Assistant to the Director-General and took on a lot of the challenge of policy research. Eugene Murray spearheaded the development of digital television. Kevin Healy became Director of Public Affairs, charged with reorganising relations with the public, the press and the political apparatus in Dublin, Brussels and Strasbourg. Helen Shaw replaced him as Director of Radio.

THE SINN FEIN CHALLENGE

Of all the issues debated by the Authority in the 1995-2000 period, probably the greatest amount of time was spent on three issues: the commercialisation of children's television, the development of a digital strategy and formulating a response to Anthony Coughlan's complaint about how RTÉ should handle referendum campaigns. These three issues occupied large blocks of time (and are examined elsewhere in this book). Passionate debate was also the order of the day when we came to discuss how RTÉ journalists were now handling Sinn Fein interviews, in a broadcasting atmosphere adjusting very cautiously to the ending of the ban – the infamous Section 31 – on granting direct access to the airwaves to a range of political groups associated with paramilitary organisations.

Michael D. Higgins and Albert Reynolds had decided in 1994, as one of the confidence-building measures driving the peace process, not to reactivate the yearly Section 31 censorship regulation. In the opinion of many commentators, but probably not a majority on the RTÉ Authority, this decisive ministerial action, reversing a policy that had been in place for several decades, was to play a major role in advancing the peace process in Northern Ireland. I believe historical hindsight will validate this judgement. But in the first few years of post-Section 31 broadcasting, I could never be sure that a majority of my colleagues didn't deeply resent the new-found freedom of Sinn Fein to speak directly to journalists and to Irish audiences. Over the previous two decades, many complex layers of self-censorship regarding "the Troubles" had evolved within RTÉ, aided by the formation of unofficial staff watchdog groups associated with Sinn Fein, The Workers' Party, which had descended directly from Official Sinn Fein (the "Stickies") after the split in the Republican movement in the early 1970s and had become increasingly sympathetic to Unionist and revisionist interpretations of the conflict in Northern Ireland. One of the most active of groups in RTÉ was the Ned Stapleton Cumann, that operated within the RTÉ branch of the Workers' Union of Ireland. Pressures towards censorship, deeply embedded in different parts of the organisation, intimidated staff into accepting, however reluctantly, forms of self-censorship that went far beyond the letter of Section 31. President Mary McAleese has given some insight into the editorial atmosphere of her time in RTÉ, sometimes encountering a tendency towards anti-Nationalist bullying in her work as a researcher in Current Affairs in the early 1980s, especially around the time when hunger striker Bobby Sands was elected to Parliament at Westminster.[7] Revisionism had also taken a grip on most of the national newspapers, to the extend that many print journalists avoided important stories like the Guilford Four and the Birmingham Six miscarriages of justice, for fear of being labelled Provo sympathisers.

The challenge in 1996 was how to sweep away the damaging aftermath of the censorious mindset of the "Stickies" and remove the fear of being a "hush puppy" (the derogatory term coined by RTÉ Producer Eoghan Harris to signify those considered to be "soft" on the Provisional IRA and Sinn Fein). The challenge was made all the more difficult because of the deeply coded way in which discussion of this problem usually took place within RTÉ, even at senior management level. It was difficult for a newcomer like myself to decode some of the talk, and some of the silences, about the internal censorship campaign waged by the Stickies. In some cases, there were obvious similarities with the anti-communism hysteria and the purges of staff in the US media industry in the early 1950s, where various layers of guilt for not recognising and resisting the danger to free speech represented by McCarthy outlasted the end of the actual purges by several years.

The question of how to handle Sinn Fein, newly released from years of broadcasting exile, surfaced in Authority discussions in 1996, initially in the form of reactions to news coverage of anti-drugs campaigns in Dublin's inner-city neighbourhoods and Sinn Fein's role in them. There is a certain irony in the fact that as journalists were adjusting slowly to the ending of Section 31 censorship, RTÉ was at the same time working to increase its transmission power northwards, in the belief that by achieving symmetry of television reception on both sides of the Border we could play a role in increasing mutual understanding between Unionist and Nationalist cultures and perhaps achieving reconciliation across the various borders of tradition, politics, religion, group memory and historical identity that had plagued Ireland for so long. We were going ahead with diplomatic negotiations and engineering field strength trials that precede full-power operations in a very low-key manner, announcing the increased television availability in the North only to television set dealers and on teletext. This was to avoid adverse reaction and xenophobic outbursts from politicians representing certain sections of Northern Ireland society who would abhor the ideological pollution that would start drenching the population from full-power RTÉ transmitters, now liberated from Section 31.

How does a journalist maintain high standards of fairness, impartiality and objectivity in some of the highly-charged, key confrontations in the Northern Ireland summer calendar, where one group is driven by fanatical feelings of group superiority, historically rooted in the need to cow neighbours, and another is organising resistance to this triumphalism, hoping that the whole island of Ireland is now at last interested in these ancient clashes? There was a certain timidity on the part of the RTÉ Newsroom about coverage of the Northern Ireland Summer confrontations over use of public space, a fear that television news, as it sought to report, might in fact inflame. This was the old Yeatsian worry that our words and our pictures might send certain young men out to die. My academic instinct was to distrust this "hypodermic" paradigm of media effects – the notion of media directly, powerfully, uniformly influencing viewers – as simplistic and already abandoned by media theorists. Whatever about a poet's verse, television output has an impact that is more inclined to be indirect, complex and biased towards cultivating a "mainstream" view. Some Authority colleagues worried about Charlie Bird's animated style of delivery, in his reports from Northern hotspots like Drumcree and the Apprentice Boys march in Derry. My fear was that an institutional timidity about reporting Northern Ireland, deeply entrenched in Section 31-induced self-censorship patterns, might continue to produce a televisual blandness that would bore and alienate and lack relevance, rather than grip and involve the core RTÉ audience. If it is to remain relevant to Irish people, RTÉ must in fact be shielded from all forms of censorship, so that it can sharpen its critical edge. The colour and emotion in Charlie Bird's reports were therefore to be valued for the way in which a real sense of the tensions in Northern Ireland could be communicated to people who rarely travel north of the Border. Within a few years, new radio and television stations would be reporting in their own graphic styles, unencumbered by any institutional memory of Stickies or Section 31.

Such was the unhealthy legacy of Section 31 in RTÉ that loose talk about "robust journalism" could be quickly recoded as "hush puppy journalism, " that gives succour to the Provos. Some colleagues on the Authority believed that the RTÉ Newsroom had a "Republican agenda" and that this was obvious in its coverage of the anti-drugs campaigns in Dublin, which did not sufficiently highlight the "sinister" leadership role of Sinn Fein in these inner-city crusades against drug dealers. But side by side with this view on the Authority was the criticism that some RTÉ programmes were treating Sinn Fein politicians in an unnecessarily aggressive way. The phenomenon of selective perception operated consistently in this area, linking commentators' personal orientations to "the Troubles" with their perceptions of how RTÉ was handling Sinn Fein. In the jargon of the time, who was in charge of the news, Stickies or Shinners? The question was something of a Rorschach test.

In 1997, our discussions about Sinn Fein on the Authority tended to focus on two questions: was Sinn Fein being given too much access on the airwaves and were RTÉ staff adequately prepared in interviews to manage the very considerable oratorical acumen believed to be accumulated within the Sinn Fein organisation? Some colleagues felt RTÉ needed clearer editorial guidelines as to when it was appropriate to interview a Sinn Fein spokesperson, as the party was adroit in managing its media exposure to suit its own circumstances. We tended to disagree over whether there was too great a presence of Sinn Fein people on air. On the one hand, the party was relatively small in electoral terms and its share of broadcast time should arithmetically reflect this. On the other, decisions made by Sinn Fein were inherently more newsworthy than the moves of most other parties, since they were the main conduit of information from the IRA about maintaining a ceasefire, and later, moving towards decommissioning weapons, two key aspects of the unfolding drama of the peace process.

There was by now no longer a strong belief among members of the Authority that there was a seriously sympathetic ethos in favour of Sinn Fein embedded among RTÉ staff, and certainly no fear of a conspiracy to promote its aims in contravention of the legal requirement for RTÉ to observe impartiality in its news and current affairs output. Eoghan Harris, long since retired from RTÉ, stridently kept alive his "hush puppy" accusations from the vantage point of a weekly column in the *Sunday Times*, but the actual debate had moved on to the notion that RTÉ staff were simply not able to handle the very sophisticated debating skills of people like Gerry Adams, Martin McGuinness and Mitchell McLoughlin. RTÉ managers were frustrated by Sinn Fein's capacity not to respond to critical questions posed by journalists, or to respond only with bland truisms, particularly when challenged to clarify the Party's relationship with the IRA. This was an obsessive question, on the lips of most journalists in 1998, and Sinn Fein was giving coy or evasive answers when challenged, or brilliant long-winded lectures on nationalist history, though many commentators today would acknowledge the necessary role played by ambiguity on all sides, including Sinn Fein, in keeping the peace process alive for so long. Every broadcast interview quickly turned into a very tense debate, and the concern about this was all about imbalances in debating skills; on the one side, naïve and poorly trained RTÉ journalists, and on the other, battle-hardened men and women whose debating skills stemmed from long years of training in survival skills, including training for the experience of interrogation in grim RUC and British Army conditions, far removed from the niceties of Dublin 4 studios.

To my mind, the bottom line for the Authority was to avoid a situation where a heavy-handed top-down regime of managerial control would be reimposed on journalists before they had the time to get to grips with Sinn Fein's debating style, similar to the rules of upward-referral put in place in the Newsroom in the immediate aftermath of the suspension of Section 31. Even a partial reimposition of censorship would be no help to the peace process. There was certainly an imbalance in many interviews on radio and television in this period, where RTÉ journalists seemed to be frequently losing the argument. Even the urbane Gay Byrne, who had interviewed kings, emperors and vagabonds with supreme confidence, seemed to some critics to come off second best in his very wary encounter with Gerry Adams on the Late Late Show.

Any realistic analysis of the situation would have to conclude that Gerry Adams and Martin McGuinness were not at this time going to clarify the exact nature of their relationship with the IRA, no matter how high the "skill levels" of RTÉ journalists might be boosted. When they were allowed access to the airwaves from 1994 on, it was inevitable that they would have long, pent-up tales to tell of oppression and humiliation suffered by the nationalist population in Northern Ireland over many decades, whether or not we in the Republic wanted to listen to these tales with some amount of sympathy. Sinn Fein had been waiting a long time to tell its side of a story that had been dominated for a very long time by the press relations skills of the British Army, aided by friends in the London newspaper establishment like the *Daily Telegraph*.[8] But RTÉ had been conditioned by decades of censorship to be unprepared for these outpourings, which were radically transforming the mix of political information available to Irish citizens. At no time was I sure that a majority of my colleagues on the Authority agreed with me, some claiming that they knew what was "really going on" inside what was called "Sinn Fein-IRA." The problem was never put on the agenda for an Authority meeting and it was never voted on. My tendency was to put the brakes on discussions that took the form of circling back towards the comfort zone of the old Section 31 mentality. We compromised on a stance of light-touch supervision by the Director-General in this sensitive and contentious area, and avoided reimposing upward-referral rules about contact with Sinn Fein.

It was important not to let these teething difficulties in the initial stages of the post-Section 31 era force us to decide prematurely on another very long-running question: should Television News and Current Affairs maintain their editorial separateness, or should they be organisationally merged, forming one structural entity where the "rashness" of reportorial impulses to chase the immediate story might be tempered by the more reflective and analytical instincts of Current Affairs? Such a hasty decision on our part might in fact have been counterproductive, in the sense of signalling that we expected Current Affairs to play the "safe" role. All of our discussions of the future of Current Affairs in fact were critical of the voices of caution which envisaged Current Affairs as essentially the location for the elaboration of stories broken elsewhere in the Irish media. We were unanimous in urging Current Affairs to listen to the accusations of blandness and timidity levelled at it by its more intelligent critics, to invest in investigative journalism and to trust the Authority to support staff when good journalistic work was done, even if that might sometimes disturb vested interests in Irish society.

The shadow of Section 31 still fell over RTÉ at the beginning of 1998 (four years after it had ceased to have legal power) when the Secretary of State for Northern

Ireland, Mo Mowlam, decided to visit Republican and Loyalist prisoners in jail, to engage with their views on the peace process. Rules for allowing the views of paramilitaries to be published were broken in at least one instance (an unauthorised interview with a UFF prisoner in the Maze prison, aired on *Today with Pat Kenny*) and were soon relaxed. But it is significant that what exercised minds in RTÉ at this time was not the intermittent airing of convicted prisoners' views but the daily challenge of dealing with Sinn Fein as it moved inexorably towards the centre of mainstreaming politics and the signing of the Good Friday Agreement.

GOVERNANCE OF RTÉ

This chapter has foregrounded the work of the RTÉ Authority in governing the public service broadcaster in Ireland. Public broadcasters are distinctly different from privately owned broadcasting companies, in that they are owned and funded by the public. The assumption is that they are also accountable to the public. But how is this reflected in the way they are governed?

The Broadcasting Authority Act of 1960 established that the members of the Authority are appointed by Government, not less than seven or more than nine, for a period not exceeding five years. Members of either House of the Oireachtas (Parliament), or candidates for election to either House, can not be members. The Authority was dismissed by Government in 1972 following official displeasure at the way it handled news staff communication with the IRA, and following some reflection on this, the Broadcasting Authority Act of 1976 stipulated that a member of the Authority may be removed from office by Government for stated reasons, only if resolutions are passed by both Houses of the Oireachtas calling for such removal. The Broadcasting Authority Act of 1993 provides for gender balancing on the Authority.

Both Eamonn De Valera and Sean Lemass, the two politicians most associated with the birth of RTÉ, were very uneasy about the advent of television and the trouble it might cause for the State. They had strong ideas about the type of programmes that should – and should not – be broadcast and in 1960, Lemass drafted very strict Policy Directives that he expected the new RTÉ to follow. This attitude helps explain his famous Dail statement in 1966 that RTÉ was "an instrument of public policy." The history of RTÉ since then, however, reveals the steady pulling away from the state-run model and the building up of a system of self-regulation in the RTÉ Authority. The Authority also acts as the guardian of the public interest in broadcasting and formulates policy in relation to broadcasting. Most of the public broadcasters in Europe are governed within a similar system. Major changes have been announced for RTÉ in legislation to be introduced late in 2003. Many of the functions of the RTÉ Authority will be transferred to a new Broadcasting Authority of Ireland, which will govern all broadcasters, both private and public. A Board of Directors will replace the RTÉ Authority. It remains to be seen precisely how new legislation will assign responsibility for the promotion of the public interest in broadcasting to a Regulator that is also responsible for promoting the development of private broadcasting.

How should the public interest in broadcasting be secured? How should its controllers be accountable, given that "accountability" belongs to the family of democratic concepts that infuses the tradition of public service in radio and television and given the powerful formative consequences of broadcasting for the fabric of democratic culture and the quality of public life? The RTÉ Authority reports regularly to the Minister in charge of Broadcasting, particularly via quarterly financial reports and periodic meetings between the Minister and the Chairman or the full Authority. It also responds to queries from Joint Oireachtas Committees and conducts frequent public meetings around the country. Is this enough to ensure public rights to participate in broadcasting decisions and obligations to respond to public appraisal of broadcasting performance? Is it enough to ensure viewer and listener protection against power abuses, including those embedded in the organisational culture in which staff work, such as the Stickies pressure group in the 1980s, already referred to? Two questions are paramount. How can a modern democratic state ensure that its public broadcaster serves real audience needs and desires, and not just a public of its own management's imagination? And how can the future of public broadcasting be guaranteed against politicians who would bend it to their will, whether they be Sean Lemass in the 1960s or Ray Burke in the 1990s or Silvio Berlusconi more recently in Italy. Berlusconi reacted to RAI's (Italian public service broadcaster) criticism of the the Governments he formed in the 1994 by removing the Governors and requiring RAI to carry Government-funded advertisements for his right-wing economic programme. He had a second chance to copper-fasten his control of RAI in 2002-2003. His control of private broadcasting in Italy was already highly advanced, raising fresh fears among commentators about the quality of Italian democracy in such a system. Could something similar happen in Ireland? It is very worthwhile to consider what more should be done to sharpen the critical edge of public broadcasting by shielding it further from Government pressure.

One concern is to remove appointments to Boards and Authorities from direct, unmediated patronage by Ministers. There are a number of ways in which appointees could be recommended by an independent appointments committee, made up of nominees from representative organisations in the country. This would favour people of talent who are drawn from a cross-section of society to represent the public. The Institute for Public Policy Research, an independent centre left think tank close to New Labour in London, has developed some ideas on devolving the power to appoint Governors to the BBC.[9] This would involve creating an Electoral College which would devolve power to the public, in order to increase the Governors' responsiveness to viewers and listeners and to strengthen its independence from Government. This Electoral College would separate power into different constituencies to reduce the risk of domination by any one group. Some Electoral College members would be appointed by national and regional Advisory Boards (Scotland, Wales, Northern Ireland and the English regions), some would be appointed by the House of Commons National Heritage Committee and some by new broadcasting societies, such as the Viewers and Listeners Associations. Such a mix of constituencies choosing members of the Electoral College would ensure that the appointment of the Governors would be influenced by the composition of the House of Commons but would not be directly subject to the patronage and values of the Government of the day. Their appointment would also be influenced by both regional and civil society interests in shaping broadcasting. This Electoral College would appoint the Governors of the BBC having regard to the representativeness of its appointees to include individuals who can speak for social categories, such as age (younger and older people), ethnic minorities, people with disabilities etc. The IPPR suggests the principle of electing BBC Governors would be a clear improvement on direct patronage. It would be the most impartial and practical way to implement the principle of election and of guaranteeing that the BBC would "pass the Berlusconi test." Should Ireland borrow some of these ideas for selecting its Broadcasting Authority in the future? RTÉ has already decided to create its own Audience Council, to facilitate better communication with the public and improve accountability.

The key to securing support for public broadcasting into the future is surely to win widespread popular support for a well-articulated mission which the majority of citizens can see is in their best interests. This would assume some power to harness new technology to the common good. It would also assume the ability to relate to global markets in television and film in ways that protect the core broadcasting system in order for it to reflect adequately the concerns, interests and cultural traditions of Irish society. The core system must be able to produce programming that is less subordinated to market dictates than what is imported from the thoroughly market saturated television systems of North America, that is capable of carrying forward in to the culture what is worth preserving from the past. James Curran suggests we should think about of a "cultural system, " in a way that is analogous to the democratic system, with requirements that need to be met if it is to function properly. These include conservation, innovation, reproduction, diversity and social access: "Public service broadcasting helps to conserve the cultural system by transmitting to the next generation works of literature, music and art which were judged to be of outstanding value by past generations. It renews the part of the cultural system represented by broadcasting by supporting innovation through the allocation of resources to original and experimental work. It fosters the diversity of the cultural system through internal cross-subsidies ... which are designed to sustain production for minorities (including, crucially, ones that are not viable in the marketplace). It helps the cultural system to reproduce itself by sustaining concentrations of craft skill, experience and talent, and by supporting creativity through the ceding of a high degree of autonomy to production teams. And it facilitates social access to the cultural system through a low, collectively subscribed cost of admission, and through mixed programme schedules that encourage viewers to try new experiences."[10]

We turn now to consider how the debate on the regulation of broadcasting in Ireland unfolded in the 1990s.

2 REGULATING IRISH BROADCASTING

With the birth of television in Ireland in legislation passed in 1960, regulation of broadcasting moved from a Government department to a statutory public corporation, the Radio Eireann Authority (it later became the Radio Teilifis Eireann Authority) whose members were appointed by Government. This was the outcome of a long debate that took place inside and outside Government in the 1950s about whether Ireland could afford to have television, how it would be funded, whether it should be privately or publicly owned and funded and how it should be regulated, if established at arm's length from Government.[11] The final decision on television was presided over by Sean Lemass as Taoiseach, who himself favoured the private broadcasting option but was out-voted by his Cabinet colleagues. For years he remained very wary of "the desirability of entrusting (broadcasting) to an Authority outside the Government, relying only on directive principles set out in legislation and on the power of the Government to appoint members of the Authority, to ensure that the direction of the service would be consistently in harmony with the highest and most enduring purposes of the nation."[12] It could be argued that this wariness of the autonomy of RTÉ has remained active in some parts of the Fianna Fail Party right up to the present. Government in the 1960 Act retained the right to decide the length of the broadcasting day, the amount of advertising permitted and of course the level of the licence fee to be paid by viewers and listeners. The law also laid down that news and current affairs programming must be handled objectively and impartially and without any expression of the Authority's own point of view. Government could issue a directive in writing to prohibit, or require, the broadcast of specified material, but beyond this, the Authority had a high level of autonomy.

Self-regulated RTÉ remained the only legal broadcaster in the country until 1987, when the then Minister Ray Burke legislated to put an end to the pirate radio stations that had become quite popular throughout the 1980s and to establish commercial radio on a legal footing for the first time. This was underpinned by the establishment of the Independent Radio and Television Commission (the IRTC, later to become the Broadcasting Commission of Ireland, after the 2001 Broadcasting Act) to regulate all commercial and community radio and television stations. This dual regulatory system has remained in place until the present, but it is about to be changed, as the Fianna Fail-Progressive Democrat coalition Government plans to fuse the regulatory powers of both the BCI and the RTÉ Authority into a single new Commission later in 2003. Here we examine the background to this decision, rooted in regulatory concepts introduced in the mid-1990s but then submerged in the debate about preparing for digital television, which culminated in the 2001 Broadcasting Act.

This 2001 Act was long in gestation, having made its way through two different Governments that held office during a time of unprecedented change in broadcasting.

The Act both responded to and gave legal shape to major transformations taking place in the media landscape. These included the perfection, after years of research and development, of digital compression technology and its incorporation into the strategic plans of major global media corporations, the growing interest of the European Commission in media and cultural politics, and the slow effects on the Irish political elite of the global spread of the neo-liberal ideology of broadcast deregulation. These transformations are examined elsewhere in this book.

The previous broadcasting bill had been enacted in 1993. It was a very slight document that focused almost entirely on two areas: the first was the removal of the cap on advertising revenue which could be earned by RTÉ, which had been imposed by the (now disgraced) Minister Ray Burke in the Broadcasting Act of 1990, in order to facilitate the launch of the country's first private radio station. This was the ill-fated Century Radio, which went into liquidation soon after launch, despite the Minister's attempts to divert advertising revenue in its direction and his success in pressuring RTÉ to make transmission facilities available to Century at a fraction of the cost determined by RTÉ. The circumstances in which these favours were carried out by Ray Burke and the possibility that serious political bribery took place was one of the major focal points in the investigations carried out by a judicial tribunal set up by the Government to examine questions of political corruption. It established that Ray Burke had received a political donation of £30,000 from Oliver Barry, one of the Directors of Century Radio, and Burke had intervened decisively in favour of Century in its dispute with RTÉ over the charge for using its transmission network. Century directors had also lobbied the Minister to close down RTÉ's second radio service FM2, so that the popular music field could be left entirely to the commercial sector. Government rejected Burke's proposals to require FM2 to vacate popular music and to divert up to a quarter of the licence fee income to the private broadcasting sector, but it agreed, in the 1990 Broadcasting Act, to impose a cap on RTÉ's advertising income, so that some revenue could be diverted to the private broadcasters.[13]

The 1993 Act also focused on the building of an infrastructure to facilitate the emergence of an independent production sector in television. This took the form of a requirement that RTÉ divert part of its television programme expenditure, rising to twenty per cent by 1999, into a special account for the purpose of commissioning television programmes from the independent production sector. In many ways, the Broadcasting Acts of 1990 and 1993 revealed official reaction to the world of broadcasting at the start of the 1990s, a world that was reasonably stable, apart perhaps from the temptation among some politicians to accept bribes and increase their personal wealth as private broadcasters emerged to bid for some of the funding that had supported public service broadcasting in Ireland for several decades. If we read the Broadcasting Act (2001) as the reaction of politicians to the increasingly globalised broadcasting environment at the end of the decade, we can glimpse the huge changes that have taken place, both in the actual situation in which radio and television programmes are produced and consumed and in the political reaction to it.

MICHAEL D. HIGGINS' GREEN PAPER

Political thinking about broadcasting was given a major boost when Michael D. Higgins, Labour minister in charge of broadcasting in the Rainbow Coalition Government, let it be known that he was working on new legislation that would put Irish broadcasting on a firm footing for the new century, going way beyond the legislative tinkering of the 1990 and 1993 Acts. Unlike most of his predecessors, Higgins was a public thinker, with his own ideas about media and the arts and passionate convictions about their role in a small nation exposed to major global trends and influences. Broadcasting was a major part of his vision and he wanted it to work at optimum capacity as a force for creativity in every genre of radio and television. He let it be known that he would be preparing a Green Paper, then a White Paper, and consulting widely before publishing a comprehensive new Bill.

My involvement in this project began in 1994. The Minister had just taken a major step in revitalising the Irish film industry and appointed Lelia Doolan as Chair of the Irish Film Board, so now he wanted to direct his attention to a radical review of broadcasting. Some time later I found myself immersed in an hour-long Sunday afternoon telephone conversation with the Minister discussing his early draft of a Green Paper. Would I come on board and rework the Green Paper, which was in danger of suffering from a dose of civil service inertia? I jumped at the opportunity, because I wanted to contribute substantively to the nation's debate on broadcasting and also because I was curious about the process of working with the civil service as an outsider on a paper intended to open up some new ideas.

In fact, my work was done in complete isolation from civil servants: no long meetings negotiating carefully towards consensus, no rephrasing each other's language, no nasty disagreements to be adjudicated by the Minister. Department adviser, Colm Ó Briain was the go-between, and sketched out the assumptions that had guided the drafting thus far. I worked on a re-write totally on my own. There was a strange hiatus of several weeks in 1994 when the Government fell and it seemed that my work and the Green Paper might come to nothing. The country went to the polls to produce another Rainbow Coalition, Michael D. returned as Minister, Colm Ó Briain and Kevin O'Driscoll returned as Adviser and Programme Manager and work on the Green Paper was completed. I was immediately told that my draft of the Green Paper was fully accepted by the Minister as it stood, complete with references to Jurgen Habermas and academic jargon. Too late I realised the jargon should have been edited out, when I heard Vincent Browne on radio try to verbally maul the Minister for the obscurantist language that infused his Green Paper.

The basic foundation of the Green Paper was the Minister's and his concerns emerged strongly in the final version that was published in April 1995, several months later than its intended launch date. It was clear to me from our conversations that he had little faith in the RTÉ Authority, which in his view had proved incapable of unleashing and managing the wealth of creativity within RTÉ, retreating instead into a position of retrenchment, regarding broadcasting merely as an industrial system like any other that had to maximise its revenues and minimise its cost base. But merely changing the personnel on the Authority would not fix the problem, which was structural and deeply rooted. He worried over the riddle of how to combine the management ethos of a public resource such as RTÉ with the management ethos needed in an organisation whose raison d'etre was to maximise continually a culture of creative productivity. How could the contradictions generated in a body that is both semi-State and essentially an engine for creativity be managed under one roof? Could success in this endeavour even extend to the successful export of Irish programming, to the Irish diaspora and elsewhere?

It became clear to me in working on the text of the Green Paper that one aspect of the original draft was untouchable, even though I had serious misgivings myself about how helpful it would be in revitalising Irish broadcasting. This was the Minister's unshakeable belief in what he called a "Superauthority", a body which would exist outside RTÉ and work to resolve some of the inertia which he perceived to be inhibiting the creative energy that should be driving production. His view was deeply influenced by his knowledge of the film production sector and his relationship with film producers, many of whom were deeply disappointed in the apparent failure of RTÉ to be the key driver in the production of fiction which could thrive even in the international media marketplace. His views were also influenced by his awareness of a low morale problem within RTÉ, especially among its producers, and an aching feeling that "public service broadcasting" needed a clear definition, not just theoretically and in the increasingly important and turbulent world of EU cultural politics but also operationally in the pragmatic context of budget allocations and editorial meetings within the national broadcasting system. If recent Authorities, too close to the actualities of management problems, had proven themselves unable to tackle these challenges, would a new entity, a Superauthority, make a crucial difference? The main challenge now was how to provide a sound theoretical base for this Superauthority and test reactions from a number of sectors.

In launching the Green Paper Michael D. Higgins emphasised that it was not about breaking up RTÉ, a key element in media debates in Ireland a decade before, but about re-focusing the national broadcaster in the context of basic values: cultural diversity, broadcasting as a public good, the linkage between broadcasting and democracy and the need to put Irish broadcasting on a sound legislative footing at a time of intense change in a vexed continent, flooded with virtually instantaneous information circulated by ever more sophisticated technologies. Reaction was mixed. Fianna Fáil called the Green Paper disappointing, saying it was no more than an ideological treatise on broadcasting. RTÉ, the IRTC, the NUJ, Film-makers Ireland and IBEC all found something of value in it. Comment from other media was also mixed. John Waters in the *Irish Times* suggested that the manner in which it attempted to re-establish the parameters of the debate was both "radical and promising" as it raised questions "not as the thin ends of ideological prescriptions but as practical steps in addressing pressing cultural conundrums of the age."[14] In the same newspaper, Vincent Browne in a more populist vein found it "suffused with post-Modernist babble ... pretentious guff" produced by a Minister who had "lost the run of himself."[15] The Green Paper attempted to ground its discussion of broadcasting issues in the notion of the public sphere, explored in the work of the German philosopher Jurgen Habermas, but Browne was having none of this "tendentious, puerile, under-graduate babble" which proved only that broadcasting policy should not be left in the hands of Michael D. Higgins. The Green Paper galvanised the Independent Group of newspapers into a bitterly antagonistic view of Michael D. and everything he did or said for the remainder of his term in office, as if it was intent on stamping out as dangerous heresy the kind of robust defence of the values associated with public service broadcasting, values which had been taken for granted in public discussion at the establishment of RTÉ in the early 1960s, again in the deliberations of the Broadcasting Review Committee of the early 1970s, and now championed once more in the Green Paper of 1995.

In the final version of the Green Paper the core notion of a Superauthority was suggested in Chapter 5 but not argued for with any degree of passion: "There may be a case for giving the RTÉ Authority a clearer policy mandate and for the separation of the 'guardian of the public interest' and 'regulator' roles from the more day to day functions and responsibilities of the Authority".[16] There may be an argument, it suggested, for merging the policy and regulatory functions of the RTÉ Authority and the IRTC to form one over-arching authority. This could assume overall responsibility for broadcasting policy, the development of broadcasting services generally and the regulation of broadcasters. This Superauthority would be able "to take an overview and balance the needs and demands of RTÉ on the one hand and the demands of the independent sector on the other". This would eliminate the need for the Minister to adjudicate between competing needs and demands rooted in the public and private systems. The Superauthority might also absorb the powers and functions of the Broadcasting Complaints Commission.

Surprisingly, this radical proposal for a Superauthority received very little attention in the media coverage that followed the publication of the Green Paper. Its significance was not lost on RTÉ however. Within a month of the publication of the Green Paper, the Minister had invited me to become Chairman of RTÉ, and I found myself immediately in the strange position of leading a team focused on unwrapping the academic jargon of the ideas advanced in the Green Paper and putting together RTÉ's response to them. My first meeting with senior staff was an informal one, sharing a pot of tea in the Director-General's office with Joe Barry himself, Assistant Director-General Bob Collins, Director of Television Liam Miller and Director of News Joe Mulholland. From the start I shared with them my role in the formulation of the Green Paper and my deep reservations about the notion of a Superauthority, notwithstanding the Minister's strong interest in it. It was not well theorised in the paper and the rationale for it was weak. Debate on a similar restructuring of broadcasting in Britain was then also circulating in New Labour circles in London. But there was a major concern in my mind that even though there might be a case for centralising some of the supervisory functions for both public and private sectors in areas of common concern (as the Conseil Superieur de l'Audiovisuel does in France), such as handling audience complaints, enforcing the right to privacy, overseeing impartiality in news and the protection of children etc., the tightly centralised regulation of both private and public broadcasting by one Superauthority in areas where they compete might seriously obscure and weaken the basic differences between the two sectors. There is a case for arguing that a regulatory body responsible for both sectors, operating in a political context ideologically infused with strong belief in neo-liberalism, might even become a powerful tool for unidirectional political and economic interests in which public service broadcasting would be the loser.[17]

As the new Authority set about formulating its response to the Green Paper, it found itself increasingly having to consider the implications of digital compression technology for the future of broadcasting in Ireland. Digital television received only a brief mention in the Green Paper and as late as the beginning of 1996 was receiving no attention from government departments in Ireland, and although the British government was moving rapidly with its White Paper to shape the policy for digital terrestrial television (DTT), but this was being considered within DG13 of the European Commission with considerable ambivalence. Colleagues in my position in other European countries, such as Markun Laukkanen, Chairman of the Administrative Council of YLE, the Finnish public service broadcaster, were highly critical of what was seen as gross complacency in Brussels.

RTÉ's response to the Green Paper, worked out over the summer and autumn of 1995, focused in particular on the proposed Superauthority and pointed out that if all dispersed references to it were brought together, it became clear that it would have a strikingly wide range of powers.[18] These would be underpinned by its role as a distributor of public funds to all broadcasters for certain types of programming in accordance with criteria set out in legislation, as discussed in Chapter 8 of the Green Paper. This system of licence fee disbursement had been suggested in the Peacock Report in Britain some years before and though never implemented there, had inspired the establishment of a similar structure in New Zealand, with very mixed results.[19] RTÉ feared that such a Superauthority in Ireland would in effect develop into a super-broadcaster, with existing channels becoming programme providers to a schedule based on policy articulated by a Superauthority, perhaps in a system, like New Zealand On Air (NZOA), whose funding was determined by the Superauthority. This would seriously undermine the autonomy of the individual broadcast companies and blur the distinction between the different roles of the public and the private sectors.

The RTÉ response proposed that a National Broadcasting Commission be established instead, with a broad remit for developing and implementing national policy on broadcasting, including issues arising in an environment where broadcasting and telecommunications are merging, allowing new technologies and new communication services to emerge. DTT in particular would require a commission to decide issues of frequency allocation, equal access to new technology, media ownership rules, local and regional digital broadcasting issues. The National Broadcasting Commission would also deal with codes for advertising and sponsorship, broadcasting complaints and standards and would establish a rate card for access to RTÉ's transmission system. But it would not play a role in the programming and scheduling functions of individual broadcasters.

Early in 1996, Michael D. Higgins informed us that some one hundred and thirty responses to the Green Paper had been received and instead of trying to balance all the competing interests in a White Paper, he would proceed directly to publishing the heads of a new broadcasting bill. Inexplicably, however, more than a year passed before the shape of a new bill began to emerge, and when it did, the Superauthority, in the form of a proposed Irish Broadcasting Commission was firmly back on the agenda. The vagueness of the Green Paper was gone, replaced now by a clearer, firmer expression of the Minister's view.[20] And it wasn't received well in RTÉ.

The Minister's proposals at this point took the form of "Heads of Bill," for which he had received Government approval to advance to the parliamentary drafting stage. The paper summarised the thrust of the Green Paper, offered a definition of public service broadcasting, established TG4 as a separate statutory entity and copper-fastened the concept of the licence fee funding of RTÉ as a reasonable payment for a national broadcasting service rather than a State subsidy. In so doing, the Minister, to the great relief of RTÉ, was rejecting the "New Zealand option" of dividing the licence fee revenue among broadcasters according to the type of programming provided. He centred on the establishment of a single regulatory and policy-making body, the Irish Broadcasting Commission, to oversee the broadcasting sector in Ireland, including the regulation of local and community services on cable television and MMDS, satellite and educational television services. The existing functions of the IRTC would be transferred to the IBC. The RTÉ Authority would be reconstituted as a broadcasting corporation, charged with operating its services consistent with the general policy objectives adopted by the new Commission. The Authority would no longer have a function in relation to the development of broadcasting policy. The Commission would approve both hours of broadcasting and advertising minutage for RTÉ, comment in its annual reports on the performance of RTÉ and formally review that performance every five years. RTÉ and other broadcasters would finance the Commission by paying an annual percentage level (1.5 percent) on its broadcast commercial income. The Commission would have no discretion in respect of passing on revenue from licence fees to RTÉ and the fee itself would be index-linked to general inflation.

It was no surprise to me that the "New Zealand option" was no longer active, as I believed the Minister never had any intention of disbursing the licence fee income to a variety of broadcasters in an "Arts Council of the Airwaves" model, despite strong pressure from the Association of Independent Stations (AIRS). The core of Clear Focus / Focus Gear was a proposal to change fundamentally the way in which RTÉ is governed. The Commission would be empowered to subject the performance of RTÉ to "rigorous scrutiny" and to initiate change if considered necessary. It would draw up a comprehensive charter for RTÉ, which might expand on the statutory objectives of the national broadcaster and amend it from time to time. It would review RTÉ's organisational structure to see if it is the best for meeting its remit and ensure that the structure promotes innovation, quality and diversity in its programming. It could require appropriate restructuring initiatives and require RTÉ to make changes to or even to cease certain commercial activities. It could generate revenue from new commercial activities if consistent with a commitment to fair trading. The Commission would review the costs of various activities within RTÉ in order to determine the comparative funding of different elements in those activities. The Commission could also establish specific elements of RTÉ's activities, such as its transmission system, as separate entities under the control of a separate board if this arrangement were considered beneficial to broadcasting in general in Ireland. Finally, it could require RTÉ to include any particular matter, including financial matters, in its annual reports. No new powers in relation to the private broadcasting sector were proposed, beyond those already embodied in the Radio and Television Act of 1998.

The new powers given to the proposed Commission were, of course, those already exercised by the RTÉ Authority. The key change proposed in the Government plan was to strip these powers out of RTÉ and bestow them on a new body with no organisational links with RTÉ but rather regulatory and policy links to both public and private broadcasting. What was the rationale for the assumption that this new arrangement, in which RTÉ would be answerable to an Irish Broadcasting Commission, would secure the public interest in broadcasting for a long time to come? What was the argument supporting the assertion that these changes would serve the public interest? The first (leaked) version of the plan merely asserted that "confidence in existing structures, where the broadcasting authority is the operator of the broadcasting service, to address a range of issues in an objective way is decreasing". None of the one hundred and thirty responses to the Green Paper was cited in support of this claim. Whose confidence? Certainly not radio and television audiences as measured in JNLR and TAM ratings, and certainly not opinion polls or feedback from town hall meetings with RTÉ, which demonstrated a consistently healthy appreciation of the national broadcaster. In the published version, this was changed a little: "there is diminishing confidence among broadcasting professionals in the capacity of the existing structures to address such issues in an objective way".[21] But where had broadcasting professionals expressed this view?

There were two principal locations. RTÉ Television Producers and Directors submitted a response to the Green Paper in 1995 in which there was a scathing attack on the previous ten years' output of television, which was seen to be driven by Authority and management policies that severely diluted programme quality and diversity in a bid to increase sheer quantity of hours produced. They described the schedule as a series of low-cost, formula programmes, many of them merely imitating what has been commercially successful elsewhere. Among the recommendations is the notion of a broadcasting charter, based on specific public service obligations, renewable by the Oireachtas every ten years, to be overseen by a new Superauthority. The Producers/Directors' paper articulated a very unhappy professional situation. Its authors were clearly frustrated and disillusioned. The root of this misery probably lies in their view of the RTÉ Authority's policy response to the Government-commissioned SKC Report of 1985, which stressed the need for a significant increase in production. In 1985, RTÉ broadcast 975 hours of home-produced television (excluding sports, news and repeats), with a staff of 303 in the Television Programmes Division. In 1996, it broadcast almost 1,700 hours with a staff of 357 (excluding the Independent Production Unit and commissioned programmes). The major increase in production actually took place in 1986-91 and the volume of production then stabilised.

During this period, competition from other English-language channels grew fierce as British television penetrated more deeply into Ireland. Satellite technology was in its infancy in Europe but cable companies, still firmly in Irish ownership (RTÉ itself was involved in cable distribution systems in the major urban areas) were expanding audience access to the BBC, Channel Four and ITV. Indeed, in the context of negotiations to end the Troubles in Northern Ireland, it became a steady complaint from Dublin that while less than 30 percent of the Northern Ireland population could receive RTÉ (due to restrictions imposed on the strength and directionality of RTÉ transmitters positioned near the Border and Unionist objections to changing that situation, often couched in engineering jargon), about 70 percent of the population of the Republic could be reached by UK television signals beamed from Northern Irland. Cable systems were also improving their competitive positions by offering their customers new channels based on American content and testing the children's television market.

It was obvious to other broadcasters in Europe that RTÉ was the star performer throughout this period in terms of maintaining a large share of the national audience in what is probably the most competitive same-language multichannel environment in the whole of Europe. Unlike comparable broadcasters in other small peripheral European countries (for example, Denmark, Finland, Norway or Greece) RTÉ faced competition from large Anglophone broadcasters, whose output was resourced initially, before successful international sales, by their large domestic audiences (in the case of the UK, an audience over twenty times the size of RTÉ's). What the Producer/Directors' paper clearly communicated was their alienation from corporate decision-making in RTÉ, something that had to be addressed urgently. And the measure of their alienation was their bypassing of management structures in RTÉ to present their views directly to the Minister.

But it is the IRTC response to the Green Paper that most clearly resembles what eventually emerged in "Clear Focus." It argued for a National Broadcasting and Transmission Authority, which would expand the existing functions of the IRTC and assume regulatory responsibility for all RTÉ channels, including TG4, as well as the licensing of cable, MMDS and local television services. It would also oversee policy for a National Transmission Company to be formed out of the privatisation of RTÉ's transmission system. Crucially, it also adopted the "New Zealand option" and recommended that the Superauthority should disburse licence fee revenue to a range of broadcasters since, it argued, public service broadcasting is no longer the sole preserve of RTÉ. The new Superauthority could be built around the current IRTC "which is the only independent body involved in the regulation and monitoring functions and is experienced in balancing the interests and needs of different operators in the independent sector".[22]

This proposal from the IRTC had been greeted with consternation in media circles generally in 1995 because of what was perceived as severe centrist tendencies and because of fears that the Superauthority would mean not only another unnecessary layer of bureaucracy but the imposition of "politically correct" ways on broadcasters. Yet it is the IRTC proposal that was essentially adopted by the Minister, minus the licence fee disbursement role. In fact its organisational chart is remarkably similar to that in "Clear Focus" (Appendix One).

While the establishment of a single regulatory and policy-making body appeared to be a neat administrative arrangement, it needed to be demonstrated that such a formidable concentration of power doesn't actually harm the public interest. After all, the Superauthority notion could attract adherence from the right of the political spectrum just as it could from the left. Michael D. Higgins, following his very good socialist instincts, saw the Superauthority as the answer to all the inadequacies he perceived in RTÉ: not doing enough to be an excellent public service broadcaster, allowing itself to become too commercial, frustrating in-house producers and foot-dragging on sharing its resources with independent producers. But a right-wing Minister, such as Ray Burke of Fianna Fáil, following his quite different instincts could also dream of a Superauthority which would address what he might have seen as a different set of inadequacies within RTÉ: its perceived anti-Fianna Fáil bias, its arrogant star presenters, its public humiliation of the Minister when he ran the gauntlet of staff demonstrations on his visit to Montrose in 1990, its stubborn reluctance to donate transmission facilities to Century Radio and its greedy gobbling up of advertising revenue needed to launch new private broadcasters.

In a lengthy letter to the Minister towards the end of 1995, I had argued against the IRTC vision of a Superauthority, on the basis that there was simply no guarantee that placing all broadcasting services, public and private, under one regulatory body would result in equity of treatment for all. It was a matter of belief, rather than something that was convincingly and self-evidently true, that a single Authority is better than the existing separation of functions between RTÉ and the IRTC. A single regulator could, in fact, face a conflict of interest between the need to ensure the success of private broadcasters and the obligation to support competitive services in the public sector. And it is easy to imagine particular configurations of political forces in a future Ireland which could radically open broadcasting to extremely detrimental political influence through the concentration of monopolistic regulatory power in one group, especially one with the power to intervene in internal organisational and budgetary aspects of broadcasting which could bring it very close to editorial influence on content. Would future ministers always balance appointments to this very powerful Authority between advocates of public service broadcasting and advocates of private commercial broadcasting and will even-handedness of approach always dominate?

One has only to compare the attitudes to public service broadcasting of two ministers in the last decade, Ray Burke and Michael D. Higgins, to see the naivety of simple belief in the efficacy of a Superauthority. Examples from overseas would also suggest caution. The Federal Communications Commission appointed by Ronald Reagan, very successfully launched a no-holds-barred, neo-liberalist onslaught on public service broadcasting norms and protections in the US. A similar gravitational pull towards working on behalf of private interests in broadcasting rather than the public interest can be seen in the history of the CRTC in Canada, where the persistent discipline and the superior resources of industry lobbyists proved far more effective in influencing policy and regulation than the dispersed array of public interest groups trying to influence broadcasting policy. Broadcasting in the UK is far more robustly serving the public interest than either the US or Canada, precisely because it doesn't have a single regulatory authority. Healthy competition between the public and private systems has been structurally encouraged since the 1950s, though New Labour has been toying with its own idea of a Superauthority.

The campaign for a Superauthority was based on persistent but diffuse critique of RTÉ. But if one looked at evidence from audience share data in multichannel areas where competition from UK channels was keen, or RTÉ-commissioned MRBI research into its corporate reputation, showing consistently high levels of public satisfaction, there was no evidence of widespread support for the notion that RTÉ was almost terminally ill and needed a blast of regulatory energy from a Superauthority to revive it. Anti-RTÉ sentiment at this level, I believe, was embedded in no more than a few hundred people, but this was a publicly articulate minority of opinion leaders: unhappy politicians, frustrated independent producers, hostile press commentators from competing media and others who make television a scapegoat for a host of social ills (including "the liberal agenda") that spring from a variety of sources besides broadcasting. Many of their criticisms are valid and challenge RTÉ to make itself more responsive, more creative, more daring, more collaborative and more open. But there are other ways to tackle these challenges besides a Superauthority.

Building the new structure on the foundations (staff, ethos, organisational memory) of the IRTC would mean that in future RTÉ's regulator would be the developer of private broadcasting, now enhanced into a five-member full-time Commission. The public/private tensions that would be built into the Commission would be particularly acute in a country as small as Ireland, where the base of advertising and licence funding is so small. It is inevitable that the neo-liberal pressures to make room for more private broadcasting would build up within the Commission and be channelled towards "down-sizing" the "State monopoly". Attractive targets would include curtailing advertising minutage, preventing RTÉ from bidding for international programming desired by TV3, stripping out, privatising or even closing down some of RTÉ's current operations, especially Network Two, 2FM or the RTÉ Guide. And the Commission would thus facilitate the weakening of RTÉ in a politically neutral way.

All of these points were put vigorously to the Minister in his office in March 1997 a few days before "Clear Focus" was published, by myself and a delegation from the Authority. The Minister was in no mood to listen. The Irish Broadcasting Commission was needed in its present form he insisted. I followed up with a letter expressing our concerns about the Superauthority, in particular our belief that the new regulator would also function as the overall developer of broadcasting in Ireland and that in this process, the inevitable demands for expansion in the private sector would have to be satisfied to a great extent at the expense of public service broadcasting. Furthermore, the extensive powers of the Commission and the full-time nature of the five Commissioners' roles would make it extremely difficult for the Irish Broadcasting Commission to remain detached from the day-to-day operation of broadcasting services and not get involved editorially in RTÉ services. It seemed inevitable to us that the regulator, given its powers to get involved in re-designing RTÉ's organisational structures, especially those relating to diversity in news and current affairs, would be drawn into ever closer involvement with day-to-day operations, an outcome of the legislation which would be directly opposed to the declared intentions of the Government that the editorial integrity of RTÉ as a broadcasting corporation would not be diminished in any respect by the new structural arrangement.

But time was running out for the Minister's plan for a radical restructuring of broadcasting. In June 1997, a general election brought a Fianna Fáil-Progressive Democrat coalition into government and a new Minister, Síle de Valera, was entrusted with the broadcasting brief. Our immediate concern was the licence fee increase of £8, which had been granted by Michael D. Higgins and which in effect went to pay for the new programme production that RTÉ was undertaking for Teilifís na Gaeilge. The Rainbow Government had agreed to the index-linking of the licence fee but had failed to put that mechanism in place before it lost office. One of the first acts of the new Government was to rescind the index-linking. This was to have disastrous financial consequences for RTÉ later, because although inflation in broadcasting in this period far outpaced the consumer price index, indexation to the CPI would go some way towards allowing RTÉ's public revenue to increase in a relatively painless way from a viewer's point of view. From a Government perspective, it would allow public support for RTÉ to increase without the usual political fear of a public backlash that has accompanied every formal decision on an increase.

There is a certain irony in the fact that Michael D. Higgins should have left office without enacting legislation which would have addressed the concerns he initially raised in the Green Paper on broadcasting. He was a man who went beyond the usual political platitudes about "supporting public service broadcasting" to raise large questions about what such broadcasting should actually be and persuaded his Government colleagues to radically restructure the regulatory environment to bring out the best in RTÉ as he saw it. It should be remembered however that his 1993 Broadcasting Act actually had a very profound impact on RTÉ, for better or worse, perhaps more than any Superauthority could have, because it changed radically the production base of television programming by channelling funds to the independent sector. No new broadcasting legislation would be passed until 2001, after he had left office. As already indicated, the preparation for this Act focused not on the dominant Green Paper question – what is the public interest in relation to broadcasting and how can it best be served in the future – but what is digital television and how can it best utilise this new medium for the benefit of everyone in Ireland? There is another irony in the fact that the notion of a Superauthority, combining the regulatory roles of both the RTÉ Authority and the BCI, originally suggested by a Labour Minister in 1995, is now official policy in a Fianna Fáil-led Government. Minister Dermot Ahern took charge of broadcasting policy after the General Election of 2002 and appointed a Forum on Broadcasting, which recommended that a new Broadcasting Commission be established which would combine all regulatory powers together. Legislation for this is in preparation in 2003.

We turn now to a closer look at the relationship between broadcasting and Government.

3

BROADCASTING AND GOVERNMENT

Shortly after Tom Hardiman became Director-General in April 1968, the Chairman of RTÉ, Todd Andrews, invited the Minister in charge of Broadcasting, Erskine Childers, to dinner to meet the new Chief Executive of the country's most important cultural organisation. RTÉ had come through its first seven years of existence, the last three of them characterised by growing unhappiness among the staff at what was seen as increasing pressure from Government Ministers to control television output in their favour. The Chairman described the new Director-General, with a certain degree of approval, as a man who enjoyed an argument, sometimes to the point of overstating his case at Authority meetings and failing to let well enough alone, who "was never willing to let his bone go with the dog". In the course of the meal, the Minister handed Andrews a plain sheet of paper containing about a dozen names of RTÉ employees and programme guests who, according to the Minister, were "lefties, if not card carrying Communists, who should be treated as suspect subversives". The Minister refused to disclose the source of the document, but Andrews immediately replied that it had been compiled by the Special Branch (recently the object of a television documentary probe) under the inspiration of the "paranoid Department of Justice", that RTÉ would pay no attention to the allegations, and that it was not the job of the Special Branch to "institute a system of thought control or act as purveyors of political gossip."[23] The Chairman made the point that as a young man he and many of his associates had suffered from harassment by the Special Branch, some being driven to emigration, and that he was determined that no one should suffer economically or otherwise for their political opinions. He later put these thoughts to the Minister in a letter and asked that it be shown to the Taoiseach, Sean Lemass. It wasn't, but secret lists were never mentioned again.

This dinner table vignette illustrates the enormous vulnerability of broadcasting organisations to manipulation by the forces of the State. In many broadcasting organisations, the methods are far less subtle. In absolute monarchies television and radio are organised as core activities of a Ministry of Information, publishing only that which is directly authorised by the palace. In transitional societies in Central Europe, journalists go on strike, as in the Czech television crisis of 2000, to protest Government interference in the selection of the young Jakub Puchalsky as Director-General. What is at stake is the demonstrated power of the media to shape the agenda of public discussion, to impose a primary definition on a controversy and to put a particular frame around issues of vital importance to the health of a democracy.

RTÉ had to learn, through several bitter experiences, how to handle pressure from Government and facilitate the emergence of an ethos that would have more in common with an ideal of "public broadcasting" rather than a "State broadcasting" model. The Enlightenment tradition that underpins public service broadcasting had fore-grounded the links between a valid democracy and a social system that facilitates diversity of opinion. Thomas Jefferson included this in his Conditions of Political Freedom and Emmanuel Kant elevated it into a "Principle of Publicity" without which the exercise of social power would not have legitimacy. Irish broadcasters and politicians had to learn, slowly and painfully and in different ways, how to reconcile the desire for political freedom, driven by the liberal value of liberty of political choice, with the need to defend the cultural preconditions and accommodations on which both depend, especially freedom of expression.

Government hesitations throughout the 1950s about supporting calls for the introduction of television had much to do with economic anxieties in that depressed decade, but it also had much to do with the putative power of television and how the exercise of authority in Ireland might shift once RTÉ would flicker into life. After all, the Catholic Church had warned in 1961 that television could, in the wrong hands, be a powerful instrument for evil. Where people had to go out of their homes to view films in the cinema, television would bring "all this Pagan propaganda" into the family circle. The *Catholic Truth* quarterly worried that "more souls may be taken away from Christ through the gospel of pleasure they absorbed through television than if the anti-Christ would start an open, bloody persecution in our country."[24]

Politicians also feared the power of television in the 1960s and for similar reasons. Television was a new conduit of information, reaching into every home in Ireland, challenging the control of public opinion previously enjoyed by the cosy duopoly of Church and State. At the inauguration of Telefís Éireann on the 31st December 1961, Sean Lemass expressed in public his reservations about entrusting television to an Authority outside the Government, "relying only on directive principles set out in legislation and on the power of the Government to appoint members of the Authority to ensure that the direction of the service would be consistently in harmony with the highest and most enduring purposes of our nation."[25] His unease extended into the script he prepared for his Minister for Posts and Telegraphs, to be delivered at the inaugural meeting of the RTÉ Authority, a script he expected Michael Hilliard to deliver without changes unless those changes were notified back to him.

There is no doubt that the Government found it extremely difficult to come to terms with the new radio and television organisation that they had created. One of the reasons for this is that the blueprint for RTÉ neglected to provide any formal channel through which Ministers could communicate with the broadcasting organisation when important national issues were at stake. So boundaries between Government and RTÉ had to be established pragmatically, by experimentation and within the political culture of the time, each side testing its power and gauging possible reactions. Before the station opened, its first Director-General, Ed Roth, asserted that RTÉ "would not be a political organ of the government of the day". After six long years of frustration, much of it with RTÉ's news and current affairs output, during which he dallied with the notion of establishing a Minister for Information to oversee the work of RTÉ, Lemass made his famous declaration in the Dáil that "RTÉ was set up by legislation as an instrument of public policy and as such is responsible to the Government....to this extent the Government reject the view that RTÉ should be, either generally or in regard to its current affairs and news programmes, completely independent of Government supervision."[26]

This well-prepared assertion of Government power was prompted by a row between Charles Haughey, Minister for Agriculture, and the National Farmers Association, which dragged RTÉ – Government tensions fully into the public spotlight. Haughey complained to the RTÉ Newsroom about the insulting juxtaposition on the news of a statement from the NFA with a statement of his own. The NFA statement was deleted from the following bulletins. The NUJ and the Dublin newspapers were incensed by this interference. Haughey responded with further pressure on the current affairs television programme *Division*, which insisted on presenting both Government and farmers' views. Haughey boycotted the programme but "Division" continued without Fianna Fáil input and its sister, the current affairs programme *Seven Days*, responded by devoting a whole week of programming to freedom in broadcasting, exploring Government and commercial interference in broadcasting in other European countries and the USA.[27]

Some flavour of the political culture of 1960s Ireland can be tasted in the language of the sarcastic reflections of Todd Andrews on the staff in RTÉ who were getting increasingly recalcitrant with Government attempts to rein in discussion of public issues on television. "There was usually a trendy priest in the background. A few wholetime academics – to the extent to which such people exist – were recruited in a part-time capacity to add prestige to the discussion programmes....Unlike civil servants, they were almost all endowed, or inflicted, depending on one's point of view, with temperament and unlike civil servants, many of them claimed to be 'concerned', which was the vogue word of the time. They were a difficult group for a Director-General to cope with – to use the word 'control' in this context would probably be considered dictatorial. 'Concerned' citizens seemed to me to be divided into different categories. Some were idealists prepared to go to the scaffold to eliminate the injustices of society....Some were parlour pinks enjoying the social cachet attached to radical chic in pubs and suburban drawing rooms...It is difficult to see how they expected so rotten a society to provide them with the expensive and complicated facilities of a television network and pay them while they rushed into the fray to establish the new Jerusalem".[28]

Todd Andrews believed in the Lemass doctrine that it was the duty of the RTÉ Authority to support official policy and this emerged clearly in his handling of the Hanoi affair. The Authority initially supported the sending of a television team to North Vietnam in April 1967, feeling that RTÉ coverage of the war generally relied excessively on British and American sources, and that it was time that RTÉ developed a more ambitious news gathering operation in its coverage of world affairs, so that an Irish point of view could replace an excessive reliance on a British or American interpretation. When the Department of Foreign Affairs objected to this, Andrews' concern was to find out if the objection was based on a Government decision or merely the personal view of an individual Minister. He considered, and then rejected, the possibility of insisting that if the Government wanted the project cancelled, it should exercise its statutory powers of veto by issuing a formal instruction. He telephoned

Jack Lynch, who had succeeded Seán Lemass as Taoiseach, and they agreed to publish a public statement to the effect that sending a news team to Hanoi "would be an embarrassment to the Government in relation to its foreign policy".[29] A short time later, a *Seven Days* team led by Muirghis MacConghail, on its way to Biafra during the Nigerian Civil War, was recalled when it was already in Lisbon, though Todd Andrews was at pains to point out to Garret FitzGerald at the time that the Irish Government was not involved in this decision. Despite this setback, a programme on Biafra was put together, combining acquired footage with an RTÉ commentary. This was criticised by the Nigerian Ambassador for giving "an unfavourable and unfair impression of the Nigerian Government" and the Minister for Posts and Telegraphs asked the Authority for a copy of the programme. The uproar that ensued inside RTÉ, in the newspapers and in Dáil Éireann, focused on both inappropriate use of Government power in broadcasting and excessive acquiescence to this power by RTÉ.

There were significant long-term consequences for the national broadcaster. Staff morale and confidence in senior management were left severely bruised. Many felt the Authority, which had been appointed to defend the rights of free expression in broadcasting, had abandoned those rights. Todd Andrews himself regretted not having insisted that the Government use its statutory veto power, though this extended only to preventing the transmission of a programme, not gathering material for its production. Yet he and the Authority went on to veto a programme dealing with the activities of the Garda Special Branch, after it had been made and scheduled for transmission. The subsequent moving of *Seven Days* to the News Division, widely seen by staff as an expression of no confidence by the Authority in the Television Programme Division, brought the organisation to the brink of an all-out strike.[30] Yet the Government assumption throughout the Sixties, that it should control RTÉ as tightly as it could a Government Department, continued to impinge on the organisation and on public perceptions of the "independence," or lack of it, in the national broadcasting organisation. When Director-General, Kevin McCourt, resigned and the RTÉ Authority was in the process of selecting his successor, the Minister, Erskine Childers, conveyed the Government's interest in knowing the names of applicants for the job, a request refused by Todd Andrews on the grounds of an obligation to observe confidentiality for all candidates.

Fianna Fáil's relationship with RTÉ reached a nadir in 1972 with the dismissal of the Authority by the Government. The ultimate method of reining in a recalcitrant Authority was invoked by Minister Gerry Collins as the pace of"The Troubles" was accelerating. RTÉ itself had been bombed and its buildings were now defended by armed soldiers. Veteran newsman, Kevin O'Kelly, was gaoled for refusing to identify the voice broadcast in a radio news programme as that of Séan MacStiofain, Chief of Staff of the IRA. Both the Irish and the British Governments were keen to pin down evidence linking MacStiofain to the IRA. The Gardaí paid a late night visit to the home of Director-General, Tom Hardiman, and asked for production materials used in the O'Kelly programme. These were refused on the grounds that journalistic sources had to be protected. The Government wrote to the Authority asking them to countermand the Director-General's order. As the linchpin in this very public crisis, Hardiman fully expected to be fired and the programme materials handed over.[31] But after an all-day meeting, the Authority decided to stick by their Director-General and resist the Government pressure. The following day, the Authority itself was removed from office. Jack Lynch later told the story that when he met Ted Heath soon after this, the British Prime Minister was most impressed with Lynch's strength of will in dismissing a public body that numbered among its members the widow of a former President (Bean Ui Cheallaigh). It would, he thought, be like firing the BBC Governors while the Queen Mother was still a member. Before this episode could sink too deeply into the collective memory of RTÉ, Conor Cruise O'Brien, as a member of a new Government, changed the law in 1976 so that in future the RTÉ Authority could be dismissed by the Government, only if the decision were approved by both Houses of the Oireachtas.

THE LOWRY-TUFFY AFFAIR

The point in referring to a small number of the many encounters between the Government and the infant RTÉ is not to lay out a definitive history of broadcasting in the 1960s but to provide something of a benchmark against present day relationships with Government can be viewed. Thirty years is not a very long time in organisational memory or in the evolution of political culture, yet significant changes have taken place since Erskine Childers worried over dinner about "lefties".

What then of RTÉ's relationship with government in the 1990s? Strong belief persists inside RTÉ and right across the public sphere, largely influenced by the experience of the 1960s, that Governments regularly use the Authority as their instrument in forcing their will on broadcasters and their editorial view on the unsuspecting public. Partly because of the peculiarities of Irish political culture and partly because no formal channel between government and RTÉ was constructed in the early sixties when the blueprint for public broadcasting was being designed (other than the crisis-oriented power to veto a broadcast or fire the Authority), relationships with Government are complex and communication often deeply coded. My conclusion after five years on the Authority is that RTÉ needs more, not less, communication with Government, but on policy rather than on programme matters. The Chairman's telephone was ringing too often in the 1960s with calls from the Minister. (Todd Andrews complained about a continual barrage of "ministerial grouses" directed at him every Thursday and Friday when the Cabinet met, and threatened to go and see the Taoiseach and ask him to exercise a restraining influence on his colleagues, to cease their "silly complaints" about programmes they didn't like). The Chairman's phone in the 1990s was much more silent. Indeed, it was too silent at times, when closer policy collaboration between Authority and Minister was urgently needed.

Five months after I was appointed Chairman in 1995, RTÉ found itself at the epicentre of a bizarre series of events described by one Government Minister as "a naked attempt to destabilise the government". The man who assumed the central role in this melodrama was Michael Lowry, Minister for Transport, Energy and Communications, who was to become the focus later in the decade of official enquiries into political corruption.

The Ministerial portfolio was a wide one, encompassing responsibility for several state companies, including the large utilities, Telecom Éireann and the Electricity Supply Board, now gearing themselves up to face novel competitive pressures as EU de-regulation policies started to bite. Lowry was also responsible for the transport companies, Aer Lingus and CIE, as well as An Post, Aer Rianta and Bórd na Móna. When Lowry became a Minister in the Rainbow Coalition, led by John Bruton, he quickly signalled his intention to shake up the semi-State sector, and in particular to root out what he called a "cosy cartel" operating in the awarding of contracts to private companies.

First in the firing line was bus and train company, CIE, where controversy dogged its attempts to sell land at Horgan's Quay in Cork to property developer Owen O'Callaghan. This led to Michael Lowry unexpectedly replacing the Chairman of CIE, Dermot O'Leary, and facing down the full board in what was seen as a victory for the Minister. During the Summer months of 1995, Lowry had been claiming that he was under surveillance in his commercial and private affairs by mysterious elements, but that he would press on with reforming procedures applied in tendering for State business. In October, he announced the winner of the much sought after second licence for operating a mobile telephone system. This was the culmination of years of telecommunications' policy changes being implemented first in Brussels and then in Dublin, and the highly lucrative contract was given to the newly formed Irish company, E-Sat Telecom and its partner Telenor, the Norwegian State telephone company. But controversy dogged Lowry in this decision too, when one of the losers in the bidding process, Persona, queried the Minister about the business ethics of E-Sat in contributing to an advertising campaign urging the Government not to award the licence to Persona because of the ESB's involvement in the consortium.

Another unsuccessful consortium led by Comcast, in which RTÉ was a partner, publicly demanded how and why E-Sat had won the lucrative franchise.

The conduct of the decision of the second mobile telephone licence was to come under scrutiny some years later in the context of judicial enquiries into political corruption. But in 1995 the controversy was overtaken by the climax of what the three leaders of the Coalition Government were taking seriously as a "dirty tricks" campaign against Michael Lowry. The Minister had been claiming that the "sinister" surveillance operation arising out of his efforts to smash the "cosy cartel" in the semi-State sector, was linked to three business people associated with Fianna Fáil, then the Opposition party. Cork-based property developer, Owen O'Callaghan and former CIE Chairman, Dermot O'Leary denied that they had placed Lowry under surveillance and threatened legal action against anyone pursuing this allegation. Government colleagues defended Lowry and called on Fianna Fáil to "stop playing politics". A whirligig of rumour and innuendo was being driven by a series of anonymous letters sent to several senior figures in public life, one of them causing the resignation of the Minister for Defence and the Marine, Hugh Coveney, after a Sunday newspaper used anonymously supplied information to accuse him of lobbying a State company, Bórd Gais, on behalf of business for his family firm.

Media and political speculation now began to focus intensely on the origin and authorship of the anonymous letters that were creating such an atmosphere of paranoia and mistrust in public life in Ireland. The bizarre claims of Michael Lowry about the "cosy cartel" he was aiming to smash and its links to the mysterious surveillance operation he was subject to, were proving difficult to substantiate. Every newsroom in Dublin thought the answer could be found in identifying the author of those letters.

The RTÉ current affairs programme *Prime Time* got the scoop. On Thursday, 2nd November 1995 it broadcast an interview with a former Fianna Fáil activist, who claimed that not only was he the mysterious poison pen writer, but that he was paid to write the letters by a person who, for legal reasons, could not be named. This was a former accountant, Pat Tuffy, well known some years previously as Treasurer in the Fianna Fáil consitituency office in Dublin South Central and an unsuccessful candidate in the previous local election. The former Chairman of CIE, Dermot O'Leary, had been Constituency Chairman at the same time. Tuffy had done some accountancy work in the early 1990s for Dublin architect, Ambrose Kelly, who was also referred to in the letters and was the "third man", along with Owen O'Callaghan and Dermot O'Leary, associated with Michael Lowry's putative "cosy cartel". Tuffy had been struck off the membership of the Institute of Chartered Accountants for practising without adequate insurance as a company liquidator and writing cheques that bounced.

Tuffy's television interview on RTÉ added to the sense of the bizarre and the melodramatic in this whole Lowry affair. He was paid to compose and send the letters, he claimed, by a handler who either met him or phoned him, using the public phone at the Avalon Coffee House on Aungier Street in Dublin. The handler gave him instructions on how to target each letter and structure the contents around the business and personal activities of O'Leary, O'Callaghan and Kelly. The handler gave him particularly precise instructions on how to structure a letter to disgraced ex-Minister Hugh Coveney to the effect that it was the fellow Cork man, Owen O'Callaghan, who leaked the information that precipitated the removal of Coveney from office. The anonymous letter, he said, should be written as if it came from within the office of Dublin architect Ambrose Kelly. Each of the letters being prepared for senior politicians contained new sets of allegations and defamations and he was sometimes instructed to rewrite them to make them "more racy". Payment, totalling £1,100, came in a number of ways, including being stuffed in his pocket at Punchestown Races.

But the question remained: who paid Tuffy to do this? Who was the real author? RTÉ's *Prime Time* programme followed the Tuffy interview with a discussion of its contents by journalists Sam Smyth and Emily O'Reilly. It was clear that they had access to more information than was released in the television interview and that these revelations could, as they dramatically put it, "bring down the Government". Before midnight, less than two hours after *Prime Time* was transmitted, a Government statement challenged the credibility of Pat Tuffy and refuted the implication in the programme that anyone acting on behalf of any member of the Government "paid or encouraged" Tuffy to write the letters. It was also confirmed that Michael Lowry had spent several hours in his Department taking legal and political advice about Tuffy's allegations about to be broadcast to the nation. The Opposition said that it was common knowledge the Government knew the identity of the person who paid the letter writer and called for full disclosure.

It was immediately clear to anyone watching *Prime Time* that night that the television audience and the political establishment were exposed to two very different sets of information at this time. One participated in a heightened television experience of great political importance, full of innuendo but still not declaring who had paid Tuffy. The other was sure Lowry was being accused of being Tuffy's puppet master. What was going on?

Clarification came the following morning on the RTÉ radio programme, *Morning Ireland*, when the Democratic Left Deputy, Eric Byrne, named Michael Lowry himself as the man who had paid Tuffy to pen the letters. It transpired that in segments of his television interview that were not broadcast, Tuffy had indeed named Lowry. The RTÉ Producer had corresponded with the Minister by fax before the broadcast, informing him about Tuffy's allegation, and Lowry had denied that he was the instigator of the letters. It was decided then not to name Lowry in the programme. Nevertheless, the Minister thought the programme was "so laced with innuendo" that he was going to take legal action seeking "exemplary damages" against RTÉ, Pat Tuffy and the journalist Sam Smyth. He repeated his denials in a full interview with RTÉ journalist Charlie Bird, which was broadcast at length on the main evening television newscast.

The Government immediately issued a statement: "we totally refute the implication in the *Prime Time* programme that anyone acting on behalf of any member of the Government, paid or encouraged the individual in question to write these letters". The Labour Party, junior partner in the Coalition Government, called the *Prime Time* programme "bizarre" and said that "the imputation, which could not be transmitted, that a certain person was centrally involved, was doubly bizarre." Bertie Ahern, Leader of the Opposition, weighed in with a trenchant condemnation of Lowry's "appalling judgement" in making unfounded allegations of surveillance and of a cartel in the semi-State sector, all based on hoax letters. Mr. Lowry must now "account for the waste of public monies" in having the Gardaí and an accountancy firm investigate his claims.

A few nights later, the RTÉ current affairs programme *Questions and Answers* fielded a team of speakers opposite John Bowman that represented most of the political parties. PD Leader, Mary Harney, said that Lowry's position was "extremely difficult". He had given the Tuffy letters too much credence and had made a mistake going public and making wild allegations about cosy cartels and surveillance without being sure of his facts.

Ray Burke of Fianna Fáil said that the Dáil Committee on Semi-State Companies should investigate Lowry's allegations about the three business men he named. Ivan Yates of Fine Gael wanted to know who had referred RTÉ to Pat Tuffy, how RTÉ "got this so-called scoop of the decade". He felt that the letter-writing affair was "a naked attempt to destabilize the government".

Even as this studio discussion was taking place in Montrose, RTÉ was bracing itself for a major embarrassment. The Tuffy story had gone badly wrong for *Prime Time*. It had indeed been correct to identify Pat Tuffy as the poison pen writer, using the name of one Denise Whelan, an employee of the architect Ambrose Kelly, for whom Tuffy had also worked as an auditor. But it had made the mistake of taking seriously Tuffy's allegation that he was actually paid by the Minister himself to write the hoax letters. The 9 p.m. News bulletin carried an RTÉ statement that it now knew the former Dublin accountant Mr. Pat Tuffy had misled the station with his allegations on *Prime Time* about being paid to write the letters. RTÉ accepted "that some members of the public understood that Minister Michael Lowry was the person who commissioned the writing of the letters by Mr. Tuffy. This was absolutely not the case". RTÉ "unreservedly" accepted that there had been no association whatsoever between Mr. Lowry and Mr. Tuffy, regretted that this false impression had been given and apologised to Mr. Lowry. It screened a second interview with Tuffy, where he admitted that the Minister "has never called to my house....has never met me in the Avalon Café...has never met me at Punchestown....and as categorically as I can make it, I have never met Mr. Lowry." When asked why he had written eighteen hoax letters, Tuffy replied they were written "out of pique and frustration about matters that go back to 1994 with some individual".

RTÉ now found itself caught in a most dangerous situation, positioned against its will in the crossfire between the Government, which found the RTÉ apology "not unexpected" and still believed Fianna Fáil dirty tricks were involved, and the Opposition, still attacking the Minister's inability to prevent the whole saga from damaging the credibility of political institutions. While apologising to Michael Lowry and regretting that some members of the television audience were misled, RTÉ stood by the accuracy of its identification of Pat Tuffy as the author of the letters.

The identification of Pat Tuffy effectively brought an end to the long saga of Michael Lowry's campaign against a cosy cartel in the semi-State sector. The threat of his libel charge hung over RTÉ for some time, though many believed the *Prime Time* programme itself could not be seen as clearly identifying him as Tuffy's paymaster. Much worse damage, however, would have been caused if the political institutions had engaged in a sustained attack on the national broadcaster for being politically partisan in the whole affair rather than merely guilty of an editorial lapse of judgement.

At the next meeting of the Authority, we concentrated on how the organisation was reacting to the Tuffy Affair and how important it was for the Authority to send clear signals to RTÉ staff as to its own interpretation of this major political embarrassment. Given the history of Chairmen and Authorities playing an active role in curtailing probing current affairs programming on RTÉ, because of real or perceived or anticipated pressures from political institutions, we had to be seen to stand squarely behind investigative journalism, encourage it as much as resources would allow and protect it from outside interference when the going got rough. With Director-General, Joe Barry, and Assistant Director-General, Bob Collins, we analysed in detail the weaknesses in the *Prime Time* programme itself and the preparations that preceded the broadcast, including the traditional journalistic pressure to beat the competitors by publishing a scoop at the earliest possible opportunity, perhaps even when background research hadn't been as complete as it ought to be. Clearer lines of responsibility were needed in Current Affairs, as well as more specific protocols to deal with the kinds of situations that arose in the Tuffy story involving Government Ministers.

But there were many positive aspects of *Prime Time* that deserved to be praised. The reporter, Ursula Halligan, was respected among fellow journalists, not as a quick-fix headline grabber, but as a steady searcher for the truth of a story. This attitude to professionalism was reinforced by the dogged persistence of Current Affairs Editor Peter Feeney, who had been consolidating a new sense of mission and higher morale in Current Affairs, building on the momentum generated by investigating sensitive stories such as Bishop Comiskey's illness and the Father Ivan Payne child sex abuse story. In the Lowry affair, it was an RTÉ reporter who had found the writer of the infamous letters that so troubled politicians in Government and Opposition, despite four months searching for him by journalists from competing media. Independent experts firmly established without doubt that Tuffy wrote the letters. Tuffy agreed to talk and responded at length to a tough, sceptical television interview. His obvious credibility problem, lack of physical evidence and dubious track record, were all continually highlighted by the reporter. The *Prime Time* team now had the man every other journalist wanted, along with his story and proof that he wrote the letters. They put Tuffy's charges to Lowry, who denied everything and threatened to sue, so they decided to run the story in a format that would not identify the Minister. The result was a programme that was confusing for some viewers and convinced others that it was an activist in Fianna Fáil who paid had Tuffy to write those letters. When *Prime Time* realised Tuffy was lying, the reporter pursued him to get a retraction on tape. No other journalist succeeded in finding him the week after the television interview. Indeed, it is ironical that journalists who later criticised the "RTÉ debacle" for being "naïve and ill judged," had themselves been taken in by the anonymous letters and had failed to find their author.

In the Authority meeting, we insisted that whatever errors of editorial judgements were made, the programme should not result in a chilling curb being placed on free thinking and investigative journalism. Some colleagues wondered how one member of the Authority, former Taoiseach Garret FitzGerald, would react to the way RTÉ had rushed to conclusions about one of his Ministerial colleagues in Fine Gael, but it is undoubtedly one of the strengths of the RTÉ Authority at this point in its history that partisan political postures play almost no role in the work of governing the national public service broadcaster, despite intense criticism in 1995 of John Bruton's appointment of FitzGerald. Garret fully supported our major concern, which now focussed on the health of the organisation as a producer of information programming whose dominant tendency must be not to shy away from poking cameras and microphones into the murky side of political life. We agreed a short press statement to the effect that errors had been made, lessons had been learned and the Authority was concerned that the Lowry affair should have no adverse effect on the investigative role of current affairs programming.

The trajectory of the Lowry affair, the biggest story in Irish political life for several years, roughly corresponded with the learning curve of this Authority, which was just five months in office when a climax was reached in the form of the Lowry-Tuffy affair. In subsequent meetings with the Director-General, members of the Executive Board and the Director of News, the Authority emphasised our strong interest in seeing a greater effort invested in investigative journalism, which should be a core value in a public service broadcasting system at any time but especially in this era of de-regulation, as a critical mass of political opinion in Ireland came to accept the arguments couched in an international neo-liberal ideology pushing for de-regulation of the broadcasting sector everywhere. These arguments, circulated domestically by a tireless group of newspaper journalists over the years, used what were essentially public service arguments to gain economic advantage for private interests. Privately owned radio and television stations were needed, we were incessantly told, so that a more dynamic journalistic alternative could be provided to the "cosy" world of the RTÉ Newsroom, to reenergize the democratic role of the media acting as public watchdogs overseeing the State. Some knowledge of broadcasting de-regulation in other countries, especially in the US, would have told us that the real dynamic behind the proliferation of private broadcasting stations is rooted in powerful international business interests and their gargantuan appetite for more ways to reach consumers with their marketing campaigns. International experience has been that in return for permission to open up broadcasting to a variety of new private companies, politicians would be guaranteed, not a robust probing of their work by journalists making a substantial contribution to the health of the democratic public sphere, but under-funded, tokenistic news services that were interested in doing little more than acting as conveyor bests purveying to the public press releases emanating from political institutions. There are some notable exceptions to this trend in so-called "independent" radio and television, of course, but not enough to negate the slide towards "infotainment" that has devastated American television and is making inroads in many European countries too. Public service watchdogs, despite their state links, can bark, while private watchdogs sleep.

RTÉ journalism would have to continue to commit itself to probing analysis of issues of public importance, despite the occasional embarrassment of "getting it wrong." I was continually surprised in my five years on the Authority, not only at how this was seen as a core broadcasting value by all kinds of employees in RTÉ but also how news and programmes staff in general monitored perceived Authority reactions to radio and television, as if haunted by residues in the collective memory of "betrayals" of staff by Authorities in the early years of television in Ireland. I have no doubt that RTÉ's pursuit of other "probing" stories later in our tenure, like the NIB tax evasion scam and the role of Beverly Cooper Flynn, daughter of former Minister and European Commissioner Padraig Flynn, would not have taken place if the Lowry affair had culminated in a great chilling effect inside RTÉ. There is no doubt that for several years, RTÉ had been slow to break important news stories, to expose scandals, to commit its best journalists to investigative projects. Too much of television current affairs depended on bland little packages lacking any sense of urgent relevance and timeliness, and on ritualised, staged confrontations between opposing politicians encouraged to indulge in theatrics in the studio, rather than help audiences dig for real content. Critics saw RTÉ current affairs programming as timid, defensive broadcasting, dominated by a conservative legal instinct in the fact of public controversy, unwilling to take risks. The established pattern was to follow up yesterday's newspaper stories rather than break new ground. So it was essential now, at the apex of the Lowry affair, to reinforce a new trend already gaining momentum within RTÉ, that recognised and fought against tendencies towards "dumbing down" in television, that threw its support behind a new programming ambition to ensure that news stories initiated in RTÉ would be followed up and elaborated upon by newspapers for days or even weeks to come, rather than settle for allowing newspaper journalism to set the pace and accept television's role as simply offering visual elaboration of important issues to those who didn't read newspapers. The Lowry affair was thus also important because of the way it touched upon public perceptions of RTÉ and its will (or otherwise) to pursue difficult stories that might even bring it to the door of the Cabinet. It affected RTÉ internally, in its organisational morale and the sense of professional pride that frequently feeds off staff perceptions of how RTÉ is performing as a crucially needed watchdog in public life. Staff could rightfully be proud of the brilliance of its latest Eurovision Song Contest production, but nothing gave as much satisfaction as acute awareness, grounded in good programming in the most powerful medium in the country, of the relevance of RTÉ as public affairs watchdog in Irish society. The Lowry melodrama generated a timely debate inside and outside RTÉ on journalistic standards and ethical procedures. And, of course, it had an impact on Government perceptions of RTÉ and the role of public service broadcasting in the political life of the country.

THE WATCHDOG ROLE

It is important to pause and consider here the crucial, triangular relationship between broadcaster, Government and the public. The classical liberal approach to analysing the democratic role of the media in society in society, shaped by Enlightenment thinkers like Immanuel Kant, John Stuart Mill and John Locke, and energised by the tradition of civic republicanism that infused the French and American Revolutions, emphasises the public watchdog role of overseeing the State, revealing abuses in the exercise of State power and facilitating a general debate about the functioning of Government. But there is a right and a left tendency in this tradition.

There is a conservative view common in mainstream American political science that regards any reform of the media, however desirable, as unacceptable "if it is at the expense of the watchdog function. And this is the inevitable cost. A press that is licensed, franchised or regulated is subject to political pressure when it deals with issues affecting the interests of those in power."[32] Arguments like these paved the way for the increasing deregulation of American broadcasting, where television channels have already been freed from the obligation to provide a mixed schedule of programmes and from the Fairness Doctrine, requiring public affairs to be reported from contrasting points of view. Rules restricting chain ownership of television stations are now being relaxed, to the point where the Federal Communications Commission is ready to eliminate the "cap" on the number of channels a single company can control nationally, end the "dual network" safeguard that prevents one television network from acquiring another network, end the broadcaster-newspaper cross-ownership rule that prevents a broadcaster from owning a major daily in the same market, remove current limits on local station ownership, kill a proposed new policy that would open network prime time to independent producers. This kind of radical right-wing deregulation has already happened in radio, allowing the emergence of huge, concentrated media power in the form of corporations like Clear Channel, the network of 1,000 radio stations owned by the Mays family of Texas. Clear Channel controversially blacklisted several musicians after they criticised the Bush administration over the US-led invasion of Iraq. Among all the criticisms of how the American news media covered this invasion is the suspicion that the overwhelmingly one-sided news viewpoint, strikingly resonating with the neo-conservative ideological programme of the American Enterprise Institute, was sustained by a corporate concern not to alienate the White House before the FCC, chaired by the son of Colin Powell, takes the landmark decision in the middle of 2003 to eliminate safeguards on media ownership, a decision that has the potential to greatly boost the profits of the giant media corporations.[33]

What has happened in the US has also begun to happen in the UK, where it was argued forcefully in the 1980s that public regulation of broadcasting inhibits critical surveillance of Government. The result was the expansion of the private broadcasting sector and the relaxation of content controls on commercial radio and television ("light-touch" regulation). But unlike the US, the basic infrastructure of public service broadcasting survived intact in Britain due to robust political and public support. As James Curran points out,[34] the public watchdog argument has a powerful resonance because it is a key element of the ideology that legitimises and printed press and is regularly invoked as the ground for opposing any additional regulation. With the diffusion of new technology, potential access to more television channels than newspapers opened up and the door to broadcasting deregulation swung open throughout most of the Western world, including Ireland. Critical surveillance of Government is clearly an important aspect of the democratic functioning of the media but the reality on many radio and television channels now is entertainment, not news. News content accounts for only a small proportion of total output and only a very small portion of this is devoted to critical scrutiny of the State. The traditional approach to the watchdog function drives from a period when a free press was a vital defence against the imminent threat of State absolutism, when conflict was thought to exist primarily between the individual and the State. This assumed the State is the main threat to the welfare of society and ignored the exercise of power through structures other than the State and the possibilities for exploitation of the private sphere, in the home and the economy and the natural environment.

The problem with using a broader definition of the watchdog role is that it weakens the general case for a free-market approach to media, since a large number of privately owned media enterprises are tied to core sectors of finance and industrial capital, and in the US, to the huge military-industrial complex. Private media are increasingly linked through private ownership to corporate structures of power in ways that compromise their independence and limit their watchdog function on behalf of the public. The trend in deregulation has resulted in television becoming increasingly embedded, as a consequence of the take-over boom of the last two decades, in the corporate structure of big business, following the media takeover pattern set by non-media conglomerates like General Electric, Westinghouse, Sony, Seagram, Microsoft and Matsushita. Diversified conglomerates now dominate the new television industries in Europe too.[35]

One of the consequences of this changing pattern of ownership is that media companies sometimes refrain from investigating critically the activities of giant conglomerates to which they belong and parent companies sometimes step in to suppress criticism of their interests. (The case of CanWest and its owners, the Asper family, is examined separately in this book, because of its involvement in commercial television in Ireland.) So it is reasonable to conclude that the free market compromises rather than guarantees the editorial integrity of commercial media, especially in its watchdog role regarding corporate power. There is also the tendency for corporate power to act like the independent power centres that they are to use their political leverage to pursue corporate gain. Chadwick[36] has analysed how a number of entrepreneurs formed an alliance with the Labour Party in Australia in the late 1980s as a way of securing official permission to consolidate their control over Australia's commercial television and press. Bagdikian claims the American media conglomerates turned a blind eye to official corruption and failed programmes during the Reagan presidency, in order to protect a political ally. The influence of the Independent Newspaper Group on the outcome of the General Election in Ireland in 1997 has received considerable comment, particularly its turning of editorial support away from the Rainbow Coalition, which was seen not to be sufficiently supportive of its corporate interest in the distribution of television in Ireland, as has the various tactical shifts of support by Rupert Murdoch's media empire in Britain, from Conservatives to New Labour. CanWest support for Canadian Prime Minister Jean Chretien, to the point of forbidding its journalists to criticise the Prime Minster, is examined elsewhere in this book.

It is difficult in situations like these not to agree with James Curran that "media conglomerates are not independent watchdogs serving the public interest, but self-seeking, corporate mercenaries using their muscle to promote private interests."[37] It is also difficult not to be aware of their bias towards conservatism, their interest in exercising informal control over the State – albeit frequently in the guise of a populist "keeping an eye on Big Government" – and their attacks on public service broadcasting as lacking the freedom to critique the exercise of political power, as furthering what they perceive as their own economic interests.

There are some brakes on this power, of course. Chief among them are countervailing influences in media organisations, especially the self-image and professional commitment of journalists and their trade unions, where these are permitted (witness the resistance by journalists in Canada to the plans of the Asper family for CanWest and their newspaper chain recently bought from Conrad Black), as well as the organisational need to maintain audience credibility and public support for journalistic independence. Public service broadcasting organisations have also resisted editorial interference from Government for similar reasons: the self-respect of journalists and the strategic long-term interest in maintaining public support for as much independence in journalism as is possible in an imperfect world. The turmoil in

Czech television and other East European media organisations in recent years, has often centred on gaining mass public disapproval of increased political control over broadcasting. Large broadcasting organisations, including those of the size of RTÉ, are difficult to control from outside because internal editorial power is decentralised or because they are protected by internal systems of checks and balances. But the vigilance of public service broadcasting can still be undermined by covert pressure from Government exercised in a number of ways. Government supporters who don't balk at exercising their partisan power can pack broadcasting Authorities. (This fear was expressed, then confounded, when former Taoiseach Garret Fitzgerald was appointed to the RTÉ Authority in 1995.) Financial pressure can be exerted, by Government refusal to grant an increase in public funding or a move (like Ray Burke's in 1990) to cap advertising income. Public flak can be generated in an attempt drive a wedge between broadcaster and the public, as when the Government established an Enquiry in 1969 to call into question the production methods used in RTÉ's investigation of illegal moneylending and State indifference to its victims. Informal and formal accusations about journalistic content can also be applied, in order to promote self-censorship, as happened with the sacking of the RTÉ Authority in 1972 with the enforcement of Section 31. And the future of broadcasting organisations can be threatened through legislative reorganisation, which has been the recent history of RTÉ. These pressures are made more acute by inflation in broadcasting costs, increased competition from other broadcasters and the growing power of market-liberalisation arguments that question the very basis of public service broadcasting.

KEEPING ONE'S DISTANCE

When we compare Government reactions in Ireland to the broadcasting of very politically sensitive material in the 1990s with the 1960s, we must feel relief that broadcasting has attained a considerable level of independence from politicians over the decades. It is in this sense that RTÉ lost the battle in the Lowry affair, but won the war. No Taoiseach or Government Minister thundered into the Chairman's office to fulminate about *Prime Time*'s take on the Lowry – Tuffy relationship or, worse, to exert pressure to prevent the broadcast. This is not to say, however, that the urge to do this is completely dead. The case of Ivan Payne, the priest gaoled for sexual abuse, illustrates this.

A month before the Tuffy story broke, I received an urgent letter from Dermot Gleeson, Attorney-General, "reminding" me of my responsibility to ensure that another *Prime Time* television programme to be broadcast that evening would not prejudice an ongoing Garda investigation or any prosecution that might result from it. The Attorney-General was reacting to a letter received that day from Arthur O'Hagan, solicitors for Dr Desmond Connell, Archbishop of Dublin (now Cardinal), expressing concerns about the programme. *Prime Time* was about to identify a Dublin priest, Ivan Payne, as the subject of allegations of child sexual abuse being investigated by Raheny Garda Station in Dublin. The situation was complicated by the fact that the Archbishop felt obliged to provide a spokesperson to the programme and was anxious that nothing this person would say in the broadcast could later be construed as prejudicing the police investigation.

It emerged later that the diocesan spokesman, Fr. John Dardis S.J., wrote directly to the producer, Deirdre Younge, on the day of the broadcast, but denied that this was an attempt to prevent the programme being aired. The nub of the programme was a loan of £27,500 made by the Diocese of Dublin to the Sutton-based priest, to settle a claim of sexual abuse brought by a young man. Diocesan advisers were concerned that if a case was brought to court, the judge might ask what a diocesan spokesman was doing taking part in such a programme. Yet there was a decision to accept the RTÉ invitation to take part, to clarify that the loan from the diocese was given to help out one of its clergy, rather than to compensate a person making allegations of sexual abuse. It was considered important also to emphasise that the loan was financed from investments and bequests rather than church collections.

It is remarkable, despite all the changes that have taken place in Church-State relations, that the Archbishop's solicitors should write to the Attorney-General to warn him, before the programme was broadcast, that RTÉ was going ahead with the story. And it is also quite remarkable that the Attorney-General should deliver this letter, plus his own reminder of my "responsibilities" to my office on the same day. Why this flurry of correspondence so close to a broadcast? Was it really to protect the integrity of a judicial investigation? Despite the denials, it is difficult not to conclude that there was a misguided attempt, perhaps in a moment of panic in the face of yet another large embarrassment for the institutional Church, to persuade the Chairman of RTÉ to do what the Producer had failed to do and to suppress the programme. Two days after *Prime Time* was aired, the Archbishop accused RTÉ of having "already gravely prejudiced the case, if a criminal case is brought." He complained that "there are people who are exercising what I would call a completely unacceptable freedom in speaking about these matters, leaving me defenceless because I have to observe the legalities". RTÉ, he complained, "feels perfectly free to say whatever it likes. I am a man fighting a battle with one arm tied behind my back because I observe the legal priorities."[38] This little exchange of views between the Church, the State and the national broadcaster took place away from the glare of publicity. I mentioned the letters at a reception some days later to Donal Kelly, RTÉ Political Correspondent, who immediately spotted the essence of a good news story. But nothing emerged in any news medium until many weeks later, when it surfaced in a question in the Dáil from P.D. Leader, Mary Harney, to Taoiseach, John Bruton, who noted that the Attorney-General had acted without consulting him, "as was proper". In writing to RTÉ, the Attorney-General had acted "as guardian of the public interest."[39]

The incident reinforced in me the belief that one of the main reasons for the decline in overt pressure on broadcasters from powerful interests in ecclesiastical and political institutions is the knowledge that what may be intended as a quiet word in the ear of the Chairman or the Director-General, may well end up on the front page of a newspaper or in a feature story in a current affairs television programme. The very real possibility of publicity is itself one of the principal bulwarks against interference.

Perhaps more significantly, the Ivan Payne story illustrates how far the power of the

Catholic Church had receded by the middle of the 1990s, if one compares the frustrations of Archbishop Connell, with the easy, even smug use of ecclesiastical power in the temporal sphere by his predecessor as Archbishop, John Charles McQuaid, the man who dismissed novelist John McGahern in the mid-60s from his teaching post in Clontarf because of the scandal surrounding his first novel "The Barracks". McQuaid was the man whose objections to the proposed Fianna Fáil health Bill in the early 1950s provoked the advice from Eamon de Valera to Sean Lemass that "every member of Government should first acquaint himself with the traditional position taken up by the Church, in Church versus State disputes" and that "each particular proposal of ours to which objection was made, be taken up with the Archbishop and that he be asked to make a draft with the qualifications which would satisfy him."[40] In 1962, Archbishop McQuaid was confident enough of his power to hold a private meeting with Lemass at which he named three individuals working in Telefís Éireann and complained about their subversive influence; former *Irish Times* features editor, Jack White, then Controller of Television Programmes, Proinsias MacAonghusa and Producer Sheila Richards.[41] McQuaid's ecclesiastical style is in sharp contrast with the tortuous circumlocution of Archbishop Connell's letter in the Ivan Payne affair and the subsequent diocesan frustration with RTÉ's decision to air the *Prime Time* programme. The contrast is, of course, also a measure of how far the Church – State – media relationships have evolved in thirty years.

Of the broadcaster – Government relationship today, it can be said that direct attempts to influence editorial decisions on content are rare. The relationship is more complex than this, however, since it encompasses a range of situations where the broadcaster proposes initiatives, such as new investments, which must then be approved by Government, or where Government proposes policy changes, which then demand responses from broadcasters. These responses are very often in the form of attempts to shape such changes to their own advantage, either as purely commercial broadcasters or as broadcasters working to a public service remit in a dual-funding situation. For the latter, Government control of RTÉ's revenue in the form of fixing the level of the licence fee and fixing the amount of broadcast time that can be devoted to advertising, demonstrates the high level of power over broadcasting exercised by Government that has a profound, though indirect effect on programme output in an overall sense. Michael D. Higgins' Ministerial championing of a licence fee increase in 1998, for example, was crucial in allowing TnaG (now TG4) to begin broadcasting. But Government control over investment decisions also plays a role in building up or running down the resources needed to maintain the core business of broadcasting, its programme output. This can be seen in RTÉ's interest in 1995 in entering the mobile 'phone business.

An ideal investment opportunity was presented to RTÉ when it was approached by Comcast, the Philadelphia-based giant US cable television operator that was becoming one of the fastest growing operators in the cellular telephone business. With the deregulation of the Irish telephone market finally becoming a reality in the mid-1990s, Comcast was keen to bid for the second GSM licence, using RTÉ as a local partner already possessing a valuable nationwide transmission service, complete with a large number of network sites and towers. This initiative was part of Comcast's overall global strategy of bidding for telephony franchises in several European countries, to extend its existing core mobile telephone business based in Brazil and the US. It also had substantial cable television interests in the UK and it was obvious that the mutual interest of both RTÉ and Comcast in broadcasting should allow RTÉ to take advantage of their involvement in cable in both the UK and the US, in order to roll out Irish cable television stations in the big American and British cities where the Irish Diaspora demand was greatest. RTÉ's CelticVision service was already in place in the Eastern region of the United States and plans were in development for an Irish cable channel in the UK.

There was initially a 20 percent stake on offer to RTÉ and 10 percent to Bórd na Móna, which could contribute a further range of transmission sites to extend the telephony network. Apart from the possible broadcasting synergies that could be achieved with Comcast in other countries, this was an excellent investment opportunity for RTÉ. It badly needed an investment outlet for funds which were then on deposit, with all the risks to which retention of cash give rise, and it was realistic to expect Government approval, since the targeted sector was within the media / communications field and would generate economies in RTÉ's transmission facilities. The first business plan fort the cellular phone project was put together on the expectation that the Department of Communications, under Minister Michael Lowry, would fix the value of the GSM licence at about $50 million. There was every expectation that the GSM business would be extremely lucrative in a short space of time, as mobile telephony, as a new form technology and a new form of social communication, was penetrating the Irish market at a rapid rate. Our prime motivation in pushing on with the bid was that the GSM business would begin to generate profits in four or five years time, when competition from other radio and television channels, advancing rapidly in line with deregulation through the 1990s, would begin to put enormous pressure on RTÉ's commercial revenue. A healthy GSM revenue stream could deliver much needed support for programme making for many years into the future.

The Comcast affair illustrates one of the major difficulties encountered by State companies in making major decisions that require Government approval. Communication with Government is slow and convoluted and this inhibits the efficiency needed in these times to respond to commercial opportunities. Decisions within RTÉ are arrived at fairly quickly, following a period of research, consultation and senior management discussion. But then the whole process must begin again in one or more Government Department, and real or imagined difficulties in communication between these large bureaucracies can frequently drain the energy from decision making on large issues that need more of the entrepreneurial mix of speed, instinct and risk taking. Written and verbal communication between RTÉ and the Department of Arts, Culture and the Gaeltacht began in early April 1995 and drew no response whatever for over three months. Then the Department asked for further information (instantly supplied by RTÉ) and stated that the Minister "would be reasonably sympathetic in principle towards the application." In a fast-moving, deregulated commercial environment, with several multinational companies and a new breed of Irish entrepreneurs getting the smell of very big money in their nostrils as the GSM bidding grew feverish, RTÉ had to make do with the ambiguities of civil service English: what real comfort could be taken from "reasonably sympathetic in principle"? This kind of sluggish response, lacking all the sharpness needed in a tense, competitive environment as the EU stick of deregulation was being rudely plunged into the hornet's nest of Irish capitalism, was to dog all the major decisions to be made in RTÉ up to the end of the century, including the extremely protracted business of shaping a digital broadcast future for Ireland.

To the great surprise of all the interested parties, the Government's bid price for the licence was lowered to £15 million. This meant that GSM business prospects were further enhanced, since the reduction in the cash bid would have a positive effect on the cost of mobile phone calls and therefore on the number of subscribers likely to commit to the new service. Predictions on the number of mobile phones likely to be in use in Ireland by 2000 varied from 250,000 to 400,000. RTÉ decided to accept a 15 percent equity stake in the Comcast consortium on the basis of a straight cash investment, since it was apparent even in 1995 that a future Government decision might require a change in ownership of the RTÉ transmission network and that if that happened, it would not require a transfer of any equity holding in the GSM franchise. But Ministerial approval had still not been obtained, two weeks before the deadline for the submission of business plans. One week before the deadline, RTÉ was informed that the Department of Finance had rejected the request to proceed with the Comcast project, on the basis that it did not have sufficient information on RTÉ's five year corporate plan. Director-General, Joe Barry, replied immediately that Arts, Culture and the Gaeltacht already had all the required information. He also made personal contact with Ruadhrí Quinn as he visited the Radio Centre for a studio discussion and the Minister for Finance promised to give his agreement. This was subsequently delivered in a letter authorising a maximum shareholding of 15 percent for RTÉ at a cost of £9.5 million.

At the close of bidding, six consortia had submitted business plans for the second GSM franchise:

> (a) the Celstar Consortium, including Comcast (60 percent), RTÉ (15 percent), Ganley Communications (15 percent) and Bórd na Móna (10 percent)
> (b) E-Sat Digifone including E-Sat (40 percent), Telenor (40 percent) and a group of smaller institutions (20 percent)
> (c) Europhone, including Kinnevik of Sweden, and Millicom International Cellular
> (d) Irish Cellular Telephones, which included AT & T (26 percent), UPC (26 percent), Independent Newspapers / Princes Holdings (26 percent), TCI (12 percent), Shannon Development (5 percent) and Riordan Communication (5 percent)
> (e) Irish Mobilcall comprising Southwest Bell (25 percent), Deutsche Telecom (25 percent), Tele Danmark (25 percent) and a group of Irish businessmen,

Martin Naughton and Loughlin Quinn of Glen Dimplex and Ciaran Corrigan, the media entrepreneur

(f) Persona, consisting of Motorola (26 percent), Sigma Wireless (26 percent), Unisource (26 percent) and ESB International (20 percent).

The Minister, Michael Lowry, announced the decision in November, the same month in which his campaign against "cosy cartels" was reaching a climax and he was grappling with the shadowy figure of Pat Tuffy and RTÉ's embarrassment over its *Prime Time* programme. The GSM licence was awarded for a fifteen-year period to E-Sat Digifone in circumstances that became instantly controversial. These circumstances returned to haunt Lowry when they were put on the agenda of the Moriarty Tribunal some years later as it probed his financial affairs for evidence of corruption during his period as Minister for Communications. The decision in favour of E-Sat also soured relations between bidding loser Independent Newspapers / Princes Holdings and the Rainbow Coalition Government (which had already expressed concern about Independent Newspapers dominant position in the Irish media) in the run up to the election of May 1997. A new Government was formed by a coalition of Fianna Fáil and the Progressive Democrats. The decision in favour of E-Sat dramatically extended the new, emerging class of Irish millionaires beginning to benefit from the role played by deregulation in the buoyant Celtic Tiger economy. The list of the newly rich now included Dennis O'Brien, who benefited from huge windfall profits within a few years when E-Sat was sold to British Telecom for the sum of £1.2 billion.

From a point of view that puts a premium on public service values in the conduct of public affairs, it is difficult to avoid some pertinent questions. Was the GSM telephony initiative all about creating new wealth among a handful of Irish millionaires and abandoning any traditional urge to keep important national assets under Irish control? Does the logic of market liberalisation, fully accepted by the European Commission and by recent Irish Governments, deliver the best value in services to the Irish people? Is there not an argument that better long-term value for Irish people would have been gained by allowing RTÉ to invest in the GSM franchise for fifteen years, in a plan that would secure for it a share of the lucrative telephony market, which would then fund programming at a time when deregulation in broadcasting would cause huge pressures on its ability to provide revenue for production? This would also position RTÉ for a vibrant partnership with Comcast in rolling out new cable channels in the UK and the US, thus achieving an important economy of scale in distributing its programming to an audience several times the size of its current one. This scenario was to reappear five years later as RTÉ struggled with Government over the shape of digital television in Ireland.

ALL-ISLAND BROADCASTING

There are more modest methods to enlarge the RTÉ audience, of course, and one of these surfaced during the elongated series of debates during throughout the 1990s collectively known as "the Peace Process". This illustrates another aspect of the broadcasting – Government relationship. Broadcast legislation requires RTÉ to be responsive to the interests and concerns of the whole community and to be aware of the need for understanding and peace within the whole island of Ireland. Yet, although it has staff based in Northern Ireland and makes radio and television programmes in and about Northern Ireland, many people who take part in such programmes frequently cannot see or hear them, because RTÉ has been unable to broadcast to the whole island of Ireland. Until recently RTÉ had been received by less than a third of the half million television households in Northern Ireland, while BBC and ITV could be received by more than two-thirds of the one million households in the Republic. By 1995, RTÉ was loudly articulating the argument that greater availability of its services would lead to better understanding between the two parts of the island and lessen the mutual ignorance stemming from the cultural effects of the Border in Irish life. Disparities in reception imply that many people in Northern Ireland do not receive very much insight through broadcasting into life in the Republic. For example, most of Belfast, parts of Armagh, East County Down, North and East Antrim and the mountainous area to the West of Lough Neagh, have almost no RTÉ reception.

These issues were raised in the mid-1990s at the Forum for Peace and Reconciliation by RTÉ Director-General, Joe Barry and were discussed over some time at the Anglo-Irish Inter-Governmental Conference. The Conference finally recommended that work should be undertaken on proposals for improvement of RTÉ reception in Northern Ireland. The arrival of TG4 (and Channel 5 in the UK) and the granting of a cable franchise to Cabletel in Northern Ireland, would provide a new impetus towards an all-island reception policy being implemented. RTÉ's response to the Green Paper on Broadcasting, aided by a very interesting paper prepared by Authority member, Anne Tannahill, editor of the Blackstaff Press in Belfast, further stressed the advantages of creating an all-island audiovisual space. The British Embassy in Dublin, the Northern Ireland Office, the Department of Foreign Affairs and the Department of Arts, Culture and the Gaeltacht were all involved in negotiations to address the imbalance in television reception across the Border. Once the UK administration indicated that there was no objection at a political level to improving RTÉ coverage in Northern Ireland, initiatives were accelerated within RTÉ Engineering to remove antenna restrictions northwards on the Clermont Cairn transmitter. This would give quality coverage for up to 50 percent of the Northern Ireland population and to improve coverage in Armagh, which is largely shielded from Clermont Cairn. At a meeting of technical experts between Ireland and the UK in January 1996, agreement was reached on increasing power. This would result in an estimated 300,000 viewers coming within the primary service area of Clermont Cairn in Northern Ireland for the first time and another 200,000 receiving good secondary service. This increase in power would bring the total RTÉ coverage in Northern Ireland up to almost seventy percent of the population.

It was agreed that since UK broadcasters get no benefit from the changes, the Irish side would bear the cost of these changes (about £350,000) that include antenna improvement in Northern Ireland. RTÉ agreed to do all the necessary planning and engineering analysis. Negotiations on getting frequencies for low power RTÉ transposers within Northern Ireland were deferred, so as not to delay progress on Clermont Cairn. RTÉ also began at this time to consider how the new technology of digital compression could further enhance all-island coverage, particularly when TV3 and TG4, not yet launched, would also go digital and if site sharing for an all-Ireland digital network could be agreed.

Much work remains to be done in achieving universal all-island reception of all television stations broadcasting in Ireland. Beyond this engineering dimension, interesting questions about audience engagement with television remain to be explored. Does selective exposure and selective avoidance operate at a significant level, for example among Unionist and Nationalist audiences in Northern Ireland? Have different television channels developed particular "brand" identities over time among different social groups on the island? For example, what does UTV signify to Dublin working-class youth and what does RTÉ signify to DUP members? How has RTÉ's apparently staunch support for Section 31, up until the abandonment of State censorship of political discussion in 1994, affected its credibility among Nationalist and Republican audiences in Northern Ireland? At the level of political economy, how will the emergence of an all-island broadcasting space be affected by the commercial objectives of the two major media multinationals, CanWest and Granada, that now exert a very significant influence over TV3 in the Republic and UTV in Northern Ireland? How well can the public service broadcasters (RTÉ, BBC, Channel 4) engage in co-production and other forms of resource sharing that will benefit all audiences across the island? And what role can be played by the European Commission's Media Programme, which provides seed funding for training, script development, production and promotion, as well as the Irish Film Board and the Northern Ireland Film Council, in fostering better cross-Border co-operation in film and television production, so that the increasingly important audience interest in good home production can continue to be addressed?

For several decades, a form of broadcasting apartheid has existed in Ireland, with the Border playing a silent but powerful role in maintaining a form of cultural partitionism that is increasingly outdated since the Good Friday Agreement was signed in 1998. Cross-Border co-operation has existed for many years between the two Arts Councils on the island and is perhaps most evident in the area of orchestral music and opera. But beyond high culture, little else has happened to open up a truly all-Ireland audiovisual space that might increase mutual understanding between the different socio-political groupings on the island and accelerate the process of post-colonial reconciliation. On the wider European front, a consensus has emerged since the 1980s, embodied in the Television Without Frontiers Directive, that forging closer cultural links between Member States through television policy (for example, insisting on programme import quotas from other European countries) should be encouraged, since some common cultural dimension of life must surely underpin enhanced political and economic union. The same logic should apply in Ireland. The two different political entities on the island may be meeting the letter of the Television Without Frontiers Directive, without the strains usually found in other parts of Europe, because they have easy access to a common Anglophone film and television market. But they are not yet meeting the spirit of the directive.

GOVERNMENT AND CABLE POLICY

If Government interest in influencing editorial aspects of radio and television had greatly diminished by the 1990s, government control over major financial aspects of broadcasting had not, as the case of Cablelink demonstrates.

Cablelink originated in the 1970s as an RTÉ subsidiary (RTÉ Relays) to help distribute BBC and British commercial television to Irish viewers. By 1990, it had evolved, under Government pressure, into a joint venture between RTÉ and Telecom Éireann, the state telecommunications company. Ireland became one of the most cabled countries in Europe: 85 percent of television households passed by cable and about 50 percent subscribing by the 1990s. With 295,000 subscribers centred in Dublin (where there is a concentration of relatively high spending power and where the up-take of personal computers is considerably higher than the national average), and another 50,000 in Galway and Waterford, Cablelink was among the top twenty-five cable companies in Europe. Other companies, including the "Denver Duo" of UIH and TCI, operating with local partnerships, brought the total number of subscribers (including MMDS/Wireless Cable) up to 490,000, or about half of all television homes in the country.

In 1994, Telecom Éireann exercised its option to increase its stake in Cablelink from 60 percent to 75 percent, which yielded £13.5 million for RTÉ, in what was largely seen as a defensive move, rather than a positive decision to develop the cable company by upgrading its old infrastructure. Now Telecom Éireann was exploring possibilities for a strategic alliance with some of the world's largest telecommunication companies (including US West, British Telecom, Bell Atlantic, Singapore Telecom and Tele Danmark) but it was also being investigated by the European Commission to see if its interest in Cablelink represented an abuse of a dominant position. Competitors were calling for Telecom Éireann to be forced to sell off its 75 percent stake in Cablelink in order to open up the cable industry to more competition, and this view was supported by the government agency Forfas. It was argued that Telecom Éireann cannot be allowed to hold what are essentially the rights to two fixed wire telephony services into the home and therefore should be forced to divest. Such a decision would force Telecom Éireann to sell off part of its stake in Cablelink, opening the way for a strategic partner to invest in upgrading the system. The cable market in Ireland was then considered mature, with good penetration – up to 80 percent in some key urban areas, compared with an average of 22 percent in Britain. But the network was in need of major overhaul and investment if it was to become "a main route in the Information Superhighway," as the dominant discourse of the mid-1990s put it. Northern Ireland, which had never had cable television, was already anticipating the building of a superior network by the newly franchised company Cabletel. This promised a thoroughly modernised, combined telephony – television system that would deliver a range of multimedia services. Cable, however, was starved of investment for many years, yet in 1996 was valued at over £90 million.

In its discussions with its Cablelink partner, RTÉ had a strategic advantage in the form of a Shareholders' Agreement which gave it the option of selling its 25 percent share up to June 1998, as disposal of its interest could provide a valuable source of funding for its digital development programme. RTÉ had reservations about Telecom Éireann continuing to hold such a large share in Cablelink, as it represented not only a possible conflict of interest regarding telephony, but more importantly for RTÉ, a barrier against the full development of cable for multimedia services. KPMG, in the Autumn of 1997, was valuing Cablelink at £130 – £150 million against a very buoyant view of cable across Europe. At the very least, the RTÉ preference was to retain its 25 percent share and see the Telecom Éireann share drop below 50 percent, allowing a third partner to come on board in order to prepare the company for the roll-out of digital television.

By December 1998, relationships on the board of Cablelink had become quite frayed. Telecom Éireann was indicating that it no longer wanted to continue its majority shareholding, though pressure from Minister of Public Enterprise, Mary O'Rourke, and the European Commission was a major factor in this change of heart. RTÉ's put option, its right to dispose of its shareholding to Telecom Éireann at full market value up to 28th June 1998, required immediate protection. At the same time, there was now an urgent need to develop Cablelink so that it could realise its digital potential to offer Internet access, e-commerce, multimedia and a full telephony service. This would require the introduction of external investment and expertise and a substantial change in shareholding. The Government was publicly admitting that "the full rigour of competition" was not evident in Cablelink. The Opposition was calling Telecom Éireann "a spoiler shareholder," not interested in providing the necessary investment of £100 – £150 million needed to upgrade the network: it should be compelled to sell off its entire shareholding to two strategic partners and to the public.

In a detailed letter to Minister for Broadcasting, Síle de Valera, early in 1998, I set out our view that participation in Cablelink represented a strategically and commercially important investment for RTÉ, particularly in the changing circumstances of broadcasting which now confronted the organisation. Our "strong desire and firm intention" was to retain RTÉ's shareholding at its present level. An added consideration was the fact that about forty Cablelink staff were in fact RTÉ staff who were on secondment to Cablelink. We further pressed the point that the renewed company should have an independent chairman. These points were put to the Minister again when she met the Authority on 30th January, 1998. The main purpose of this meeting was to emphasise the urgent need for the development of government policy on digital television (the Minister expressed the hope that new broadcasting legislation, mooted since Michael D. Higgins' Green Paper in 1995, would be drafted by the end of 1998, a hope that would not in fact be realised for a further three years). The Minister and her officials expressed support for the RTÉ position on Cablelink and its preference for remaining as a shareholder. They expected no Government opposition to this. They were to be proved wrong.

In April, 1998, the Government decided to require both Telecom Éireann and RTÉ to divest themselves of their shareholding in Cablelink. They were permitted to retain the proceeds. The Minister for Public Enterprise, Mary O'Rourke, would lead the trade sale. Attention on the Authority now switched to ensuring that RTÉ would actively participate in the management of the sale of the shares and oppose a decision to allot control of that process solely to Government Departments. The Government agreed this to. Obstacles to be tackled in the sale process included achieving regulatory clarity, so that operating licences could be obtained from ODTR to develop all new activities (digital services, telephony, interactivity), and achieving a suitable arrangement with seconded staff who had originally been employed by RTÉ. By Spring 1999, financial advisers were valuing Cablelink at £350 – £400 million.

Because of the scale of the Cablelink network, its buyer would be positioned as one of the largest telecommunications players in the country, particularly after the impending completion of deregulation of the telecommunications sector. Two Irish companies emerged as serious bidders. Cable Management Ireland, which operated about 30 small cable and MMDS operations across the country, with a total of 60,000 subscribers, declared its interest, as did E-Sat Telecom. Three large international groups were also interested: TCI – Telecom Ireland (in which the Independent Newspaper Group had a 25 percent share and an existing 150,000 subscribers to its Princes Holdings cable system), British-based cable company NTL (owner of Cabletel, the franchisee in Northern Ireland) and the Dutch cable firm UPC, which declared its interest in buying both Princes Holdings and Cablelink. By March 1999, these were all willing to pay up to £360 million and also to face the likelihood that a further £200 million would need to be invested in Cablelink to upgrade its aging infrastructure to broadband standard, so that it would be able to offer telephony, high speed internet and advanced television services. The winner that finally emerged was NTL, which had to fight off a legal challenge from E-Sat that went all the way to the Supreme Court.

The final sale price for Cablelink was £538.18 million, or £1,500 per subscriber, one of the highest yields ever achieved in such inflated sales in Europe. RTÉ quarter share of this amounted to £133.797 million, more than double what had been expected only a few months before. Although this represented a very substantial injection of funds to public service broadcasting, there was a danger that it might work to the long-term disadvantage of RTÉ in being perceived either as a free gift from Government or as diminishing the requirement for increases in public funding in the future. Plans were immediately put in train to invest in major new development of RTÉ in a number of areas, including digitisation of its production capacity and new investment in programmes, particularly drama, children's programmes, documentaries and archive development. But most importantly, the Cablelink windfall meant that RTÉ now had the financial flexibility to fund the major early retirement scheme that would be needed to drive the "downsizing" of RTÉ then being negotiated with staff through the Transformation Agreement.

Following NTL's purchase of Cablelink, a great deal of media speculation in Ireland centred on why it had paid such a high price for a modestly sized cable system badly in need of upgrading. But a glance at the global cable industry at the time shows that in the US, cable acquisitions often operated on a valuation of television homes ranging from $2,500 to $4,000. It was also evident that US cable television companies in 1999 generally considered that most European media companies (and Governments) are steeped in the concept of cable as a utility, like the supply of electricity or water or gas, and usually undervalue their cable assets, particularly their subscriber base. These companies believed Europeans would follow the American lead, that European consumers of television could be induced to spend more on what they perceive as better in-home information (digital television, Internet, telephony) and that they would become accustomed to paying premium prices for higher speeds of delivery. Some of these expectations proved to be highly inflated.

Despite the presence of several large over-capitalised media conglomerates in Europe, the European cable market is being dominated by a number of aggressive US groups that are changing the European landscape dramatically by transforming what had been a television-delivery utility service into a pay TV model, that deploys the so-called "triple play" of television, telephony and Internet. The US-style business practice of these groups is acquisitive, as we see in the case of NTL bidding up the price of Cablelink to a very high level, and it is based on borrowing capital directly linked to equity markets, in business plans frequently underpinned by high debt loads.

Four large US-based media groups with complex links to each other now directly control or have strong operational influence over sixty percent of all cable subscriptions in the sixteen European countries where they operate. This amounts to over 35 million European cable subscribers. Their market share at the end of the 1990s range from 10 percent in Romania to 85 percent in Germany and 99 percent in the UK and Ireland. The dominant trend in the European cable industry is towards further rapid consolidation, which in turn confers on the US conglomerates enhanced bargaining power, economies of scale and power to exploit content rights. An enhanced drive to acquire more small local cable companies will see this figure grow but as growth stabilises, the focus will shift more clearly to extracting more revenue from each existing subscriber. The strategic goal of the "triple play" is to increase average revenue per subscriber (ARPU) across very large networks. United Pan European Communications reaches over nine million subscribers in twelve different European countries, and is itself controlled by the Liberty Media Group, which reaches another 11 million European subscribers, mostly in Germany. It reaches 24 percent of the Irish cable market through its 50 percent stake in Chorus Communication, and 35 percent of the presently small UK market through its interest in Telewest. (Telewest was to become a partner with RTÉ in Tara Television, an Irish programming channel aimed at the British cable market.) Both Liberty and UPC have expanded their operations into investment in television content, in order to feed their expanding cable networks. Many of their channels, such as Discovery and Animal Planet, have been "versioned" all across Europe, from Romania, Hungary, Poland and Slovakia to Ireland.

NTL, the new owner of Cablelink, presently reaches about 6.5 million subscribers across Europe (Switzerland, France, Germany, UK and Ireland). Its Irish operation is directly owned by the US parent NTL Delaware Inc., which has based its expansion on a strategy of boosting revenue by bundling telecommunication services with its cable TV package. NTL's influence in Europe could deepen if it is successful in its bid to provide a broadband distribution system across Europe for AOL – Time Warner, the world's largest media content group.

These US based cable companies follow a similar strategy in pursuit of global market dominance: grow quickly through acquisition of local cable companies, which expand the subscriber base. Then upgrade the cable infrastructure to broadband capability and deploy the triple play, cut costs and increase ARPU. The strategy then would include moving upstream into acquiring television content and controlling distribution rights, so that programming can be fed in sufficient quantity into the expanding global cable empires, where a very large customer base makes it easier to finance and exploit content assets. Since the mature US cable market is not open to new entrants, and both European satellite and free-to-air markets are also difficult to access, the European cable market, often undervalued by its traditional operators (such as Telecom Eireann and RTÉ), offers new opportunities to acquire subscribers at a cheaper rate than in the US and in numbers large enough to support steady increases in revenue when new technologies are bundled into one integrated cable service.

National Governments and Regulators have so far been supporting these moves, perhaps more frequently by default and in confusion, rather than by first carefully sifting through a cost-benefit analysis that is infused with concern for the social good and calibrated to respect public service criteria in informing policy on the appropriate parameters of deregulation. There is now some reason to worry that unhealthy trends in the US cable market may spread to Europe. These include the impact on the US cable subscriber of regional monopolies, which produce the predictably negative outcomes of higher prices and poorer service. But there are two negative outcomes in addition that must also be considered.

Firstly, the dominant business practice of these US based media conglomerates is to rely on equity financing and large debt burdens, so they are linked firmly to finance markets whose fluctuations directly affect cable industry strategies. We have already seen in Ireland a clear impact on the digital roll-out strategies of both NTL and Liberty / Chorus of the downturn in global technology stock markets. UPC has also dramatically scaled back its operations in Eastern Europe and the roll-out of digital services generally in Europe has been well below expectations. Stock market fluctuations influence roll-out or pull-back in the build-out of cable operations, as they adjust their expansion plans in response to the interests of their stockholders and creditors. This overrides Government audiovisual policies in individual countries and the demands of Regulators. When Cablelink was purchased by NTL, global technology stocks were reaching an all time high and confidence in new media was peaking. Cable systems were valued on the assumption that new owners could raise pay television penetration and ARPU to generate the additional income needed to pay back bank debts.[42] Within a year, however, the Irish Regulator, the ODTR, was warning the cable companies not to abandon their digital roll-out plans. This cyclicality in expansion and retrenchment, directly linked to finance market turbulence, has a huge impact on Government plans for steady digital roll-out, open access of broadcasters to digital platforms and analogue switch-off timing. Politicians in some European countries are already beginning to question the increasing monopoly power of US-dominated stockmarket-driven cable conglomerates.

There is also some justification in querying the strategy of boosting ARPU rather than increasing the number of subscribers in a cable system, especially where the latter demands a higher investment in spreading broadband capability over a wider area. An ARPU strategy alone would focus on opening premium services at higher speeds to premium customers who can afford to pay ever higher subscription fees, rather than offering the benefits of cable TV to as many households as possible across a franchised territory. The current European experience seems to be that it is easier to increase ARPU in satellite television systems but not in cable, where subscribers tend to purchase only the basic tier of service.

PARTY RELATIONS

While playing almost no role in shaping editorial policy in broadcasting, the political apparatus of the state has considerable influence over the future of RTÉ through reserving consent to major investments that might enhance the revenue of the organisation. For this reason, it is vital that careful attention is paid to how the organisation communicates with politicians.

With the appointment of Bob Collins as Director-General in 1997, a number of changes were made in RTÉ at senior management level, including appointing Kevin Healy Director of Public Affairs, and focusing attention on communicating with both Government and Opposition deputies and senators, as well as key civil servants, in a number of modes: small group briefings, one-to-one conversations, lunch visits to Montrose, informal contacts in the Dáil, seminars for politicians. A crucial part of this strategy was to focus on back-benchers who would not be as familiar with RTÉ plans and the challenges emerging in the media landscape as their Ministerial or front-bench colleagues. Public meetings organised in major towns every eight weeks or so, opening up direct communication between senior management in RTÉ and local communities, also provided opportunities to communicate with local politicians. A number of key issues highlighted in the late 1990s included the following: the level of the licence fee, its indexation and the cost of its collection; shaping new legislation which would define public service broadcasting and prepare for the transition to digital television; interpretation of the 1993 Broadcasting Act which sought to open up the independent production sector; the funding of TG4. These issues are examined in more detail elsewhere in this book.

Because television in particular is such a high profile medium in Ireland, there are times when broadcast material can have an impact on individual politicians to such an extent that organisational anxieties focus on how the national broadcaster may be perceived by political parties, especially Fianna Fáil. Every party complains from time to time that it gets unfair coverage from RTÉ, but there is no doubt that Fianna Fáil in particular sees itself as "always getting a raw deal" from RTÉ, a belief fuelled inside RTÉ by former Minister Ray Burke's hostile "capping" of the organisation's income in 1990 and his perhaps overly enthusiastic encouragement of the launch of the ill-fated Century Radio, Ireland's first privately owned national commercial radio station. In

1996, Eamon O Cuiv (who became a Minister in a Fianna Fáil led Government soon after) complained to the Broadcasting Complaints Commission that during a discussion on television (This Week, 31st March 1996) about Labour Party funding, his grandfather, the late Eamon de Valera was described as owner of the Irish Press newspaper and "a millionaire" and that the RTÉ interview should have corrected this untrue statement. RTÉ pointed out that his cousin, Deputy Síle de Valera, a participant on the programme, was invited to comment on these remarks but did not do so. The Commission dismissed the complaint. It is unusual for politicians to hold their fire in criticising RTÉ, especially in proximity to elections, as we saw a little while later when the Taoiseach, Bertie Ahern, publicly blamed RTÉ for the loss of a Fianna Fáil seat in a Cork by-election, because of the way his candidate was interviewed on air.

Preparations for the public access programme *Questions and Answers* were almost always arduous, when politicians saw an election looming. During the Spring 1997 General Election campaign, RTÉ planned a special *Questions and Answers* which would present the studio audience with a panel of representatives from all the major parties. Fianna Fail objected, on the basis that the Government parties would have an unfair advantage over the Opposition, and in spite of strenuous efforts over a long weekend by Peter Feeney and Betty Purcell, no solution could be found. So an alternative panel faced John Bowman for the Monday night slot, with no politicians present. The Authority let it be known that we had major concerns about allowing one political party effectively to veto a programme at an important time like this. But we supported the decision of the Editor, because in the context of an election, it would have been more questionable to proceed with a *Questions and Answers* edition having only Government parties involved.

Eamon De Valera returned to haunt us again when Síle De Valera, now Minister with responsibility for Broadcasting, attended a meeting with the Authority in January 1998. RTÉ had just broadcast a television documentary on the Civil War in Ireland, "The Madness from Within," which depicted Eamon De Valera in a very unflattering way as a man traumatised by war. Before his granddaughter arrived in Montrose, we had an intense discussion on the way the documentary depicted the major protagonists, Michael Collins and Eamon De Valera, and their role in the Civil War. Should we mention the programme during her visit? Garret FitzGerald considered the documentary biased and factually wrong in a number of places and felt it might have caused undue stress in the De Valera family, particularly as it built on the strong anti-De Valera sentiment that had already emerged into popular culture in Neil Jordan's film *Michael Collins*. Professor Tom Garvin of UCD was the consultant historian on the project and also a participant, and there was a feeling on the Authority that these roles should in future be separated. We agree not to mention the programme during the Minister's visit, that I would raise it with her privately. When she was leaving, I escorted her to her car and mentioned our misgivings about the editorial balance of the programme. The Civil War was a very complex period in modern Irish history and RTÉ would be returning to it in several new programmes. Síle De Valera listened to me politely, said she hadn't seen the documentary but would get a copy, and left. The whole episode left me pondering not only how the events of 1922 are still so difficult to depict in the popular medium of television seventy-five years later, but also the decency with which a member of a prominent Fine Gael family could worry about possible hurt caused to the De Valera family, and about the grace with which De Valera's granddaughter listened to my explanation and held her fire. This episode too is part of the story of the relationship between broadcasting and politicians in contemporary Ireland and how the personal cuts across the political. But respective official roles are also generally maintained with a high level of scrupulousness. I would hear only indirectly of a ministerial criticism in the Dail bar of how *Questions and Answers* was "stacked" against the party of the complainant. When George Lee, Economics Correspondent, referred on television to the "Thatcherite" budget plans of Finance Minister Charlie McCreevy in December 1999, Síle De Valera lashed out in the Dail at this "unacceptable" level of criticism. But I sat beside her that night at a Russian performance of the ballet "Sleeping Beauty" and there wasn't a mention of anything untoward.

Direct Government attempts to influence editorial decisions on output are rare but suspicions remain and always will. Sometime these surface not just in the excited prose of an eager reporter in a Sunday newspaper, but in the very centre of RTÉ itself, around the boardroom table during RTÉ Authority meetings. One major example of this will be examined in this last section of the chapter, because it intensely involved myself and several Authority colleagues, along with the Director-General, Bob Collins, and has been described from a particular point of view in Bob Quinn's book *Maverick*, which is argued for passionately but erroneously.[43] My own account here is intended to set the record straight as I see it, lest the Quinn version be accepted as further myth-building proof of just how subservient RTÉ is to the Government of the day. What ended up as a Supreme Court case gets to the heart of the operation of the public sphere in Ireland, because it centres on how public policy is made through the democratic mechanism of the referendum, and how the broadcast media should facilitate the use of referenda by granting, or denying, access to the airwaves by those who want to reach the electorate with their arguments.

THE COUGHLAN APPEAL

Trinity College lecturer, Anthony Coughlan, made a formal complaint to the Broadcasting Complaints Commission in 1996 that RTÉ had breached Section 18 of the Broadcasting Act (1960), which requires RTÉ to be objective in its reporting of current affairs and matters of public importance. This breach occurred, he complained, during the previous year's Referendum on Divorce, when RTÉ had granted uncontested political broadcasts to several political parties, most of whom supported a 'yes' vote in the Referendum, with the result that far less broadcast time was given to those groups advocating a 'no' vote. The Commission rejected the argument that RTÉ coverage breached its statutory obligations and Coughlan sought to have this decision quashed by the High Court. He argued that the Commission had misapplied the law in finding that RTÉ had not breached its statutory duty. He argued that RTÉ should have either refrained from offering uncontested political broadcasts during a referendum or else afforded equal broadcast time to both 'yes' and 'no' sides.

High Court Judge Carney gave his decision in April 1998, and it was in favour of Anthony Coughlan. The Government, he noted, has no role to play in the submission to the people of a proposal by way of referendum, as decided by the Supreme Court in a case taken by Green Party MEP, Patricia McKenna in 1995 against Government funding of one side in a referendum. Similarly, political parties are given no role under law or by the Constitution in the referendum process. Any interference with the free exercise of the people's prerogative to amend the Constitution would itself be unconstitutional. RTÉ would be acting in an unconstitutional fashion if it transmitted uncontested political broadcasts weighted on one side of a referendum argument. The imbalance in time allocated between both sides in the Divorce Referendum indicated that RTÉ had thrown its weight behind one side of the argument. RTÉ was wrong in using political parties as its starting point in the allocation of broadcast time during the referendum campaign. This amounted to unconstitutional unfairness, which would not have arisen if RTÉ had afforded both sides of the campaign equal broadcast time. The decision of the Broadcasting Complaints Commission was therefore quashed, as Anthony Coughlan had requested, because it had fallen into error in its interpretation of RTÉ's statutory and constitutional role.

On the face of it, this appeared to be a wise judgement. In the case of elections, it is proper that RTÉ should grant political parties the facility of uncontested broadcasts, since elections for the most part revolve around party political issues. In Constitutional referenda, however, it is the people who are legislating directly and it may well be the case that the balance of opinion among parliamentary parties bears little relation to the state of opinion in the country. All the parties favoured a 'yes' vote on divorce in 1995, while almost half of those citizens actually voting voted 'no'. There was even evidence that in some parties the leadership favoured 'yes' while a majority of the members and supporters favoured 'no'. There was, therefore, an obvious logic to Judge Carney's view that RTÉ was wrong in using political parties as its starting point in the allocation of broadcast time in a referendum campaign.

And yet there were aspects of the Carney Judgement that made us pause and consider whether we should lodge an appeal to the Supreme Court. Initial legal advice to the Authority cautioned that there was an issue for RTÉ in the High Court's decision to equate "fairness" with equality of broadcast time, and there was good reason to worry about how this principle might be interpreted in the future. Under the Broadcasting Acts, the Authority had the discretion to decide how to be fair to all interests concerned. Legislation made no mention of equal time. Was RTÉ's discretion now being superceded by a new principle never before deployed in broadcasting in Ireland? There was a now also considerable concern that Judge Carney's invocation of the McKenna Judgement might result in the principle of "fairness equals equality" being broadened out into news and current affairs output generally, including coverage of election campaigns, even though Carney had specifically confined his judgement to referendum broadcasts.

At the May 1998 meeting of the Authority, it was agreed that the Director-General should seek further legal clarification and then make a decision on lodging an Appeal. This was done and an Appeal was prepared by RTÉ lawyers and lodged in June. But this was far from being the end of the matter. Arguments over whether we should go ahead with the Supreme Court Appeal or withdraw it, were to occupy a great deal of discussion time in RTÉ over the next several months and lead to some very acrimonious allegations widely publicised by Bob Quinn. These included the allegation that the Executive and Director-General, not the Authority, had authorised lodging the Appeal in the first place and that this decision was taken "in consultation with the Government". Both accusations were rejected at the time and have to be firmly rejected again here. They are based not only on an erroneous interpretation of the actual decision-making process within RTÉ in 1998 but, even more damagingly, on a deliberate ignoring of the very substantial legal arguments widely debated within RTÉ, leaning clearly in favour of sustaining an Appeal against the Carney Judgement in the interest of good political broadcasting in the future. Even though a great deal of time and effort was expended in familiarising the Authority with these broadcast based arguments, Bob Quinn chose to see instead a hidden conspiracy in which the Government was able to influence an RTÉ decision to appeal, so that it could return to the status quo ante, where political parties would have favoured access to the electorate. He acknowledges hearing from me, very early on in our long debate on the Appeal, that while most people in RTÉ, including the Authority, agreed with the broad conclusion of the High Court decision, the purpose in appealing against it was to seek clarification from the Supreme Court about the broader implications for political broadcasting.[44] Yet over the next several months he continued to ignore these implications for future broadcasting that needed to be clarified in the Supreme Court and instead focused all his energies on building the charge that there was a Government – RTÉ conspiracy here and we were all guilty of covering it up.

The Appeal was lodged before the Summer in good faith by the Director-General, on the understanding that it would be far easier to withdraw it later if we wished, having had more time to digest legal detail, than to seek to lodge the Appeal long after the High Court decision had been issued. RTÉ's future organisational and editorial independence in the light of the High Court judgement would need very careful analysis. This we continued to apply into the autumn, until a decision to maintain the appeal was finalised at the end of October. What was the major legal issue that demanded so much attention throughout much of 1998?

The core of the legal problem for RTÉ was the requirement that responsibility to be fair amounts to a responsibility to be equal. The principle enunciated in the High Court was that in uncontested broadcasts, RTÉ must afford equal time to each side of the argument. This adds a new dimension to the legislative concepts of "fairness to all interests concerned" and presentation in "an objective and impartial manner," embodied in the Broadcasting Authority Act of 1960 (as amended in 1976). The Carney Judgement was based on the Supreme Court ruling in McKenna versus An Taoiseach (1995), rather than on the statutory obligations imposed on RTÉ by the Broadcasting Act, and here was the origin of our anxieties. The McKenna Judgement referred broadly to "a democracy free from Governmental intercession" where "public funds should not be used to fund one side of an electoral process, *whether it be a referendum or a general election,* to the detriment of the other side of the argument" (emphasis added).

An obvious interpretation of this in the future would be that the Supreme Court did not intend that its dicta be applied only in a referendum. It could be argued that the same principle would apply equally well to any other exercise of the democratic suffrage. By applying *equality* in broadcast coverage as the guiding principle in covering a general election, individual candidates or political parties could claim with some justification that they were not being treated fairly unless coverage for their views was equal to that provided to the larger parties. Before the High Court judgement, disparity in broadcast treatment could be justified (and has been since 1960) by the principle of being "fair to all interests", having regard to the extent of electoral support for small and large political parties by reference to the last election results. But now, such disparity would be extremely difficult to justify, if the guiding principle is based upon allocation of equal time. In most General Elections, there are multiple candidates and multiple parties. It is likely that any dissatisfied minority party or independent candidate could institute legal proceedings to ensure coverage equal to the major parties. This would substantially inhibit RTÉ's general editorial independence in deciding its broadcast treatment of future elections.

Since the Broadcasting Complaints Commission was continuing with its appeal, the Supreme Court was being asked to adjudicate on issues that would have important consequences for RTÉ. If RTÉ now withdrew its appeal against the Coughlan Judgement, this would in effect confirm that it accepted the correctness of that decision and was satisfied with Judge Carney's interpretation of the Broadcasting Acts. Our legal advice was that it would be an "extremely dangerous" strategy for RTÉ not to proceed with its appeal. It would risk a significant judgement from the Supreme Court in relation to future broadcasting, without any RTÉ contribution to the arguments made before the court. In these circumstances, we decided to pursue the Appeal.

Bob Quinn refused over several months to recognise the severity of this legal problem being teased out with us by what he called "two solemn faced lawyers" (Mary Finley S.C. and John Trainor S.C.) He focused instead on supporting what he saw as the David-against-Goliath victory of Anthony Coughlan over the political establishment. He insisted on seeing any deviation from the emotional comfort of this position as devious RTÉ collaboration with that establishment (the main political parties) against the plain people of Ireland. Colleagues on the Authority who insisted on tackling the legal complexities that had a bearing on broadcasting were, at best, "making an ass of RTÉ" in a public relations disaster of monumental proportions, or at worst, responding to hidden Government pressure on behalf of the larger political parties by indulging in clever delaying tactics to ensure that the Appeal could not be withdrawn.

Wisps of circumstantial evidence loomed very large in the Quinn worldview. The Director-General had had an informal discussion early in 1998 with the Taoiseach, Bertie Ahern, at which the matter of the licence fee was discussed. RTÉ had been lobbying Government to amend the 1993 legislation governing its relationship with independent producers, and it had been arguing for a central role in developing Ireland's digital future. Might all this have made RTÉ more susceptible to subtle Government pressure? In addition, Anthony Coughlan had intimated that after an appearance on the current affairs programme *Prime Time*, he had been told by the Director of Television, Joe Mulholland, when asked why RTÉ was appealing the High Court decision, "if I had my way, we wouldn't. But there are pressures...."[45] And it was clear that the Attorney-General could not appeal in his own right but would wish to be associated with the Appeal. All of this amounted, in the Quinn view, to the charge that the RTÉ Executive had decided on the appeal "in consultation with Government and the major political parties". When this was directly challenged by Bob Collins as utterly untrue, we were told by Bob Quinn that "consult" was being used not in its primary dictionary sense of "seek an opinion from / ask the advice of," but the secondary sense of "take into consideration". The truth was that we all consulted, in the most active sense, not politicians at all but some of the best legal minds in the Law Library to help us sort out the complexities of the Coughlan Appeal.

The long debate within RTÉ in 1998 centred on the extremely important question of how political communication should function within the public sphere in Ireland in the future. But there were times when that debate veered towards hysterics that threatened not only to destroy the trust that should exist between the Authority and the Director-General it appointed, but to spread widely the false notion that here, yet again, was evidence of Government interference in RTÉ's editorial independence, interference of a most pernicious kind. Nothing could be further from the truth in this case. The only communication from Government to me in all this period was a brief telephone call from Sile De Valera a week after the Carney judgement, extremely polite and non-directive in tone, saying she didn't want to interfere in what was an RTÉ matter but I might like to know the Government's current view of the situation, that it didn't see the need for maintaining uncontested political broadcasts in referenda campaigns in the future. This coincided with my own view at that time. But because of all the previous cases, by now well rehearsed, where Government power could genuinely be felt in RTÉ, there was a danger that the Coughlan case could be added on to these and taken as one more thread in the pattern.

Those well rehearsed cases included: the famous Sean Lemass statement in 1966 that RTÉ was set up as an instrument of public policy and therefore both generally and in its news and current affairs programmes could not be completely independent of Government supervision; Charles Haughey's direct intervention in the Newsroom in the same year to object to the way RTÉ was covering the farmers' dispute with the Government, an intervention that triggered the Lemass dictat; Government accusations of bias in current affairs coverage of the proportional representation debate and the issue of emigration in 1966; Government refusal to allow an RTÉ news crew to travel to North Vietnam and suspicions about Government involvement in the decision not to send a news crew to Nigeria during the Civil War there, both in 1967; the Government's establishment of a public enquiry in 1969 to examine how RTÉ produced a programme on moneylending; the sacking of the RTÉ Authority in 1972 for what it regarded as its breaching of the Section 31 censorship directive.

To a large extent, Government controls the economic and competitive environment in which RTÉ exists, originally by establishing RTÉ and granting it a monopoly in national television broadcasting for several decades, and continually, by controlling its level of income from licence fees and the amount of broadcast time it can allocate to advertising. Government decides on allowing competing channels in radio and television, though the detail is delegated to the Regulator. Government has even intervened to block the appointment of a Director-General in RTÉ.[46] Given that Government can set limits to RTÉ's income, it is inevitable that there will sometimes be reluctance within some parts of RTÉ to allowing its output to offend politicians, though this reluctance has radically diminished over the last decade.

As Peter Feeney argues, RTÉ's dependency on Government is balanced by broadcasters' awareness of their obligation to provide fair and objective programming, an independent stance that can at times bring RTÉ into sharp conflict with politicians.[47] If programming does not hold up to scrutiny those who hold public office and their policies, programme makers are failing to justify the privileged position that has been created for them by those in public office. This conflictual relationship is at the centre of the balance that must be maintained between broadcasters and politicians. RTÉ's highlighting of health issues in the 1989 general election earned it the wrath of Fianna Fáil and probably created the environment for the devastating assault on RTÉ's advertising income by Broadcasting Minister Ray Burke in 1990 in an effort to help the ailing Century Radio. This was tolerated, if not encouraged, by certain elements within Fianna Fáil, where a deeply embedded antipathy towards RTÉ still survived from the early clashes over Section 31.

Broadcasting is obviously a purveyor of debate but it is also frequently a participator in the debate itself. It is both inside and outside the political process. The conservative civil service ethos that carried over from Radio Éireann can still have an influence on decisions within RTÉ, as can be seen, for example, in senior management reluctance in the mid-1990s to employ the very considerable journalistic skills of Vincent Browne in radio and television, because of the fear that his maverick instincts could not be editorially controlled. But more usually, the conservative disposition that some of its critics see in RTÉ can be traced to a sense of professional responsibility that induces caution, especially in the area of political communication. Because RTÉ still occupies a dominant position in Irish broadcasting, and because the role of broadcasting in public debate is so important and influential, there is a necessary caution about "getting it wrong".

This was the overriding tone of the long debate on the Coughlan Appeal in 1998. Frustrated with this debate, Bob Quinn sent copies of all his correspondence with myself and Bob Collins to Broadcasting Minister, Síle De Valera, a futile gesture of appealing to a higher authority regarding his "statutory position", an unwise move for anyone supporting the need for never-ending vigilance and struggle to consolidate the hard-won distinction in Western Europe between the categories of "state broadcaster" and "public broadcaster". The copies were returned unopened to RTÉ. Bob Quinn resigned from the Authority six months after this. The Appeal went ahead in the Supreme Court and was rejected, as we expected. The implications of this judgement are still being worked through, for party political broadcasts during referenda, for non-party interest groups seeking broadcast time, for the Referendum Commission and its own provision of balanced broadcasts, and for small political parties and independent candidates struggling to get broadcasting time during elections.

4 THE ECONOMICS OF BROADCASTING

In Europe's most competitive same-language market, RTÉ's television channels hold a national, prime time audience averaging 50 percent, a figure that betters the performance of public service television in France, Germany, Italy, the Netherlands and the UK. Month by month over half the programmes in RTÉ 1's top twenty most watched programmes, as measured by A.C. Nielsen, are home produced. RTÉ's radio share of national listening is 50 percent in a country where private commercial radio at local and national levels has made impressive advances over the last decade. But the size of the population to support all this broadcasting is small, at 3.6 million people, and audience expectations of RTÉ are very strong, given that seventy-five percent of the 1.1 million television households in Ireland receive all the major British channels, which draw their resources from a domestic audience that is about twenty-five times larger than Ireland's. Despite audiences being able to compare the output of Irish with British channels and expect the same standards and levels of output of domestic programming, RTÉ is clearly never going to be able to match the economies of scale and the sheer volume of resources available to its competitors. About two-thirds of RTÉ's income is commercial revenue, the balance coming from the licence fee. It has often been pointed out that over-reliance on commercial income is not healthy for a dual-funded broadcaster with a public service remit, because of the danger that the pressure to maximise audiences as often as possible will exert a powerful gravitational pull on programme schedules and soften the commitment to provide a diversity of programme genres aimed at stimulating both small and large audience interest. Buoyant commercial revenues sustained RTÉ throughout most of the 1990s but underlying trends in this period pointed to a more demanding and less certain broadcasting environment, as the rate of cost increase began to overtake revenue from licence fee and advertising sales and RTÉ began to head into deficit.

Consider the following ten-year trends. Revenue from the licence fee increased by a factor of 44 percent in the ten years between 1989 and 1999, while the take from advertising sales on radio and television increased by 84.5 percent. At the same time, the proportion of the total revenue accounted for by the licence fee dropped to about 33 percent. Overall revenue (television and radio advertising, plus other broadcasting income, plus income generated by RTÉ Commercial Enterprises) grew over that decade by 61.5 percent. But expenditure over the same period inflated at an even greater rate – broadcasting expenditure by 83.5 percent and total expenditure by 88 percent. In 1989 there was an operating surplus of £8.4 million, and by 1999 this had turned into an operating deficit of £16.7 million at a time when surpluses of at least £10 million should have been generated for capital expenditure and new programme development.

NEW COMPETITION

In the Autumn of 1995, the new RTÉ Authority tackled the question of the likely economic impact on RTÉ of the imminent launch of the new national, private, commercial radio and television channels. RTÉ had successfully adapted to the arrival of local commercial radio in the early 1990s, a new broadcasting sector that proved very popular in some parts of the country where the need for local programming was most intense. These local stations had a significant impact on Radio 1, eroding its market share considerably, especially outside Dublin and Leinster. But now the memory of the failure of Century Radio in 1990 (despite the inappropriately strong backing it had received from the Minister for Broadcasting, Ray Burke) was fading and the IRTC was again inviting applications for a national commercial radio service. It was also advancing negotiations with the TV3 consortium with a view to launching a national commercial television service. The TV3 consortium indicated its intention of providing twelve hours of programming per day, with 15 percent (about two hours) of total output being home-produced at the outset, increasing to 25 percent (three hours) by year five. At this stage, it looked as if UTV would be the dominant force in TV3 and it intended to rationalise its advertising sales on an all-island basis by offering advertisers attractive UTV / TV3 packages. The arrival of the new channel would have at least a strong novelty value for audiences in the so-called "dual-channel" area with access only to the two RTÉ services. It would probably be more difficult for TV3 to have a significant impact in the multi-channel terrestrial and cable – satellite areas, where competition was already fierce.

Audience share would be vitally important for both radio and television services if they were to attract sufficient commercial support. RTÉ research in 1995 estimated a potential loss of £3.2 million to the new radio station by the year 2000 and £10.8 million to TV3. TV3 would also have an impact on RTÉ in the international television programme market, as each channel would struggle to acquire broadcasting rights to the most attractive programming. In every country where competitive television services have been established, the cost of acquired programmes has increased sharply and Ireland would be no exception, as competition for the same material would enable distributors to increase their prices, perhaps by as much as fifty percent.

The Irish advertising market is characterised by two dominant suppliers of advertising time and space in the three major media: RTÉ in both television and radio and Independent Newspapers in the press. So there are relatively few gateways for advertisers to gain access to large audiences. But while new entrants in radio, television and the press tend to attract only small market shares at present, the ongoing process of market fragmentation slowly erodes the position of the dominant players. As cable, MMDS and deflector systems serve more areas with multi-channel television, access is continually improving for TV3, Channel 4, UTV and Sky Television (which developed an advertising opt-out in 1999). But the total advertising market in Ireland was growing very strongly in the late 1990s, by between 10 percent and 19 percent annually. In 1998, the year of the launch of TV3, RTÉ was holding 77 percent of the total nett television advertising market, TV3 had 3 percent and UTV and Channel 4 had 20 percent between them. While there tends to be a linear relationship between television advertising revenue growth and GNP growth, this pattern can be disrupted. The total advertising market in Ireland grew by 30 percent between 1996 and 1998 but RTÉ's revenue grew by only 16 percent. This is because television advertising relies heavily on what the trade calls "fast moving consumer goods" (FMCGs), demand for which does not tend to increase in line with general economic growth. RTÉ's top ten advertisers in 1998 were Unilever, Proctor and Gamble, Guinness, Master Foods, C & C Group, Nestlé, Kelloggs, National Lottery, Cadbury and L'Oreal, representing 44 percent of its total television advertising income.

Even without new competitors entering the marketplace, and assuming there would be no significant slowdown in wider economic activity, it was already clear in 1999 that audience fragmentation would continue and that a slowdown in the rate of growth in RTÉ's advertising income would take place. Since the early 1990s, Radio 1 had suffered a steady decline in market share as local stations began to broadcast across the country and became particularly strong in Munster, Connacht and Donegal, though the arrival of the private national station, Today FM, (previously Radio Ireland) after a slow start began to have a larger impact on the local stations than on Radio 1. Local radio stations in Dublin, offering mostly pop music, attained a share of over 70 percent from 7 p.m. to midnight, while RTÉ held on to its commitment to minority interest programming in this period and generated its large audience share during the morning, its radio prime time. Independent Radio News began to sell advertising along with news across all local stations, and this proved to be popular with national advertisers, while the advent of breakfast TV was seen as a threat to radio advertising revenue during radio's most important segment of the day.

In the late 1990s, RTÉ's television channels between them had a 56 percent share of the market, far in excess of its competition as illustrated in Table I.

Table 1: National Market Share: Adults: Prime Time.

Channel	Jan – June '98 percent	Jan – June '97 percent
RTÉ 1	42	40
Network Two	14	16
TV3	6	n/a
BBC 1	9	10
BBC 2	3	5
UTV	11	9
Channel 4	4	5
Sky One	4	4
Others	7	11
TOTAL	100	
Total RTÉ	56	56

Source: A.C.Nielsen

In order to be able to develop market share, a broadcaster must first be able to reach the audience with a television signal. As Table II indicates, the level of market penetration of competitors varied a great deal in the 1990s but is steadily increasing as distribution technologies proliferate: satellite, cable, MMDS and deflector.

Table 2: Television Channel Penetration

Channel	1998 (percent)	1996 (percent)
RTÉ One	100	99
Network Two	100	99
TV3	85	n/a
BBC One	70	69
UTV	64	62
Channel Four	62	62
Sky One	50	46
Sky News	48	45
Eurosport	39	28
Children's Channel	32	26

Source: A.C.Nielsen (Note: some broadcasters claimed higher levels of penetration, including UTV and TV3.)

Cable systems, offering Irish and UK terrestrial and some satellite channels, gained high penetration in newly built housing estates and apartment blocks in the mid-1990s. The huge increase in this kind of concentrated housing, as the economy expanded, favoured the cable companies. The addition of new channels, as capacity increased, further enhanced the attraction of cable, even before broadband technology held out the promise of carriage of telephony, the Internet and digital television. Subscription television, availed of by about 15 percent of Cablelink customers in the late 1990s, would probably grow rapidly, as digital capability was rolled out. Along with Internet services, this would create new in-home competition for RTÉ, in terms of both further audience fragmentation and advertiser spend. There was little cable carriage of RTÉ in Northern Ireland at this time, where only 20 percent of households were cabled, but the NTL-driven roll-out of cable in Belfast and elsewhere could increase RTÉ penetration there to 75 percent. Political sensitivities had militated against a strong RTÉ effort to market its channels in the North and its desire to increase its market share from the current level of about 5 percent to a more respectable level of at least 10 percent. A campaign to recruit Northern Ireland viewers launched in Summer 2000 resulted in up to 50 percent of households adjusting their television sets to receive RTÉ.

For much of the 1990s, there has been a shortage of commercial airtime in the advertising market of the Celtic Tiger. Due to the economic boom, demand for airtime increased dramatically but there was little increase in supply, despite the arrival of TV3 and Today FM, which haven't yet been able to attract large shares of the market. Despite this strong demand for airtime, RTÉ is prevented from fully exploiting the possibilities for revenue generation by minutage restrictions imposed by the Minister, which prevent it from increasing the length of commercial breaks. Newspapers can launch new supplements and magazines to provide new vehicles for advertisers, but broadcasters can only increase the number of minutes per hour, a process subject to two major restrictions. Firstly, there is a real limit to the number of minutes in any hour that can be tolerated by audiences, above which viewers begin to rebel against excessive commercial clutter by switching channels. Viewer behaviour provides an economic brake on the pressure to maximise advertising minutage by threatening audience share, the vital statistic that guides advertiser's decisions on how to apportion their budgets among broadcasters. In the very lightly regulated US television system, this limit is reached at about 20 percent of television time, or an average of twelve minutes per hour of advertising time.

The second limit on advertising minutage can come in the form of Government regulation applied with a view to engineering what legislators see as appropriate levels of competition between broadcasters. Regulation of advertising minutage was applied with some ferocity by Ray Burke, Minister for Communications in the Fianna Fáil Government that came to power in 1987, with the intention of delivering on its long-standing promise to support commercial radio. The judicial tribunal set up in 1999 by the Government to investigate allegations of political corruption, revealed the intricacies of the relationship between Mr. Burke and Century Radio, the first national station to be licensed as a direct competitor of RTÉ for audiences and advertising. Mr. Burke intervened personally in favour of Century in a lengthy dispute with RTÉ about the amount to be charged for the right to use RTÉ's transmission network to ensure national reception of Century's signal. Century's directors had intervened directly with the Minister in an attempt to get RTÉ's pop channel, 2FM, closed down. One of the directors, Oliver Barry, made a political donation of £30,000 to the Minister. When Century found its financial situation deteriorating rapidly not long after its launch in December 1989, Mr. Burke intervened dramatically with three new policy proposals: 2FM should become a cultural and educational service (thus leaving popular music completely to the private radio sector); a quarter of the licence fee should be diverted from RTÉ to support the new private broadcasting sector; and RTÉ's advertising income should be capped to divert revenue to the private sector.[48] These proposals generated intense controversy at the time, including a threat by the NUJ to embarrass the Government by refusing to cover an upcoming EU Summit to be hosted by the Taoiseach, Charles Haughey. The first two proposals were dropped, but the capping of RTÉ's income was implemented in the Broadcasting Act of 1990. Advertising minutage was reduced by a tenth to 7.5 percent of total daily programme time. Maximum hourly minutage was reduced from 7.5 minutes to 5. RTÉ's maximum advertising revenue was to be limited to the amount received from the licence fee, These measures gave the Government hands-on control of the total revenue of RTÉ, but they failed to save Century Radio, which closed down in November 1991, having achieved a mere 6 percent of the national audience. The result of Government intervention was to divert advertising revenue out of the State, particularly to UTV.

The Broadcasting Act of 1993, the creation of a Labour Party Minister,
Michael D. Higgins, removed the cap on RTÉ advertising generally but did not

restore the pre-1990 level of advertising minutage in radio. On television, RTÉ can now broadcast up to six minutes of advertising per hour on average, up to a maximum of 7.5 minutes, provided this is compensated for at other times, so that the six minutes average is maintained over the day. UTV and Channel 4 broadcast seven minutes per hour, TV3 is allowed nine minutes and satellite channels vary. There is no indication that the Government will allow RTÉ to increase its minutage and in fact Sile De Valera, successor to Michael D. Higgins, turned down such a request from the RTÉ Authority in 1997. Partly to compensate for these restrictions, RTÉ has moved to twenty-four hour broadcasting, but there is limited scope for attracting sizeable audiences, a realisation that led RTÉ to pull back from launching a full breakfast TV service which would probably not be commercially viable in the small Irish broadcasting market, well served in the morning by popular radio schedules, though TV3 now has a three-hour breakfast show in place.

There is probably still a considerable amount of frustrated demand for television and radio advertising space in the Irish market. The development of TV3 and the Sky Television Irish opt-out will satisfy some of this demand but it is inevitable that pressure will increase on RTÉ's advertising revenue, though this is difficult to predict. Attempts to determine the link between advertising revenue and the wider economy through examining correlations across the previous decade, to find out under what market conditions an increase in GNP can predict the total value of advertising in the country, are notoriously unreliable. It is increasingly difficult to predict the dynamics of the advertising industry as competition in broadcasting gains strength and audience fragmentation accelerates. By 2001 there were indications that forecasts of growth in RTÉ advertising revenue would not be met. The least that can be assumed is that it is highly unlikely now, as private broadcasting is well on the way to maturing in Ireland, that any Government in the near future will develop a passion once again to control RTÉ's advertising revenue so blatantly, as well as its licence fee.

PUBLIC FUNDING

If advertising revenue had the effect of constantly pulling RTÉ in the direction of designing its programme schedules so that it could reach as large a segment of the population of viewers and listeners as possible, thus aligning itself with the agenda of advertising agencies, its second source of income, the licence fee, pulled it in a very different direction, towards that powerful but vaguely articulated and always contested ideal known as public service broadcasting. Indeed the majority of the most bitterly argued differences in RTÉ Authority discussions centred around the inevitable contradictions generated by the tension between these two opposing forms of financing and their influence on programming. It is worth recalling here briefly the origin of this tension, since dual funding is at the core of how RTÉ behaves as an organisation dedicated to cultural production and is an essential key to explaining how it responds to the pressures of globalisation.

After nine years of debate about the basic structure that would be used to build and operate a national television service in Ireland, the Cabinet meeting on July 31st 1959 finally opted for establishing a State-owned and operated public television service, without the involvement of any commercial concerns. Up to this point, it had seemed certain that the operation of Ireland's television service would be privatised, taken on by an American, British or European corporation and financed solely by advertising. The terms of reference given to the Television Commission established in 1958 to advise the Government, were carefully crafted by Sean Lemass to stipulate that no charge should fall on the Exchequer, on capital or current account. This presented the Commission with an impossible challenge, as entrusting television to a commercial company was the only obvious way to ensure it would be cost free, yet effective control of television programmes had to be exercised "by an Irish public authority." The actual proposal that was finally accepted, however, put together by Leon Ó Broin and his colleagues at the Department of Posts and Telegraphs, argued that a State-owned service could quickly be got up and running with financial support from the government that would be repaid through licence fees and advertising.

As Savage points out, "the dismal fiscal and economic realities that haunted Ireland throughout this period influenced the service that was established."[49] While many opinion leaders were inclined to support a State financed system, "the grim realities of a State troubled by economic stagnation and relentless emigration, forced a strict evaluation of priorities. The desire to avoid spending precious State funds on television, when it was apparent that other more critical issues had to be addressed, had created strong opposition to state involvement in the new medium." This opposition included the Department of Finance, editorial boards of national newspapers, various Government leaders and Members of the Dáil (Parliament), semi-State bodies, wealthy industrialists and even the Catholic Church. The final Government decision in 1959 did not establish a public service comparable to the BBC (which took a keen interest in the television debate in Ireland throughout the1950s) but in adopting a State-owned commercial public service model, it avoided turning the airwaves over to foreign commercial operations.

When we look at RTÉ thirty-five years later in the mid-1990s, we find Irish households paying a licence fee of £62 through An Post, which has acted as the collection agency since the origins of Irish radio in 1926. This rate was close to the lowest in Europe at that time: only former Eastern bloc countries Poland, the Czech Republic, Slovakia and Romania charged less. At the top of the scale was Austria, Belgium and Denmark, charging their citizens almost 5.5 times more than Ireland. Throughout the early 1990s the relative importance of public funds, as compared to commercial revenues, was declining (from 38 percent in 1993 to 36 percent in 1994 to 33 percent in 1995). Only Spain (25.9 percent) and Portugal (31 percent) had a lower proportion of the funding of public broadcasting organisations coming from public funds.

In July 1996, the Government announced an increase of £8 in the licence fee, bringing it to £70 after a ten year freeze at £62. When one looks at international comparisons, it is extraordinary that successive Governments have been so loath to increase the public funding of broadcasting in Ireland. The myopic view of this is that Governments live in constant fear of the electoral effect of declaring an increase and when it has to be done, tend to want to minimise the public impact by announcing it in

July, as the political (and much of the media) apparatus is preparing to wind down and go on vacation. If this were the full explanation, a relatively painless way to ensure that the licence fee matches inflation is to link it to the Consumer Price Index. The Minister in1996, Michael D. Higgins, decided to do, this but left office before indexation was implemented and left the way open to his successor Sile De Valera, to decide against indexation, preferring to have RTÉ make a specific argument for each increase it requested. Ministers of Finance have typically been cool to the idea of increasing the licence fee, because it increases the expenditure of the Department of Social Welfare, which pays the licence fee for a range of different people on very low incomes. Increases also tend to affect the inflation level in the economy, since the licence fee is one of the services included in the "basket" of goods and services used to estimate the rate of inflation.

A more realistic explanation for the very low level of public support for broadcasting in Ireland is the desire of politicians (of all parties) to feel they have some leverage over, if not control of, RTÉ and that this is manifested in a public way. Politicians tend to receive very favourable, uncritical treatment on local radio stations and this has now become a major new force in political communication in Ireland, a fact acknowledged in such phenomena, for example, as the number of politicians publicly celebrating the launch of the new lobby group, the Independent Broadcasters of Ireland (IBI), in 1998. But RTÉ had built up a good record of critiquing politicians, of challenging them in studio discussions in well-prepared interviews or confronting them with some of their colleagues from other parties in staged rituals that sometimes look like the modern equivalent of bear-baiting. For some critics of broadcasting, much of this political wrestling is sterile, predictable, set-piece ritual that doesn't go far enough. But for very many politicians themselves, it generates an aggressive love/hate relationship with RTÉ, whose passion I found palpable as Chairman meeting politicians, once pleasantries had been dispensed with. Controlling the level of the licence fee is a favoured political expression of the hope that RTÉ can be "tamed" by fiscal restraint. Many politicians declare themselves to be dedicated supporters of strong public service broadcasting, but they then go on to express their love/hate relationship through the form of dismissing any appeal for financial support as "crying wolf" and assuming that RTÉ is so adroit at looking after its own interests that ever more obligation can be squeezed from it, whether that be to providing 365 hours of programming *gratis* to TG4 or slicing 20 percent off its total television programming expenditure to develop a private production sector in Ireland, both major pressures on RTÉ in the 1990s.

Political attitudes to the licence fee reveal a lack of consistent attention to policy formulation and revision across the whole administrative system, from political parties to the recesses of the civil service. It should have been obvious to all political parties in the mid-1980s, as Thatcherism and Reaganism peaked on each side of the Atlantic, that Ireland was finally prepared to listen to the globalising message of market liberalisation, reverberating throughout the Western world first, then the former Communist Bloc and finally the developing world. The decision to opt for "deregulation" was part of the liberalisation gospel being preached by OECD, IMF,

World Bank and other powerful organisations. To deregulate broadcasting meant in effect to end the monopoly position RTÉ had enjoyed for decades and allow rivals to compete for the same advertising revenue that sustained RTÉ. There should have been – but there wasn't – a political debate about the future funding of broadcasting, about the need to look anew at the role of the licence fee in a deregulated broadcasting market. There was already plenty of evidence, backed by solid academic research mostly from the US, that it is not so much a dependence on advertising that degrades programming, as the intensity of competition for advertising among different broadcasters in the same market. It wouldn't have taken a great deal of political imagination even to anticipate that private broadcasters, once allowed on air, would have plenty to say about sharing out the proceeds of the licence fee. Rupert Murdoch was already floating this idea as his fledgling Sky Television struggled to survive in the 1980s. It should have been foreseen by Irish politicians at that time, as arguments in favour of deregulation swept in from Europe and the US, that RTÉ would need a firmer foundation in public financing once competition from private broadcasters began, and that this would mean, as it did in other parts of Europe, a firmer approach to increasing and indexing the licence fee.

Most of the increase of 8 percent granted by the Rainbow Government in 1996 actually went towards financing the new Irish-language television service, TG4, and did little to ward off the evil day when pressure to capture advertising revenue would become intense. (Chapter 7 outlines the forces working against the launch of TG4 and the pressure on RTÉ to provide one hour of programming per day, at no cost to the new channel.) In effect, this means that in the fifteen-year period between 1986 and 2001, (when an increase of £14.50 was granted) there was no increase in the licence fee, despite a rise in the CPI of about 50 percent over the same period. From 1990 onwards, the cost of broadcasting in Ireland was met increasingly by advertising and the share of RTÉ's revenue coming from the licence fee dropped dramatically. In 1996, we estimated that the licence fee increase approved by the Rainbow Government would bring in an extra £7.7 million per annum immediately and grow to £8 million by 2001, by which year indexation would expand this to £15.3 million (even allowing for what RTÉ considered an exorbitant fee of £7.3 million per annum charged by An Post for the job of collecting the fees). At my first meeting with the new Minister, Sile De Valera, over lunch in the Dail, she told me that the new Fianna Fail-Progressive Democrat Government did not agree with indexation and would deal with RTÉ's application for licence fee increases on a case by case basis.

The effect on RTÉ was immediate and devastating. Already it was becoming clear that the organisation would be slipping into deficits very soon. Indexation, a relatively painless way to ensure public funding increased in line with the Consumer Price Index, was gone. Pressures in the global television markets were leading to hyperinflation in the cost of sports and other programmes rights. Increased support to the independent production sector was mandated by the 1993 Broadcasting Act. There was no sign of the promised Government support for TnaG programme costs. Soon TV3 and Radio Ireland would have an impact on commercial revenue. If large deficits were to be avoided, it was becoming clear that a comprehensive review of all RTÉ's activities and operating practices must be undertaken and that inevitably the size of the workforce must be reduced. This would be a long and painful process.

In the meantime, the actual value of the licence fee had to be maximised, beginning with the efficiency of the collection system. In 1997, RTÉ and An Post jointly commissioned a review of the television licence collection system and its cost. The first draft of the report by PriceWaterhouse was quite critical of many of the practices current in An Post and suggested that considerable changes could be made in what was charged to RTÉ and in the collection process generally, to bring about savings of £1.75 million annually. The Draft Report went to both organisations for review and then the Final Report was issued. This was much less specific on the precise savings that could be achieved and An Post announced it could not agree that the Final Report indicated RTÉ was being overcharged, suggesting that many of the conclusions reached by Price Waterhouse were very subjective.

RTÉ was also now taking a much more pro-active role in maximising licence fee revenue, focussing on all aspects of collection, including its own interface with the public and its perception of value for money, analysis of evasion and inspection methods. Because of the history of collection, RTÉ never had any input on methods used. An Post collects the fee for the Government, which then pays RTÉ by way of Exchequer grant, first deducting collection costs, the cost of the Broadcast Complaints Board and other administrative charges. The key issue now was the significant infrastructure costs within the Post Office network, whether RTÉ needs this network to issue television licences and whether it should in effect be contributing to An Post's infrastructure costs. If selling television licences at the counter is regarded as marginal activity, then this should attract only direct marginal costs. But throughout the 1990s, An Post charged annual amounts for collection that varied between 10 percent and 12.3 percent, representing income for An Post rising from £5.9 million in 1990 to £7.7 million in 1998. Throughout the decade, the number of licences sold increased by 17.7 percent, due to changing demographics, increases in household numbers, changes in home ownership patterns and new housing developments. None of the new revenue was due to an increase in efficiency in the collection method. An Post was still not implementing a robust inspection system. Evasion levels remained too high, estimated variously between 10 percent and 16 percent, while the European average is 8 percent. By contrast, the Licence-Fee Collection Department in the BBC had succeeded in getting the UK evasion rate down to 5.4 percent. If both evasion levels and collection costs in Ireland could be halved, and if indexation were restored, RTÉ could be receiving an extra £12 million per annum without any formal increase being granted by Government.

By the end of the 1990s, RTÉ had moved to the conclusion that the collection of the fee should be put to tender by Government or by RTÉ, in accordance with current best practice for large contracts. This would almost certainly result in a more robust inspection system and lower evasion levels, as well as lower collection costs. It is likely that the Irish Government will inevitably be pressured by the European Commission to accept the principle of public tendering in this area, but this will take time and will be resisted, because of its implications for the survival of An Post in its present form. We adopted a shorter-term strategy, focussed on RTÉ working more closely with An Post to recognise the existence of a previously "missing" 200,000 television households which had never paid a television licence fee. This could generate a further £14 million if this sector were to be targeted vigorously via direct mail and localised advertising on poster, local radio and local press, along with concentrated inspection visits in particular areas. Digital television held out the possibility of using encryption technology to identify evaders, but this solution was a long-term one.

In the early 1990s, RTÉ was generating surpluses and with no national competitor in sight in either radio or television, its future looked secure. Chairmann John Sorohan's Annual Report for 1994, for instance, announced a broadcasting surplus of £4.25 million, with an extra £5 million income from Radio Tara, Cablelink and CEL delivering a healthy group surplus of £9.4 million (down slightly from the 1992 level). But 1995 marks a watershed in the evolution of broadcasting in Ireland, because in that year, the large surplus of £14.8 million, fed by a once-off injection of funds arising from the sale of part of Cablelink, masked the fact that broadcasting itself was in deficit to the tune of £2.43 million. What was emerging strongly by the mid-1990s was an accelerating convergence between year-on-year trends in broadcasting revenues and broadcasting expenditures. In 1995, for instance, revenues increased by 8 percent over the previous year, but operating expenses grew by almost 13 percent.

COST DRIVERS

What were the cost drivers operating behind this convergence in the Consolidated Accounts? Firstly, 50 percent of RTÉ's prime time schedule is built on acquired programmes, an achievement resulting from a policy adopted after the SKC Report of 1985, to increase the volume of indigenous programming. But the proliferation of new television channels in Europe at this time began a steady climb in the cost of acquiring programmes in the global market and, of course, this increase would be accelerated once another Irish channel would enter the market, after the launch of TV3. This cost pressure was felt most keenly in sports rights, as the arrival of scores of new channels, including specialist sports channels, encouraged television sports right holders to seek ever bigger fees from broadcasters. The significant spending power of the multinational specialist channels forced up the price of major sports events to a level almost beyond the reach of terrestrial, publicly funded broadcasters like RTÉ.

Secondly, the effects of the 1993 Act were being felt acutely as the decade advanced. The Act was designed to privatise parts of the television production apparatus and move RTÉ closer to being a publisher-broadcaster, by directly feeding production funds to new companies in the independent production sector, some of them managed by former RTÉ staff. The Act stipulated a schedule of payments by RTÉ, rising from £6.5 million in 1995 to 20 percent of television programming expenditure by 1999. The "downsizing" of RTÉ as a production organisation was debated hardly at all as the 1993 Act was being passed, but it was an inevitable consequence of this legislated requirement on RTÉ to fund the independent production companies. The problem now was that the Act pegged the expenditure to a percentage of "television programming expenditure" and this opened the door to a long and bitter argument with Film Makers

Ireland (FMI), the independent sector's professional association, on how this should be interpreted. If taken at face value, it meant that instead of reaching a stable plateau in 1999 when the formula reached the full 20 percent, RTÉ would find itself on a moving escalator, paying out ever larger amounts to the independent producers. This was because the base on which the 20 percent was calculated would continue to be subject to the rampant inflation in the global television programme market that was manifest in the spirally cost of acquiring programme and sports rights.

Neither this hyper-inflation nor the cost of RTÉ's commitment to TnaG could have been foreseen when the 1993 Act was being framed. James Hickey, the vary able public voice of FMI during this period, objected strongly to my proclivity to highlight the impact of the 1993 Act on RTÉ, arguing that it was by now a "done deal" and RTÉ should get on with adjusting itself to the new reality. But I insisted on pointing out at every opportunity that we were approaching a severe crisis as 1999 neared and RTÉ would be unable to afford 20 percent of a value that was getting more unstable by the week, as the globalising forces of the large television programme markets continued to bear down on RTÉ's small budget. Broadcasting itself, as the core business of RTÉ, was losing money increasingly from 1995 on – the broadcasting deficit quickly reached £5 million by 1998, the year of the arrival of both TnG and TV3 – and there were no easy ways to stop the financial haemorrhaging once the spend on broadcasting had overtaken the income from broadcasting. RTÉ and the independent sector took time to develop a mutual respect after a very stressful relationship at first, particularly when the independent demand for access to RTÉ funds outstripped the supply by a large margin. But the relationship began to work more smoothly from 1997 on, through the pragmatics of collaboration. Significant strains continued to be felt in the budget area, however, as the start up of national competitors in radio (Radio Ireland, later Today FM) and television (TV3), as well as the aggressive targeting of Irish audiences by UK broadcasters, jangled the nerves of everyone in RTÉ. The combination of commitment to TnaG and the independent production sector, as well as the increasing fragmentation of Irish audiences as more channels became available, contributed to a palpable sense in Montrose of RTÉ as an institution becoming unsettled as never before.

The pace of change affecting technology – no one could predict what way digitisation would change the way people use television – and public policy regarding broadcasting, were accelerating in Ireland and throughout the EU. Not so long ago, Britain was the most powerful external influence on broadcasting in Ireland, but now, it was just one of the many complex realities to be kept in view by smaller countries such as Ireland. Wherever we looked, the broadcasting environment was unpredictable, nervous, agitated by change. The certainties of earlier decades, when Governments could shape broadcasting to suit local conditions, were replaced by the apprehension that no one was in control. In Europe, deep anxiety was the reaction to the continuing cultural and economic dominance of the US, and academics argued over whether this could still be called cultural imperialism or cultural globalisation. Sometimes the latter term meant little more than recognition of the fact that other large centres of production had grown up outside the Anglophone television world, to parallel American cultural power in specific language markets, such as Spanish, Portuguese, Arabic or Mandarin, in Mexico, Brazil, Egypt and China.[50] Small European countries worried about their cultural identity. Would anything distinctly local survive under the shadow of richer and more aggressive powers in production and distribution, beaming dozens of new television channels into their territories and tightly controlling valuable content rights? True, a similar fear had accompanied the global growth of Hollywood power in film between the two world wars, but when television arrived, it had beaten back American dominance in cinema in a dramatic shift towards the restabilisation of national media systems, based on indigenous production appreciated by audiences far larger than what the cinema could muster even in its heyday in the 1940s.

Within the EU, debate on the future of broadcasting was dominated by the idea of digital convergence, as the Commission gathered in responses to its Green Paper on Convergence, published in 1998. RTÉ's input emphasised the social responsibility of public service broadcasting and the need to keep in view values that go beyond those of the market place. Later that year, the Commission circulated a discussion paper exploring the criteria by which public service broadcasting might be defined, so that programming on dual-funded systems like RTÉ could be divided into types which could be funded by a licence fee and types which could not. A brief and fierce debate ensued and the paper was hurriedly withdrawn when it was obvious that most Member States rejected its basic premises. But no one was in any doubt that these funding issues would surface again as competition between public and private broadcasters in Europe intensified and the latter issued more frequent complaints to the Commission about public service broadcasting being fundamentally at odds with the free market because it receives public funding. The DG4 tilt towards private broadcasters was corrected somewhat at the end of 1998 by the Report of the High Level Group on the Digital Age and European Audiovisual Policy (the Oreja Report), in its recognition of the role of Member States in determining the precise balance between public and private broadcasting in each country.

The large deficits being incurred by broadcasting from 1995 on, as costs rapidly outpaced revenue, were sustained within the larger group finances of RTÉ, especially healthy earnings generated by CEL under the able leadership of Conor Sexton. RTÉ's 25 percent share in *Riverdance*, the Eurovision Song Contest interval act that was developed by its producer, Moya Doherty, into a global show that drew its power from traditional Irish music, earned considerable income over six years for CEL and the sale of its share in Cablelink also ensured that RTÉ was far from bankruptcy. But the underlying trends were alarming. The level of public funding was static, unlike other European public service broadcasters that received increases in the licence fee every year or two. Advertising income was based structurally on a strong market demand for more airtime in the early 1990s, which weakened a little with the coming on stream of national and local broadcasters. These were inexorably shrinking RTÉ's audiences and providing alternative routes to consumers for advertising agencies. Meanwhile, RTÉ's cost base was experiencing hyperinflation, just like all other European television companies. The question was what could be done about all this.

ORGANISATIONAL REVIEW

After one year in office, the Authority had come to grips with the full complexity of the two main questions that focus on the economic life blood of the organisation, which either allows great programming to be broadcast or prevents it: what drives costs and what drives revenues? Our search for answers was fully entwined with the search for a new Director-General to replace Joe Barry. Mr Barry had served RTÉ admirably in a variety of roles since entering the organisation forty years earlier as a technician in the Engineering Division and making his way up the ranks to the position of Chief Executive Officer. His deep knowledge of the organisation, combined with his interpersonal abilities to relate to a great variety of employees, was highly valued by the Authority in the aftermath of the early 90s' RTÉ strike, which left many organisational bruises in need of healing. The search for a new Director-General took six months in 1996-7, from initial discussions with a recruitment consultant to define the search more precisely, to the final speech in the farewell for Joe Barry and the installation of his successor. This six months allowed the Authority to focus on the question of broadcasting costs, always more difficult to analyse than revenues because there are a myriad answers, most of them buried in the detailed workings of a large and very complex organisation of very creative people.

The choice of Bob Collins as Director-General was welcomed in Government and among all political parties and was a very popular choice within RTÉ itself, given the man's exceptional intellectual and verbal abilities and the belief that he had a clear view of what public service broadcasting should be all about.

The phrase "a root and branch review" trips easily off the tongues of job applicants as they sit in the interview chair but this is precisely what Bob Collins now set about, with full Authority backing, when he took up office in April 1997, carefully explaining to staff what was involved. A fundamental review of RTÉ's structures and operations was set in motion, with the purpose of identifying the essential conditions of change and the significant performance improvement options available to RTÉ in securing its position. The broader context of this review was the ever-increasing domestic and international competition facing RTÉ and the transition to digital broadcasting technologies that would have to be tackled immediately. The review would form the basis for a strategic plan which would take the national broadcasting organisation into the new millennium with confidence, but in a broadcasting environment that was radically different from what existed just a few years previously. A significant level of production was being transferred into the independent sector, driven by the 1993 Broadcasting Act. Large investment would be needed to make digital broadcasting a reality, as technological convergence redefines programme making and changes the relationship between broadcaster and viewers / listeners. And new competitors were steadily fragmenting the audience, as greater access to more television stations replicated the pattern established over the previous decade by the arrival of new private radio stations, small and agile competitors providing local services that ate into what RTÉ used to regard as its exclusive revenue base. As the cost of entry to broadcasting in the 1990s was tumbling, RTÉ had no option but to prepare itself to be as agile at several levels as its smallest competitor.

The most remarkable aspect of this review was that in contrast with the externally imposed SKC Review of 1985, this one was created and executed in-house by a project team, led by Eugene Murray, which utilised a variety of methodologies including weekly meetings of a review panel drawn from the Trade Union Group and the RTÉ Managers Association. This was to ensure that staff consultation would be at the core of what promised to be an exercise in radical self examination. The organisation was abuzz for five months with meetings, focus groups and user panels, concentrated on self-analysis and the establishment of agreed corporate objectives. These included the generation and evaluation of different options for the future in each Department and Division, activity analyses, priority-based resourcing exercises, visits to other broadcasting organisations facing similar major challenges, programme cost comparisons and a consultant-led examination of specific areas.

The results of this tremendous effort at organisational self-analysis were published in June 1998 in the 250 page Review of RTÉ's Structures and Operations, which became known as the *Blue Book* as it circulated through every office, workshop and studio. The hard realism of its assessments was shocking to some people. Television programme costs, for example, had risen 30 percent over the three previous years, at a time when audiences – and therefore advertising revenues – were shrinking and Governments were as reluctant as ever to increase the television licence fee. This alone, along with the statutory requirement to outsource a significant amount of television production, meant that the cost base would have to be reduced quickly, by reducing staff numbers. The dreaded "downsizing" option was already hovering over Montrose. But the *Blue Book* was also bullish about the future, arguing that RTÉ should avoid retrenchment and work to develop programme services further, in a more cost effective manner, by adopting new technologies, organisational structures and work practices. This would mean that revenues could be better utilised to provide Irish people with radio and television programmes that would match the best offered by other public broadcasters across Europe.

To get to that point, however, some bitter medicine had to be swallowed. If large parts of RTÉ were in denial about some of their shortcomings, the *Blue Book* laid out its truths with devastating clarity, including its view of how many staff reductions should take place in each area. Quality radio and television would have to be supported by a focus on value for money, as well as on a renewed commitment to public service values. Managerial roles and organisational structures did not always allow this and there was no shared vision about how RTÉ would address competitive threats. Resistance to change, the *Blue Book* emphasised was influenced by inertia, lack of trust between management, staff and unions and fear of the impact of change.

An important measure of the effectiveness of the *Blue Book* probing was the level of dismay, anguish and sometimes anger with which it was greeted by staff, feelings that then largely developed into a sense of the realism about the need to radically reform work practices. In the Radio Division, for instance, the sense of shock at the *Blue Book* recommendations was palpable. Staff could quickly deconstruct the dry language of administration analysis and translate the criticism into terms (and individual names) that were relevant to their daily work experience. The roles and functions of senior editorial managers urgently needed more clearly defined responsibilities, so that informal and unofficial lines of communication would no longer encourage those at producer level to withdraw from the decision-making process entirely. Too much of the work involved in preparing daytime radio programmes was carried out by producers rather than researchers and broadcasting assistants, so not only were people's skills not being utilised fully but programme costs were too high, driven by an imbalance between producers (15 in all to produce *Today with Pat Kenny, Gay Byrne, Liveline* and *Five Seven Live*) and researchers (only 7 for these key daytime programmes) and broadcasting assistants (only 8). But in other parts of the Radio Division, it seemed that some producers were being under-utilised, as became obvious when a significant proportion of their salary was costed against one programme.

This level of detailed analysis was not to be seen in the SKC Report of 1985, commissioned by Government and imposed upon RTÉ from outside. The achievement of the *Blue Book* was that its analysis was undertaken by RTÉ staff themselves, so it was more difficult to hide uncomfortable information and therefore the quality of the analysis was far better than what could be produced by external consultants. The internal dynamic behind the fact finding and the analysis, driven by the new Director-General and Executive Board, also meant that it was more likely that staff at all levels would respond positively to the final recommendations and agree to implement changes, in full awareness of the economic need for reform.

This is in fact what happened. After a thorough analysis of the accounts and management predictions about slowing revenue streams and cost inflation, the RTÉ Trade Union Group agreed a process, built on industrial partnership principles successfully implemented in other Irish industrial sectors and in other countries. This process led initially to agreement to bring about over three hundred voluntary redundancies, and then to reconfigure work routines so that resources could be deployed more efficiently towards one goal: maintaining high quality programme output in radio and television and, where possible, improving it, for instance, by implementing a badly needed increase in home produced television drama.

GOVERNMENT REACTION

It is important here to emphasise that the *Blue Book* initiative, and the Transformation Agreement that followed it, was entirely an RTÉ-originated action. As Authority Chairman, I submitted quarterly reports to the Minister along with commentary and trend analysis that teased out the long-term significance of the figures. In every Annual Report during this period, my introduction went into considerable detail on the economic environment in which public service radio and television operated and warned of dangers ahead that would radically unsettle RTÉ if not addressed. Never once did anyone from the Department ask for more information or for an informal chat to discuss trends in broadcasting. The initiative for briefings was always taken by RTÉ. When we were summoned to discuss broadcasting with the Joint Oireachtas Committee on Broadcasting in 1997, Joe Barry, Bob Collins and I spent several hours poring over documents spread across the large boardroom table, preparing for an intelligent interrogation about future developments in broadcasting and the long-term implications of digital convergence between the Internet and television. The main concern on the Committee, however, was why we did not release information on the salary of Gay Byrne and other well-paid presenters. The Committee Chairman pressed us hard on this, along with the familiar reproach that "it's the people's money and therefore should be revealed." This was populist politics at its best, responding to editorials in the tabloid papers rather than to any real concern for broadcasting as a public good. Senator Shane Ross used the occasion for some public sector bashing, castigating RTÉ for consistency in always being a year late in releasing its Annual Reports. This was a sure sign, in the Senator's mind, of the usual public sector laziness and ineptitude that would one day soon have to face the wrath of the savage (and saving) god of privatisation. Our answer to this was that publication of the RTÉ Annual Report was delayed in the Department, not in RTÉ, as the Senator had already been told more than once.

The only time the Cabinet showed an interest in broadcasting budgets was when Bertie Ahern, again presumably responding to the populist pull of tabloid politics, instructed Síle De Valera to demand information from RTÉ on the salaries of Gay Byrne and others. It was somehow insulting to senior politicians that one of their state companies would not release such information, on the basis of commercial sensitivity. After protracted manoeuvring worthy of Monty Python treatment in its silliness, the information was eventually presented in a form that would not identify individuals and would not generate a paper trail that could be followed by any tabloid journalist. A formal meeting between Bob Collins and myself and the Minister and her staff yielded a list of salary amounts arranged in bands, which passed from one side of the table to the other, was copied by hand into jotters by the civil servants and passed back again. The information was then shown only to the Taoiseach and the Tánaiste, and they reported to the full Cabinet that the deed was done, to the satisfaction of all, a bit like John de Chastelain reporting to David Trimble that he had witnessed a significant act of IRA arms decommissioning but could say no more.

The sheer silliness of the Gaybo salary saga illustrates the weakness of politicians for tabloid populism, where newspapers give the impression that the whole country is convulsed with the question of RTÉ salaries and challenges politicians to "put manners" on RTÉ. But it also illustrates a strange lack of interest in the economics of broadcasting and in the implications of the new technologies for programme making and distribution, technologies that were then being deployed in other countries. RTÉ housed the best expertise in these areas and was very eager to share its knowledge with policy-makers. But few were interested. A charitable explanation is that politicians have overreacted to the fear of being exposed by journalists as meddlers in RTÉ affairs, since most newsrooms in the country work to a news value that highlights any tension, however trivial, between politicians and RTÉ. This news value is deeply embedded historically, conditioned by memories of the 1960s and 1970s when politicians had no qualms about trying to influence RTÉ editorially. When Michael D. Higgins was Minister and we would meet at receptions or book launches, he would jocosely mention after a few minutes conversation that the Minister must now maintain his "statutory distance" from the Chairman of the Authority. But there was also a serious edge to the remark.

My own feeling is that it is possible, and desirable, that senior politicians and civil servants should be able to meet senior RTÉ managers and the Chairman informally to brief themselves on key challenges facing broadcasters in an atmosphere of mutual trust, without in any way compromising RTÉ's editorial independence. Trust was important, but not always maintained. Early in my term of office, I was invited to lunch in the Dáil by Liam Lawlor to brief him on broadcasting matters. He then used my briefing solely to attempt to embarrass and score trivial political points against the Minister, Michael D. Higgins, in the Dáil chamber later that afternoon. Liam Lawlor would never receive a briefing from me again, given his total inability to resist the easy temptation to trivialise the information he received from me for micro political gain – perhaps a brief tabloid mention of a "wound" inflicted on the Minister by the intrepid T.D. from Kildare – rather than educate himself as a public representative on the complexities of broadcasting.

Given the almost total lack of interest among those staffing the political apparatus of the State in the future of broadcasting in Ireland and given the self-starting initiative of RTÉ, in responding to its own economic predicaments and putting its own house in order via the *Blue Book* and the Transformation Agreement, it was therefore somewhat disingenuous of Government to use RTÉ's own housekeeping agenda to justify refusing it the licence fee increase it requested in 2001. In 1985, the Government of the day commissioned the SKC Report but then did nothing to oversee the implementation of its recommendations. Fifteen years later, Government showed little interest in RTÉ's financial affairs but when RTÉ undertook its own reform, initiating a long and difficult process of change by staff consent, Government then jumped belatedly on the band wagon of reform and used the necessary slowness of the RTÉ consensual process to whip the national broadcaster still further. There is no doubt that the digital debacle of early 2000 and the frenzy of blame shifting that followed, damaged relations between RTÉ and the Minister and this may have coloured the harsh tone that iced her public utterances in 2001. By November of that year, for instance, it was clear that costs were mounting very quickly in RTÉ (largely driven by bad euro/dollar exchange rates) and advertising revenue was plummeting. Bob Collins predicted that advertising revenues, already down by £12 million in that year, would be £15.5 million below projections for 2002. Yet, Síle De Valera declared in the Dáil (8th November 2001) that RTÉ still had to "get its act together" and "face the real market realities". The Government would not consider another licence fee increase until RTÉ got on with its Transformation Agreement: "RTÉ must arrange its financial affairs and that is what the RTÉ Authority is there to do."

This was Government response to the crisis of late 2001, in which RTÉ decided on further cuts, including eliminating a further 160 jobs, closing down a number of Departments and selling off its Outside Broadcast operations. Political ignorance and lack of interest in broadcasting meant that external factors, over which RTÉ had no control, were being ignored in the Government's response to the crisis in RTÉ. These factors included currency exchange rates in US programme purchases, the success of British channels in sucking out television advertising money from the Irish economy, and the success of Sky Television in signing up 185,000 households to its digital service. Government ignorance of the significance of the inroads of Sky in the context of the stalled development of digital terrestrial television in Ireland (see Chapter Five) can be seen in the boast of a senior civil servant in November 2001. He told a group of visiting telecommunications executives from Mediterranean countries, that the enthusiastic, popular acceptance of a foreign digital satellite service was a very positive sign of "how the digital infrastructure in Ireland is increasingly being modernised." He made no reference to the damage to the national interest that might be caused if Murdoch's satellite expansion closed down the option of developing an Irish digital terrestrial platform.

An emerging external factor, from RTÉ's point of view, was the steady development of TV3, now guided by foreign owners CanWest and Granada, and its emergence as a serious competitor for both acquired programmes and advertising revenue. Many voices in Irish public life had argued throughout the 1990s for an alternative television system, so that "another point of view besides RTÉ" could improve life in Ireland. Now, in the winter of 2001, as it became clear that TV3 had acquired a firm hold in the very competitive Irish television market, the Broadcasting Commission of Ireland signalled that it would make permanent its practice of "light touch" regulation of private broadcasters. This confirmed what many in RTÉ already knew: that TV3 was investing very little in Irish-made television and therefore would be making few contributions to "an alternative view" to complement RTÉ's, and that the BCI was unwilling and unable to monitor TV3's output to determine if it lived up to the legislative requirement for content diversity. The implications of all these developments pointed towards a running down of the quality of broadcasting in Ireland right across the public-private spectrum. We now turn to consider how the arrival of digital technology in broadcasting is about to complicate still further the economic structure of television.

5

DIGITAL TELEVISION

LOCAL FORCES IN A GLOBAL CONTEXT

When digital compression technology emerged in its perfected form out of the electronics laboratories of universities and large companies ten years ago, it was a technology in search of a purpose. The public was unaware of it and there was no consumer demand for any of the services it might provide. The story of digital television today is largely the story of who gains advantage by controlling terrestrial, cable or satellite platforms and how consumers will be persuaded to part with their money for a new kind of communication and entertainment that will be available on more channels and will have some form of interactive capability. Six years on from the launch of the first digital television services, major questions still remain. How attractive are at the new uses of digital technology being developed every month by electronics laboratories? How many of us are interested in them to the extent of paying for them? Will the future be driven by consumer use as planned by global media corporations or by surprise uses generated unexpectedly by the early adopters, like the SMS "texting" phenomenon in mobile telephony that no one could foresee? Will service providers be able to survive the awesome competitive forces that are being unleashed in this period of corporate shake out and consolidation and will they be able to develop a business model which allows the benefits of digital technology to be provided on a near universal basis?

By 1998, the promise of digital television was huge and much of the early excitement centred around Digital Terrestrial Television (DTT). The British Government published a White Paper, then new legislation, allowing the most affordable distribution platform with the potentially widest reach in the population, to take off quickly. This was digital terrestrial television (DTT). Michael Green, Chairman of Carlton, declared that "every single television household will be watching DTT at some point in the future. It's only a question of time." Today, like the dotcom hype, the huge optimism about DTT has collapsed. Headlines in respectable broadsheets announce the end of digital television. On the same weekend in March 2002, Kirch in Germany was in freefall towards bankruptcy, ITV Digital was placed in administration by its owners Carlton and Granada, and the cable giant NTL was heading for receivership under the weight of its massive debts. Misjudging the cost of content and the rate of subscriber growth had devastated ITV Digital, as the value of many television companies across Europe started to fall sharply in a process that has now turned into a massive shake out, fuelled by fierce competition and the strains of carrying expensive debt. The demand for Hollywood product on premium channels remains very slow and there is no sign of profits from television for hopeful football clubs. Kirch's demise, as a conglomerate controlling newspapers, film production, cable and broadcasting, was the larger corporate collapse in German post-war history.

In the last few years, heavy expenditure on content (mostly Hollywood films and football) was gambled in order to lure new subscribers. In Italy, Murdoch's Stream channel and Vivendi's Telepiu competed furiously on this basis. It is now likely that pressure from bankers will force them to merge. ITV Digital invested almost one billion pounds sterling in its service but attracted only 1.2 million subscribers out of 25 million households. Kirch had failed to lift its subscriber base over 2.4 million subscribers. The mistakes (as well as the high stakes) in recent digital television strategies are acutely captured in one telling transaction: ITV Digital, having paid 350 million pounds sterling for Lower Division football rights, found itself paying £1.2 million for a Nottingham Forest versus Bradford City match which attracted a total of 1,000 viewers.

The collapse of DTT in Britain in 2002, with millions of pounds owed to football clubs, was a blow to UK ambition to be the first fully digital television nation by 2010. The British Government had hoped that 80 percent of the population would have switched to digital television before then and the remaining "analogue refuseniks" (as the Murdoch tabloids call them) would be pushed into digital television by an impending analogue switch-off date. This would then allow the Government to raise large sums of money in "spectrum farming," as the wasteful use of the electromagnetic spectrum would yield to its more efficient use to provide new generation telephony services.

So, who gains from the present failure of DTT? This chapter takes a detailed historical look at how digital television policy was shaped in one country – Ireland – so that we can better understand the forces at play, both local and global, in the initial stages of the development of a major new communication technology. The two chief protagonists in this case are Government and RTÉ, which took the lead role in establishing a digital policy in the mid-1990s. In effect, this attempt at policy-making is now in disarray and market forces are presently the primary drivers in the rollout of digital television. In summary, the Government rejected RTÉ's plan for DTT in 1999 and imposed its own: RTÉ was required to sell 72 percent of its transmission system and it would be excluded from the business of marketing and managing a DTT service. RTÉ's argument for a "unitary model," where both the transmission and the multiplex operations would remain in a single company that would attract private investors into partnership with the public broadcaster, was set aside, after successful lobbying from the private broadcasting sector. Now, there is little interest among investors in buying RTÉ's transmission network and only a single bidder for the multiplex operation licence who, unable to attract the investors he needed, has already withdrawn. The Government's decision in effect put DTT on the back foot and opened the way for two rival platforms, both of them controlled by multinational media conglomerates: cable and satellite.

A great deal of press discussion of digital television assumes that the larger countries in Europe will drive the agenda for all the others. This may not always be the case and it is worthwhile to examine the different regions of Europe separately to see how the global dynamic in digital television is bedding in with local political and economic interests. This chapter examines the debate about digital television that took place in Ireland between 1995 and 2000, most of it behind firmly closed doors in the Boardroom in RTÉ, the Cabinet Room in Government Buildings and the Ministry in change of broadcasting. This debate illustrates how local policy issues in a small corner of the European Union reverberate with concerns about how the challenges presented by digital technology assume the dimensions of "influence at a distance" at the heart of globalisaton theory.[51] .

THE BEGINNINGS

The first formal consideration of digital television and its implications for RTÉ took place in November 1995, in response to a management document which expanded on RTÉ's response to the Green Paper on Broadcasting, published earlier that year: "The impact of Digital Technology on the Transmission of Television Services."[52] This had been written by the then Group Head Programme Services, Eugene Murray, who was one of the earliest and most persistent advocates of a proactive approach by RTÉ in shaping the national digital television strategy, which at this stage did not exist even in embryonic form outside RTÉ. The 1995 document focused on digital terrestrial television (DTT), comparing it with cable, MMDS and the satellite technologies to determine where the thrust of a public service interest should be aimed. Each platform has a different configuration of advantages and disadvantages in respect of technical capabilities, number of channels delivered, interactive potential via a "return path", affordability, subscriber management system and crucially, ownership and control. Unlike the earlier debate about the establishment of analogue television in Ireland, which took place in the 1950s, the debate about digital television originated in and was profoundly shaped by RTÉ, as the first and main mover of new ideas regarding the future of broadcasting, without any contribution from politicians or Government departments until near its denouement. But like the debate in the 1950s, this one was driven by the belief that doing nothing about developments in television technology would lead to Ireland being colonised by British television interests because of the accessibility of Irish audiences to signals originating north of the Border or from transmitters across the Irish Sea in Wales. Interest in UK television services gave some impetus to the development of significant investment in cable in Ireland in the 1960s and 1970s and it was likely the same could happen with digital television. UTV analogue terrestrial overspill reached as far south as Dublin, Mullingar and Sligo and was of low quality, especially during difficult atmospheric conditions, but its digital signal would be perfect up to the outer limit of the overspill boundary. In withdrawing from the TV3 consortium, UTV was already signalling its interest in concentrating on an all-Ireland digital strategy.

Both the UK Government, through its White Paper, and broadcasters like the BBC, with its exploration of plans that would be published in its "Extending Choice in the Digital Age," were very actively involved in planning strategies for digital television. We decided to identify RTÉ staff who could keep abreast of developments (Eugene Murray principally, and later Peter Brannigan, then Director of Production Facilities and Engineering) and also to work towards stimulating relevant Government Departments to formulate a national plan.

The private sector was also getting interested in what was coming to be known as "new media." RTÉ had been having discussions since 1994 with ICL, for instance, about building a comprehensive web site with semi-automatic feeds from existing electronic sources, to minimise staff costs. I was involved myself in discussions with ICL with a view to building a partnership to exploit the total value of RTÉ productions (including unedited material, stills, source documents, background research etc,.) as multimedia content for electronic publishing via CD or the Internet. In the jargon of the time, this was "repurposing" archives so that new revenue could be generated from existing assets. ICL was already involved in building a multimedia data base for the vast collection held by the Victoria and Albert Museum in London and was collaborating with British Telecom in building a broadband educational network in Britain, while its major shareholder, Fujitsu, a leading advocate of interactive television in Japan, owned the largest number of multimedia titles in the world.

One year later, a great deal had been happening in the development of digital television in Britain and mainland Europe, but there had been no development of official thinking in Ireland, as was obvious from the draft memorandum on new broadcasting legislation Clear Focus, which charged the new Broadcasting Commission with the task of advising the Government on new media policy. In fact, a great deal of Ministerial energy was taken up defending the effort to launch the new Irish-language television station Teilifís na Gaeilge, against the attacks of a virulent media campaign, particularly in the O'Reilly newspaper group, despite almost universal political support for the venture.

RTÉ's first communication with the Government on digital television, its response to the Green Paper on Broadcasting published in 1995, highlighted the national interest and the danger of leaving this whole field of cultural and economic activity to international market forces alone. The government was urged to outline at an early stage its position on the introduction of digital broadcasting services and the new regulatory arrangements that would be needed. This document also highlighted the need for appropriate alliances, if RTÉ was to meet the challenge of new production and transmission opportunities. Senior staff in RTÉ throughout 1996 were visiting British broadcasters to establish contact with the principal players there. It was beginning to emerge early in 1997 that a strategic alliance with a commercial partner would be needed, to develop the digital transmission infrastructure and also to ensure that links with broadcasters in Northern Ireland should be considered, with a view to providing an all-island transmission system that would guarantee universal availability to all parts of Ireland. Major questions for RTÉ itself were beginning to arise, including the investment needed, the impact on advertising revenue of universal multichannel reception, audience fragmentation and the cost of providing new services. Major decisions would also have to be made regarding the cable company Cablelink, jointly owned by RTÉ and the (not yet privatised) telecommunications company Telecom Eireann, as it moved towards digital television. Should RTÉ sell its share or think of investing in a capital investment programme to enhance the cable infrastructure and bring it to digital capability? The BBC had decided to spend two-thirds of the 150 million pounds it received from the sale of its transmission system to NTL to fund its new digital services. Since digital television would run in parallel with analogue services as an extra cost with no immediate revenue, it was emerging as an imperative for all broadcasters to plan to induce audiences to switch from one to the other in as short a space of time as possible.

By the middle of 1997, the RTÉ planning process was firing on all cylinders. Scenarios were being developed with more confidence. The major questions were being asked and then focussed on the decision-making bodies, especially the Executive and the Authority. Both the Minister and the telecommunications Regulator were advised that a major RTÉ policy paper was in preparation, so that these other state organs could also function their attention on the relevant issues. It was an exciting environment. DTT had the potential to serve 95 percent of households within a cost-effective and short time frame. Building a transmission system would cost £35 to £45 million. Over a five-year period, £30 million would convert production facilities to digital widescreen capability and ensure the digitisation of all material in the total supply chain from production, archives and acquisition through to consumption. It was now obvious that RTÉ should seek a strategic partner to jointly own and operate a new digital transmission company, to be known from this point on as DIGICO. Given the pace of British developments, a sense or urgency was quickening. There was also the sense that the new centre-fight Fianna Fail-Progressive Democrat Government would have little sympathy for the notion of protecting a "public interest" (for instance, universal, affordable access, education and community channels, all-island audiovisual initiatives) in the ownership structure of DIGICO. In fact, we anticipated that there might be a strong argument from Government that the RTÉ transmission system should be fully privatised. There might be some hesitation, however, particularly at Fianna Fail grass-roots level, if privatisation meant that the system might pass into non-Irish hands. We were soon to see, however, towards the turn of the millennium, part of the meaning of globalisation in an Irish context was that at an ideological level, traditional notions of economic nationalism were rapidly dissolving in the media and telecommunications sector, as major foreign interests took control of Telecom Eireann, Esat Telecom, Cablelink and TV3, without protest from any significant political sector including Fianna Fail, which would traditionally have regarded itself as more the custodian of the nation than any other party.

In the development of its digital strategy, RTÉ still had some months before the June 1998 Cablelink option deadline in which to consider which digital platform it should develop. Could a mix of digital cable and MMDS deliver universal access to new television and Internet services? Would the provision of integrated telephony and television services, as in some of the new regional digital cable systems rolling out in England, such as Nottingham Diamond cable, provide the crucial user interest to drive uptake and could we realistically plan on a switch-off date of 2010, so that costly simulcasting in digital and analogue could be ended? We would need action on three fronts: a political framework in which digital television could be structured as a new industry, a business plan that might well include strategic alliances, and an on-going review of technological developments in the different technological platforms on which digital television could be launched.

It was envisaged in 1997 that RTÉ would have majority control of any new structure, which would reflect its historical and current position in providing the transmission backbone in Irish broadcasting. Requesting a once-off capital grant from the government might be sufficient to kick-start the conversion of the transmission system to digital capability, but in the balance of opinion in RTÉ at that stage, it was more realistic to expect the Government to require RTÉ to bring in a partner who would supply the necessary capital. An astute reading of the ethos of the centre-right government then in power was that RTÉ would never be given total ownership of the digital system. This would be either completely in the private sector or placed in the ownership of a public-private partnership of RTÉ along with other interests.

The first major plans for digital television was submitted to the Government by RTÉ in October 1997,[53] urging swift Government action to the light of British plans to upgrade the Northern Ireland transmission system to DTT operations by the end of 1999. It suggested Government policy should embody some key principles: universal access for all households; reception throughout Ireland of all television services originating on the island; early introduction of digital services; national regulation of digital broadcasting; maximisation of Irish content; a competitive market for delivery systems; better use of existing assets (spectrum, transmission infrastructure, reception antennae); compatible standards throughout the island of Ireland. First estimates put the cost of the DTT transmission system at £35 – 40 million, which might be as little as 1/10 the cost of a cable or MMDS system. RTÉ would need to spend a further 35 million pounds to fully digitise production operations.

This key document is very tightly framed within a discourse of "the nation." This is true of many RTÉ policy documents and indeed most internal debates in RTÉ in this period. The introduction of digital television is seen as a defining moment in the development of mass communication in the country, as the new digital delivery systems of cable, satellite, terrestrial and telecommunications networks begin to alter fundamentally the public's access to new ICTs. A coherent national strategy is advocated, so that Ireland can have a viable long-term presence in the broadcasting and multimedia industries, with a digital agenda that avoids control by multinational interests situated outside the state, with all the subsequent loss of strategic control that this implies: introduction of dependencies on foreign content and likely damage to indigenous audiovisual industries. The emphasis in this discourse is on ensuring that the new technology will carry Irish content and that the public interest will have a controlling influence on media performance.

THE DTT DECISION

After much research and consultation with broadcasters elsewhere, RTÉ was opting very firmly for DTT. There were both economic and technological reasons for this. DTT is the most economic means of delivering digital signals to everyone, since it builds on existing transmission networks and achieves penetration levels closely matching existing analogue patterns of reception. It achieves very high population coverage for a relatively small investment, so using the "legacy network" as a primary delivery system meets universal service obligations in a cost-effective way.

Satellite transmissions, on the other hand, cannot effectively serve viewers in urban apartment buildings because of zoning restrictions on dishes or lack of "line of sight" to enable receiver dishes to "see" the satellite arc on the equator from north-facing buildings or where shadows from other buildings intervene. Direct TV in the US reported that only 60 percent of TV homes could get line of sight to its satellite orbital position because of "urban clutter" and UK estimates put a theoretical upper limit on satellite access at 70 percent. The active, electronically amplified antennae for satellite leads to higher costs than passive DTT receivers, as they require maintenance periodically.

Could hybrid cable/MMDS systems achieve the goal of a universal service obligation? Cable penetration has now reached saturation penetration level of 50 percent of Irish homes and this situation is not likely to change with the introduction of digital television, since additional capital and operating costs will be needed to upgrade from analogue services before any attempt can be made to reach new subscribers where homes are not already passed by cable. In rural areas, cable is obviously an uneconomic option because of large distances between homes creating diseconomies of density. And MMDS "fill in" would require a much better network of transmitter sites at high cost to compete with the universal coverage potential provided by the terrestrial network that requires far fewer transmitters. MMDS has a further economic limitation, in that it is restricted by hilly terrain, dense foliage and high-rise buildings, as Bell Atlantic was discovering in north-eastern US. In Europe generally and particularly in the UK, the consensus was emerging in 1997 that DTT was the preferred platform for discharging the universal service obligation of public service broadcasters, because it benefited from intensive transmission re-use and did not require expensive cable upgrading.

RTÉ originally envisaged that a Broadcasting Act would be passed in 1998, which would allow for a search for a strategic partnership to be completed and DTT to be launched by September 1999. But the Broadcasting Act wasn't passed for another three years. Whence the delay? The possibility was raised in 1997 that different Irish broadcasting interests pulling in different directions would create a scenario where policy-making fails to promote an effective and timely framework for the implementation of digital television service. From a contemporary perspective, it is worth revisiting those 1997 predictions of what would happen if no government action were taken.

Firstly, Ireland would suffer a loss of sovereignty in the management of spectrum usage and the creation of media policy, because of the imminent roll-out of digital satellite and DTT services in Britain and Northern Ireland. BSkyB was ready to launch its digital satellite service and the BBC, not yet in agreement with BSkyB, planned to offer on the same Astra 2A satellite a range of current free-to-air services, new digital free-to-air services and a number of subscription services in partnership with Flextech. Both Sky and British Digital Broadcasting were free to market themselves in the Republic of Ireland, as they held all pan-television rights for both the UK and Ireland.

Divis transmitter near Belfast was about to become the first DTT station on the island of Ireland, with extensive over-spill into the Republic of Ireland. In the absence of an Irish digital television service, Irish viewers would purchase equipment to receive the British DTT and digital satellite services, accepting de facto both Electronic Programme Guide and Conditional Access standards established in Britain to facilitate British channels. Commercial pressures on British broadcasters would lead to an increase in the power of their DTT transmissions, in order to serve their target markets better, with the effect of considerably extending the over-spill into the Republic. The West and South of Ireland would be digitally disenfranchised, being out of reach of over-spill, and a "digital deflector" problem would be likely to emerge, with all the political problems that attended Government attempts to shut down illegal analogue deflector operators in the mid-1990s in order to recover spectrum for other uses. All the British broadcasters would be likely to set up subsidiary companies in Ireland to market their wares and collect subscription revenues from DTT over-spill and digital satellite, thus taking more of the media budget out of Ireland, with subsequent damage to the whole Irish film and television production sector.

Secondly, the Government's ambitious plan to exploit the benefits of the Information Society depended on its ability to accelerate the convergence of television and interactive services delivered via the Internet. New telecommunications systems, including GSM, UMTS and ADSL, were being developed so that interactive broadband services could be delivered to mobile hand-held devices and through the "local loop " to homes and offices. But none of this technology had the ability to reach 95 percent of the population in a short space of time. DTT could do this and thus extend the Internet potentially to the whole population once analogue TV became a thing of the past. Several West European countries were rapidly developing policies and regulatory framework for DTT for these very reasons, including the US, UK, Sweden, Denmark, Norway, Finland, Germany, Spain, Australia, New Zealand, Canada and Japan.

FINANCING THE VISION

The RTÉ proposal in 1997 was that a National Broadcasting Commission should be established to regulate the new system and deal with issues of pluralism and media ownership, licensing conditions for new broadcasters, ensuring competition policy and monitoring content to safeguard broadcasting standards and program diversity. Creating a competitive market in digital delivery systems would bring a number of strategic benefits to Ireland, including faster roll-out of infrastructure, a wider choice of services and (perhaps) lower consumer prices. This would also be in line with European Commission policy. Competition Policy Directorate DG 4 had already vetoed a number of digital television platform proposals that would have created national monopolies or damaged the development of competing digital infrastructures, in Germany Scandinavia and Spain. The regulator would also, of course, deal with technological issues, including the building of a common technology area with the UK. Economies of scale and scope in production of television receivers could be achieved and benefits of large-volume UK receiver price reductions could be passed through to Ireland. Roll-out in Ireland would be accelerated through early delivery of transmitters and related equipment. Interoperability with Northern Ireland would be easier, as would access to UK audiences of Irish originated services.

The early vision of digital television articulated in RTÉ's key 1997 document set out a preliminary notion of what new Irish channels could be developed: a 24-hour rolling news service, offering an alternative with an Irish perspective to BBC News, CNN, Euronews and Sky News; RTÉ Plus, allowing viewers an opportunity to catch up with programmes already broadcast; regional, local and community access; full coverage of Oireachtas debates; and an educational channel.

In the light of later public debates and acrimony over the question of why RTÉ wasn't established in the Broadcasting Act (2001) as the sole operator of the DTT system, it is interesting to note that, as early as 1997, RTÉ recognised that it was unlikely that public finances would be made available to fund what would probably become a viable commercial business and that RTÉ would not be able to finance in any realistic timeframe the entire digital supply chain directly from its current revenue sources. After all, it would also need funding to upgrade its production infrastructure and to generate new programming. So it suggested that what was becoming a dominant trend in other parts of Europe should be adopted in Ireland too – an alliance with other interests which would bring in funding and new expertise, thus sharing risk and reducing the requirement for public money. The RTÉ transmission system was already a common carrier for other television and radio services, so this model could be extended quite easily to facilitate all licensed DTT services, with the service charges determined by an independent regulator, thus reducing competition policy problems. Because of Ireland's small size, in terms of television households, GDP/capita, and the penetration of VCR, cable and satellite, models evolving in Scandinavia, especially Finland, were closely observed. YLE, the public service broadcaster in Finland, owned the network for all commercial and public radio and television transmission. In the middle of 1996, the Ministry of Communication asked YLE to establish a separate transmission company to operate at arms length from YLE, and also a separate company for DTT multiplex transmission. Ownership of this multiplex company would include YLE and the commercial companies TV 3 and Channel 4, and it would use the existing YLE network to roll out DTT. These developments at YLE were being closely studied in RTÉ.

The RTÉ plan argued that important economies of scale could be achieved in a small country by integrating subscriber management, viewer navigation systems, multiplex operations and the transmission function in a unitary operation. This single business entity would also be more likely to roll out the service more effectively than a separate set of operators at each point in the value chain. Strategic partners in this DTT company – DIGICO – might include telecommunications operators, or other transmission companies, pay-TV operators and investment institutions as equity partners. RTÉ would retain the largest shareholding in the new entity, which would market and operate six multiplexes, including the Conditional Access System needed for pay-TV services, the EPG and the subscription management system, though some of these functions could be sub-contracted to third parties, as was happening in the US and UK. DIGICO would be regulated by a National Broadcasting Commission, within the framework of Irish and EU competition law, to ensure fairness in relationships with all service providers. RTÉ could make a contribution in kind to marketing the take-up of digital television through use of its airtime on the existing analogue channels. Assuming a launch of DTT in September 1999, the Millennium celebrations would create considerable national interest in the benefits of wide-screen digital television.

RANGE OF INTERESTS

It was difficult to enthuse senior civil servants about digital television and convince senior politicians that now was the time to move, wisely but quickly, on building this part of the Information Society vision. It was as if the vision embedded in the international jargon of proposal documents and commissioned reports, was itself paralysing rather than energising. When actual decisions were needed, the apparatus of Government froze. This was partly due to the lack of expertise in Government departments in new challenges such as digital television and the increasing tendency to reach for the Yellow Pages and call the local branch of one of the international consultancy groups. But it was also due to the slow recovery in the Civil Service from the regime of the previous Government, where the emphasis had been on protecting the core values of public service broadcasting at European level and intensifying supervision of RTÉ at home via a new regulator, rather than getting fixed on the challenge posed by digital compression and convergence technologies.

The full Authority didn't have an opportunity to meet the new Minister, Síle De Valera, until the end of January 1998, seven months after her appointment. On our agenda were the crucial pressures then being felt inside RTÉ: the emergence of clear evidence of a dangerous financial trend, in which broadcasting costs were rising at a rapid rate and revenue was falling; the implications of the non-indexation of the licence-fee and problems in both setting its level in a realistic way and tackling wastage in the inefficient manner in which the fees were collected from households by An Post; the glaring inability of RTÉ to meet what Film Makers Ireland claimed was its obligation to the independent production sector under the terms of the 1993 Broadcasting Act; and the need to establish TnaG's fragile financing on a more secure and stable footing. But at the top of our agenda was digital television and the need to convince the Minister that time was not on our side in launching a DTT system and that the Government needed to get its act together in forming a policy on regulatory structures and strategic alliances. At this stage, we were also arguing for retaining RTÉ's existing shareholding in Cablelink, because of the long-term benefits, strategic and commercial, that would accrue to public broadcasting from involvement in an important complementary platform for the delivery of new digital channels and interactive multimedia services, as well as telephony and electronic commerce. But Cablelink would needed a complete overhaul before it could meet the digital challenges, including the involvement of appropriate strategic allies to bring in much needed investment and new skills to secure the company's future. RTÉ would accept some dilution of its shareholding to facilitate this, in a scenario for instance that would see Telecom Eireann withdraw completely from Cablelink, so that public broadcasting in Ireland in the future could benefit from revenues generated by digital cable. As we will see elsewhere in this book, this was not to be. Department officials were reasonably supportive of RTÉ's position but there had been no formal statement of this support at political level. There was a painful awareness in RTÉ, in fact, that most politicians had a complete lack of awareness of the support that RTÉ had given to Cablelink over several decades, in spite of the competition for RTÉ audiences that built up through Cablelink's multi-channel services in major urban areas.

At this meeting, Síle De Valera reiterated her support for public service broadcasting and in conjunction with the Minister for Public Enterprise, would prepare a policy for Government by mid-year and could envisage legislation drafted by the end of 1998. This would mean that DTT might be launched before the end of 1999. She enquired particularly about our plans for control of the transmission system and the trade union attitude to those plans. We emphasised the changed circumstances since the Green Paper discussions (where it was assumed RTÉ would retail full control of the network), which now suggested that RTÉ would need partners in order to fund developments. We were left with the impression that there was no indication of Government opposition to RTÉ's preference to remain a shareholder in Cablelink, though we were also conscious that in all major decisions affecting media policy in Ireland, the Department of Public Enterprise was now playing a major role, and the Department of Arts, Heritage, Gaeltacht and the Islands was serving as a conduit for RTÉ views. It was also obvious that the European Commission was also emerging as a major player in all discussions about media policy.

A few days after the meeting with the Minister, an important report commissioned by RTÉ from BDO Simpson Xavier was delivered.[54] It confirmed the costings put forward by RTÉ, under the stewardship of Peter Brannigan, and placed a valuation on its transmission network in the event of a possible sale of its assets. The business plan it developed assumed RTÉ would sell the existing network to a new joint venture company – DIGICO – comprised of RTÉ and other investors and then pay this company an annual fee for the analogue and digital transmission of its services while the period of simulcasting lasted. The proposed transaction structure would allow RTÉ to convert assets, which have a diminishing value, into a significant equity interest in this new entity without any conditional cash requirement. DIGICO would acquire a working network and be able to defray the start-up operating deficits of the digital operation with positive cash flow generated by the analogue distribution fees. If the assumptions of the projected financial performance were valid and if the projections were achieved, RTÉ would participate in the success of a potentially very profitable company. As the BDO report put, DIGICO would represent the marriage of the highest market share content provider in the Irish market and the largest concentration of technical expertise in DTT in Ireland, with private investment capital.

The BDO analysis supported the RTÉ argument that DTT has a competitive advantage due to a low capital cost for distribution in comparison to satellite and cable. This cost advantage would be passed through to viewers, enabling DIGICO to offer them a more competitively priced service, both in areas not currently served by existing subscription services (because not economically viable for alternative means of delivery) and in markets currently having access to subscription services. DTT would offer lower infrastructure capital costs and wider market coverage than is economically feasible for cable (though not satellite). It would offer less interactivity capacity than cable but perhaps more than satellite, assuming the wireless return path for DTT over a large customer base can be successfully deployed. (One system in development is the EU-funded Wireless Return Channel System, using Synchronous Frequency Division Multiple Access technology.)

The dominant Government interest in digital technology is the desire to realise the full value of the spectrum, replacing inefficient analogue television spectrum consumption with more efficient digital distribution. The Irish Government was slow, however, to develop this interest in the late 1990s. The dominant consumer interest is in increased choice of television channels and in reaping the rewards of the convergence of the Internet with digital television. This interest was beginning to grow in the popular press in Ireland at this time. The dominant commercial interest is driven by opportunities created by the interactivity of digital delivery in such areas as product marketing and Internet services. The dominant external pressure, apart from terrestrial over-spill from UK transmitters into some parts of Ireland, was coming from the market entry of dominant satellite distributors such as BSkyB, which can increase the geographic size of their markets with very little additional capital expenditure. Not only would a foreign "gate-keeper" have a large degree of control over what people watch, by controlling the selection of channels carried, but if the dominant platform is a foreign operation, a significant amount of economic activity will also transfer overseas.

One of the key contributions of the BDO report was in calculating a range of value for the RTÉ network and therefore the purchase price in the event of RTÉ separating its distribution function from its existing organisation, as the BBC had done, and then outsourcing its transmission to a new entity in which it would be a stakeholder. This would allow RTÉ to convert a cost centre into a profit centre, increase the residual value of RTÉ assets and achieve a higher rate of return for DIGICO than if it were to pursue digital distribution independently, with a separate digital television network in which RTÉ would have no equity interest, paying an annual fee to access its own sites. If most of the elements of the BDO business plan held up, the creation of DIGICO as a new economically viable entity would secure the development of a national platform for Irish broadcasting in the digital age, provide a new domestic alternative to foreign competition and retain some control over the future economic potential of interactive marketing in what would be called "e-commerce" a few years later.

CHALLENGING THE UNITARY MODEL

While the BDO report was in preparation, the Office of the Director of Telecommunications Regulation was also commissioning a report on the economic, spectrum management and other technical implications of DTT, from London-based consultants National Economic Research Associates and Smith System Engineering Ltd (Nera/Smith, 1998). This report raised the question of whether the small Irish market is likely to support all digital media platforms and if not, whether DTT or a digital MMDS will be used to provide universal coverage in rural areas (assuming the cable sector will be a cornerstone in future competition for telephony and interactive services in urban areas). Competition from digital satellite will exist in any future scenario, driven as it is by UK market forces, but, the report suggests, it is unlikely to carry Irish national broadcasting services. (This prediction would prove to be the most unsound of all the forecasts generated in this period, when RTÉ radio and television services began to be offered on the Sky system in 2002.) The Nera/Smith report went on to warn that delaying the launch of DTT beyond the expected date of 2000 would dampen its prospects seriously, making its financial performance deteriorate as the other transmission systems established an early lead in the battle for digital subscribers. DTT would lose around 50,000 subscribers by delaying its launch to 2002 and 100,000 subscribers by delaying until 2004, shifting its break-even point back to 2010.

The major new element introduced into the Irish digital debate at this period is the recommendation from Nera/ Smith that there should be a separation of the transmission and the multiplex operator functions for DTT. No rationale is provided for this, especially one to match the very small broadcasting market in Ireland, beyond mentioning the potential for discrimination against other broadcasters exercised by an RTÉ-controlled company for its own advantage, though the report admits this problem could be controlled a regulator. As the RTÉ (1998) response pointed out, Nera/ Smith actually seemed to confuse the separation of functions here with a very different separation of functions between transmission and broadcaster already implemented in the UK, Australia and New Zealand. But this intervention is the origin of the idea in the Irish digital debate of breaking DIGICO in two. Nera/ Smith provided the opportunity, as a UK-based (therefore perceived as a highly respected and independent) consultant, to those who would go on in 1999 and 2000 to argue – successfully – that RTÉ should be excluded from multiplex operation completely, a notion that was subsequently written into the new legislation.

The RTÉ response to Nera/Smith sent to the Regulator in April 1998, challenged the Report on a range of issues. Just two will be examined here. Could Nera/Smith be interpreted by Irish policy-makers as support for abandoning DTT entirely? The finding that DTT is likely to be less financially attractive than digital cable as DMMDS is based on assumptions arising from incomplete market and financial models which are open to question. The combined DMMDS/Cable route to universal service is at least ten times more expensive in total infrastructure costs than DTT and has a very slow route to universality compared to any option that includes DTT as part of the overall portfolio of delivery systems operating in Ireland. The number of DMMDS transmitter sites would have to be increased very considerably, which would have a negative impact on the economics of DMMDS as well as having a significant adverse environmental impact. DMMDS has several technical shortcomings, which led quickly to DMMDS market failure in the US, using the same frequency band as Ireland. At the reception end, unlike DTT, DMMDS would have only a small "legacy network" leverage, as only 6 percent of Irish homes had MMDS antennae compared to 60 percent of homes with existing terrestrial antennae. Analogue MMDS has met with only limited consumer success in Ireland and there are no specific reasons to assume that DMMDS will perform differently. Cable networks will be digitised but upgrades will be patch and timescales depend on investment capacity. Major urban areas will be digitised first, with smaller towns and suburban areas last to digitise. In contrast, DTT would commence with 95 percent population coverage and its low-cost package would enjoy considerable take-up. It would acquire current deflector customers in time and be driven forward by the television set replacement life cycle.

Secondly, assuming a decision in favour of DTT, how should the transmission function and the multiplex operation function be organised? Equitable treatment of all delivery systems in Ireland would indicate that DTT should be treated similarly to digital cable and DMMDS, where the roles of transmission provider and multiplex operator are in practice integrated. To ensure fair and non-discriminatory markets for delivery systems, DTT should be permitted to integrate all functions in the supply chain in order to maximise its commercial prospects. It should be licensed as a common carrier, as with digital satellite systems in the US and DTT in Sweden and Finland. The fragmentation of a start-up business introduces diseconomies of scale and scope, ignoring commercial necessity for the sake of a theoretically competitive model. These diseconomies impact on the timing of roll-out and the efficiency of the business by creating companies artificially contesting markets at all points along the value chain. The importation of this aspect of the UK model, we argued, is inappropriate in Ireland because of its smaller market size (about one twenty-fifth of the UK market). The distinction between multiplex operator and transmission operator is an administrative device peculiar to the large media market of the UK and the importation of this aspect of the UK model would be inappropriate for Ireland. The suitability of the uniquely British regulatory model had not been critically assessed against other options. RTÉ suggested that Ireland should seek to avoid the structural complexity inherent in the UK approach to DTT regulation advocated by Nera/Smith, based as it is on artificial segmentation of a number of functions which are quite appropriately vertically integrated in other delivery systems. Ireland should benefit instead from the approaches adopted in other countries: in the US, Spain, Sweden and Australia, the service provider and the multiplex operator functions are integrated in DTT.

In the second half of 1998, the Irish Government agreed on the heads of a new Broadcasting Bill. RTÉ would form part of a new digital company, with a 40 percent shareholding, as the Government decided to go forward on the basis of a public-private partnership. The Minister was influenced she said, by RTÉ's expertise, its infrastructure and its universal service argument in favour of DTT. RTÉ would have access to one multiplex, TG 4 (the Irish-language channel) and TV 3 (the commercial channel) would share another multiplex and the remaining four would be at the disposal of the multiplex operator.

A Project Management Group was immediately put together from several Departments (Arts, Heritage, Gaeltacht and the Islands; Public Enterprise; Trade and Employment; and Finance) as well as RTÉ. (Liam Miller, Managing Director of Organisation and Development, became the RTÉ representative on this important group and also the link with a corresponding in-house group consisting of Peter Brannigan, Paul Roche, Ray Maguire and Liam Miller himself.) This Government/RTÉ group would plan the way forward in detail, including the determination of the value of RTÉ's transmission system, RTÉ's contribution to the digital company and the process of identifying a strategic partner. The RTÉ Authority would retain its present role and responsibilities: there would be no "quango," as the Minister put it, by which we understood she meant that Michael D. Higgins Superauthority was now dead and buried.

RTÉ moved immediately to set up its Network service as a stand-alone Business Unit, to isolate all activities and assets in facilitating a shift from a cost centre to a profit centre. This was to become the nucleus of DIGICO. Already staff involved in transmission and their trade unions had begun to raise the question of employee share options in the new company, on a gifted and purchased basis. Huge organisational changes would need decisions. Would the Donnybrook tower, emblem of RTÉ since its inception, become part of the new entity or remain par of RTÉ, to be used as always as an injection point for Outside Broadcast link facilities? Where would programme contribution links fit in, as part of Network or Programmes? Should RTÉ retain a Frequency Planning capability? TnaG too would have to be treated as a separate contract, accurately costed, so that the impact of its separation from RTÉ would be minimised. The experiences of BBC and ITV, as well as the two UK transmission companies NTL and CTI, would have to be explored.

As momentum began to build, driven by very real changes in RTÉ's organisational structure as it began to prepare itself for digital television, the danger now was that the Irish public would opt in large numbers for satellite or cable delivery, unless they could be convinced to wait for the roll-out of DTT. The vision of digital convergence was finally emerging off the pages of Information Society policy documents and engineers' technical reports and actually beginning to change the structure and behaviour of the most important institution in Ireland's cultural industry. Tom Quinn, Director of Corporate Affairs, chaired a group which sifted through the applications of 13 firms responding to RTÉ's call for expressions of interest in tendering for the provision of financial, commercial, legal and technical advice in connection with the setting up of DIGICO. The winner of this contest was A.D. Little.

In January 1999, the Authority saw a draft text of the proposed Broadcasting Bill on a confidential basis and declared itself quite satisfied that most of our suggestions on how to proceed had been taken into account, not only on the central issue of DTT but also on the definition of public service broadcasting incorporatd into the Bill, the establishment of of the BCI and the future of TnaG, though the draft Bill made no mention of the future funding of TnaG. Our consensus in 1999 was that it was a very positive Bill from RTÉ's perspective. There was no hint at this stage that the Bill would take another two years to be passed and only then after a major unravelling of the carefully assembled plan for DTT had taken place.

There was now a real sense of urgency in RTÉ about being prepared for a launch of DTT. Each component of the DIGICO formation process – technical, business and legal – was managed by the Project Team led by Liam Miller and co-ordinated by Ray Maguire. Plans were reworked for filling the new digital capacity with programming and interactive content, including a possible Department of Education involvement in a new digital learning channel. The development of digital television on competing platforms in the Irish market was continually monitored, as were developments in other European countries that had committed to the early roll-out of DTT. NTL's investment in Cablelink at that time indicated a strong belief in the commercial viability of digital cable. Developments in Digital Audio Broadcasting (DAB) was also being closely monitored by a group headed by Helen Shaw, Director of Radio, especially as the radio industry generally remained cool about the long-term commercial viability of the transfer from analogue to digital. Despite the BBC's strong championing of DAB and the launch of Digital One in the UK as as joint venture between Classic FM and NTL, there were still substantial risks in investing in the necessary substantial capital needed as long as the cost of receiver sets remained out of reach of most radio listeners. If this obstacle could be overcome, DAB could yet emerge as a technology that brings not only superior sound but also a range of new services incorporating image, text and data in an audio stream that converges with the Internet. But unlike digital television, the market had responded very slowly to the technological possibilities since 1996. Large European countries like the UK, Germany and Sweden had made DAB available for most of their listeners but there were still very few digital receivers on the market. This was a classic new technology chicken-and-egg scenario, where manufacturers wait for 100 percent broadcast coverage before putting DAB receivers into new cars as standard and pushing the roll-out of receivers in retail outlets.

By Summer 1999, senior Civil Servants were confident that the Broadcasting Bill would be passed before Christmas. RTÉ was still lobbying for a change in the text that would give it (instead of DIGICO) full technical control of its multiplex and the allocation of bandwidth among its range of television channels, as was the practice in Britain, because the bandwidth needs of different television programmes could change several times throughout the broadcasting day. (Typically, a televised football game with multiple cameras and wide range of movement across the screen, would need much more bandwidth than a studio discussion involving few cameras covering a narrow field of vision and fixed speaker positions.) RTÉ's adviser A.D. Little predicted digital penetration would reach 33 percent by 2015, with a positive cash flow position by 2002, assuming an investment of £80 million. But finalising a sales structure was complicated by a number of factors, including the size of RTÉ's shareholding in DIGICO, the need to avoid the question of "state aid" and the Government's need to maximise sale proceeds. The core RTÉ concern was that it should receive a reasonable market price for the business and it would have to be the final arbiter of this decision. By autumn 1999, there were already signs that the process was slowing, as was the passage of the Broadcasting Bill through the Irish Parliament. Substantial differences of approach to the sale process and to the valuation of RTÉ network assets were now emerging between the Government's advisers and those of RTÉ. A major difficulty had arisen in identifying exactly where the line should be drawn between the value of the network and the overall value of DIGICO, which would have two broad areas of activity – the transmission system and the content provision or retail system, each with a quite separate profile.

AIB, the Government's advisers, tended to see the network in terms of depreciated value (Net Book Value) of the physical assets, with very little value attributed to the earning potential inherent in the network as a distribution system. They therefore wanted to place a modest value on the network and seek agreement that any value above this which might be gained in the actual sale of the network should be regarded as a "digital premium," that is, attributable entirely to the licence to operate the digital multiplexes and therefore to accrue to the Exchequer. But here, some ambiguity emerged over whether AIB had instructions from the Government to seek a digital premium for the Exchequer. AIB insisted it had, but the original Information Note prepared by the inter-Departmental Project Management Group did not identify any such requirement.

The key issue for RTÉ was its responsibility to ensure that it would get the best possible price in the sale of its assets, in this case the transfer of its transmission network as a going concern. The issue of state aid in European competition law also loomed large in its deliberations. To sell the network at less than its full market value could constitute state aid to DIGICO in the minds of cable and satellite operators, its would-be competitors. RTÉ's legal advice was that securing full market value for the network would not constitute state aid, even where the purchaser might be the owner of the multiplex licences and where RTÉ would retain a shareholding in the new company. There was also a significant issue of public and political perception arising from the successful sale of Cablelink, the cable company partly owned by RTÉ and sold to NTL at full market value, and this had an important influence on how the Government side was approaching the digital challenge. The task of the RTÉ team now focussed on finding and agreeing a valuation for the network which would go beyond AIB thinking, recognising that some value of potential future business (new media, data, interactivity, Internet services etc.) as well as current business must be attributed to the network value, without claiming that the total value of the entire DIGICO operation had to be ascribed to it. The recent sale of the terrestrial transmission facilities in Australia suggested that a factor of one and a half times the replacement value of the network was a market-tested process.

The draft legislation did not specify the size of the RTÉ shareholding in DIGICO but the Government decision was that RTÉ would have up to a 40 percent share. The value of the network would then be the basis on which RTÉ's equity participation in DIGICO would be decided. If the price paid for the network exceeded 40 percent of the total value of the company, then RTÉ would receive a 40 percent equity participation and would expect to get the balance returned to it. This might, however, be contested by the Department of Finance, which could overcome any suggestion that the Government was challenging the property rights of the RTÉ Authority through a mechanism in the Finance Act which would in effect impose a levy on RTÉ, for instance by altering the basis on which the licence fees are paid over to RTÉ after collection by An Post. But if the value of the network were set at a level less than the value of 40 percent of the company, then the Government's decision implied that RTÉ would not be able to use additional resources to secure the 40 percent and the Authority would end up with a lesser shareholding.

Rather than paying a "digital premium" to the Government, RTÉ argued that any cash accruing to itself from the sale of its network should be used exclusively for introducing new digital services, supporting them in their introductory years until their viewership could sustain a claim for public funding for them. This would also ensure there was no "digital licence fee" (a notion then being considered by the BBC as a means to fund the roll-out of digital television in the UK), which would in any case yield very little return in the early years and perhaps act as a disincentive in persuading viewers to switch from analogue to digital receivers.

SQUEEZING RTÉ OUT

There was still another way to make a play in the preparation for digital television, a radically different approach which would involve pressuring RTÉ to make a complete U-turn in its digital strategy. At the margins of the negotiations involving senior Civil Servants from several Departments, RTÉ executives, AIB Capital Markets and A.D. Little (and in the background Government Ministers and other politicians contributing to the debate on the Broadcasting Bill as is went into Second Stage), there arose unfocused but persistent talk about RTÉ's assumed automatic entitlement to a shareholding in DIGICO and concern about the unfair advantage this conferred, relative to any other broadcaster in Ireland. In the eyes of some participants, the involvement of the publicly funded national broadcaster in the state's only terrestrial distribution system was inappropriate. For them, it was even more inappropriate that RTÉ should seek to get the full market value of the network as well as an automatic legislative right to a shareholding, even if this was being paid for. The accusation could be made that RTÉ was in a favoured position vis-à-vis other broadcasters. This was becoming a source of real political difficulty and an inhibition to realising the full value of the network, though there was no direct communication from politicians on this.

We had a full debate on the Authority in the autumn of 1999 on the possible merits of seeking, or not seeking, a shareholding in DIGICO, though leaving the field to somebody else would reverse everything we had argued for since the Green Paper. There were significant pros and cons in having, and not having, a shareholding and we were acutely aware of the significance of our decision and how future generations might judge our wisdom, or foolishness, through perfect 20/20 hindsight. If RTÉ had no shareholding in DIGICO, it could deal with the company at arms' length, maximise the value of the network and use the proceeds to fund new digital services, thus avoiding the need to seek additional public funding in the early years. Securing maximum value would not constitute state aid. Being a shareholder also carried the burden of being liable for substantial cash calls if further capital injections were needed to fund further development of DIGICO. (Previous unwillingness to invest new cash in Cablelink when both RTÉ and Telecom Eireann were shareholders, had led to the running down of the cable network and the eventual Government decision to privatise it.) The need for cash calls might require RTÉ to dilute, or in time, even sell its shareholding. And in any case, RTÉ's minority position on the Board would greatly reduce its influence on strategic decisions. Moving away from a policy which RTÉ had itself proposed to the Government would be embarrassing and difficult to explain to staff, but a *volte face* could be managed if it was in the best interests of RTÉ and secured public interest goals in the service provider of new media.

Much concern centred on the long-term performance of DIGICO, which even the most assiduous economic modelling could not assure. If digital television was not going to be an outstanding success in Ireland – and who could predict how this technology would develop in an environment where there was at present little public demand – maybe it would be best for RTÉ to realise the economic value of its transmission system now and concentrate on being a production and broadcasting company, leaving the uncertainties of digital platform management in a small economy to others. If, on the other hand, DTT was going to fulfil even some of the visionary promises made for it, and if some form of national public service involvement was essential to ensure that Irish viewers in future would be able to find Irish programmes to watch, then RTÉ should fight for its shareholding. So the question was short-term gain or long-term investment, in an untried technology that had huge potential but not yet any clear model of successful operation in any part of the world. Would it matter, for instance, if Rupert Murdoch turned DIGICO into a private monopoly, one small part of a vast global digital media conglomerate? Would the Irish Regulator, even a combination of the proposed BCI and the ODTR, be able to protect the public interest in such a scenario?

My own instinct was to fight for a substantial involvement in DIGICO as a long-term investment. All the indications at the end of 1999 were that digital television would become a significant platform for the mass roll-out of the Internet and e-commerce. RTÉ pressed on with elaborating its plans for new digital channels (RTÉ, 1999). Stock market confidence in new technologies was peaking just then and the number of new entrepreneurs entering the "dotcom" business was accelerating. There were no signs yet that the overproduction of PCs and mobile phones would send this whole sector into decline within the year. In this mood of optimistic expansionism in the new media sector, it would be foolishly short-sighted to strip RTÉ of its network, a major national asset in public ownership, and allow only private interests, whether these would be domestic or global, to reap the benefits of new communication and information services to emerge at the point of convergence between digital television and the Internet.

Arguments about whether future users would "lean forward" to access the Internet on their PCs, or "lean back" to enjoy convergence in traditional, relaxed television-viewing mode, were being resolved in the empirical conclusion that PC penetration of the population had probably peaked but both modes of screen interaction would survive. It is still probably a fair assessment of future access to the Internet to conclude that a majority of the population will use the digital television set (or in the short term the analogue set augmented with a set-top-box), albeit within "walled gardens" controlled by platform managers or broadcasters, where minimal interactivity will be needed for low-cost, easy-to-use access to a wide range of services. A sizeable minority of the population will continue to use the PC for information seeking that requires a greater amount of interactivity.

It was clear to us that DIGICO would own and control an essential gateway to Irish homes for a range of services beyond traditional radio and television. These would be based on a converged television-Internet base and include electronic commerce and other commercial services, including on-line banking and betting. Banks were already investing by then in digital platforms with enthusiasm, though it was impossible to say with certainty when e-commerce would become a dominant force in the digital Irish economy and therefore when DIGICO might become a major toll-gate n the so-called Information Highway. By 1999, about 70 percent of Federal Express parcel orders originated on-line and the direct delivery of digital content to PCs (software, travel and financial services, music, education and training, multimedia etc,.) was also growing steadily, as distribution costs were lowered substantially. It was clear that DIGICO would probably accelerate the up-take of e-commerce, especially when its integrated return wireless path could be perfected.

The strategic issue was who controls the gateways to the digital economy, those points of contact between households and the burgeoning world of digital information, entertainment and communication services? Digital cable in large cities clearly had a bright future and RTÉ would have retained its interest in Cablelink if it could, so that it could benefit from new revenue streams, just as the film industry developed interests where it could in multiplex cinemas and video rental chains. Sweden, with its strong tradition of supporting the public interest in broadcasting, was drawing up plans to allow both public and private television, SVT and TV 4, to become shareholders with the state-owned broadcasting network Terracom in the DTT company Senda, so that there would be some sharing of future profits and market power, as well as some allowance for a substantial public service voice to be heard in decisions about the future development of a major multi-service platform in the context of a Digital Society vision. It was also possible that the present very substantial inefficiencies in collecting the licence fee could be overcome in the digital regime by incorporating the fee in the annual rental of a "smart card" that would be necessary to gain access to digital television where all content is encrypted.

Meanwhile, AIB was advising Government that RTÉ should have no share in DIGICO, that the disaggregation of what had been a vertically integrated system since the foundation of RTÉ in 1961 (programme production, acquisition, scheduling and delivery into homes) was now appropriate. This would side step "state aid" issues, strengthen the rationale for future licence fee increases, avoid the problem of exposing RTÉ to future cash calls for investment in DIGICO and maximise the value to RTÉ of its network. If RTÉ insisted on keeping a shareholding in DIGICO, the sale price of the network would be lower, as buyer interest would weaken in a situation where full ownership of the digital platform was not available. If RTÉ could abandon its hope of sharing in future digital revenue streams, Government advisers argued, it would realise a higher asset value now for its network. But RTÉ knew that accepting this argument about reducing the network asset value would mean withdrawing from having any strategic control over the future direction of digital television and being able to ensure that public service goals, as distinct from purely market goals, would play a role in shaping the Information Society. Major decisions would be made in the future by the DTT service provider, including how access to television programmes and channels would be favoured or discriminated against in the design of the EPG and other navigation systems, how consumer choice in e-commerce could be constrained and directed towards particular services, who would be able to "push" targeted programme material, advertising and direct purchase opportunities at viewers, how cross-promotion of services would be regulated and how return paths would be controlled.

By this time, an RTÉ Working Group led by Gerry Reynolds, Head of Broadcasting in Cork, had delivered a very impressive, well-researched plan for new digital services. These included a 24 hour information channel "Ireland Today," a youth channel "Zap TV," music focussed, strongly interactive and offering accelerated learning at second level, and a broadly based education and learning channel "Eolas," providing both formal and lifelong educational services with strong interactivity. The driving motivation here was the recognition that digital television will fragment audiences still further and therefore RTÉ must ensure that its services are available even more than at present in a fragmented television world, to increase the chance that viewers are watching an RTÉ channel. This is crucial if RTÉ is to maintain public support for the idea of adequate licence fee funding, on which the whole notion of public broadcasting depends. RTÉ would also need to avail of opportunities to create revenue-generating new services in e-commerce. "Enhanced text" services providing add-on information to currently running programmes could readily link to RTÉ's on-line News web site and create two-way television programmes that incorporate audience interaction. The huge resource embodied in the Programme Library, if properly digitise an managed, would be critical in differentiating RTÉ's digital offerings from those of domestic and international competitors and should form the cornerstone of a successful digital strategy. These services would form the backbone of RTÉ's multiplex on the DTT system but would also be offered on cable and MMDS platforms to meet its universal service obligation. "Ireland Today" and "Eolas" might be offered for carriage on international platforms on a subscription or pay-per-view basis.

We continued to be troubled by one of the many major unknowns in modelling how digital television would roll-out in Ireland. If RTÉ retained a significant shareholding in DIGICO, how significant would be the cash calls made on shareholders in the early years to secure the level of capital necessary for the development of the company and the extension of its services to the entire population? These could impose severe financial strain on RTÉ at a time when digital take-up could still be weak and they could even result in diluting RTÉ's shareholding. A related, but more immediate concern was whether the shareholding could become a barrier to securing the maximum market value of the network assets. The Authority had a responsibility to make sure that the best value is received for assets it would transfer to the new company. Transferring the network for less than an appropriate value could be considered a form of state aid to DIGICO, disadvantaging cable companies and other platform operators and therefore infringing European law. Legal advice suggested that giving a shareholding to RTÉ, for which it would pay, could not in itself be deemed to be state aid, but if any element of the price could be deemed to be the so-called "digital premium," this could be regarded as state aid to RTÉ. Several voices had already been raised as the draft Broadcasting Bill was making its way through Second Stage debate in the Dail, particularly at hearings organised by the Committee on Heritage and the Irish Language, arguing that it was inappropriate that RTÉ should hold any level of shares in DIGICO. The RTÉ Executive was leaning towards a recommendation that the Authority's best interest lay in being detached from DIGICO, being free to dispose of the network and secure the highest possible value for that transaction without being inhibited by the requirement to obtain a shareholding. This would eliminate the competition question and defuse some of the political opposition to a shareholding. The Executive agreed in addition that RTÉ, as a minority shareholder, would have little leverage on the Board of DIGICO if serious differences arose, for instance on the most appropriate range of services to be carried, and that public policy interests could best be secured in drafting the licence to be granted to DIGICO. RTÉ staff transferring to DIGICO might not like this new scenario, feeling that their interests were now more vulnerable, and the staff in general would probably be reluctant to see RTÉ lose an expected shareholding. Any change in policy at this stage would also have to be conveyed to the Minister quickly, so that she could reflect the new circumstances in Amendments to her Bill as it entered Committee Stage in the New Year.

Behind all this rethinking of our digital policy in RTÉ was the protracted disagreement, now running into six months, on the value of the network. The Government's advisers proposed a value of £34 million, where RTÉ's advisers calculated a "base case of valuation" of £66 million, although RTÉ was slow to communicate this to the Government since there was still the possibility of a decision to let the market decide the value of the network. In either case, the process could not go forward until this large difference could be reconciled. The Government's view was that where RTÉ had a shareholding, there appeared to be no possibility of it getting more than the Government-predetermined value of the network, because of state aid complications. Where there was an agreed market value, there arose the possibility of the Exchequer receiving some or all the excess over the Government's figure. RTÉ still had the reserve power, granted to it in the Broadcasting Bill, of deciding which assets it would transfer to the new company and therefore in effect of refusing to sell.

FINAL DECISIONS

The consensus in RTÉ at the end of 1999 was to insist on its shareholding in DIGICO, in the belief that even if it could be certain that no public policy objectives would be secured thereby, RTÉ should be able to benefit financially in the long term by being part of the revenue-generating platform. If the prospect of long-term commercial potential looked uncertain in any time in the future, it could withdraw from the company. It wanted to obtain a high value from the sale of the network and it wanted to be involved in DIGICO to benefit from long-term revenue streams. By the end of the year, it signalled very clearly to the Government that it was opposed to withdrawing from the shareholding. This set it on a collision course with the Government.

It was a busy Christmas for Director-General Bob Collins, as a series of letters was exchanged with the Department almost on a daily basis. Each letter from RTÉ set out clearly and firmly our decisions, and prompted rapid responses from the Minister's

Director-General Tadhgh O hÉalaithe. Nothing was agreed in these letters beyond the admission that the roll-out of digital television was being seriously delayed by these protracted negotiations. For the first time, a revised a launch date of "early 2001" was mentioned. Bob Collins reiterated that the Authority wanted to achieve full market value for the network by exposing the transaction to the determination of the marketplace. As a statutory corporation, RTÉ is obliged by the Broadcasting Authority Acts and by law applicable to statutory corporations to obtain full market value if it proposes to dispose of its assets. Legal advice had already been sought for the Government by the Project Management Group for a situation where the RTÉ Authority might conclude that the valuation of its assets did not represent its valid interest. "Best practice" in the disposal of property by public authorities, as laid out in a European Commission communication, was an unqualified bidding procedure, which Government Departments themselves normally adopt in the sale of Government property under the terms of its own Public Procurement Guidelines. It would be particularly unconscionable for the Authority to dispose of the network where its own advisors had identified a significantly higher range of values than the Government's advisors. The sale of the network should be no different than the sale of Cablelink, where both shareholders, with the agreement of the Government, secured the full market value of their assets.

The Department's response via Tadhgh O hÉalaithe a few days before Christmas revealed a little of how Government decisions tend to be made in these times, by appointing an outside group to advise and then accepting this advice as the foundation for a decision. The decision is defended on the basis of the integrity of the tendering process and the assumed neutrality of the advice, rather than on the wisdom or otherwise of what is delivered by the consultant. The Department emphasised that "the Government Advisers were selected after an onerous competitive tender process as the most suitable consortium to advise and manage the sale process to a conclusion. In these circumstances, to set aside the advice of the Government Advisers without compelling and transparent reasons ... would jeopardise the integrity of the entire process." Plenty of compelling evidence reasons to question AIB Capital Market's advice were provided by RTÉ but the Secretary General still failed to find any common ground on why AIB was raising questions about a "digital premium" and even the very notion of RTÉ having any shareholding at all in DIGICO, saying they failed to see a rationale for this, even though a shareholding was an essential part of its client's plan announced five months previously and incorporated into the drafts of the Broadcasting Bill. One could only wonder what the senior politicians and civil servants who made the first major decisions about RTÉ in 1960 would make of this form of government-by-consultant – Sean Lemass, Eamonn De Valera or Leon O Broin. Of course, it was difficult to query in public why the Government should put so much trust in the banking sector as it in turn drew on discourses and assumptions located in that most globalised part of Irish life – the heart of corporate Ireland. But public trust in the banking sector was weakened at this stage by various scandals revealed on television and other media. Indeed, a question arose in Dail debates about the role of AIB Capital Markets in advising the Government on the sale of RTÉ's transmission system, while it was also advising a possible customer in that sale, the US company Crown Castle, which had already purchased the BBC's transmission network. When I raised the possibility of a conflict of interest in conversation with a senior civil servant, he spluttered in exaggerated horror at the mere suggestion that advice the Government bought and paid for might not always be one hundred per cent neutral, that an advisor might have an interest in keeping down the value of an asset so that another client could benefit. Given all the recent exploration of white-collar crime in Tribunals of Enquiry in Dublin, it was a reaction that was either too naive or too knowing.

By the end of January 2000, it seemed that all the Government Departments involved in the Project Management Group had accepted RTÉ's view about the valuation of the network and the expectation was that RTÉ would sell the network and retain the proceeds. This was good news. But it was balanced by an ominous development. It now seemed likely that the Minister would advise Government that there was no longer any public policy need for RTÉ to have a shareholding in DIGICO, since universal coverage could be guaranteed in the licences issued by the Regulator. A strong lobby organised around TV 3 was arguing against RTÉ having any shareholding. Drawing on the very successful lobbying experience of its parent company, CanWest in Canada, TV 3 had already lodged a complaint with the European Commission soon after its launch in 1998, alleging that unwarranted state aid is given to RTÉ through the licence fee and also through "gratuitous" access to the national transmission system. Now it reorganised the loose federation of independent radio stations, formerly known as AIRS, into a new body, the Independent Broadcasters of Ireland (IBI), and convinced them that they too would in time have to work through DIGICO dominated by RTÉ, despite assurances from RTÉ that this debate was not about radio or DAB. IBI hired a lobbying firm and a competition lawyer and began a political campaign against an RTÉ shareholding that involved local radio stations around the country putting pressure on politicians in their local area. An indicator of how seriously this campaign was being taken in Leinster House came when 50 politicians turned up at the Shelbourne Hotel at the height of the campaign to celebrate the name change from AIRS to IBI. RTÉ simply couldn't match the power and reach of this countrywide public relations machine and its influence over politicians.

Within a month, the Government's digital policy took a new turn. Síle De Valera decided that the transmission system would now be separated from the multiplex management function, an idea that originated some years previously in the Nera/Smith report (1998) but had been rejected because no convincing business rationale was offered for such a separation in a very small television economy such as Ireland's. Furthermore, RTÉ would sell its transmission network on the open market and retain the proceeds for digital developments. But it would have no shareholding in either new company. This was a devastating blow to RTÉ's plans: its principal interest in DIGICO was a commercial one, to secure an income stream in future years for investment in programme production. Its approach to developing strategic alliances was in line with strategies in other state-sponsored companies. Not only would this change of policy cut RTÉ out of any involvement in digital distribution and delay an already seriously late Bill from becoming law, but seeking private investment for separate companies might well deprive the whole digital venture of the necessary commercial drive.

Early in March, an RTÉ delegation consisting of myself, Chairman-designate Paddy Wright, Director-General Bob Collins and Managing Director Liam Miller met for breakfast in Mespil Road prior to meeting the Minister in her office. We were all conscious that this was probably the single most important Ministerial meeting in the term of office of this particular Authority, due to expire in three months. It was important to me to have the newly appointed Chairman-designate at this meeting, so that RTÉ could be seen to be speaking with one voice both in this and in the next Authority, especially since I had been told back in January that the Minister's adviser Michael Ronayne had asked Paddy Wright to go to see the Chairman of the Project Management Group "because RTÉ is fucking up DIGICO."

As we focused on the issues over breakfast, we noted the front-page headline in the *Irish Times* (3 March 2000) "Cabinet Opposition to de Valera's Plan for RTÉ." The story by Kevin Rafter centred on opposition among several Ministers, including Taoiseach Bertie Ahern, to De Valera's plan to sell off RTÉ's network on the private market. Senior Government sources indicated her proposal "would not fly." Some Ministers were reported to be annoyed at the Minister's "solo run," since the "new policy" came into the public domain (leaked to the *Irish Independent*) before Ministers were circulated with a new recommendation. Michael D. Higgins, the former Minister for Broadcasting, had described the proposal for privatisation as "outrageous," making the national broadcaster "a tenant on sufferance" in a system which it had built. Was this all an indication of major mismanagement of the DIGICO project by the Minister and her senior civil servants and advisors, or mischief-making from another Department (tensions with Public Enterprise were well-rumoured), or even an outcome of lobbying by third parties?

On the way in to the Minister, we met Colm Connolly, RTÉ Media Correspondent, and his cameraman, silently shooting our entry, waiting for an interview for the evening News. Certainly our meeting would be news for the Newsroom, but does the rest of the country care a whit? We were ushered into the Minister's office at 9 a.m. sharp and left admiring the large Martin Gale picture that adorns one wall of the meeting room. It is a very still, formalised landscape without movement, in the style of the American painter Andrew Wyeth, without strong colour, like a dreamscape, rigid, isolated human figures staring at a lone deer in the distance. It is perhaps a fitting emotional correlative of our feeling of extreme alienation now from the Department's plans, the worst I have felt in five years as Chairman. No one comes near us for half an hour. We imagine the *Irish Times* has just landed face up on the Minister's desk and its significance is being analysed by a handful of advisers in a room somewhere nearby. The waiting seems interminable. Will we ever see DTT launched? All of 1999, at least, wasted in squabbles on the Project Management Group. Whose advice to take? How to value the network? Who's behind Síle De Valera's change of mind? Parallel with all this drama, another crisis back in Montrose that morning over the leadership of the Television Programmes Division, already shaken by the departure of Helen O'Rahily back to the BBC. Lawyers called in this week, tense, meticulous negotiations with Joe

Mulholland, old tensions now coming to a head, the canteen abuzz with rumours. Decisions to be made: if Cathal Goan moves to the Television Division from Connemara, what's the likely impact on TG4, where he's had an enormous impact? The Sunday newspapers already lining up their stories: will Mulholland's departure divide staff? Old loyalties, old enmities? What have the producers to say? Inevitably, the dominant news frame around all this will be "RTÉ in crisis. Privatisation to succeed?" I fear the self-fulfilling prophecy of all this repetition of a single news frame: if we say it often enough, we can bring about a crisis. It happened already in Portugal, where political and public support for RTP collapsed.

Finally, after half an hour, the door opens and the Minster joins us, along with adviser Brigid McManus, senior civil servants Michael Grant and Brian Millane, and newly appointed Secretary General Phil Furlong. The Minister makes an opening statement from notes, probably written in the last few minutes huddled over the *Irish Times* headline. She is emotional, exhausted, but controls her anger. No eye contact, glancing at notes. She is annoyed, very annoyed, about RTÉ spreading rumours and inaccuracies about her handling of DIGICO. She is especially upset about comments made by RTÉ director of Public Affairs, Kevin Healy. We defend the right of RTÉ to defend itself in public and explain its position. She asks for confidentiality now, at this delicate stage in our negotiations, and we agree. Colm Connolly will have to wait. We begin. The Minister sits at the top of the table and says very little. We probe to find the core of the problem as the officials see it. Why does the plan articulated by the Government twenty months previously, in July 1998, now seem to be falling apart and why do we get to know about it only in the newspapers? The answer is amazingly simple: they are afraid of "trouble" from "the Commission" if the original plan goes ahead. There will be complaints (no names are mentioned) and they "already know" from informal comments made by officials in Brussels that the original plan won't work.

I don't say it out loud but I am amazed there is so little resolve among these Civil Servants in shaping European broadcasting politics, in following what is right for the public interest, in going beyond a service attitude of kowtowing to a politics that hasn't yet by any means solidified among Brussels administrators who are still coming to terms with the national protections for public service broadcasting built into the Protocol to the Amsterdam Treaty that was so resented by the Commission staff. Are we to forget so quickly that it was these same Civil Servants and other colleagues, led from the front by Michael D. Higgins, who a few years before, had worked doggedly against sleep in the wee hours of the morning, as the last bits of Amsterdam Treaty were being finalised, to get approval for the precise language of the Protocol, which gave the Irish Government (and all the others) the power to decide themselves how they wanted to define and protect public service broadcasting? There was now a breakdown in political leadership, and in the vacuum, officials lost their nerve, put all their energies into anticipating "trouble from Brussels," avoiding a fuss, seeking to please other forces with far less interest in the welfare of public service broadcasting. The strong, confident discursive frame imposed on his staff by Michael D. Higgins is missing now, rooted in a personal passion to defend a public interest in a national space.

From my side of the table, I deal with the public interest first, asserting my scepticism about trusting future regulators to protect public service values in broadcasting when the going gets rough and private broadcasters complain that they need more space. Witness the IRTC's inability to require TV3 to invest in Irish programming as promised, or its failure to prevent the new generation of radio stations from colonising the airwaves with an extremely narrow range of music that does nothing for the public need for musical diversity. Appeals to Brussels will trigger competition law, not concern for the public interest.

They listen to me in silence and say nothing.

We table our plan. Our preferred option is the Government's DIGICO model of 1998, based on the conviction that the future success of DTT in Ireland can best be assured if the operator of the transmission network is also charged with the DTT rollout obligation. Given the small scale of the Irish market, it is unlikely that a stand-alone multiplex operation will be sufficiently attractive to an investor to generate the expenditure necessary for viability, given the slow return on investment that can be expected in digital television uptake. But if the Government in its wisdom decides the best approach is to have a twin structure, that is, separate transmission and multiplex companies, it is then highly desirable that there be a linkage between them, to ensure the early arrival of investment in the multiplex operation. If the multiplex operator's licence is offered first, the criteria used to shortlist applicants could include the requirement of an interest in also bidding for the network. If the Government opts for the twin structure, two separate companies, then RTÉ should retain 40 percent of the transmission company. The multiplex company would be 1000 percent owned by strategic investors and the participation of RTÉ in the transmission company would not in any sense preclude the multiplex and 60 percent of the network being in the same hands. RTÉ's participation in the transmission company would not give it any role of influence in the multiplex company. The digital network will expand into the provision of new services, such as "third generation" UMTS telephony and what some American commentators call PANS (Pretty amazing New Stuff), to ensure a continuing stream of income to RTÉ for investment in home production.

Again and again, we put the argument for a 40 percent RTÉ share, and each time, there was a feeble attempt from the other side of the table to pick it apart, in this small meeting room dominated by the big Martin Gale painting of the frozen deer-gazers. We have to struggle continually to reframe our discussion away from the Department's basic question: "Why should RTÉ retain a 40 percent (or indeed any) share in DIGICO?" towards what we in RTÉ regard as the more fundamental question: "Why should RTÉ have to sell more than 60 percent of this important asset, built up carefully with judicious investments over the years, which allows RTÉ to be just as vertically integrated as all the other platform operators (satellite and cable), who will be involved in both programming and distribution?"

I can't help making comparisons between these public servants and their Minister, with their lack of conviction and vision and their immersion in this volatile, enfeebled political process that has become broadcasting policy-making at the end of the twentieth century, with the enduring vision and negotiating skills of Leon O'Broin, another Civil Servant, who persuaded Sean Lemass and Eamon de Valera in the 1950s to opt for a public service system. Without a broad, historical, global view, the women and men in this room are lost, at the mercy of AIB advice and in unnecessary fear of Eurocrats in Brussels. I also feel the absence in these people of theory, that is, of an explanatory framework within which to understand the global ideological forces at work on all of us, arguing through the pervasiveness of a rejuvenated discourse, that privatisation is always good, that public ownership must be treated with suspicion, that breaking down regulatory oversight of the media into something called "soft regulation" will improve media content.

It's over. The Minister must leave to answer a telephone call from the Taoiseach. "But it's not about this," she adds. We laugh, uneasily. We reiterate our resolve not to abandon our involvement in the network. We stress the urgency of a DTT roll-out. We agree to meet again within a week. (This didn't happen.) As we leave, one of the Civil Servants mutters in my ear: "Who's meddling in this?" To tease, I say it might be a third party interested in getting a prime asset at a basement bargain price. He shrugs. The RTÉ News crew is waiting outside. Someone jokes that there's a side entrance if we want. I faced Colm Connolly's camera and mindful of the promise of confidentiality, uttered inanities into the microphone for five minutes, which went on the Evening News without adding one whit to public understanding of how digital media will be developed in Ireland.

The public position at this point was that the Minister was suggesting that RTÉ be excluded from retaining an interest in its own transmission network when it was sold through public auction. RTÉ's shareholding would be reduced from the proposed 40 percent to zero. Síle De Valera noted in a speech that current legislation regarded transmission as an essential element in the broadcaster's operation – implying that any modernisation of legislation would have to eliminate this anachronism. The familiar discourse of market liberalisation originating in right-wing parts of the US and the UK, expressing itself through this particular syllogism, was that public ownership of an asset like this was a foolish throwback to a more primitive way of managing public affairs, one that would have to be put right by modernisation, typically in the form of selling such assets to private companies. Dail debates continued to refer to other actors in this complex drama: TV3 and private radio broadcasters, unhappy with the prospect of RTÉ sitting on the board of DIGICO; one or more prospective bidder who may have balked at having to establish a strategic partnership with RTÉ, preferring a total buy-out of the transmission network; and the possibility that one of the clients of the Government's chief adviser had an interest in bidding for the network. In all these debates, much of the blame for the delay in launching DTT was directed back at RTÉ, where, among other things, it was said there was no unified position between the RTÉ Authority, the Trade Union Group and Network employees, whose jobs would be affected by any change.

The employees' concerns about leaving state company employment for the private sector were new factors in the complex mix of interests and Phil Flynn was appointed by the Government as facilitator to "clarify the issues" here. The former Sinn Fein Vice-President, ICC Chairman and Rights Commissioner had the reputation in Government circles as a good "Mr. Fixit." At his initial engagement with Department and RTÉ officials, however, he found the situation, and his own assignment, "thoroughly confusing." And so it was. Network staff, some unionised and some not, were arguing towards an Employee Share Option Plan (ESOP) and differed from the main Trade Union Group in supporting a lower valuation of the network assets rather than RTÉ's higher value. The size of the ESOP would also affect the ultimate size of the shareholding allotted to RTÉ, since the ESOP would be contained within RTÉ's share. Confusion about RTÉ's share continued for some time. Department officials insisted that the only way to pursue the original DIGICO proposal was as advised by AIB, but they were aware that this would not be acceptable to the Authority, which insisted on a 40 percent share. They also expressed confidence in finding interested parties to invest in the separate multiplex operation and would impose conditions that would guarantee the projects' viability and early roll-out.

The final stages of debate on the Broadcasting Bill did little to unravel the rationale behind the Government's position in abandoning its original DIGICO plan. It was conceded that there were strong arguments supporting RTÉ's insistence on exposing its transmission business to the marketplace in order to maximise its value, but it was also asserted repeatedly that this was impossible to achieve without changes to the original plan. If the wishes of the RTÉ Authority were to be satisfied (that is, only its wishes regarding getting full market value for its network, not its wishes to maintain a commercial interest in digital television so as to enhance funding for public service broadcasting in the future), then the Minister must change the original plan. Frequent rhetorical reference was made to Britain, where the BBC was obliged to sell off its network in 1996 to Crown Castle. And it was pointed out that Rupert Murdoch's BSkyB managed to achieve a position of strength without owning either the satellite or the cable systems on which its content is distributed (though it was not pointed out that in Ireland, deregulation would allow new digital cable and MMDS systems, as well as telecommunications companies using ADSL, to become involved in both content and distribution.

Síle De Valera's own contribution to the Dail debate framed the problem as being entirely the result of RTÉ changing its mind about selling its network when the Project Management Group decided that the proper way to proceed was to predetermine the value of the network business. No mention was made of the enormous difference in the valuation arrived at by AIB (£34 million) and A.D. Little (£66 million) and there was no questioning of why a predetermined value for the network should be calculated when this procedure seemed to go against normal Government and EU guidelines for selling public property, and to be at variance with the method of selling Cablelink, another valuable asset held in trust for the public by RTÉ. The question of RTÉ's shareholding as treated as simply a pragmatic decision for RTÉ as to when to sell one of its assets, rather than as a strategic approach to guaranteeing for public service broadcasting a long-term revenue stream from all the new broadcasting, telephony and Internet business to be carried on the new interactive transmission system. "It is simply a question of practically determining whether it is better for RTÉ to cash in the full value of its asset now, at a time when it would be open to full competition, or hold back a minority share in the hope that it will increase in value in the future ... It is a simple, practical choice as to which option is best for RTÉ and which will best deliver the Government's objectives in rolling out access to digital offerings as quickly as possible."[55]

What remains hidden in this debate is the role of TV3/Canwest in organising the lobbying clout of the IBI at grassroots political level and threatening EU competition law on the issue of "state aid." An essential confusion and paralysis remained in the Department throughout this period, despite RTÉ's argument that opting for the AIB solution (a predetermined network value of £34 million) would be far more likely to generate "state aid" accusations against DIGICO than allowing market forces to decide the price. This Departmental confusion and delay was exacerbated by an inability to withstand pressures within the Project Management Group from two other interested Departments, Public Enterprise led by Mary O'Rourke, and Enterprise, Trade and Employment, led by Tanaiste Mary Harney. It was also worsened by an inability in the political system to maintain a courageous vision of what was good for public service broadcasting in the face of criticism from the private broadcasting sector, or a determination to test the new protective power of the Protocol of the Amsterdam Treaty, secured by Irish diplomacy but not yet put to use. Its advocate, Michael D. Higgins, pointed out in the Dail (23 March, 2000) that "not a single technology company in the known world is selling or valuing its assets in terms of current earnings. Every one, including those involved in mad speculation, is based on potential value. Why is RTÉ to be treated differently?"

It was clear that Phil Flynn's intervention was driven by the Taoiseach's Department, with the intention of working with, rather than against RTÉ, in sorting out not only the ESOP issue but also the related problems of the shareholding and the methodology to be used for network valuation. In the space of a single month, perceptions of the DTT drama had evolved significantly, from digital television being seen initially as an EU competition problem, through a period of intense gossip about private broadcasters lobbying against the public interest for the sake of gaining a foothold in DTT, and finally to the whole saga collapsing into a squabble within RTÉ, involving internal disagreements with Network staff who had opened up their own very effective lobbying pathway to the Minister. No wonder Phil Flynn would find it all very confusing. The key Civil Servants on the Project Management Group seemed preoccupied with shifting blame away from themselves for the AIB-delivered mess and the delays. RTÉ management meanwhile knew the focus had now shifted to the Department of Finance: could Minister Charlie McCreevey be persuaded of the need to agree even a 30 percent share? Direct contact was opened up between Bertie Ahern's advisers and Bob Collins, where the notion of a 25 percent share was floated, only to be rejected by the Director-General as too small to allow RTÉ to influence policy at board level. How far should compromise on this figure go, in order to speed up the launch of DTT?

The final Government decision came in June 2000. RTÉ would retain a 28 percent share in the new transmission company and its network employees would get another 5 percent. RTÉ would hold no stake in the separate company to be established to retail digital television services to viewers.

CURRENT PROBLEMS

In the middle of 2003, there is no sign of development in the proposed DTT platform, which was legally provided for in the Broadcasting Bill that eventually became law early in 2001. RTÉ has abandoned its two-year attempt to sell its network, as the value of it plummets in an uncertain economic climate. There has been only one bidder for the multiplex operator licence – a former RTÉ executive who played an important role in shaping RTÉ's digital strategy – but he has not been able to attract the 100 million investment that is needed and has now withdrawn. As Ireland's DTT strategy sank slowly under the weight of inertia, aided by the collapse in confidence in new media prompted by the rapidly falling technology stocks on major global markets in 2002, both cable and satellite operators are moving in to fill the vacuum, one with more success than the other.

Cable in Ireland is dominated by two major operators, NTL (which purchased Cablelink from RTÉ and Telecom Eireann for what is now seen as a very inflated price) and Chorus, jointly owned by Denver-based Liberty Media and Dublin-based Independent News & media. By the middle of 2003, NTL had 365,500 subscribers and Chorus had about 240,000. An wireless network running on microwave technology (MMDS) serves a small proportion of these and has just gone digital since April 2003. Both companies have been experiencing poor cash flow problems, which prevent them from drawing down more investment funds from banks, which in turn delays the full roll-out of digital cable and its related wireless network. This brings them into conflict with the regulator, the ODTR, because they cannot meet the deadlines agreed when they received their licences. The Regulator has already removed Chorus' and NTL's exclusive right to broadcast in their franchise areas in a bid to promote greater competition, but the severe downturn in the technology sector has prevented competitors from taking advantage of this. Its parent NTL Group in the US emerged from Chapter 11 bankruptcy protection in January 2003. Chorus is pulling out of a number of state-backed broadband infrastructure projects, based on high-speed fibre-optic rings serving twenty regional towns around Ireland. These cable companies are failing to increase their average revenue per subscriber (except by persuading the Regulator of the need to increase basic subscription fees) because they can not afford to build out so-called "triple play" services: telephony, television and Internet. NTL has less than 45,000 digital subscribers by mid-2003, compared with 280,000 Sky digital subscribers, and it still suffers from a substantial churn rate in its general subscription base: in the first quarter of 2003, it gained 116,000 new subscribers but lost 89,000. In yet another shake out and consolidation scenario, it is likely that Liberty Media will rescue NTL, along with Telewest, its UK cable competitor, by buying them out at bargain rates and forcing them to merge. The fact that NTL and Chorus in Ireland run different, incompatible versions of Open TV middleware on their set-top-boxes may present problems in developing interactive services in the future.

Meanwhile, the difficulties in cable and DTT open the way for satellite television. BSkyB is the big winner at this stage, as it already dominates the move to digital television in Ireland. In a short space of time, it had signed up 280,000 households by the middle of 2003, or 25 per cent of the Irish market, and is now the most significant multichannel digital platform, even though, being based in Luxembourg, it is not regulated in Ireland, does not pay VAT at Irish levels, does not pay a levy to the regulator ComReg (the licensed cable companies pay 3.5 per cent of their revenues) and is not subject to price controls. All of its customers are digital. Its success is based on its existing subscriber base, on the delays in launching DTT and in rolling out digital cable, as well as on the large economies of scale it can avail of in providing free set-top-boxes and controlling sports rights. Impending changes in media ownership rules in the UK may see News Corp, its parent group, consolidate itself further in this part of the world by gaining its first foothold in terrestrial television through a bid for Channel 5. Sky's uptake in Ireland can be largely attributed to its success in persuading embattled RTÉ to expand its reach across the whole of Ireland (including Northern Ireland) and therefore to increase its viewing figures and advertising revenue, by putting its radio and television channels on the Sky satellite platform. Sky Ireland, the subsidiary of parent BSkyB, has been contributing to the overall profits of the group and helping it to rise towards the end-of-2003 target of seven million subscribers, but there were indications in the middle of 2003 that growth was slowing. Its subscriber list is skewed towards rural areas, it still hasn't been able to sign up UTV and Channel Four and the number of desertions from ITV Digital has slowed. The roll-out of the BBC s "Freesat" will put it under further pressure. Sky's entry into the Irish market – which would have been regarded by those working on digital television policy back in 1996 as a "doomsday scenario" for Ireland – happened very quietly and very quickly, with almost no public discussion, until the eruption of public anger in the middle of 2002 when Sky purchased the television rights to all Irish international soccer home matches, removing them from free-to-air television. A very embarrassed Government is still attempting to make up for its past negligence, allay football supporters' outrage and implement a "Listed Events" policy, in keeping with the rules of the Television Without Frontiers directive.

There has clearly been a major overestimation of the potential of digital television, the Internet and telecommunications expansion over the last four years right across Europe, so predictions for the future must be very cautious. What will viewers gain in moving from analogue to digital? The dominant European trend at present is against enhancing the high-resolution capability of digital television in favour of increasing quantity of channels and promoting interactivity as part of an enhanced viewing experience. Two models of interactivity are emerging, the "walled garden" concept and the "enhanced programming" model. Each includes e-mail, EPG, limited Internet browsing and the ability to interact with programmes in real-time by choosing alternative camera angles in sports programmes and voting on programme content (Big Brother as a prototype). Sky customers in Ireland will soon go online via a set-top-box connected to a fixed line home phone which will route transactions – banking, betting, financial services, home shopping – via a network operated by Nevada Telecom using Eircom switching, and share revenues with private firms.

What share of the total television market will want these interactive services? Will Early Adopters be followed quickly by an Early Majority, then a Late Majority (to use the jargon of new product research), leaving the Laggards to be pushed into digital television when governments switch off the analogue signal? Crucially, will a small economy like Ireland – with 24 times fewer television households than the UK – be able to offer information and entertainment on television in the future that has anything recognisably Irish in it? Will the new forces of globalisation unleashed by digital technology enhance or destroy the capacity for content creation in this country that has steadily developed since the foundation of RTÉ in 1961?[56] In the evolution of all cultural industries to date, audience taste for information and entertainment has been notoriously fickle and difficult to predict. There is no reason to think it will be different in digital television. Already Video on Demand is no longer being touted as the "killer application" with the same level of confidence as four years ago. "Churn rates" (the proportion of subscribers cancelling subscriptions) are already high in European premium digital television services, as audiences sample, grow bored and opt out. The big question for digital television companies is whether new services made possible by digital technology will be attractive enough to generate sufficient revenues, particularly in a situation where audiences want more local and national content from a digital regime that runs increasingly on globalised content. We may yet need more affordable, locally controlled DTT systems.

What is incontrovertible is that in Ireland, DTT received the most detailed attention from planners since 1996 and yet the Government's digital policy is now in disarray. In the UK, Government tenacity in pursuing two high-level objectives – efficiency in radio spectrum management and promotion of on-line connectivity – has led it back to a decision to place the BBC at the centre of its digital television policy after the recent collapse of ITV Digital.[57] But Government inertia in Ireland has allowed DTT to recede as a real option for the majority of Irish viewers who continue to want free-to-air television. This is a worrying development for the future of the biggest revolution in broadcasting since the introduction of colour television, but it is positively alarming if it also means the further weakening of a public service presence in broadcasting and the rise to prominence in every part of Europe of global corporations who find no place on their agenda for investment in indigenous television production and probably for diversity in programming either.

These are not considerations for the long finger. An immediate threat to broadcasting in Ireland is posed by the British Government's support for the new BBC "Freesat" digital strategy, announced in March 2000, along with the decision to withdraw all BBC channels from the BSkyB system and offer them on a free-to-air basis via the Astra 2D satellite. This means the new BBC digital channels already being distributed in the UK by DTT on Freeview, and a host of radio stations, will now be available in Ireland for the first time using Sky receivers, without encryption and the need for a smart card: BBC News 24, BBC3, BBC4 and BBC1Scotland, in addition to BBC1 and BBC2 Northern Ireland. Replicating the BBC's DTT strategy via satellite makes good sense for the BBC: it frees it from platform control dependencies on BSkyB in respect of encryption and conditional access systems (the BBC was already in dispute with BSkyB about EPG numbering and regionality issues) and frees it from the costs entailed in involvement with a platform it doesn't own. The mixture of DTT and satellite distribution, both controlled by the BBC, also forecloses conversion of BBC to a subscription based funding mechanism and preserves its universal service, free-to-air, and public service nature. The approximately 20 percent of British homes outside the Freeview (DTT) area will be able to use the Freesat (satellite) offer to gain access to multichannel television. If the public respond in sufficient numbers, this is a perfect solution for the BBC to all the challenges posed by the arrival of digital technology ten years ago. With 25 million households in the UK, the size of the market provides the economies of scale and scope that allow a complementary digital terrestrial/satellite strategy to work. It is also a perfect solution for the British Government, which first decided to trust private companies (Granada and Carlton) with the task of rolling out DTT, and when this failed, committed itself to the only obvious alternative, the BBC, in order to achieve its own twin objectives: bringing the benefits of the Information Society to Britain in the form of television-Internet convergence, and creating a real possibility now for switching off analogue television for ever in Britain in the not so distant future, for the sake of "farming" the electromagnetic spectrum space saved by this move and exploiting it for future telecommunications use.

But in this instance, what is good for Britain is not good for Ireland. ITV is also considering moving towards free-to-air broadcasting when its current contract with BSkyB contract expires. Other terrestrial broadcasters in Britain (Channels Four and Five) will do the same. A strong free-to-air satellite service will emerge side-by-side with BSkyB's pay-TV service and this will have far reaching consequences for other adjoining countries within the Astra 2D footprint, where English is the first or second language. Crystal clear UK television services offering over 100 channels will be available in every corner of Ireland by 2005, rural and urban, for a one-off charge of about 300 for purchase and installation of a satellite receiver system (which compares well with the 150 charged in Britain for DTT) and many subscribers will cancel their cable or MMDS services for the very attractive and completely free package from Freesat. RTÉ and other Irish channels will remain encrypted until 2007 on the BSkyB system, until the current contract expires, requiring Irish satellite viewers to pay for a Sky family pack subscription. RTÉ's audience share in homes that were previously analogue terrestrial only – about 30 percent – will be eroded. The business case for an Irish DTT service, discussed at length here, will be undermined because it will lose the critical advantage of carrying UK terrestrial services, that will be available long before any Irish DTT service could be launched, since full UK/Irish coverage is in place already and the technology used is mature, already tried and tested in BSkyB. Much of the service that could be offered on an Irish DTT system will be available already nationwide for free, with a low-cost receiver.

Furthermore, there is reason to believe that television rights holders for third-party product (US films and popular television series, and the most sought after sports) will renegotiate acquisition rights with UK broadcasters for both Ireland and the UK. This would mean that RTÉ and other Irish broadcasters would have to sublicence rights and lose brodacasting sovereignty they previously enjoyed. This will be less of a problem for TV3 than for RTÉ, given its relationship with its major shareholder Granada. The Olympic Games of 2006 may well prove to be an important test case.[58] Some precedent for handling this conundrum may be discerned in the German-language area where this problem is mirrored. SRG (Swiss German public service broadcaster) and ORF (Austrian public service broadcaster) are in a similar relationship with Germany's ARD/ZDF. German broadcasting is already dominating its linguistic neighbours in audience share, market leverage and rights acquisition. The cable, deflector and MMDS sectors in Ireland will also be adversely affected, as they depend on their retransmission rights for the four UK terrestrial channels. It is likely that a significant part of their subscriber base will migrate to the free satellite system in order to escape from subscription payments. This is already happening in the UK analogue television market, where customers are defecting from NTL and Telewest for Freeview. Independent production companies in Ireland will also be adversely affected in the longer term, as audience shares and revenues begin to diminish and reduce the ability of broadcasters to commission programmes. Finally, the development of Freeview and Freesat will have large consequences for plans to ensure that there is no longer a fundamental asymmetry in All-Ireland broadcasting, since the DTT system in Northern Ireland currently does not have the capacity to carry RTÉ and other Irish terrestrial channels.

6 **CHILDREN AND TELEVISION**

One effect of the new media order that has been emerging over the last decade is that information flows ever more freely across the globe, with ever looser ties to place and time. The volume of information conveyed by new digital media technologies continues to grow exponentially and to move across various media – television, radio, books, magazines, computers, the Internet – as they converge into conglomerates mostly controlled by multinational corporations headquartered in the USA, Japan and Europe. Media markets around the world are being restructured comprehensively to the point where national markets, still recognisably distinct up to about 1990, are becoming integrated into a global media power system. Youth and children's culture is at the cutting edge of this development. Fewer global corporations deliver more products of mass culture in a continuous flow to more far-flung audiences of young people than ever before in world history.

What does it all add up to? Probably no aspect of the media has received as much sustained scrutiny by researchers as the relationship between children and television. This body of research in turn fits alongside academic reflections on youth sub-cultures, broad historical patterns in the evolution of childhood. Neil Postman in his very influential 1982 book *The Disappearance of Childhood* suggests that while the invention of printing led to a strong division between childhood and adult life, television has eroded this division. Under conditions of almost total illiteracy in the Middle Ages, all information was available to everybody, there were no secrets and there was no concept of childhood. Typography however, created a new definition of adulthood based on literacy. Children were a group of people who did not know certain things adults knew, so there were no "children" since adults do not have access to information that they alone could possess. Johann Gutenburg changed this in one direction, television changed it back again, because of its tendency to homogenise. Ways of dressing, eating, speaking, entertaining and playing all moved towards a homogenised lifestyle, according to Postman. In the television age, there are three stages of life – infancy, adulthood and senility – where adulthood is synonymous with the "adult -child". Relationships between young and old people have changed radically in recent decades, compared with earlier societies, and young people leave their mark on culture ever more strongly than before. Television in Postman's view is central to this social transformation as it makes previously unfamiliar phenomena known to all age groups.

The notion that television is "bad" for children comes out of both a conservative and a left critique. The conservative critique is often based on nostalgia for a pre-television era and a privileging of elite cultural forms. The dominating influence of F. R. Leavis on the teaching of literature in the middle of the last century can still be felt in resistance within educational establishments to the idea of introducing the concept of visual literacy into primary and secondary school curricula and in arguments about the canon of "great texts" to which children should be exposed. At the opposite end of the spectrum of cultural politics, the left critique stresses the ideological power of the media to define young people's world views very tightly and traces this manipulative influence back to questions of ownership and control of media companies and their global links today to conglomerates involved in producing and marketing a wide range of consumer goods – fast food, clothes, music, films – that view children as just another market.

From the inception of television after World War II in the United States, parents, academics and teachers succeeded in influencing the political agenda so that the issue of media violence could be highlighted. Congressional hearings explored violence in television from 1952 to 1955 and in the 1960s, in response to anti-Vietnam War agitation on university campuses and riots in black ghettos in American cities, the National Commission on the Causes and Prevention of Violence pointed a finger severely at television. Television's relationship with children and young people became a health issue in the following decades, as first the Surgeon General,[59] then the National Institute of Mental Health and finally the American Psychological Association added to the approximately 4000 books, articles and reports that had accumulated by 1990. By now, concerns went beyond violence to include worries about the impact of television viewing on school performance and the emotional development of the child, as well as how television influenced children's knowledge of the world in its portrayal of different gender and ethnic roles.

Recurring themes in media research include the extent to which children are helpless victims in the glow of the television or PC screen and whether, or under what conditions, they can master the challenges posed by contemporary media content that is now available around the clock. Only a decade ago, children's television in Ireland consisted of a few after school and Saturday morning hours, plus a little morning cartoon sequence for pre-schoolers. But now an increasing number of Irish children in homes linked to satellite or cable systems have access all day to dedicated channels like the Disney Channel and Nickelodeon. The formula is cheap and simple and thrives on small children's insatiable delight in repeat viewing of cartoon and live action comedies linked together by studio inserts. RTÉ struggles to maintain an Irish voice in this format with Network Two.

Critical analysis of the impact on children builds on earlier concerns with cinema in the US, where the Payne Foundation funded the first large-scale examination of how cinema might be affecting audiences' values, attitudes, behaviour, relationships with others and even physiological reactions to the big screen. Today a variety of methodologies are used – including experiments, content analysis, participant observation, in-depth interviews, surveys and attitude scales – to explore a range of questions with contemporary relevance. Does television inculcate in children sexist, racist or ageist views of their world? How well do children of different ages and family backgrounds follow and understand television? What does excessive use of television displace in the child's waking hours or do we need to fear television dependence? Should we be concerned about young children's fright responses to television content?

What are the implications of young people's exposure to pornography? Does television improve children's knowledge of the world and does it have an impact on other ways of knowing their world including schooling, reading and creative play? What does it teach them about social roles, about handling frustrations?

The emergent view in the US is that violent content on television or video games can be a causal agent in relation to the development of aggressiveness in children, that this influence is felt before the child begins to go to school and that it continues into adolescence where the damage is the result of cumulative exposure. This cause-effect explanation is not accepted to the same extent in many European countries but there is still a concern about the form taken by violence in television, film and computer games and how it relates to violence in society.[60] Does television also have beneficial and desirable pro-social effects on children, on their moral and imaginative development and even on their ability to "purge" their aggressive impulses through fantasy or daydreaming? A major set of questions concerns the possible effects of advertising on children. How are they affected cognitively, emotionally and behaviourally by commercial messages on television? To what extent do these messages create conflict in families through "pester power", where youngsters are led to pressure parents into unnecessary purchases? Can young children distinguish between programme and advertisement to the extent of recognising the persuasive intent of the commercial and if they cannot, must the *caveat emptor* principle be abandoned as a starting point of a new ethic? Is the impact of advertising so great that children are likely to be socialised into overly materialistic worldviews?

In the late 1990s, advertising agencies have emerged more clearly as "brand stewards", identifying, articulating and protecting the corporate brand, not as a product but as a way of life, an attitude, a set of values, a look, an idea, an experience, a lifestyle. So, polaroid is not a camera – it's a social lubricant. Swatch is not about watches, it is about the idea of time. Benetton is not about clothes, it's about risqué art and progressive politics. Nike's mission isn't to sell shoes but to "enhance people's lives through sports and fitness", to "keep the magic of sports alive" so that "the inspiration of sports allows us to rebirth ourselves constantly."[61] Advertising is only one vehicle, along with sponsorship and logo licensing, used to convey the core meaning of a corporation to the world. Does television advertising focused on children at an early stage in the development of their identity cultivate them as "fashion victims" in thrall to the very set of trans-national corporations with very high brand name recognition that are now the focus of the outrage of the global anti-capitalism movement? Is the ultimate impact of advertising therefore ideological, in inculcating at an emotionally satisfying level an identification with and loyalty to fully globalised consumer capitalism? We will examine advertising in Irish television later in this chapter.

CHILDREN'S TELEVISION AS INDUSTRY

Children's television has been one of the most dominant genres of TV since the beginning of broadcasting. No other genre of programming generates a spectrum of professional talk and writing about itself that varies so widely from extremes of inspiration to extremes of cynicism. On the one hand educators, parents groups, public service broadcasters and campaigners for better media in civil society (the best known being Action for Children's Television in the US and Voice of the Listener and Viewer in the UK) articulate the vision, the possibilities, the needs of a child-centred production strategy. Television has a potential, they say, to break down inhibitions about the unknown, to open up controversial issues and experimental adventures, to activate the intellectual and creative potential of children, to inspire learning through active play and exploration. Good children's television is an introduction to the broader world outside the home, a catalyst for the process of learning that is geared to the emotional, physical and intellectual perspective of the child.

In sharp contrast with this kind of visionary discourse is a newer kind of talk about children which has come to the fore in trade conferences and in the trade press, which parallels the proliferation of new global television channels and production companies specialising in entertainment for children. Many of these are already well versed in the art of localising a global product. Chum City International, for instance, advertises itself to broadcasters as "now available in assorted cultures, formats or franchises. Tailored to meet your needs. In your local language. Covering your local scene. Find out why our style of TV is a success wherever it travels."[62]

The way such new companies talk about children is an indicator of how extensively the discourse of market liberalisation has proliferated, given earlier taboos on speaking about children in purely commercial terms. Broadcasting and Cable Magazine's supplement "Television Europe" (September 1998) analyses the challenge of "building multi-national kid's brands" onto key "properties" such as Britt Allcroft Group's "Thomas the Tank Engine and Friends", in terms of developing "the multiple applications of the character" through television, cinema, video, website, publishing, toys, promotions and "tie-ins", all in the "key territories". Success is measured solely by the ability to generate "a hit". "The international media says that a children's show encourages addictive behaviour (Pokemon), subverts formal learning (Teletubbies) or condones violence (Mighty Morphins Power Rangers) and you know you have a hit on your hands. That's not because these shows are fundamentally different from anything else seen by children on television but because they are so loved that grown-ups are desperate to work out why." In a different context, offering a new twist to arguments about "pester power", children are seen as one of the most significant factors, along with the lure of movie and sports channels, in persuading people to subscribe to pay television delivered via either satellite or cable. One of the major problems in the pay-TV sector in many countries in Europe is that not enough subscribers can be signed up to premium channels and of those that do, not enough can be persuaded to renew their subscription beyond the trial period – the problem of the so-called high "churn rate."

Commercial research companies persuade pay TV operators that they can reduce their churn rate in homes with children by offering channels for children, such as the global brands Fox Kids, Disney and Nickelodeon, which tend to be watched by girls and Cartoon Network, which tends to be preferred by boys. In the new aggressively market-driven environment, it becomes a question of seeing children solely in demographic terms and supplying more entertainment for children (including, crucially in the new digital environment, child-friendly interactive features). A Merrill Lynch report on digital pay TV prospects in the UK,[63] describing the "generational wash-through effect", points out that in the US, children raised in cable homes are more likely to subscribe to cable when they become adults. Initial penetration of pay TV starts in the young adults and family households. As parents grow older and children leave home, they keep the service and like it. The children start their own homes and also subscribe because they enjoyed it when they were younger. Hence the pursuit of the child viewer by the new generation of television companies and pay TV operators, not only for the additional revenue to be generated by advertising but also because of the value of children's television in persuading parents to abandon terrestrial TV, to initiate and then maintain a subscription to pay TV and because of the "generational wash through effect" as today's children become tomorrow's customers.

Of course, this new market-centred way of talking about children as customers, a very far cry from the way children's needs and well-being are discussed in the Children's Departments of public service broadcasters, is an extension of attempts (by major companies in several industrial sectors) to extend brand identity even to children under ten. The Journal of the American Medical Association published research that underlined the ability of the R. J. Reynolds tobacco company to make its cartoon character Old Joe Camel, associated with its Camel cigarette brand, as identifiable among American six year olds as Mickey Mouse.[64] Even Porsche, the German luxury car manufacturer has made attempts to influence children with positive messages about its cars. It ran a series of focus groups in elementary schools in San Francisco in 1998 "to see if kids regard Porsche as a dream car" and then a television advertising campaign tailored specifically to the ten year old customer.[65] The company was bombarded with requests from children for Porsche free gifts, evidence enough for the company to conclude with confidence that "kids decide what's cool and Porsches are cool again."

TOYS AND TELEVISION

Childhood is an age-defined early stage of human development, between infancy and puberty, but it is also a social, cultural and economic construct, as can be seen from comparative studies of childhood in different contemporary societies and across different historical epochs. In our present world, at least in those relatively wealthy societies represented in the OECD, childhood is increasingly being shaped by the forces of globalisation working through the cultural industries, especially television. The parameters of children's entertainment today is largely defined by toys and television, with some input also from records, films, video, books, video games, PC software and the Internet. The predominant influences shaping the global children's TV market today originate in certain lifestyle changes that have been taking place in American society since the 1970s and in corporate adjustments in the entertainment sector to the changing constructions of childhood in the US. The prime mover here is the toy industry and the increasing role it began to play from 1980 onwards in the larger child entertainment industry.

A number of events converged in the US in the late 1970s which contributed to the shape of the current children's entertainment industry: the desire for new markets by independent television programme producers; the tightening advertising market and the demand for additional points of contact with consumers; the availability of new independent television stations to serve that market, following the deregulation of broadcasting by the Reagan administration; the huge appetite for cheap programming among new broadcasters and the growing market of young consumers with more disposable income than ever before. Thus, children's imaginations and the entertainment that sustained them are tied ever more closely to the imperatives of the market economy and it is this set of values that is now being spread globally as broadcasting channels multiply beyond the United States.[66]

The earliest examples of a vibrant children's market in entertainment date from the US in the late nineteenth century, as mass production techniques were applied to magazines, comics, dime novels, trading cards and paper cut-outs. Public (and Congressional) reaction to the targeting of children focused not on the economics of children's entertainment but on the supposed effects of particular kinds of content, especially where this was violent. These reactions were frequently driven by moral panics and crusades. A further wave of expansion came in the early 1930s in the new medium of radio, as the number of children's radio hours doubled each year when sponsors (but not yet advertisers) grew more eager to come on board. In the 1970s, as television achieved just about one hundred percent penetration of every corner of the US, media reformers lobbied for a reduction in the number of minutes per hour of advertising allowed, the production of more age specific television programmes and the elimination of the practice of "host selling", whereby the hosts of children's television programmes also starred in advertisements, thus completely blurring the distinction in the child's mind between advertisement and programme. At this stage, toy companies began using names and icons developed in television programmes, in return for paying a fee to copyright holders and a percentage of toy sale profits. From this point on, pressures peculiar to the toy industry became key drivers of change in television, change which directly affects Ireland today.

Up to the 1970s, eighty percent of toys in the US were sold from November to December, to adults rather than children, and the years marketing focus was firmly on the fourth quarter of the business year. But changing demographics were working to alter this seasonal demand to the extent that toy sales would shift from providing the once off Christmas surprise to supplying a year long stable in the consumer market. The creation of a massive, radically new child market in toys replicated an earlier industrial phenomenon: the construction of the "teenager" as a new market was made possible in the expanding US economy of the 1950s and the maturing of the post-World War II "baby boom". By the 1970s, the toy industry had become extremely volatile and was ripe for adopting strategies to increase market consolidation by reducing the high up-front risk inherent in new toy production costs and encouraging year-round sales. Its volatility was influenced by some key demographic changes, related to increases in the birth rate, in the number of new households using toys created by a rising divorce rate, and in the number of older parents with more money to spend on more expensive toys.

The higher cost of toy production required that the industry be able to anticipate eighteen months in advance what the whims of five-year-olds will be, hence the increase in research and development departments – though there was still a place for "gut instinct" – and the sub-contracting of production to low-cost foreign facilities. One of the sensational successes of the 1980s, Cabbage Patch Kids, was "intuitively" developed but rejected by five major toy companies and a television network. Its producer, Coleco, was investing 77 percent of its business in the Kids but the quick failing of interest in this toy soon after, along with the flurry of mergers and acquisitions that gripped the American toy industry in the 1980s, soon forced Coleco to file for bankruptcy.

The 1980s saw a shift from generic toys to toys licensed across a range of media to extend their life cycle. The most successful of these were the Care Bears, Smurfs and Teenage Mutant Ninja Turtles, supported by a year-round media marketing blitz. The shelf space problem in department stores was overcome with the development of another innovation, the specialised large volume toy store designed to stock toys year-round, such as Toys 'R' Us, which quickly spread to all fifty US states and over seventy other countries. Thus, an unstable market for toys was made less volatile by the restructuring of the industry via mergers and also by extending the shelf life of toys, thus reducing the "fad" factor.

How did these huge changes have an impact on television? Major restructuring of the toy industry was achieved by linking it much more closely with television and exploiting its power to extend the consumer memory for characters. Television was also crucial in the corporate move from producing single toys to creating multiple lines, each with their own "accessories". Now the Muppets have babies, Care Bears have cousins and Barbie has power cars and wedding cakes. Disney was the first to utilise licensing successfully in the 1930s, to exploit the popularity of Mickey Mouse, but since 1980, we have seen the wholesale licensing of character properties across a wide range of different media. Typical of this strategy would be the Care Bears, originally constructed by a greeting card company, now licensed across TV specials, book promotions, movies, venues, web sites, day care centres, hospitals, radio programmes, cough medicines. The licensing agent is the bridge between toy character rights owners, whose wealth is a legal entity, the actual manufacturers of toys and the widely scattered child entertainment industry, with television at its epicentre, because of its ability to supply large audiences to advertisers. These are among the key dynamics that drive what we experience today as the globalisation of children's media in Ireland.

American television itself had been going through fundamental changes, which allowed it to converge with the toy industry over the course of a quarter century. These were driven by technological changes being adopted in the television industry for the distribution of its output. Cable TV finally hit its stride in the US after several decades of humble existence as "community antennae TV" scattered throughout rural areas. In 1980, only eight percent of the population had access to cable television. Home Box Office, the first dedicated national cable channel, distributed by satellite, looked like an idea whose time had not yet come. But in little over ten years, the percentage of cable subscribers had grown to sixty-two. This meant on the supply side that many new television channels were now coming into being in response to the increased carrying capacity of cable. But it also meant that the large audiences of the old networks would now fragment and distribute their patronage over a wider set of channels, thus increasing substantially the competitive pressures building up inside the television industry.

One solution to these business pressures, one that would have an impact far beyond the coast of the United States over the next two decades, was the positive response of television executives to the overtures of licensing agents who worked for toy manufacturers in their quest to stabilise the sales cycle of toys traditionally subject to children's whims. This convergence of interest allowed the new generation of television stations to spread the risk associated with programme production costs between content producers and toy manufacturers. For children, however, it meant a further blurring of the distinction between sponsorship and programme content, between imaginative play and commercial exploitation. New animated television programmes were being developed, with the consultation and financial backing of toy manufacturers and licensing agents. Independent television stations pioneered this new wave of animation, tied to new or existing toys, that also served to establish in children brand awareness of consumer products marketed on tee shirts, activity books, story books, shoes, lunch boxes and other paraphernalia.

The 1970s' children's television market in the US was limited to three national networks, plus some independent stations in major cities. But in the following decade the deployment of cable and satellite distribution systems, combined with deregulation decisions in the Federal Communications Commission, meant that a whole new range of channels became available, general programming channels as well as specialised ones such as Disney and Nickelodeon. In 1970, for example, children in New York City, the largest television market, had access to 36.9 hours of network children's programmes per week, plus 48 hours from local stations. Twenty years later, children in New York City had access to 300 hours of television per week.[67] Much of this increase in programming was animation, but in the 1990s, television channels began to focus more strategically on the so called "tween" market of nine- to eleven-year-olds, by filling late afternoon hours with reruns of situation comedies, game shows, soaps and serials based on familiar books like the Nancy Drew series.

Animated programmes were the mainstay of this expansion, however, for a number of reasons: young children enjoy multiple viewings of the same content; cartoon characters are easy to replicate and spin-off as toys; they can be recycled every three years to a new generation of young children, as older siblings move on to different kinds of content; the simple drawings of animation make dubbing into other languages easy; and their neutral cultural background make them ideal for the export market. Animation also involves no payment of expensive royalties to film stars, except where well-known voices are used.

The toy company Mattel and the production house Filmation Studios made the first weekly series based on licensed characters in 1983. This was the fantasy cartoon "He Man and the Masters of the Universe", shunned by the networks for fear it would be challenged by the Federal Communications Commission as an advertisement for toys but eagerly accepted by the new independent stations desperate for first run programming. Thus new content for the new stations involved minimal capitalisation, yet made them competitive with the networks in the children's television market. In its first three years alone, one hundred and twenty-five million "He Man" character dolls were sold on the principle of collectibility. Adding new characters took place both in the television cartoon and on the toy shelf. Several television episodes were combined into a feature length movie which was premiered Hollywood-style in ten major cities. Its phenomenal success in the US was matched in the forty-eight countries it was sold to, including England, Germany and Ireland.

"He Man" was a significant milestone in the evolution of children's television because of the innovative type of cost-sharing co-operation it represented, between toy manufacturer, the advertising industry and the emerging cable networks. It was a milestone in a different sense also, because it defined more clearly the dominant trend towards linking the world of children's entertainment to market forces alone, and thoroughly commercialising the notion of children's developmental needs. As William Melody pointed out in an earlier period of commercial television, when competition increases in the media industry, the need for strong programming intensifies, in order to attract the child audience and supply it to advertising agencies.[68] After 1980, the dynamics of the television-advertising market exchange system changed, as new television stations began to compete with the established networks for both programme content and advertising revenue and as advertisers and companies like Mattel, Hasbro and Fischer Price moved into the supply side of the market structure through co-financing and bartering deals with the television industry and their production companies. This laid the foundation for the globalisation of children's television, as conditions changed in Europe too.

GLOBAL CHANNELS

The major changes taking place in the entertainment sector in the US in the 1980s spawned another innovation that has had a huge impact on the globalisation of television in Europe and in Ireland: the emergence of dedicated children's channels, such as the Disney Channel, Nickelodeon and Time Warner's Cartoon Network.

Since its origins in cable in 1984, the Disney Channel quickly developed the ultimate model in blurring the lines for children's entertainment, with its vertical integration of advertiser, licensing agent, programme supplier, television station and market manager all in one. The Disney Channel is not the major source of revenue for the corporation but its importance for corporate branding is huge, with characters being developed as media stars first, then as age-specific toy sales (through its partnership with Mattel) and icons licensed for use on everything from babies' nappies to candy bars, restaurant chains, theme parks and hotel resorts. Each display of the Mickey Mouse or Donald Duck icon is essentially a commercial message whose branding power has resonated around the world for many decades even before the Disney Channel acquired a global reach. Disney's long-established dominance of the global animation business is only now being challenged by Steven Spielberg's

Dreamworks, the first major new studio established in Hollywood for fifty years, backed by Microsoft and the giant Asian media group, Samsung of Korea. Its aim is to overtake Disney in the production of digitally animated feature films, though it also works in joint ventures with Disney, as if seeing the wisdom in Rupert Murdoch's famous comment on global competition among media giants: "we can join forces now, or we can kill each other first and then join forces."

Nickelodeon originated in Warner Cable's experimental Qube Station in the 1970s and launched itself in 1982 with a strong corporate philosophy of offering pro-social children's television in a commercial-free environment. It was later taken over by Viacom, one of the four largest media companies in the world (which includes the global networks MTV, Showtime and The Movie Channel). Its business plan now resembles Disney's, in moving from a reliance on live-action to cartoons, in carrying advertising and in exploiting product tie-ins that license television characters into various merchandising lines (shampoo for pre-teens, clothing, stuffed animals, tee shirts). Its evolution away from its original pro-social philosophy has followed commercial principles for children's programming, stressing age-specific specialisation. This strategy is based on child audience availability at different times of the day, demand from advertisers and the pricing of commercial time, rather than any consideration of the cognitive or developmental needs of the child.

One of the key drivers in the formation of global media conglomerates over the last two decades has been the opportunity for cross promotion of products across a wide range of radio and television channels, films, videos, software, print publishing, theme parks, sports teams and sports stadiums. Most of this vertical and horizontal integration has proceeded without serious hindrance from the public media sector. A rare exception was the decision to close down Nickelodeon in Germany in 1998 because it couldn't compete with the Kinderkanal, launched by public broadcasters ARD and ZDF.

American media corporations regard overseas markets as providers of supplementary revenue, "icing on the cake" of handsome profits generated in the large domestic entertainment market. The domestic environment has by now become so crowded that the internationalisation of media products is planned in from the very start of the production and marketing cycle. This is a major accelerator in the bundle of processes that drive cultural globalisation. But there are brakes in this process too. One of them is what media scholars call "cultural discount " in the international flow of television programmes.[69] The audience appeal of a programme or film diminishes as it crosses national boundaries. This translates economically into a percentage reduction in potential value to the exhibitor or distributor, compared to what a domestic product of the same type and quality could earn once put into circulation. Aesthetically, cultural discount describes the difficulty viewers will have with a television programme or film made in another culture, where there is a substantially decreased ability to identify with the style, values, beliefs, history, myths, institutions, physical environment and behavioural patterns embedded in the foreign content.[70]

Animation largely circumvents the problem of cultural discount, and translates well across cultural borders, though some media corporations have found creative ways to do this with live-action programmes too. Saban Entertainment is among the largest international producers and distributors of children's programmes in the world. One of their most successful programmes "Mighty Morphan Power Rangers," which at one point could be found in over one hundred national television markets, achieves the same dissociation from reality – generic time and anonymous landscapes, stylised characters spending most of their time in fantastic costumes – as animated action adventure programmes that feature multiple characters suitable for international merchandising. Saban borrowed the basic concept from one of the major Japanese media companies Toei, whose Zyn Rangers was a very successful example of the popular *Sentai* genre (the exploits of super-hero teams) on Japanese television. The American company brought the idea back to the US, replaced Japanese actors with American ones and used the action sequences and special effects from the Toei productions to launch a new US-made product with very low cultural discount for the international market. Toei is now co-producer and also distributor to the Asian market. The fact that "Rangers" generated so much controversy in the 1990s because of its violent content served only to increase its appeal. It was banned in New Zealand, Norway and Malaysia. UK regulators judged it to be extremely dangerous because of the danger of children imitating its karate displays. It was blamed for the killing of a girl in Norway by teenage boys in 1994 and banned there. New Zealand also banned it and the Australian regulator forced a re-editing. In Canada, the Broadcasting Standards Council ruled that it broke the Code on Violence and it was dropped by several television stations. CanWest (part owner of TV3 in Ireland) asked Saban to re-edit it for Canada but then dropped the programme. In Malaysia, it was banned because the name "Morph" suggested "morphine". By contrast, *Parenting* magazine in the US called it one of the ten best children's programmes on air and then Leader of the House, Newt Gingrich gave it a rousing public endorsement, declaring "I'm a Power Ranger too."

The internationalisation of children's entertainment is not new and Disney cartoons have long been a feature of the international marketplace. But the 1990s witnessed a major globalising thrust by American media companies, producing not only children's television but all its associated merchandise as well. Non-US markets presented new opportunities and a lucrative escape route from an increasingly crowded and well-worked domestic US market. The population figures alone are tempting. In 1990, there were approximately forty million children under the age of ten in the US but seventy-one million in Europe, fifty-five million in Russia and one hundred and thirteen million in Latin America. It is sobering, of course, to juxtapose these statistics, fuelling new global market challenges for American entertainment corporations, with another set of International Labour Organisation figures showing two hundred and fifty million working children aged five to fourteen in the developing world, one hundred and twenty million of these working full-time.

The major expansion of the American children's television market into a global one in the 1990s was facilitated by changes in technology (limited terrestrial broadcasting now vastly expanded by cable and satellite), by the corresponding increase in distribution outlets as more venture capital was invested in new television stations and by the arrival of an era of government deregulation. This was fuelled by the ideological triumph of market liberalisation, driving more and more government decisions in the U.S, the EU and far beyond them. Satellite distribution, throwing a footprint that crosses national borders, augmented by cable and MMDS has fuelled a new demand for children's entertainment and encouraged American corporations to move into foreign distribution more aggressively. Expansion in the media sector is paralleled by the consolidation overseas of toy companies such as Mattel and Hasbro and the establishment in European countries of specialised retail outlets like Toys 'R' Us. It is worth noting that the huge outward thrust of international children's entertainment is not matched by any reverse flow into the US from other countries, although there is one exception. The BBC's "Teletubbies" began to enter the US television system in the late 1990s, but the BBC had given up its right to licence-related toys in the lucrative US market.

CHILDREN IN PUBLIC SERVICE TELEVISION

A key question now needs our attention: what impact has the globalising of children's television had on public service broadcasting? The essence of public service broadcasting is the notion that public funding is used to ensure that the output of radio and television caters for a wide variety of interests and that the tendency to programme for the majority case is tempered by the obligation to serve a range of audiences that measured in themselves are accurately called minorities. It might well be asked, for example, what television delivers that is explicitly of interest to senior citizens, though it can also be acknowledged that television in general – soap operas, films, situation comedies, documentaries, news, current affairs discussions, game shows, sports – is also accessible to older people. The situation is a little different at the other end of the age spectrum, where children require the special attention of society because of their vulnerability, where a great deal of mainstream television is not accessible to them for a variety of reasons that have to do with the cognitive development of young human beings, as well as with family and societal norms regarding what is acceptable for child consumption. This is why there is a particular obligation on public service broadcasters to attend to the needs of children and why the health or otherwise of children is often taken as a barometer of the health of public service broadcasting.

The question of the impact of globalisation on children's television in public broadcasting systems must first be examined in the context of the influence revenue can have on programming decisions, both the amount of revenue available and the source of that revenue, whether it comes from advertising or public funding. Canada is an interesting example of how the pursuit of advertising revenue has affected programming. The CBC in Canada has traditionally generated about twenty percent of its budget from advertising and receives the remainder in the form of parliamentary appropriations. From the mid-1980s, the real level of these appropriations has declined and the CBC has had to pursue advertising more aggressively. The Mandate Review Committee found in 1996 that the CBC English-language network "has subtly reduced its emphasis on children's programming and more serious drama; produced or commissioned less high profile arts programming and provided less money for local and regional programming."[71] At the same time, there was a tendency to replace children's school programmes with old US series and to increase the percentage of sports in prime time output from eighteen per cent in 1985 to thirty-seven per cent a decade later.

The situation in Europe is a little different. The tradition of public service broadcasting co-ordinated cross-nationally by the European Broadcasting Union, has always emphasised the special nature of children as television audiences, their vulnerabilities and special needs. In some countries, organisations in civil society, such as the Voice of the Listener and Viewer in Britain, nourished the ongoing debate that is needed around the question of how to secure children's interest in broadcasting. But in other countries, including Ireland, there is effectively no debate in civil society, which leaves the field clear for broadcasters, public and private, along with advertising and other media interests, to sort out the tensions in practice between the commercial and the cultural imperatives.

In Ireland, the Green Paper on Broadcasting (1995) included a separate chapter on children and television that raised a number of important questions. What special measures need to be taken to ensure that within the economics of television, sufficient resources will be made available to provide a healthy mix of programmes for children in terms of genre and place of origin? Should we be concerned if television for very little children fails to offer viewers an opportunity to connect in any meaningful way with life in Ireland, because this opportunity has been pushed aside by a large volume of imported programming? How well are different levels of childhood being served, from pre-schoolers to adolescents? Should advertising minutage regulation make special provision for hours during which programmes are directed at children?

There was no public or media debate on these issues when the Green Paper was published, nor did any part of the apparatus of Government, (such as a Joint Oireachtas (Parliamentary) Committee on Broadcasting, initiate a debate on how to preserve a broad range of programming genres for children, within the mandate of informing, entertaining and educating, that would address them as young citizens and introduce them in age-appropriate ways to the complexities of the world in which they will grow up. The danger is that in the absence of public debate, children's interests will be no match for the lobbying power of big business, keeping its corporate eye firmly fixed on the huge earnings to be made from global entertainment and character tie-ins, operating behind the rarely questioned orthodoxy that children's taste extends only as far as animation and "we only give them what they want".

Two facts are incontrovertible: firstly, only a broadcasting system with a public service remit can provide the necessary infrastructure for producing a broad range of television programming for children. Secondly, severe damage has already been done to that infra-structure across Europe in a number of ways: under-funding; an increasing reliance on advertising revenue; pressure to concentrate on audience-maximising programming at the expense of a fully diverse range of genres; and a growing need, because of cost inflation in other aspects of programming, to emphasise low cost imports in television schedules. The working out of these economic pressures in television generally over the last decade has seen the steady lightening of prime time, as current affairs, documentaries, politics and the arts are moved out to less popular times and more soaps, quizzes, talk shows and "reality" programmes are moved in. Related changes in children's television across Europe in the early 1990s have been documented in a report by Jay Blumler and Daniel Biltreyst, which is well worth summarising here.[72]

Firstly, as the secondly generation of commercial television stations began to emerge in Europe from the 1980s on, new competitive forces led public service broadcasters to increase their overall hours of broadcasting. The average number of hours per channel Europe-wide was 4,342 in 1991. Four years later this had jumped to 5,571 hours. In the Romance countries, it grew to 6,509 hours. But children's television was not marginalized in this process. On the contrary, children's share of the total increase was maintained as broadcasters relied more upon children's programming to facilitate their general increase in output.

Secondly, the increase in hours in children's television programming was greatest in channels that relied more on advertising for revenue. Pressure from competitors induced public service broadcasters to stay on air all day and to structure early evening viewing so that the family audience could be held on to in the run-up to prime time. In channels with high levels of public funding, children's share of the total output was significantly less.

Thirdly, domestic production levels declined in absolute and in relative terms. European children's TV overall offered an average of 203 hours of home production per annum in 1991. This declined to 177 hours in 1995 as production budgets decreased. In small countries, the decline was steeper, from 205 down to 117 hours. Channels with a heavy reliance on advertising displayed a lesser commitment to home production. The corollary of this decline is an increase in imported programming. The share of total children's programming enjoyed by public service broadcasters varied from a high of 40 percent in the Nordic countries to a low of 27 percent in the Romance countries and was greater in channels with high levels of public funding (40 percent) than in channels with low levels (19 percent). The volume of US imports exceeded domestic production in several European channels, including RTÉ. In fact, US imports dominated channels with low levels of public funding (51 percent) compared to channels with strong public funding (20 percent). Imports from other European countries was highest in the Nordic area and lowest where English was the dominant language: the BBC, ITV, Channel 4 and RTÉ.

Fourthly, these structural changes led to a shrinking in the range of programme genres offered to children with significant regional variations. Nordic countries maintained a strong commitment to drama (35 percent of children's output) and a low interest in cartoons (17 percent), compared with Romance countries (17 percent and 56 percent respectively). A reliance on high levels of public funding was associated with strong output in drama, while channels with low levels of public funding were associated with strong output in animation. Channels with the least interest in both drama and factual programming were those that inserted commercial messages within children's programming.

These correlations allow us to discern a pattern emerging in programming which is associated with funding patterns. There is a close relationship between the amount of children's TV in a channel's total output and its reliance on cartoons to fill the schedules. High output channels (those with over one thousand hours per annum) relied on cartoons to fill 53 percent of their needs, while low output channels (500 hours or less) used animation to fill only 16 percent of their needs. Only half of the channels studied in this report could be said to offer an appropriately diverse range of programming to children. Cartoons, of course, are easy to schedule, are available on the international market in enormous volume at low cost and have a broad appeal among younger children. But used in large quantities to fill out expanded schedules, they displace other genres that should also be in children's schedules – drama, documentaries, news, arts programmes etc. Children have more to view but there is less diversity in it, considered either by genre or by geographic origin. Competition increases pressure for ratings across the full schedule, including children's television, and diffuses a commercial ethos throughout public service broadcasting organisations, if levels of public funding are allowed to decline.

This is the problem in RTÉ. And in Ireland, neither civil society nor the national parliament considered this to be something to get agitated about. Nor can the European Commission be depended upon to act as a guardian of children's interests. In fact, since it became interested in cultural matters in the mid-1980s, the Commission has tended to shy away from public support for public service broadcasting and to see its main role to be defender of the notion of competitive markets solving all problems, even in broadcasting. The correlation between the health of children's television and the general health of public service broadcasting is as obvious in Northern Europe, where we have most reason to be optimistic about both, as it is in Southern Europe, where the opposite is the case. Ireland fits in somewhere between these two extremes and we now turn to examine the case of RTÉ against the backdrop of global trends in children's television and youth subculture. Again, personal experience working within RTÉ on its Authority provides some important insights. Every Authority is dominated by a handful of major issues. Between 1995 and 2000, children's television – and in particular advertising on children's television – absorbed very many hours of discussion without producing spectacular changes. The frustrations inherent in the situation in which we found ourselves in the late 1990s produced more heated passions than well-lit solutions to problems, but an exploration of this tension opens up the wider contra-dictions in Irish broadcasting. One version of these discussions is offered by my Authority colleague, Bob Quinn, in his book "Maverick". I present an alternative view here which tries to set the issues in a wider context, so that our frustrations regarding the improvement of children's television can be understood at a level that goes beyond merely the clash of personalities within a regulatory body.

BOARDROOM BATTLES

The issue of Children and Television erupted onto the agenda of the RTÉ Authority on three separate occasions in the late 1990s, first in a long debate that stretched over six months in 1995-96, then in a short period in the middle of 1997, and finally in a four month period in 1999, leading up to the resignation of Bob Quinn from the Authority.

In July 1995, the new Authority debated the merits of the recently published Green Paper on Broadcasting and in that context, Bob Quinn tabled a motion that RTÉ "cease treating children as targetable consumers, that is, as a market, and remove forthwith commercial messages from the context of children's programming."

A long discussion followed, with many members expressing their personal reservations about advertisements aimed at children but also their worries about the loss of revenue that a total ban would bring about. We returned to the issue in September, aided by a paper prepared by Director-General, Joe Barry, which set out the context of children's television in Ireland and other countries and included a survey of parental attitudes to the question of advertising.

The principal advertisers addressing Irish children through television in 1995 were Weetabix, Mattel, Lego, HB, McDonalds, Jacobs and Ribena, along with a range of less dominant advertisers of breakfast cereals, toys, games, children's publications, ice-cream, restaurants, health drinks, biscuits and confectionery. Almost all the advertising revenue for toys and games was earned on RTÉ television and this market was expected to grow annually by 7 percent – 10 percent. It was immediately clear that a ban on advertising aimed at children would be increasingly ineffective in achieving its goal if advertising were to switch from RTÉ to the other channels which could be accessed by increasing numbers of children — UTV, Channel 4, Sky One, the Children's Channel and MTV – whose codes of practice were less restrictive than RTÉ's existing practice. Moreover, audience research data on children's viewing habits showed that the majority of their viewing takes place outside the traditional children's timeslot of 2 – 6 p.m. In April 1995, 93 percent of children's viewing on all stations took place outside children's time. Even with a ban on advertising in children's time, there is no doubt that children would be exposed to a large amount of advertising at other times on RTÉ and other channels. Only an agreed policy among all broadcasters to reduce advertising, or the imposition of a ban at EU level, would produce the desired result to preventing access by advertisers to children. A go-it-alone policy, however, would have the effect of minimally reducing children's advertising while at the same time expanding a market for RTÉ's competitors. Given the perilous state of RTÉ's finances, this would inevitably have an impact on levels of programming and therefore employment at the national broadcasting station.

Bob Quinn's motion was proposed again but there was no seconder and the motion lapsed. The Authority adopted instead a set of measures proposed by the Director-General that was aimed at restricting, but not banning, advertising. The new policy included the following:

(a) No commercial break to be permitted immediately before, during or immediately after any programme aimed at pre-school children.

(b) Sponsorship to be withdrawn from all children's programmes.

(c) Commercial breaks in children's programmes to be reduced to a maximum of two in any hour, with a minimum of twenty minutes between breaks.

(d) Short public service "infomercials" to be included in commercial breaks with the aim of giving children some awareness of how advertising works, in order to moderate their expectations of material goods and to support the relation-ship between parents and children in making consumer decisions.

These measures would be monitored and reconsidered within two years. The thinking behind (a) was that since research in child psychology showed clearly that pre-school children were not yet cognitively equipped to understand the persuasive intent of advertising, the traditional assumption of "caveat emptor" should not be applied in their case. There was a clear majority on the Authority generally sympathetic to Bob Quinn's sentiments about advertising but unwilling to adopt an outright ban. We also considered, but did not impose, a moratorium on advertising in the pre-Christmas season and there was plenty of comment on Gay Byrne's Special Late Late Show devoted to toys, particularly on its proclivity to promote expensive toys and increase "pester power" directed at parents. When all the dust settled on this debate, however, it was frustrating to realise that the move to inject a stronger public service spirit into television advertisers access to children generated very little positive press reaction. Such support from other media might translate into stronger public support for a badly needed increase in the licence fee and less reliance on commercial revenue. Several advertising industry voices, including the Institute of Advertising Practitioners of Ireland and the British Toy and Hobby Association, were emphatically hostile to the new policy and this dominated and framed press reaction. They articulated their "disquiet" at what the RTÉ Authority was doing, warning of "a major crisis of confidence" in RTÉ's relationship with the advertising industry in the future. Advertisers' main goal, of course, is to increase, not diminish, the opportunities to reach audiences. RTÉ's limit of six minutes of commercial airtime is regarded by the advertising industry as too restrictive (it is far less than the minutage allowed on RTÉ's Irish and UK competitors, both terrestrial and satellite channels).

A review of this new RTÉ policy in 1997 showed that it led to a 37 percent reduction in advertising in the traditional children's time, representing a drop of £1.2 million revenue on the previous year, though overall television revenue grew by 5 percent. But audience fragmentation had also advanced, especially among children, and it was obvious that if RTÉ's appeal to children diminishes as the overall television environment gets more competitive, so does its relevance to advertisers. With multi-channel homes representing 70 percent of total homes at that time, the ability of RTÉ unilaterally to influence what Irish children watch is declining. Total multi-channel audience share for the 2 – 6 p.m. period in 1996 was divided as follows:

RTÉ Network Two	21 percent
RTÉ 1	07 percent
The Children's Channel	16 percent
BBC 1	13 percent
BBC 2	06 percent
UTV	12 percent
Sky	07 percent
Channel 4	07 percent
Others	11 percent

As RTÉ's finances declined still further in the late 1990s, its ability to manoeuvre around a children's policy inspired by public service values but likely to generate a negative financial impact, was severely curtailed.

Should RTÉ still bite the bullet and adopt more radical proposals on advertising, no matter how rapidly its financial situation was deteriorating? Bob Quinn returned to the fray at the end of Joe Barry's trial period for the new policy. The Director-General's chair by this time (April 1997) was occupied by Bob Collins, who himself had worked on the new children's policy eighteen months previously.

Bob Quinn now linked toy advertising with the deplorable sweat shop conditions in Asian countries where toys were manufactured for the large Western toy companies. It was a sordid business, he argued – very low wages and very poor working conditions – and RTÉ was colluding with it by continuing to advertise toys in a process he called "imaginative paedophilia". This time, there was less sympathy among Authority colleagues, partly because of reactions to Bob Quinn's deliberate raising of the emotional temperature. "Were we all paedophiles? Had the whole Authority realised the vague immensities in which they were involved, followed the Chairman's lead and gone native?"[73]

In fairness to the Authority, several opinions were articulated which deserved a listening. Firstly, many other products, including especially clothes and food, are produced in sweatshop conditions. For the sake of consistency, advertising for these too would need to be banned. Secondly, should only children be protected from advertisements for such products and how late in the evening should a ban exist, in a family viewing environment, where adults and children together watch television up to 9 p.m.? Could RTÉ survive a cutback of such magnitude in the advertising of all products produced in appalling conditions? And would such an act of financial hara-kiri actually achieve much, beyond making a friendly but ineffectual gesture towards ending sweatshop conditions? A dominant position among Authority members was deeply sceptical of "gesture politics," but advocated a stronger role for RTÉ in public consciousness raising through its radio and television programming, so that it would converge with similar efforts being made by development agencies like Trocaire and the Trade Union Movement to expose sweatshop conditions.

Bob Quinn returned once more to the question of children in advertising early in 1999, noting the tension building in the EU legal system between the major European advertisers and the Governments of Sweden and Greece, because of the limits they imposed on television advertising. He was appealing for further action to be taken, going beyond the changes made in 1996, to eliminate advertising aimed at children. The Authority, he urged, should assert that RTÉ was not simply a moneymaking activity and had responsibilities to children.

But little had changed in our debate on the Authority. It was still true that children see advertisements wherever they watch television, with the exception of the two BBC channels that carry no advertising. And children see advertisements whenever they watch television. Our audience research showed that 33 percent of children watched Network Two up to 7 p.m., 23 percent up to 9 p.m. and 15 percent from 9 p.m. onwards. The problem was that when RTÉ was established after a decade-long debate in the de Valera and Lemass Cabinets of the 1950s, it was decided against strong arguments from the Department of Finance that Ireland could not afford a broadcasting system funded like the BBC, that it would have to be dual-funded, by licence fee and advertising.[74] And there was obviously no political will now, forty years later, to emulate the BBC by abolishing advertising and tripling the licence fee to maintain current levels of funding.

So what Bob Quinn was refusing to accept was that as long as advertising remains part of the process by which television is funded, not only in Ireland but also in the UK (BBC excepted) and in the global channels now steadily increasing their share of the Irish child audience, then children will continue to be exposed to commercial messages. To continue to rail against this was Quixotic, or as

Bob Quinn put it himself, "baying at the moon."[75] There are many people in RTÉ who deplore the commercialisation of television but who have to get on with the job of providing television programmes within a system that is highly commercial or else leave the organisation and get involved in work that produces lower levels of cognitive dissonance.

Bob Quinn was also refusing to accept that beyond advertising, the very activity of watching television programmes generally, with their steady portrayal of lifestyles and attitudes to personal possessions embedded in the seductive values of consumer capitalism, is capable of generating acquisitive desires and consumer demands for material goods. Consumerist values saturate the life-world of children as well as adults, in the totality of television they watch and beyond television in all the other manifestations of consumer capitalism. Removing advertising from television would do very little to change this. The loss of even four million pounds, which was then the advertising revenue generated by Network Two between 3 and 6 p.m., would have had a major detrimental impact on television schedules and would have reduced still further the resources RTÉ needed to make improvements in children's programmes.

Bob Quinn's best argument actually was the link he emphasised between the marketing of goods in the Western world and the appalling conditions under which many of these goods are produced. Currently, a shirt that sells in Dublin for fifty euro is produced by a worker that is paid five cent in Bangladesh. There the official minimum wage of seventeen euro a month is ignored by local employers on contract to Western companies that have a global reach into every market they target and an enormous power to market their brand. Basic safety standards are also often ignored, with catastrophic consequences for the life and health of workers. Other Western companies contract their manufacturing activities to factories that operate in South China within a few hundred miles of Hong Kong, fortified like garrisons by armed guards behind high fences, who turn away journalists curious about allegations that the workers inside live lives little different from slaves. The situation in Burma is no better. Pharmaceutical companies engage in biopiracy in developing countries, acquiring legal ownership of natural medicines that have been used by local communities for centuries. Other companies make huge profits by patenting anti-AIDS drugs and pricing them out of the reach of the most poverty-stricken areas of the world, where AIDS flourishes.

Much of this misery is facilitated by the emergence of global policy-makers, like the World Trade Organisation, that have no democratic accountability, and international agreements structured to help the wealthy minorities in the world's population at the expense of the poor majority, like the Trade Related Intellectual Property Agreement. Indeed, it was one of these Agreements, the North American Free Trade Agreement, which triggered the Zapatista resistance among poor peasants in Chiapas in Mexico, from which the "anti-globalisation" movement grew, aimed at highlighting the privatisation of power that lies at the heart of corporate globalisation. This form of globalisation is not constructed on the egalitarian value of fairness to the developing world, does not alleviate poverty and eschews principles of peace and justice. But inadvertently, it is producing a countervailing civil society movement around the world to raise the ethical issue: what kind of globalisation should we have? Should it, for instance, be a "globalisation from below", which would harmonise workers' rights across every continent, not just in Europe and North America?

The issues raised in the debate about egalitarian globalisation are much larger than Irish broadcasting and the solutions are more far reaching than any simplistic belief that improvement will come if RTÉ eliminates access to its audiences by advertisers. To most of his colleagues on the RTÉ Authority, Bob Quinn's insistence on going in this direction became ever more quixotic, time wasting and obstructive.

His other set of arguments concentrated on the notion that advertising was harmful to children. These also failed to convince because they were high on emotion but low on evidence. Child targeted commercials were, quite simply, "evil". Analogies were made with the sexual abuse of children in institutions, paedophilia, Victorians' turning infants into chimney sweeps and mine workers, child slave labour and so on. Most of the members of the RTÉ Authority did not like the idea of advertising aimed at children and in the ideal world, wished that RTÉ could operate like the BBC. This was a fantasy that could never be actualised in a small country like Ireland, with one-thirtieth of the public funding the BBC could access. But the Authority did not believe that advertising was "evil" and no research evidence was presented that would change the Authority's mind.

IMPACT OF ADVERTISING

It is worth reviewing here briefly the academic research which examines the impact advertising has on children. A great deal of research has been conducted, mostly in the US in the 1970s and 1980s, stimulated by the realisation that the standards of production in television commercials are generally equal to or better than those applied in programme production, highly attractive visually and skilfully worded and musically scored. Major questions arise about these sophisticated, persuasive messages. How are children affected emotionally, cognitively or behaviourally by them? To what extent do commercials lead children to pressure parents into buying products unnecessarily, causing conflict within families, and to what extent are they socialised into over-materialistic habits?

Most research now steers clear of a simple, direct, uniform, cause-effect relationship between message and behaviour, though this was the dominant approach in research up to the 1940s. This early twentieth-century "magic bullet" or "hypodermic syringe" approach ignored children's ability to evaluate and cognitively process both commercials and programmes before they come to believe their appeal and act on them. Separate subsections of the information processing involved need exploration. Are children aware of advertising as distinct from programmes, even when the same host or the same characters appear in both programmes and commercials? Do children understand the persuasive intent of advertising and at what age? Do they remember and then believe what advertising tries to tell them? Do they respond by wanting the products that are being promoted to them? How do such factors as age, gender, social class and family communication patterns impinge on these responses?

Research evidence confirms that very young children usually have difficulty in defining the nature of advertisements and distinguishing between programme and commercial message. This conclusion is based not only on youngsters' personal accounts but also on monitoring levels of visual attention during viewing.[76] This is a general age-related finding. There is consistent evidence that younger children, below the age of six, do not understand the persuasive intent of advertisements and are more likely than older children to regard their claims as truthful and be more vulnerable to the influence of advertisements, while British research suggests that girls are a little better than boys at understanding that the main purpose of advertising is to sell something.[77] The general thrust of the conclusions in these and other research projects formed the basis for the RTÉ policy put in place in 1996, relating to the "caveat emptor" principle already discussed. Variations in response will be found among children, depending on the amount of visual scene changing used, including action and characters, changes in the amplitude of the soundtrack, such as lively music, unusual voices, sound effects, laughter, use of women's and children's voices. Tempo of editing, such as rapid cutting between camera shots, or zooming in and out of close-ups, can also be significant.

Other research notes that by five years of age, children can consistently distinguish advertisements from programmes,[78] while research that does not rely on children's verbal responses suggests that children as young as three know the difference between programmes and advertisements.[79] Product Symbolism (for example, the ability of children to describe the kind of child they think is likely to own certain products) tends to be stronger in girls than in boys and is better developed in middle-class children. After the age of nine, children grow in their understanding of humour and ambiguity in advertising.

Does television advertising affect children's purchasing of goods? Academic research is ambiguous on this. There is some indication that children's requests for products they see advertised can result in conflict within families, especially where children are heavy viewers of television, but this is reduced if parents discuss television and advertising with them and involve them in family purchasing decisions. Choice of methodology in studying children and families must also be considered when evaluating findings. Studies using an experimental methodology suggest that the impact of advertising is considerable, whereas use of survey research usually indicates that advertising effects operate at a fairly low level.[80] This is because experimental research is generally limited to measuring short-term effects that take place immediately after exposure to advertising and does not explore any of the processes that mediate between watching television and eventual product purchase. Because of the necessarily artificial environment of experimental research, it replicates very poorly the "real world" activity of television viewing and consumer behaviour and thus has limited external validity.

Survey research, on the other hand, uses correlational data (for example, on the relationship between television viewing and consumer purchasing) but is typically weak at attributing causality or assessing the direction of cause – effect relationships between viewing and purchasing. Does heavy viewing of commercial messages cause an increase in purchasing behaviour, or could it be that people that are heavy consumers are attracted in that direction by other forces, not part of this research design, which also induces them to pay particular attention to advertising? Similar problems of causality also appear in research into television and violence. Survey researchers generally highlight a range of factors influencing decisions to buy, including consumer's own personality characteristics, ability to weigh up different sources of information about different brands, family background, current fashions and pressure from peers to conform to trends, as well as levels of disposable income. They stress that the effects of advertising are mediated by styles of parental discipline, how members of a family interact with one another and whether parents socialise children to develop "resistance" to commercial persuasion.

A great deal of American research has focused on the impact of television generally, programming as well as advertising, on children's health and their ability to stay healthy. This is a concern that is only beginning to be articulated in Ireland. If lifestyle plays a prominent role in chronic illnesses, such as stroke, high blood pressure and heart disease, and in other problems such as obesity and tooth decay, media influence on nutrition and dietary patterns, smoking and alcohol consumption needs to be placed on the public and policy agenda.[81] These concerns go beyond advertising. George Gerbner has produced long-term studies about how American television depicts the world and how it cultivates an effect on different audiences which "mainstreams" them into a television-centred world view.[82] One study, for example, shows how American prime time drama depicts three-quarters of all characters eating or drinking, or talking about doing so. These behaviours occurred on average nine times per hour. Snacking behaviour was found to be particularly frequent on children's programmes, where regular meals were seldom depicted and snacks most often comprised high calorie, high fat food, yet young people were rarely depicted as obese. In a great deal of social scientific research, however, it has proven difficult to produce research evidence that singles out the specific influence of television from other factors in the home and social environment.

It is difficult to justify, from research evidence alone, a ban on advertising as the sole solution to many of the worries about the impact of television that have been articulated over the years. This is not to say that we should have no concerns about the impact of advertising. There is close to a consensus in academic research that advertising does not directly influence its audience, but also that indirect influences are very difficult to prove with empirical evidence. There is therefore always a place for social norms, levels of acceptance specific to particular societies, lines drawn in the sand beyond which a dominant social viewpoint does not want advertisers to go. Of particular interest is the socially consensual notion of "immorality" applied to specific techniques to sell goods. Explicit sex scenes involving adolescents probably fall into this category. So would the famous commercial for Pirelli tyres, where the male protagonist sets out on a journey in his car unaware that the woman in his life had tampered with the breaks: thanks to Pirelli tyres, he survives her murder attempt. As audiences grow accustomed to the style of advertising, do they become less aware of its gradual influence on their sense of right and wrong? While using dramatisations of immorality to sell goods, are advertisers also selling the immorality?[83] And then there is the very large question of the role of advertising as ideology, subtly infusing every corner of the culture with a "common-sense" that legitimises the dominance in contemporary life of consumerist values, quietly and insistently consolidating a hegemonic belief in "the magic of the market" and the attractions of closer integration into a global, capitalist economy and culture, with all the dangers to democratic politics that can flow from this.[84]

PROGRAMMING

The RTÉ Authority of 1995-2000 spent a considerable amount of time discussing advertising aimed at children and to some extent this displaced discussion of children's programmes. The findings of Blumler and Biltereyst's research (already discussed) alerted us to the extent to which RTÉ was seriously exposed to fallout from the globalisation of children's television. In the middle of 1999, we focused on the problems and began to move towards some solutions within the budget constraints of that time. Children's output had been under pressure right across Europe for most of the 1990s. There was a growth in output but not in local production capacity. Resources for children's programmes had decreased as public broadcasters were forced by new competition to invest more heavily in prime time programming. This meant for children a marked shift from domestic production to acquisition of content produced for a global market, particularly animation. The following table shows the hours produced in RTÉ's young people's programmes department and direct programme costs (excluding cost of facilities) from 1988 to 1998. The significant increases from 1995 to 1997 reflect the development of "The Morbegs" for young children and Finbarr's Class, a drama series for adolescents

Year	Hours	Cost (£)
1988	381.25	664,840
1989	220.75	609,440
1990	213.55	619,159
1991	189.75	555,388
1992	182.00	621,127
1993	157.75	591,185
1994	170.25	817,472
1995	155.00	1,161,782
1996	161.50	1,259,271
1997	198.70	1,305,131
1998	143.08	1,140,894

The most remarkable trend here is the drop in production from 381 hours in 1988 to 143 hours in 1998, a plunge of 38 percent. Behind these figures should be read not only the globalising pressures referred to, which had a massive impact on most other European public service broadcasters, but also local pressures, including (a) the capping of RTÉ's income in 1990 by then Minister Ray Burke; (b) pressure on RTÉ to produce 365 hours a year of Irish-language programming for the new channel TG4 from 1996; (c) anticipation of the launch of TV3 in 1998 and serious inflation in the cost of acquiring rights to sports and other programming.

Throughout this period, most children had access to other channels, especially BBC and ITV, which could afford a substantial output of children's programming in news, drama and documentary. By the end of the nineties, access to multichannel TV had increased from 66 percent of households in 1990 to 73 percent. The number of homes with VCRs doubled and access to satellite increased from 35 percent in 1990 to 54 percent. Homes with more than one TV set had already trebled. MTV could now be accessed in a third of Irish homes. The Children's Channel, then Nickelodeon that replaced it 1998, was available in a quarter of Irish homes. Audience figures told a similar tale. RTÉ's combined national children's share in the afternoon declined from 69 percent in 1990 to 51 percent eight years later, as the global channel Nickelodeon grew in popularity to reach a share of 20 percent of the multichannel audience.

Children's viewing taste was also changing with the growing popularity of programmes produced for older audiences now attracting more young children. It was a little surprising in 1998 to note that the highest rated programme on Network Two for children was an episode of Australian teen soap opera "Home and Away", followed by an episode of "Friends", a serial and a series which find their core audience in people who have long since left childhood. These viewing patterns reflect the changing tastes of young people in Ireland and a growing convergence with styles of television viewing in the US, where children and adolescents have numerous opportunities for exposure to sexual themes in the media. Indeed, the effects of sexual content on children is now emerging as a major theme in media research.[85]

The problem in RTÉ, then and now, is that resources are not sufficient to yield the variety of programming that is needed by children. Children's needs have not represented a significant element in the Independent Production Unit's commissioning decisions, though some material was commissioned for inclusion in the series "The Morbegs" in the mid-1990s. The vast bulk of the output for children is provided by Programme Acquisitions, and it is fortuitous that Dermot Horan, Head of this Department, was sensitised to the range of issues affecting children by his previous experience as Head of Young People's Programmes. The goal now needs to be to reverse the trend of the 1990s which saw a big increase in children's programmes acquired from other countries and a decrease in home production. Greater diversity of programme types is needed, including a regular news service tailored to children's needs, to expand their awareness of the country and the world they inhabit. Closer collaboration with TG4 and with other broadcasters in the EBU would help to improve the situation by providing a greater range of quality programming in the schedule.

An obvious partial solution to the problem of the deficit of home production for children was to ensure that all the income from advertising aimed at children could be invested in producing programmes for them. But the deterioration in RTÉ's finances at the end of the 1990s would not allow even this modest adjustment. Increasing competition from other broadcasters, detailed elsewhere in this book, have led to the transfer of resources slowly but surely into adult prime time programming. How were these externally caused pressures now to be reversed? We decided in July 1999 that for the next three years, the budget for children's programmes would be increased by £1 million by transferring resources within the television division and that some rearrangement of staffing would occur so that overall responsibility for all children's output could become more centralised. (At that time, decisions about programmes for children were being handled across a number of Departments, including Variety and Young People, Presentation, Acquisitions and the IPU). Children's needs would also in future have a more structured place in independently produced programmes and the News Division would devise a way to produce some level of regular news content specifically tailored for children. A Programme Development Fund of £25 million – £5 million per annum over five years – would be established with a portion of the proceeds from the sale of Cablelink and this fund would be used to improve programmes for children especially in drama, along with improvements in other parts of the TV and radio schedules, particularly in drama and documentary.

It is difficult not to be pessimistic in assessing the real possibilities of improving children's TV in Ireland. RTÉ cannot afford to make further cuts in advertising aimed at children, even if it were generally agreed that it should. Until recently, it had very little room within its current funding to make significant changes to programming. The Programme Development Fund is a limited initiative and is not resourced from current funding. The reduction of RTÉ staffing means that fewer people are available to make improvements, such as the creation of a news service for children, though efforts are now under way to produce news tailored to children's needs. The obvious solution is a political one – appropriate increases and index-linking of the licence fee, tied to specific programming commitments. With the substantial fee increase approved in late 2002 and the response of RTÉ in the form of its publication of a "Statement of

Commitments" in May 2003, there are now hopeful signs that more resources can be provided for children's television.

The political culture in Ireland has never shown much interest in the welfare of broadcasting for children. This is in sharp contrast to other parts of Europe, especially Scandinavia, where control of advertising is stronger, funding of public service broadcasting is more robust and interest in broadcasting for children is keener. Sweden typifies this difference with its clear political will to improve the provisions for children in the Television Without Frontiers Directive currently under review by the European Commission. There are signs in fact, that the EU is seriously reviewing the advertising industry's power to self-regulate, especially in marketing to children. This in turn has led advertisers to prove to the EU that they are capable of acting responsibly, particularly in drink advertising and advertising aimed at children. One initiative is the Media Smart television campaign in Britain funded by advertisers, including global toy manufacturer Hasbro and the British Advertising Association. The Media Smart campaign will help children to deconstruct advertising and look beyond the hype of marketing strategies, using experience gained in a Canadian campaign which urges children, through a mixture of television "infomercials", educational material for schools and Internet activity, to "watch carefully, think critically and navigate safely".

Political interest in both the protection of children from the harmful effects of television content and the provision of better programming doesn't exist in a vacuum. In my five years as Chairman of RTÉ, at the receiving end of a constant stream of feedback about RTÉ output from a great range of Irish organisations and individuals, I was conscious of a huge lack of a civil society presence in Ireland that would speak up for children. This does exist in some other countries, including the US, where organised pressure on Congress from parents and teachers led to the passing of the Children's Television Act of 1996 (though broadcasters moved immediately to find ways around its weakest directives), and the UK, where The Voice of the Listener and Viewer regularly gets the attention of broadcasters and Government ministers. Certainly, I see little pressure from parents and teachers in Ireland that could build steadily into a powerful lobbying organisation for the betterment of television for children.

There is, of course, a need to go beyond the periodic battles over the licence fee. There is increasing pressure on public service broadcasters to remain true to their mandate to provide a comprehensive service to all children on a free to air basis. Competition is growing in the private sector, in the form of new childrens' channels based in the US, such as Nick Junior, Noggin, Playhouse Disney and HBO Family, all of which have developed "early learning" streams for pre-school children. These channels appropriate the very terms that once defined public service media uniquely – non commercial and educational – and use web sites to integrate games, creative tools and activities designed to stimulate learning, with their television content. But they have two disadvantages from the Irish point of view: they will never be available to all children, free to air, and they will not provide recognisably Irish content with which Irish children can identify. The ideal development is an RTÉ children's channel available on all digital platforms, which allows children to interact with content in new ways and to communicate, build, simulate or play in ways that were never possible with analogue television.

Competing against the American-based global children's channels is possible but it requires greater resources than are currently made available in Ireland. One of the great European success stories is the joint ARD / ZDF Kinderkanal launched in 1997, at a time when the public broadcasters' share of the child audience had shrunk to 20 percent in the face of intense German commercial television competition, especially from Leo Kirch, and formidable digital expansion plans among the main global television groups with an eye on the large German market: Disney, Nickelodeon / Viacom, Fox / Murdoch and Time Warner / Turner. Kinderkanal is now firmly established among German children, under the slogan "no violence, no advertisements, free after three". ARD and ZDF have stopped showing children's programmes during the week and consolidated their efforts in the new channel, which broadcasts from 8 a.m. to 7 p.m. It is financed by the licence fee and emphasises age specific programmes and a wide diversity of genres, topics and production styles, including news and current affairs and children's feature films. Cartoons make up less than 30 percent of the schedule. Private broadcasters in Germany took an action against the public broadcasters in the Federal Court of Justice, claiming unfair competition, but then abandoned the action to avoid the risk of protests from German parents. Soon after, Nickelodeon bowed to the inevitable and pulled out of the German market. This inspires a fantasy for Ireland: a publicly funded, advertising free, dedicated digital channel for all children, showing less than 30 percent cartoons.

Meanwhile, the debate about the effects of a market obsessed culture on children has moved on beyond television advertising to include the "branding" of adolescents by major corporations and industries, despite the potential consequences for self-esteem and physical health. New sites of teen branding in the US include the teen movie and magazine, youth literature, school social events, video games, extreme sports and the dressing room.[86] It can also include the classroom and total school environment, as programmes like Channel 1 (mandatory, sponsored television newscasts and marketing beamed into American classrooms) augment moves by desperate school officials, unable to pay for textbooks and teachers, to give Coca Cola and McDonalds direct entry to their schools. The founder of Channel 1 is also CEO of Edison Schools Inc., a for-profit publicly traded New York-based company that operates more than 133 public schools in 22 States. This experiment in privatising schools is attracting corporate investors interested in reaching a child and teen market.

Advertisements in teen girls' magazines now promote breast enhancement, exploiting youth anxieties about body image already raised in the fashion industry. A recent poll in *Seventeen* Magazine found that 25 percent of respondents had considered liposuction, a tummy tuck or breast augmentation, a poll that in effect exploited its impressionable readers' anxieties, instead of helping to diminish them, through analysis and comment. Film plots and product placement in films also attack children's self esteem by exclusively celebrating personal popularity as a prime value for children, emphasising the role of branded products in maintaining their social class.

Where adolescent films from Hollywood in the 1980s depicted freaks and losers as heroes and addressed their audiences as united youth against self interested mainstream authority, more recent Hollywood movies celebrate popularity and status quo. Participating in the world is subtly but powerfully identified with consuming corporate products. Recent concerns about children and cigarette smoking in Ireland also highlight the role of branding in the tobacco industry. Cigarette advertising is not designed to convey information about the physical characteristics of smoking but to create a fantasy of sophistication, pleasure and social success. This becomes the "personality" of both the cigarette and those who smoke it, providing emotional security, however illusory, for young people precariously situated in that not-so-safe, psycho-dynamically incomplete world of adolescence, that hormonally charged transition phase that hovers between childhood and adulthood.

7 THE DIFFICULT BIRTH OF IRISH LANGUAGE TELEVISION

Ireland's first Irish-language station TnaG (now TG4) came on air at Hallowe'en 1996 with a spectacular display of fireworks and bonfires that lit up the windswept terrain outside the studios in Baile na hAbhann, Connemara. The exuberant celebrations of the launch unashamedly made the visual link with the early winter Celtic festival of Samhain, traditionally associated with fire. To those of us present for the celebration in County Galway, it was unbelievable that after so many years of bitter argument about our native language and its role in radio and television, we were now raising the champagne glasses with smiling faces and wishing the new television service a long and happy life. As I listened to the various messages of goodwill being broadcast by a succession of politicians and dignitaries, including President Mary Robinson (using the theme of fire herself in her address to the people of Ireland), I thought about my predecessor Eamonn Andrews, first Chairman of the RTÉ Authority, and the bitter ironies woven into our long and painful relationship with Irish in modern times.

Andrews resigned from his post in 1966 because of irreconcilable tensions on the RTÉ Authority regarding the place of Irish in the new channel's television schedules. He believed the Irish language was being promoted too zealously by its supporters and that his colleagues in RTÉ were pursuing a language policy in broadcasting which would alienate Irish audiences and send them scrambling for cross channel television from Britain. And here we were now, thirty years later, proudly announcing that the new television channel would provide "suil eile", a different vision, an alternative view, through a minority language. But the mood of celebration in Connemara that night belied the bitter words that the Irish language could still elicit from supporters and opponents alike as it moved from its nineteenth-century association with poverty, cultural inferiority and economic depression in post-Famine Ireland to take its place at the centre of a new mood of self confidence in the Celtic Tiger economy. Before considering in detail the struggle to establish TG4, let's consider the position of Irish itself in a global context.

One of the factors which facilitated the launch of TG4 after a long period of gestation was the fact that although actual levels of linguistic competence and use of Irish in everyday life is relatively low compared to the dominant language, positive attitudes to Irish as an ethnic marker have remained high for several decades. This is remarkable, given its close geographical relationship with English. Irish shares with thousands of other smaller languages among the world's overall estimated five thousand languages its exposure to English, the dominant language which occupies a central position within the global linguistic system. Geo-linguists estimate that as many as six thousand languages were wiped out since the explosive expansion of European colonialism in the sixteenth century, as people abandoned their languages and did not pass them on to their children. Unlike Dutch and Japanese, English did not lose ground after the decolonisation of its former possessions but went on, in that earlier surge of globalisation, to become second numerically to Mandarin as the world's first language. More significantly, English has also become the world's largest second language, the *linguafranca* of the other major supranational central languages – Bengali, French, German, Japanese, Spanish, Portuguese, Russian, Hindi, Arabic and Malay. These themselves play a key role as *linguafrancas* for more than half of the world's population, facilitating communication between people having different regional, national, sub-national or local languages. But English is the single most important medium of communication across these very large language groups. It occupies an unique place in the world as a super-central language, that is a central code, facilitating communication between bilingual speakers competent in their own supra-national central language and the super-central language of English.[87]

The dominant position of English is best represented in a Venn diagram which places it in the centre of a set of overlapping circles, representing a dozen or so supranational languages, each overlapping with further circles representing national or sub-national languages. This demonstrates the dynamic role played in global communication by English as the super-central language, where translation is available directly or indirectly into and out of every other language. This unique position is not occupied by Mandarin, the world's largest language, but by English, the world's largest second language and the communication code of the wealthiest global language community. Its influence spread around the world in earlier phases of globalisation – colonial trade relations, military expansions of empire, the expansion of American economic, political, military and cultural interests, the internationalisation of stock markets, currency markets and the oil industry.

Current globalisation processes are consolidating the position of English, in the computing and telecommunications industries, in the trans-border flow of scientific knowledge and especially in the expansion of the global entertainment and media sectors, where English is rapidly becoming the dominant language. The majority of internationally traded advertising, popular music, film and television originates in the Anglophone world and English-language publishing accounts for more than half the world book market. Despite experiencing persistent sizeable deficits in their overall trade balances for many years, the US, Britain and Australia produce huge surpluses in overseas trade in the global information sector. As the Anglophone world rapidly loses interest in learning second or third languages, because it has little to gain from doing so, interest in learning English elsewhere intensifies as speakers of peripheral languages are motivated to learn the one super-central language from which translation to every other language in the world is available. Of course, this often presents regional governing elites with a dilemma, because if they open their cultures widely to the language of the metropolitan centre, cultural autonomy and self-determination can be eroded, but if they refuse contact, they may be left behind in the race towards the modernisation that they desire.

In this analysis, English is destined to go on consolidating its dominant position by gaining speakers from other languages motivated to expand their communication potential in a more globalised environment. This is the geo-linguistic situation in which

Irish exists, as a very small language in a post-colonial relationship with Britain, within a nation state that is very much part of the Anglophone world and uses its unique position as the only Anglophone member of the Eurozone to attract multi-national corporate investment by utilizing its non-British Anglophone gateway relationship with the European Union.

USAGE OF IRISH

How frequently do Irish people speak Irish? One of the notoriously difficult tasks in any part of the world, but especially in bilingual areas, is to arrive at a reliable quantification of the frequency of use of a language and the levels of ability in that language. The survey of Ó Riagáin and Ó Gliasáin (1993)[88] gives the following profile: outside the Gaeltachtaí (official Irish-speaking areas), seventy to eighty percent of the population does not use Irish at all and does not interact with people who speak Irish in their presence. One in ten claims to have spoken Irish in the previous week and less than five per cent report speaking Irish frequently at home or at work or reading / writing Irish. However, attendance at leisure events where Irish is used – music, dance, sports – has doubled over the last twenty years, as has the numbers claiming reading ability. About 1.4 million people, or a third of the national population, were reported in the 1996 census to profess an ability to speak Irish, but the census gives no information on levels of actual use for everyday communication.

In his influential (and controversial) book "The Death of the Irish Language", Reg Hindley concluded that of the 58,000 people who then lived in the Gaeltachtaí, only half of these claimed to maintain Irish as a mother tongue and a majority of these do not transmit it to their children as their first language.[89] He suggested an upper limit of about 10,000 on the number of habitual native speakers living in communities with sufficient attachment to Irish to transmit it to a substantial majority of their children as the language of home and community. Many language activists contest Hindley's gloomy forecast from his 1980s fieldwork that many Gaeltacht people share grave doubts about the advisability of continuing to speak Irish. Hindley suggests that many of them may well end their lives more fluent in English than in Irish and in normal circumstances no longer using Irish. Inward migration to the Gaeltachtaí by English speakers, new marriage patterns, tourism and economic forces will undoubtedly put Irish under severe pressure as a community language in the future. But it was precisely such observations as the increasing use of English by children and young people in the Connemara, West Kerry and Donegal Gaeltachtaí that helped to fuel a media-centred view of language change and to add impetus to the campaign for more broadcasting in Irish. There is some truth to the observation that language survival or revival in other countries is influenced by the broader political context of support or indifference. Thus, it is often argued, the Welsh language grew stronger because it was a language of opposition, whereas Irish floundered because of the new state's policy of revival smothered it in bureaucrace, compulsion in the school and civil service systems and its elevation generally to "official" status. But this argument ignores the devastating impact of the British colonial project on the whole Gaelic cultural system (in law, literature, folkways, politics, education, language) since the triumph of the Tudor campaign in Ireland in the early 1600s and the almost total collapse of popular will, from the nineteenth century onwards, to pursue the recovery of the national language with vigour. It is significant, however, that the drive to create Irish-language radio and television in the twentieth century came out of an oppositional culture, this time a Gaeltacht opposition to what was perceived as East Coast indifference.

Statistics on language use, of course, do not tell the full story of people's relationship with language. The forging of a close affinity between language and national identity formed the core of the decolonisation project of the Gaelic League since its foundation in 1894. It strove to reverse the older association of Irish with backwardness, derived from the ideological codes imported from England in the high imperial era, which represented the Catholic Irish as a biologically inferior species whose nationalist ambitions had to be discredited. In his famous essay "The Necessity for de-Anglicising Ireland", Douglas Hyde argued for the need to be rid of the central Irish ambivalence of imitating England yet apparently hating it, resulting from the erosion of the Irish language over the course of the nineteenth century, which left people "ceasing to be Irish without becoming English".[90] This concern with a crisis in identity foreshadows current academic concern about psychosocial pathologies which are the legacies of colonialism, including the loss of the native language, with its implications for consciousness, creativity and identity.[91]

If use of Irish has been diminishing throughout the twentieth century, despite government attempts to revive it, positive feelings about the language have remained fairly constant. About two-thirds of respondents in polls taken in 1973, 1983 and 1993 agree with the statement "Ireland would not really be Ireland without Irish speaking people" and almost as many people agreed that "without Irish, Ireland would certainly lose its identity as a separate culture".[92] Survey evidence that a large number of people place considerable value on the symbolic role of the Irish language in ethnic and national identity corroborates Reg Hindley's observation that speaking Irish in the Gaeltacht gives many non-Gaeltacht people a sense of completeness, of oneness with Ireland's historic and cultural traditions which they cannot experience elsewhere. There is a real danger, of course, that these kinds of attitudes can lead to Irish assuming primarily a ceremonial role, as a cherished but little-used national treasure. Irish would then be on the way to becoming what Findahl[93] fears Swedish may become after another one hundred years of pressure from English, a quaint mother tongue kept in the family chest, a relic to be dusted off, polished up and displayed on national holidays and other festive occasions.

But such good will can also be used by language activists to build support for practical measures needing Government involvement, including minority-language media policy. National surveys show a substantial public opinion shift from 1973 to 1993 in favour of more state support for Irish and the belief that the government has a crucial role to play in the fortunes of the language, even if this entails increased public expenditure on language organisations, all-Irish schools, and conducting government business through Irish. Between 1973 and 1993, support for the proposition that the Government should support Irish on television grew from 66 percent to 75 percent and those who would be somewhat / very sorry if Irish were not spoken on national radio or television grew from 47 percent to 58 percent.[94]

LANGUAGE RIGHTS

It has become clear over the last two decades that the old ways in which we thought about Irish have been changing. The urge to insist on a highly prescriptive sense of Irish identity, based on intolerant and claustrophobic cultural policies, which was dominant in the first half of the last century, began to wane, as did its opposite, the inferiority complex that associated Irish with backwardness. A newer discourse began to take hold with membership of the EEC in the 1970s when Irish was granted limited official status. This was the notion of the right to communicate of linguistic minorities, given ideological and material support by the European Union when it established the European Bureau for Lesser Used Languages in 1983, as well as the MEDIA and BABEL projects which provide support for minority media, including funding for dubbing and sub-titling. The Council of Europe has also developed a charter for regional and minority languages, which encourages the creation of television channels in minority languages.

The demand for an all-Irish television channel had its roots in earlier campaigns for an Irish-language radio station, promised by various politicians since 1926, including Éamon de Valera, but not delivered until 1972. During the late 1960s demand for a radio station became more focused, fed in part by a growing interest in language rights as a spin-off to the civil rights movement and partly with frustration at the low level of Irish programming provided by RTÉ, especially on television. Cearta Shibhialta na Gaeltachta was formed in Connemara to fight for a radio station as a right. Inspired by Radio Caroline, a pirate radio station, Saor Raidió Chonamara went on air in May 1970 and within months, the Minister for the Gaeltacht, George Colley, announced that Raidió na Gaeltachta was to be established at a cost of £250,000. It came on air in April 1972.

Many of the original campaigners played key roles in the next struggle – to establish a Gaeltacht television service. Irish-language programming was one of the first casualties of the dual-funding nature of RTÉ. RTÉ's early reliance on advertising to augment a licence fee that governments were loath to increase meant that Irish-language programmes were increasingly pushed to the margins of the schedules away from prime time, where the pressure to maximise audiences was intense. The concept of TnaG evolved out of frustration with RTÉ's inability to satisfy the demand for more Irish on television. The organisation Freagra was formed to lobby for better television and members embarked on a series of direct action gestures designed to change public attitudes by calling national media attention to their demands. Their methodology included graffiti spraying, refusing to pay television licence fees, public marches, climbing the RTÉ transmitter mast in Dublin, chaining themselves to the General Post Office and breaking into the RTÉ news studios during transmission.

Coiste ar san Telefís Gaeltachta was formed in 1980, and Meitheal Oibre ar son Telefís Gaeltachta in 1987, with the aim of demonstrating via pirate television what a new service could look like. The establishment of S4C in Wales was decisive in shifting the campaign focus from demanding more Irish on existing channels to establishing a separate television station. The campaign was further energised in 1987 when a working group established by the Government reported that a separate television service was too expensive to consider but that RTÉ should provide more Irish-language programmes especially at peak time.

More programmes on RTÉ, however, was not now what Meitheal wanted, nor did the organisation believe that RTÉ could sufficiently cater specifically for Gaeltacht needs and interests. A delegation visited the Faroe Islands off the coast of Denmark to examine how a Faroese television station could provide for a tiny population of speakers on the shoestring budget of £3,000,000 start-up costs and £1,000,000 per annum running costs. As Meitheal founder, Donncha Ó hÉalaithe put it, "if a TV station could provide for 40,000 speakers, why couldn't we do likewise? This, together with the growth of multichannel and pirate links, provided us with the incentive for experimenting with a possible pirate transmission."[95] Money was quietly collected in Connemara, a transmitter was successfully installed in the hills near Rosmuc and coverage of the Oireachtas na nGael Festival, directed by Bob Quinn, was illegally beamed to homes in a twenty-mile radius, a direct riposte to the Government's television report.

Then began the extraordinary series of promises, commitments and procrastinations that marked Charles Haughey's interest in the issue of Irish- language television, as Taoiseach and as Minister for the Gaeltacht. Soon after the Connemara pirate transmission, he promised £500,000 from National Lottery funds to pilot a new channel. This never materialised. In 1988, he commissioned a report from Údarás na Gaeltachta and Stokes Kennedy Crowley accountancy firm, which recommended the establishment of a Gaeltacht based service on UHF, to be available nationally on cable and MMDS. It would need £4.5 million for start-up costs and £9.6 million for annual running costs. Campaigners living outside the Gaeltacht argued against an exclusive Gaeltacht service and a title that would reflect this exclusivity.

Another report, Telefis 92, was drawn up by Padraig Ó Muircheartaigh, former Chairman of RTÉ, and Proinsias MacAonghusa, President of Conraidh na Gaeilge, which recommended that a new service be established with headquarters in the Rathcairn Gaeltacht in County Meath. This too divided the campaigners, some like Donncha Ó hÉalaithe pointing out that Rathcairn was a tiny "invented" Gaeltacht near Dublin with very few native speakers. Its inevitable dominance by Dublin-based Gaelgoirí – producers, technicians, presenters and journalists – with their particular view of news and current affairs, would alienate the new service from natives of Kerry, Galway and Donegal Gaeltachtaí. It would become too reliant on Dublin and fail to develop a more appropriate Gaeltacht ethos and agenda. Conraidh na Gaeilge insisted on calling the new service Teilifís na Gaeilge, while the Connemara based Meitheal insisted on calling it Teilifís na Gaeltachta. A new campaigning group, Feachtas Naisiúnta Theilifíse, sidestepped the issue completely by using the initials TnaG, allowing the G to stand for whatever people wanted it to mean, Gaeilge or Gaeltachta. But they argued it should be Gaeltacht-based, though providing for all Irish speakers in the whole island of Ireland. It should initially be controlled by RTÉ and should focus primarily on the needs of children, which the group felt was the audience most deprived by RTÉ's long neglect of Irish-language programming. Feachtas proposed an initial two hours of programmes daily, with the surplus airtime being used for other programming, and that it could be funded by raising the "cap" imposed on RTÉ's advertising revenue by Ray Burke, the Minister placed at the centre of corruption charges by the Flood Tribunal for accepting bribes from Century Radio in return for curbing RTÉ's income.

Meanwhile, RTÉ itself was coming around to the idea that a separate channel was the best option, rather than attempting to increase the Irish-language output on Network Two, provided new funding was forthcoming. But although Haughey had announced at the Fianna Fáil Árd Fheis in 1991 that the new channel would be established the following year, his commitment was always questionable. There was no mention of a new channel in Ray Burke's 1990 Broadcasting Bill, which concentrated on capping RTÉ's income to help the private broadcasters. Burke preferred to regard the new channel as someone else's responsibility. Campaigners were being appeased rather than being taken seriously and doubts were being raised continually about the Government's ability, or willingness, to meet the costs required. The Haughey Government resigned in January 1992, to be replaced by a new administration led by Albert Reynolds, in which Máire Geoghegan-Quinn took over the communications portfolio. Ray Burke did not receive a ministerial post.

TEILIFIS NA GAEILGE TAKING SHAPE

The pace now quickened. RTÉ was asked to cost the new service and its former editor of An Nuacht, Padhraic Ó Ciardha, was appointed special adviser to the Minister. His report strongly advocated that TnaG be established immediately and the Minister met representatives of Feachtas Naisiúnta Teilifíse, affirming her intention to act swiftly. This Government collapsed before plans were finalised and was replaced by a Reynolds led Fianna Fáil / Labour coalition, in which

Michael D. Higgins took over responsibility for broadcasting. Higgins had a good record of supporting the television project while in Opposition and he now pushed on with implementing Ó Ciardha's plan, even retaining the RTÉ man as special adviser. The new "Programme for a Partnership Government" announced that the Government was committed to the establishment of Teilifíse na Gaeilge as a third channel with limited broadcasting hours. The start-up costs were to be provided from the accumulated surplus in excess of the "cap" which would be removed. The aim was to provide two to three hours of Irish-language broadcasting a day, with some element of subsidy for running costs from a contribution of the Lottery, the European Commission and / or the licence fee. The new channel would be headquartered in the Connemara Gaeltacht and would broadcast nationally. Initially, Irish-language programming would be provided by RTÉ and independent producers.

TnaG was now inevitable, though many disputes still lay ahead, including the question of how the new programming provided by RTÉ would be resourced. The Budget in 1993 allocated £4.5 million for TnaG's infrastructure and later that year the Broadcasting Amendment Act was passed, which was designed to undo the machinations of Ray Burke by eliminating the "cap" on RTÉ's advertising revenue. The Act also boosted the independent production sector on which TnaG would depend for much of its programming, by requiring RTÉ to move towards allocating twenty percent of its television production expenditure to independent production. Meanwhile, Údarás na Gaeltachta had initiated training schemes and disbursed grants to independent production companies setting up in the Gaeltacht regions. Telegael was the first of these and later attracted investment from RTÉ for its production and dubbing facilities in Spiddal. The ultimate aim of Údarás policy was to establish an audiovisual industry in the Gaeltacht in the belief that the single greatest influence on Gaeltacht life is the media industry, and television in particular. It established a script fund, to encourage new programme ideas, and was instrumental in persuading the European Commission to locate its Media Antennae initiative in Galway, so that this EU funding too would achieve synergies with local efforts to provide a suitable infrastructure for TnaG.

The momentum was now building steadily. Two advisory groups were set up and produced reports in 1993 which reflected a growing consensus between the different constituencies involved: RTÉ, Gaeltacht representatives, independent producers and civil servants. The Coiste Bunaithe report fleshed out the model for TnaG contained in the Programme for Government, emphasising that the new station would be mostly a publisher-broadcaster with its signal available countrywide. RTÉ's authority over TnaG was accepted in order to speed up the project but TnaG itself would have full control over its schedules, which would emphasise the needs of young audiences. The Coiste Teichniúil recommended use of a UHF transmission system and this was to cause difficulties in the future as most of the West of Ireland, including the Gaeltachtaí, had only a VHF reception capability. People who wanted to receive TnaG would have to install a UHF aerial. In 1994 RTÉ established Comhairle Teilifíse na Gaeilge to advise the Authority and in effect to take charge of the new channel as a board of directors. It set about initiating executive action on personnel, programming, scheduling, staff training and, crucially, the recruitment of a Ceannasaí, commissioning editors and other senior staff. The following year, the Government formally accepted Michael D. Higgins' plan for the station. It would be a national broadcaster rather than a Gaeltacht service. RTÉ would build the technical infrastructure and accept responsibility for the running of TnaG through the Comhairle, until such time as it could be established as an independent entity on a statutory basis. The capital cost would be met by a grant of £16.1 million and £10 million per annum would be provided by government for running costs. RTÉ would provide one hour of programming per day free of charge, and this decision too would become a source of tension between RTÉ and the Government.

Meanwhile, what of the context of public and media opinion in which these developments were taking place? Did they trigger an outpouring of national pride in the fact that an Irish-language television service, discussed and argued for since the inauguration of a mostly English-language television service in the early 1960s, was now about to become a reality? Within the corpus of supporters of broadcasting in Irish, divisions had centred on a number of areas: how to break political inertia, by legal or illegal means; whether broadcasting in Irish should be integrated into RTÉ channels as seamlessly as possible or given an independent existence, which would guarantee an alternative programming policy but risk ghettoising Irish; and whether the new channel should cater to a national audience or address a local Irish-speaking audience by being consolidated as a specifically Gaeltacht channel, onto which the rest of the country could eavesdrop if it wished.

But now a public debate much wider than these concerns erupted in the national press in the lead up to the TnaG launch date of Hallowe'en 1996. The State's policy on resourcing Irish-language initiatives generally came under scrutiny and the entire TnaG project was called into question, mainly on the basis that all previous Government initiatives on Irish had failed and that it was a waste of money to build a new television channel for the small number of people who spoke Irish. Some argued that TnaG would never appeal to a sufficiently large audience to attract advertising revenue and that it would also drain resources from RTÉ at a time when it was facing increasing threats to its income from UTV, Channel 4 and Sky.

The *Sunday Independent* was particularly hostile and encouraged from its journalists a tone of sneering and debunking that increasingly focused with personal invective on the Minister, Michael D. Higgins. TnaG was framed as a sacred cow that needed radical de-sacralisation. *Sunday Independent* columnists ranted passionately about TnaG as the personal obsession of an arrogant and undemocratic minister, who was going to press on with his project despite the opposition of an overwhelming majority of right-thinking Irish people. The people could stomach no more pandering to that failed entity, the Irish language. These themes and the vitriolic tones in which they were elaborated, chained out into the tabloid newspapers and local radio stations, constantly alert to the possibility that TnaG could diminish the national advertising pie on which they all nibbled and the possibility of being able to draw on public funding for what they saw as their own contribution to "public service broadcasting".

Michael D. Higgins hit back at his critics at the sod-turning ceremony in Connemara, where the studio was to be built, rebuking those who believed nothing creative was worth doing and who regarded broadcasting as no more than delivering a mass audience to advertisers. He defended the right of Irish speakers to have access to their language in the most powerful medium of communication available today and poured scorn on commentators who portrayed TnaG as "an extravagant personal gesture which I am pushing through in the teeth of government, political and public opposition."[96] Both RTÉ and the *Irish Times*, however, were highly supportive of TnaG in their interventions in the debate, emphasising the question of minority language and the progress on the TnaG project that preceded the intervention of Michael D. Higgins.

Almost every part of RTÉ was involved from the beginning in preparations for TnaG, but this involved an element of either pride in the achievement or gloom about the financial consequences, depending largely on people's commitment to the notion of language rights. There were worries from 1995, when TnaG seemed finally to come out of the realm of political rhetoric and take on a real budgetary and staffing existence, that the quality of independent productions in hand were not high enough and that the independent sector would need far more supervision by RTÉ than its name suggested, if it were going to produce new streams of television programming that improved on what already existed. RTÉ training was heavily involved in preparing the dozen or so production companies that would be feeding the TnaG appetite for content. A great deal of translation into Irish was achieved, including RTÉ's legal guidelines and terms of trade and an Irish glossary of new broadcasting terminology.

THE QUESTION OF RESOURCES

But behind all the activity and goodwill was a concern about who would pay for RTÉ's new commitment to TnaG, especially the 365 hours of programming it was asked to supply. The Authority raised this several times with the Department, aware of the general anticipation of Government cutbacks and of RTÉ's urgent need to inject new investment in its own TV schedules. Michael D. Higgins' declaration in the Dáil in November, that he did not intend that RTÉ's budget will be adversely affected by providing Programming for TnaG, were quoted back to him many times by the Authority. What was needed was direct Exchequer funding for new programme production or an increase in the licence fee of about £10, but this would have to be in addition to a long overdue increase for current production activities. John Sorohan, my predecessor as Chairman, insisted in his annual report for 1994 that new production for TnaG "must be supported by revenues additional to those currently available to RTÉ."[97]

Suspicions that the government was not going to advance any new funding were confirmed when Michael D. Higgins announced towards the end of 1995 that Exchequer funding was available for direct grant to TnaG itself to produce two hours a day and RTÉ would be expected to provide one hour daily from its own resources. At prices then charged to the Independent Production Unit by independent producers, this quantity of programme content for TnaG would cost RTÉ £8.7 million, an amount that the organisation could not find in its budget. The fear was that RTÉ would have to provide low quality material to TnaG, perhaps drawing heavily on its archives, and that this would be the kiss of death for the new channel. RTÉ's own finances were already deteriorating and there was no sign of a long-awaited licence fee increase, while some serious competition for RTÉ was about to begin with the coming launch of TV3 and Radio Ireland (later Today FM), the privately owned national television and radio channels.

In December 1995, Michael D. Higgins came to Montrose and had a meeting with the entire Authority. It was a tense meeting. It was clear that the Minister was encountering a lot of opposition to TnaG from several quarters, both inside and outside Cabinet. The Department of Finance, under Ruairí Quinn, regarded RTÉ as "cash rich" and had its eye on RTÉ's reserves, which were then in a healthy state. The *Irish Times* was generally supportive of TnaG, with the exception of Kevin Myers, who used a heady mixture of insult and intolerance of Irish speakers in his columns to sneer at the whole TnaG project. This sneering tone was amplified week after week by almost all writers in the *Sunday Independent*, who had no tolerance for talk about minority language rights and repeated *ad nauseum* the line that TnaG was an expensive personal gesture being insisted upon undemocratically by an arrogant minister.

The Minister was determined to see TnaG launched on his watch, because he believed in the importance of language rights that lay at the core of the argument since the 1980s and because it was now time to end the political dithering, prevaricating and posturing that characterised government interest in TnaG since the Haughey period. He told us in our Montrose meeting that now was the opportune moment for making TnaG a reality. It might not come again if it was not grasped firmly now. As an Authority, we all agreed with him. The only problem was finding the resources. He promised that he would work on a licence fee increase and on indexing the licence fee to the cost of living, a move for which RTÉ had been lobbying for some time. This lobbying had been intensified especially since inflation in broadcasting costs began to accelerate dramatically with the arrival of new broadcasters who bid up the cost of access to sports rights and to the most attractive imported fiction. Any increase that would be granted, however, the Minister insisted should not be seen as linked to TnaG, as this would be very damaging to it and would further influence media criticism of the entire project.

I agreed fully with this analysis, as did my colleagues. It was better to build a house now, even if we didn't yet have, in Michael D's words, the money for carpets and curtains. There was a danger that shoddy work would be the order of the day, at every level of preparation for TnaG, but in fact the Executive Board and all other parts of RTÉ – Engineering, Television Production, Newsroom, Public Affairs, Finance, Personnel and other support areas – swung in behind the project with tremendous zeal, as the realisation sank in that the time had come for TnaG, and RTÉ's reputation would be on the line. Organisational pride began to build solidly behind this huge challenge. But it was clear to me how vulnerable many projects of national importance can be while they are in gestation, how easy it is for human willpower to be sapped, especially by politicians' estimates of what public perceptions may be. As Chairman, I encountered no opposition to TnaG from any group in the country except for a handful of journalists, unable to lay aside old prejudices about Irish inherited from previous generations, who had already sold out to a lazy, opinionated way of reporting the nation and the world to their readers, motivated by the desire to find controversy and negativity purely for their own sake, in the belief that such writing sells newspapers. John Pilger calls this "anti-journalism."[98] Its main home in Ireland was the *Sunday Independent*, whose columnists poured out their scorn week after week for this Minister's attempt to redress the neglect of Irish speakers that had preceded his arrival in Government. The danger was that back-benchers, civil servants and others in the political system would slowly come to the conclusion that the constant carping of a handful of hacks somehow reflected public opinion like a barometer, or stood in for it.

After that crucial December 1995 meeting with the Minister, I wrote immediately to Comhairle Theilifís na Gaeilge, the *de facto* Board of Directors of the new channel, to point out on the one hand the gloomy financial situation and the lack of any Government commitment to fund what RTÉ would contribute to it, but also to underline the genuine enthusiasm in RTÉ for doing its very best to prepare for a successful launch. This triggered, unwittingly, what could have been a major rift between RTÉ and TnaG. My downbeat analysis of what could be achieved in programme production without a licence-fee increase produced a heated discussion in the Comhairle, which now began to doubt RTÉ's commitment to the whole project.

We quickly called a meeting to clear the air and clarify all misunderstandings: Joe Barry, Bob Collins and I met with Cathal Goan and Brian MacAongusa of TnaG. I explained that the Minister gave RTÉ no comfort at all in relation to adequacy of funding for TnaG. But had there not been a promise of a licence-fee increase, they asked. Immediately I could see a peculiar RTÉ problem raise its head, one that I would have to deal with several times in the years ahead: the difficulty of maintaining confidentiality in Boardroom discussions in Montrose. I explained that there was a possibility of a licence-fee increase but that it would be earmarked for improving RTÉ programmes generally. While it could not be explicitly earmarked for TnaG, it would of course help us to provide a top quality programme stream to the TnaG schedule. Thus reassured, we parted on good terms, agreeing that the Authority and the full Comhairle should meet soon, to allay any further misunderstandings and to focus completely on the launch date of Hallowe'en, now only nine months away. But I was left with the peculiar suspicion that there was mischief-making in operation, in parts of the Dublin media environment, and this could destroy the atmosphere of trust that was needed to see TnaG successfully launched.

This suspicion was reinforced a few days later when I took a call from Michael D. Higgins while I was in London, preparing for a round of visits to the BBC and Channel Four. The Minister was angry that continuing press criticism of him now seemed to be nourished from within RTÉ itself, as some members of staff were spreading stories about him interfering inappropriately in Authority decisions about TnaG. He let me know in no uncertain terms that if RTÉ didn't have the will to reverse its shameful historical pattern of neglect of the Irish language, he would find some other means to channel the proceeds of an increase in the licence fee to TnaG. On my return from London, I took the opportunity of a letter to the *Irish Times* to put on public record my assertion that the RTÉ Authority functioned independently of politics, that in my time as Chairman there had never been any interference in programme content or programme policy from any Government Minister, that the Authority was committed fully to the successful launch of TnaG by providing the very best programming we possibly could.[99] The Minister followed up with a letter to me expressing his concern about the rumours circulating regarding the programmes RTÉ would provide. These rumours suggested that not only had he approved the nature and content of the programmes, but also that he accepted that programmes of a relatively low standard would be provided and that the Nuacht (News) service would have to be based in Dublin. He pointed out that " it is not my function (nor indeed the function of any Minister) to become involved in detailed programme arrangements." He went on to say that he found my letter to the *Irish Times* "most helpful in this unfortunate climate of rumour and counter-rumour."

Could we all keep our nerve in the run-up to Hallowe'en? Could we calmly prevail of mischief-makers and rumour-mongers sowing seeds of doubt and the continuing frontal attack from the *Sunday Independent*?

The Department of Finance was inexplicably slow in allowing RTÉ to advertise for new positions, but key appointments in TnaG were being made – including Neasa Ni Chinneide as Head of Irish Language Programmes and Michael Lally as Head of Nuacht – and staff training was getting under way. This yielded the multi-skilling, much derided in traditional broadcasting organisations and trade unions, which lay at the core of TnaG's success, as a mostly young staff was trained across a wide range of new broadcasting technologies and could accomplish on their own production tasks which would necessitate involvement by several people in traditional broadcasting environments. In October, the Minister's official letter arrived, formally allowing broadcasting to take place, up to a maximum of 4,290 hours (and a minimum of 730 hours) in the first year of operation. On Hallowe'en night, TnaG came on air and reached 480,000 viewers, launched from a marquee erected beside the new studio building on a rocky promontory in Baile na hAbhain in Connemara, accompanied by the sound of Celtic drumming and the mother of all firework displays. Everyone involved knew it was never going to be easy to launch T na G, not just because of resource limitations but because of a hostile ideological environment, policed by a small number of commentators struggling to be heard above the message from opinion polls showing broad support for Government expenditure on broadcasting in Irish.

TnaG exists today because the democratic value of respect for the rights of minorities whether religious, political or linguistic, has taken root in Ireland and we now recognise these rights in modest but real ways. The rights of lesser-used languages have already been recognised in other European countries, where a fully developed sense of national self-respect and confidence includes guaranteeing access to broadcast facilities for regional languages. Indeed, European observers of this country are frequently bemused by our love-hate relationship with our older language, when they contrast TnaG's ability to win awards at international television festivals with the periodic outbursts of bitterness directed at Irish, under-girded by a post-colonial shame more appropriate to mid-1800s post-Famine social trauma that to late 1990s confident multiculturalism based on economic prosperity.

The rationale for TnaG's existence is this: to deprive the Irish-speaking community of what is available to the majority language users – the means of public debate and entertainment in their own language – is to deny its very existence, since television is the most powerful medium for producing people's sense of who they are and who others are across many dimensions of everyday life. Far from being a sop to unfocused national aspirations well past their sell-by date, or another sad twist in the saga of language revivalism, TnaG is based on the recognition of the language rights of an important minority that speaks Irish as its first language and a growing number interested in speaking it as a second language. It is noteworthy that attacks on TnaG never discuss either the quality of its output or the question of the language rights of viewers. If we recognise these rights as important, how much is too much to pay for them? Compared with S4C in Wales of similar channels in other European countries, TnaG provides a high quality service on a minuscule budget. As a publisher-broadcaster, its core staff is very small and independent producers make the bulk of its programming.

FROM TnaG TO TG4

Six years after launch, TnaG – now rebranded as TG4 to position it as the fourth national channel in an increasingly crowded space, especially in cable company menus and newspaper television listings – has earned the respect of most press commentators, albeit grudgingly in some cases. Some would even argue that the channel has been consistently outmatching RTÉ in the quality and imagination of its factual programming, mainly by concentrating on local, personal stories. Most of the independent production companies providing programmes to TG4 praise the open-door policy and the staff enthusiasm that persists despite the very tight budgets. It is not unusual to find an entire 15-part factual series made for less than what it costs to produce one hour-long BBC documentary. Well-made but tightly budgeted documentary productions costed as low as 30,000 per half hour broadcast, is emerging as TG4's core strength, as it avoids too much expensive drama it cannot afford and too much studio-based programming that is affordable but visually less interesting. Prestigious international awards have also helped to boost respect for TG4 as a new source of programming, such as the UNESCO 1998 Award for "I gCillin an Bhais," a documentary on the hunger strikes in Long Kesh in the early 1980s, or the Bronze Award of the Houston Worldfest in 1999 for "Michael Hartnett – Muince Dreolin," a biography of the Limerick poet, or the Best Documentary Award at the Irish Film and Television Awards 2000 for "Mad Dog Coll." TG4 has developed the travel documentary genre with particular success, as is evidenced by John Murray's "Siberia – An Bealach o Thuaidh," Manchan Mangan's exploration of the Middle East, "Manchan sa Mhean Oirthir," and Hector O hEochagain's "Amu."

The arrival of lightweight, accessible, affordable digital technology allows great innovation and flexibility in production without the expense of large production crews that are still an essential part of some of the operations of traditional broadcasters. Digital cameras and editing also allow more people to get involved in making documentaries and factual programming, which moves TG4 closer to being a community television station than any other television service in Ireland. TG4's late arrival as one of the newest television stations to be built in Europe means that it was able to leap-frog over many of the work practices and set ways of making programmes that have become traditional in this part of Europe. And its minuscule budget (about one-fifth of what S4c has for Welsh-language programmes) means that it had to find new programme niches that were both affordable and attractive to audiences.

Within one year of launch, TG4 had achieved an average daily reach of 220,000 viewers in the official statistics (separate research indicated "regular or occasional" viewers of 500,000) despite the fact that fifty per cent of television sets in Munster were still not tuned to UHF. It also created three hundred new jobs. Its goal was to build its audience up to a two per cent share in prime time. It was actively exploring synergies with Raidió na Gaeltachta, especially in coverage of politics and sport and enjoying the benefits of close association with RTÉ (for instance, Nuacht co-production, access to archives, co-ordinating commissioning activities with the Independent Production Unit in RTÉ, drawing on RTÉ expertise in engineering, promotion and audience research) while officially favouring operational independence from RTÉ. It was the only station in Ireland ready to engage in community TV when circumstances (that is a digital terrestrial infrastructure) would allow and it was also positioned to increase its programme commissioning for Northern Ireland once the British government would see its way to establishing a television production fund for Irish-language television in Northern Ireland, to replicate the fund established in Scotland for Gaelic television. TnaG was also emerging in a way that no one could have foreseen, as a favourite channel for the new immigrants attracted by the boom economy of the Celtic Tiger. Research in other countries had long established the heavy use of television by immigrants, partly for language learning purposes and partly to accelerate a gain in understanding the new host society. Anecdotal evidence in Ireland suggests that immigrants find the sub-titling of programmes on TG4 into English an accessible way to learn about Irish society and culture and also to increase their reading skills in English.

Right from the launch, the future of TG4 was far from secure. Its funding was quite inadequate for the job it was expected to do and the deteriorating financial situation in RTÉ, with the increasing fragmentation of the Irish audience for its programmes, meant that RTÉ's supply of 365 hours of programming without any increase in funding was becoming a very heavy burden. But an even more fundamental question was whether TG4 was satisfying its primary audience, including those who had been waiting for a long time for a television service in Irish.

Two years after its launch, a blistering attack on TG4 was launched in Force 10 magazine by Donncha Ó hÉathlaithe, member of Comhairle Theilifís na Gaeilge and long-time campaigner for Irish television. "Why was TnaG a monumental mistake?" he boldly asked and equally boldly proceeded to answer the question in terms of audience size: the channel was attracting a modest 100,000 viewers for its flagship Nuacht programme and this was clear evidence that after two years of effort, it had failed to attract an "East-coast" audience. Ó hÉathlaithe suggested two possible solutions. One was to admit that there is little interest in Irish- language television outside the Gaeltacht and to re-invent TG4 as community television for the Gaeltacht (the original impetus in the 1980s had leaned in this direction). Since this solution would be "ideologically impossible in the prevailing cultural climate", dominated by those who would like to "ethnically cleanse the few remaining Gaeltacht communities from the linguistic landscape", the more realistic solution was to let TG4 become a commissioning agency, funded by Government for programmes to be broadcast on RTÉ. This would free up a channel for alternative RTÉ purposes, such as a dedicated sports channel.

The RTÉ Authority was taken aback by this broadside delivered very publicly and forcefully by a member of a body appointed by the Authority itself to develop TG4 to its full potential. As Chairman, I pointed out to Donncha Ó hÉathlaithe that the station was still in its infancy and that such an airing of reservations in public by a board member must be hugely demoralising for the young staff working so hard for the success of the channel. I reminded him that the primary rationale for establishing TG4 was based on minority linguistic rights and that using an argument about low audience share was to adopt the very posture of those East-coast critics whose enmity towards the channel was anchored inside a market ideology that respected only audience size. Cathal Goan, Ceannasaí of TG4, pointed out in public that the audience for TG4 was in fact growing. The average daily reach was now (October 1998) 436,000 and weekly reach was one and a half million. Survey data showed that eighty percent of Gaeltacht viewers rated the news (stories, issues and style) as "good" or "very good". A review by IBEC, the employers' organisation, pointed out that TG4 spending at that point was underpinning 1,419 jobs, or 64 percent of the total number employed in the independent television sector, and accounted for 52 percent of hours worked in that sector. It generated 44 percent of the Exchequer returns from independent production. There was little enthusiasm at this stage, on either East or West coasts, for the notion that TG4 was a monumental mistake.

A year later, TG4 made further strides into niche broadcasting by using its commercial income to fund national television coverage of Minister's Question Time from Dáil Éireann (Parliament) and the proceedings of the Public Accounts Committee, which was exploring the very controversial issue of tax evasion by prominent citizens. It was offering a daily schedule of Irish-language programmes for pre-school children throughout Ireland, filling a huge gap in television that was one of the most compelling original reasons for setting up the station. It had reached a daily output of six hours programming in Irish in prime time. Its re-broadcasting of old GAA matches, with the original Irish commentary, proved to be very popular, as was its successful foray into soap opera with "Ros na Run" and it scheduling of late-night film classic. All of this was achieved with a core staff of 50 people, who rose to the challenge of balancing the needs of the local Irish-speaking Gaeltacht audiences with the needs of a national audience, many of them children. By March 2000, TG4 had achieved a daily reach of 670,000 people, a market share of 2 percent in multichannel areas (where several British television stations could be received alongside stations from the whole island of Ireland) and a share of 3 percent where only the four Irish national channels could be received (about a quarter of all households).

TG4 was, of course, generating new enemies in other parts of the broadcasting sector by its success. TV3 was into its second year of operation in 1999 and finding great difficulty in attracting audiences with schedules that had very little content that was produced in Ireland. It was already beginning to complain that TG4 was using its non-prime time hours to broadcast films in English, or European films dubbed into English, which potentially offered "unfair competition" to TV3. As if to reinforce this point, I received a letter from Minister Síle De Valera in August 1999 saying "I would be concerned if the service were to begin to see itself as in serious competition for audiences for programming in the English language against other national broadcasting services. Such a vision of the service would in my view undermine the arguments for the establishment of the service." The Minister's letter made no mention of the very low levels of funding for TG4 (for example, compared with S4C) and the consequent pressure on the station to build audiences beyond prime time Irish-language programmes, so that the meagre commercial income thus generated could be re-invested not in shareholders' dividends but in further Irish-language programmes.

CELTIC LANGUAGE CONTEXT

Comparisons with other Celtic languages – Welsh and Scots Gaelic – are more apt than comparisons with other lesser used languages such as Basque, Galician and Catalan in Spain, if only because of the different relationship with English that pertains to each set. Scots Gaelic is more confined to the Western Seaboard and Islands of Scotland, spoken by about sixty-five thousand people, while Welsh is spoken mostly in the Northern half of Wales by up to five hundred thousand people, or one-fifth of the population, and has a stronger urban base than Irish.

S4C provided the closest module to emulate for TG4 and was generous in offering advice and expertise. Its history was similar to TG4's, coming as it did out of a long and bitter campaign by Welsh language activists – petitions, protest marches, sit-ins, climbing broadcasting masts, refusing to pay television licences, threatening hunger strike – to its eventual launch at Hallowe'en 1982, sixteen years before TG4. S4C was established as publisher-broadcaster, producing very little television itself but commissioning from the independent production sector and receiving content produced for it by both BBC and Harlech Television. Current Welsh language output is about thirty-five hours per week. The move to digital television will allow S4C to gain much more broadcasting space from Channel 4.

Scots Gaelic broadcasting is in a less robust condition. The BBC broadcasts about 35 hours of Gaelic programmes per week on radio and has transmitted a small amount of television material since the 1950s, as has the local independent television station, Grampian. The combined annual television output now totals 350 hours. This includes the soap opera "Machair" which is shown with sub-titles on TG4. A campaign is currently underway for an independent Gaelic television station based on the S4C model, though some activists favour the continuation of Gaelic programming on mainstream channels.

The BBC's policy regarding Irish in Northern Ireland, where ten per cent of the population claims a knowledge of Irish, has been far less positive than it has been with Welsh or Scots Gaelic, despite activists reminding the Corporation of its public service responsibilities to minority audiences. Recent improvements in the analogue terrestrial signal beamed into Northern Ireland from the South and the carriage of TG4 on the Sky satellite system, mean that Irish-language television emanating from Connemara now has the potential to reach all 32 counties in Ireland. This reach may be consolidated more easily when digital terrestrial television is fully rolled out. The Good Friday Agreement of 1998, which laid the foundation for the current peace process in Northern Ireland, included commitments by the UK Government to explore with both British and Irish broadcasting authorities how TG4 could be made available more widely in Northern Ireland. The Ultach Trust formed an ad hoc advisory group (including the then head of TG4, Cathal Goan) to examine the implications of all the language issues raised in the agreement and publish their views in "How to Broadcast the Irish Language in Northern Ireland – Irish Language Broadcasting and the Belfast Agreement." It called on the Irish and UK Governments to guarantee digital reception of TG4 all over Ireland and pressed the British Government to establish an Irish language fund in Northern Ireland, similar to that which exists in Scotland and Wales, so that production of television and film could be adequately funded. This fund could be used to finance programmes produced in Northern Ireland for TG4.

Meanwhile, the issue of the number of Irish speakers living today refuses to go away. A report prepared by the Gaeltacht Commission in 2002 warned that the use of Irish was declining at a steady rate.[100] Of the 154 district electoral divisions in the Gaeltacht, only 18 have a 75 percent population which speaks Irish daily – 12 in County Galway, four in County Donegal and two in County Kerry. If the criterion for re-drawing Gaeltacht boundaries is that 80 percent of the community must be Irish speaking, as was the case in 1926 just after independence from Britain was achieved, then only 14 electoral divisions would be eligible for Gaeltacht status. If the Government accepts the report, large areas would lose their Gaeltacht status, including Conamara, leaving only 11,150 daily speakers in a redefined official Gaeltacht. The Commission recommended a comprehensive education and training system to give priority to Irish as a first language and argued that its status as an official EU working language should be secured. Gaeltacha areas should be given seven years to reverse the trend or lose Gaeltacht status altogether. Analysis of Government data in February 2003[101] shows that only 25 percent of eligible households in the total Gaeltacht area are judged to have a fluency in Irish during the 2001/2002 school year, suggesting that the number of fluent Irish speakers has dropped from 250,000 at the foundation of the State to between 20,000 and 30,000 now. Officially, 80,000 live in recognised Gaeltacht regions, but only 20,000 now live in areas in which a majority of the households eligible for an annual Government grant to support Irish-speaking, school-going children are actually judged to be truly Irish speaking.

At the start of the nineteenth century, there were more speakers of Irish than speakers of Welsh, Swedish, Norwegian, Danish or Dutch, but the Irish jettisoned their native language in the belief that it was an obstacle to progress and because they no longer had traditions that might give them sustenance. The Penal Laws of the previous century robbed them even of the last vestiges of a native leadership.[102] Only at the end of the nineteenth century, when just about 50 people could write in English, did some people, led by Douglas Hyde, conclude that with the disappearance of the language went a social framework and what Kiberd calls "a hold on the world, a basis for self-belief and ultimately economic prosperity."[103] There are still persuasive arguments for a connection between language-based cultural self-confidence and economic success, including the fact that many of the most successful "business achievers" in Ireland in the twentieth century have been enthusiastic Gaelgoirí, speakers of Irish. And it may well be, as Kiberd argues, that the cultural confusion, diminished sense of enterprise and stagnation through lost sense of self-belief that characterised the generation living in the early decades of independence, despite their successful dislodging of a mighty imperial army, can be traced in part to the experience of losing Irish.

TG4 was planned not as another measure to revive Irish as the community language but the result of a case made on the basis of minority rights. In a broader sense, it can be seen also as a reaction to the increasing sense of cultural globalisation widely discussed at the end of the twentieth century. Its branding of itself as "Súil Eile" (another view, an alternative perspective) builds upon the embracing of Irish by many people outside the Gaeltacht as a force for a "counter culture", distinct from purely nationalist values. Contemporary forces of globalisation go beyond those operating in the nineteenth century which led more and more parents who spoke only Irish to each other to see to it that only English was spoken by their children. Media contents, with their roots in trans-national systems of production and distribution – television, music, advertising, films, video games, magazines, public relations and the discourses of international politics, economics, trade, science, sports, fashion – daily cross national borders that are increasingly transparent, porous and meaningless when it comes to global capital and information flow. It will be an interesting experience to evaluate the impact of TG4 after its first ten years, against the historical backdrop of the very old relationship between the Gaelic language and English, and the contemporary backdrop of the increasing globalisation of the media.

8 GLOBALISATION

In 1998, *Foreign Policy* magazine joined with management consultant A.T. Kearney to initiate a series of surveys to measure the level of globalisation – defined as integration into the world political and economic system – of most of the countries of the world today. Ireland at that time ranked sixth but reached first place in the 2000 survey and maintained that position in 2001. At the other end of the index, Iran and Peru barely register while Argentina, Mexico, South Africa, Turkey, Pakistan, China, India and Brazil are all among the twenty least globalised countries.[104]

Ireland's high level of trade and multinational investment and high telephone call volumes with the rest of the world were the key factors maintaining its position at the top of the league. Irish trade (imports and exports combined) amounted to almost 150 percent of annual gross domestic product and Ireland continues to win a disproportionate share of mobile investment capital as institutional firms use their Irish base to target export markets in the EU and beyond and repatriate their profits in massive financial flows.

Ireland also scores highly on indices of "personal contact", the high telephone volumes in and out of the country reflecting not only business but also tourism both ways and the large number of people with relatives abroad, (which relates to the fact of previous periods of high emigration from Ireland in the past, and more recent trends among young people doing a twenty-first-century version of the Grand Tour, heading off travelling for prolonged periods to Southeast Asia and beyond.) Ireland is one of the world's biggest beneficiaries of the boom in information technologies, with huge foreign direct investment by companies such as Intel and Microsoft. But it ranked 24th in Internet usage, although Government investment in the major broadband Global Crossing project improved the general level of inter-connectedness. Ireland was also down the league in terms of political integration, based on indices measuring membership of international organisations (ranked 15th) and the number of foreign embassies hosted in Dublin (ranked 38th).

Is globalisation a good thing or a bad thing? Since its first appearance in the 1990s (in official form in the 1992 edition of *The Oxford English Dictionary*) the term has become highly contested and an "anti-globalisation" movement has spread across the globe. This backlash against globalisation emphasises the need for a new ethical approach to global relations, so that they serve all of the world's people, and the benefits of encouraging a "globalisation from below" to counter the huge expansion in private, as opposed to Government power across the world. The privatisation of power is seen mainly in the growth of multinational corporations, which now comprise more than half of the top economies in the world, and their influence on global regulatory institutions. A great deal has been written over the last few years about corporate globalisation or globalisation from above, a term capturing an awareness that in the last third of the twentieth century, large corporations became more single-mindedly transnational in focus, reorganising their operations to coincide with a vision which perceived their home country as only one among many profit centres within a globalised world economy. They used their considerable power to influence governments to accept rules favourable to their views about how trade and investment should be organised. Globalisation from above also points to the increasing power of world governance institutions – the World Trade Organisation, the World Bank, the International Monetary Fund, the World Intellectual Property Organisation – and their domination by corporate concerns rather than the needs of nation states. These world governance organisations operate in parallel with the United Nations but are not answerable to it. A reaction to globalisation from above has also made its appearance, in the form of the global justice movement, the global environment and human rights campaigns, organisations in civil society that work across national borders to reduce Third World debt, find solutions to the AIDS epidemic in Africa and promote labour rights and so on.[105]

GLOBALISATION AND COMMUNICATION

Social theory throughout the 1990s has positioned communication and culture in new ways at the centre of analyses of globalisation. This development is in sharp contrast to the paradigm of international communication that dominated the previous two decades. This highlighted a virulent Western form of cultural imperialism that imposed its shadow over all nation states in proportion to their ability to resource their own media.[106]

The epitome of this neo-colonialism was seen in the international flow of news, a global system structured in dominance since the nineteenth century by the large news agencies, or today by the news gathering and disseminating power of News Corporation's Sky Television or Time Warner's CNN.[107] It is ironical now that a great deal of analysis of cultural globalisation tends to ignore news as an essential contemporary cultural product with enormous power to shape government agendas – seen again most recently in the Anglo-American invasion of Iraq, carried out without UN Security Council backing. Issues of information dominance were central to the discourse of the last attempt to impose some democratic shape on global communication through the New World Information and Communication Order (NWICO), an initiative that collapsed along with the leadership role of UNESCO in this area, when the US and the UK withdrew from this organisation in 1985 in protest at what they saw as excessive promotion of NWICO by the Non-Aligned group of nations.

Most contemporary thinking about globalisation begins with the phenomena of "distanciation" or "time-space compression,"[108] which tend to occur in short and intense bursts, bringing rapid social change and increased uncertainty and feelings of risk. Interpreted very liberally, this suggests that globalisation means simply everything in the world affects everything else – and a lot faster than it used to. Social relations become more stretched across greater distances, radically freed from local contexts, and distance becomes less important, disappearing altogether at those moments of experience when live, global, television coverage pulls together large numbers of people worldwide into the same view of the siege of Baghdad or the implosion of East European Communist governments, or the nuclear accident in Chernobyl, or the student confrontation in Tiananmen Square in Beijing. Sometimes it is the common experience of the same mega-sport event, and frequently the shared view of millions is actually framed through a single camera lens, operated by a global television company. The global television experience of the spectacular attack on the World Trade Centre in New York on 11 September 2001, was the quintessential moment of time-space compression. Symbolic meaning (including, crucially, the framing and agenda setting that worked powerfully to shape public opinion) is shared widely at a world level, intensifying new forms of global consciousness and new arrays of ideologies that Arjun Appadurai calls "ideoscapes."[109] Cultural Globalisation is facilitated not only by the emergence of transnational mass media, such as CNN, Sky Television, BBC Worldwide, ESPN and so on, but also transnational personal media, especially e-mail and the World Wide Web.

Transnational commercial media have an ideological interest in framing globalisation in the language of privatisation and social divestment and in pursuing their own self-preservation by perpetuating the political and social systems that permit them to exist. Rupert Murdoch's News Corporation is prototypical of the large media company that has become de-linked from its home nation state and become a global conglomerate with unprecedented concentration of corporate strength, based on new forms of vertical and horizontal integration. News Corporation began as a print enterprise in Australia, spread into television in the UK in the 1970s and then into network television (Fox) in the US in the 1980s. It is now poised to take advantage of the huge Chinese and Indian markets with its Star TV system. The new global conglomerates have enormous borrowing power and the ability to minimise financial risk by managing their media products across different world markets both inside and outside their geo-linguistic area of influence. Their borrowing power can also become their Achilles heel however, as we have seen in the near collapse of Rupert Murdoch's News Corporation in the early 1990s, due to its difficulties in raising revenue to meet bank costs. We can see this paradigm closer to home in the cable systems Chorus and NTL in Ireland: their inability to face satellite competition from BSkyB means they lose customers and revenues and face huge hurdles in servicing their large bank borrowings.

Some academic writing on globalisation makes much of the fact that new media production centres and exporters have grown up to challenge the media dominance of the US that used to be described in academic literature as "cultural imperialism" or even "electronic colonialism". These new centres include Mexico (Televisa), Brazil (O Globo), India (Zee TV and Doordarshan), Egypt, Taiwan and Hong Kong.[110] Some academic analyses, however, that tend to contrast a "bad" cultural imperialism of the past with a contemporary "benign" globalisation, ignore the fact that Azcarraga of Televisa and Marinho of Globo, for instance, have become two of the world's largest media moguls, selling millions of hours of television to more than 150 countries and buying massively into foreign television stations across the world. They too are cultural imperialists, spawning close to home alternative video distribution networks and cooperatives that try to combat the stifling impact of the giant media companies on the freedom of information. In essence, there is a certain truth in Henry Kissinger's blunt assertion that "what is called globalisation is really another name for the dominant role of the US,"[111] augmented now, we should add, by newer media conglomerates that extend the American corporate model to all corners of the globe. In Europe, it is still the case that the US enjoys a growing trade surplus for audiovisual products (television, video, cinema) with the EU, much of the expansion being attributable to increased US exports to new satellite television channels. US exports of feature films to the EU are about ten times greater than imports to the US and television programme exports are more than fifteen times greater. Globally, the US counts for about 75 percent of all television programme exports, the bulk of this being drama, in which national content is confined to internationally current stereotypes and expectations, mostly melodrama in which the values of capitalist business and family are heavily featured, both positively and negatively.[112]

"Localisation" is a key term in globalisation theory that deserves some attention in analysis of the television industry. Localisation has become an important mantra in the international television trade press, signifying the many ways in which pressures within global TV markets respond to the evidence that domestic content has become more popular than imports.[113] It now refers to a range of adaptive manoeuvres applied across different world regions that include the following: franchising formats; providing "produce-it -yourself" kits to local companies for "reality-based" programmes; shooting local sequences for insertion into current affairs programmes (like CanWest's reuse of ABC's weekly current affairs programme *20/20*); selling localised versions of game shows that have attracted large audiences elsewhere, like *Who Wants To Be A Millionaire*; designing different versions of content in the production of drama, in order to reflect local accents and attitudes and eliminate what might be seen as "an American slant;" including local hosts and voice-overs in natural science programmes designed for global audiences. These ways of locally customising and culturally adapting what is designed essentially as an international product builds on well-tried economies of scale established by US-based global companies like Coca Cola over the course of the last century. They pay close attention to local partnerships that market the brand in a local accent. The Australian-based company Grundy International (now owned by the British Pearson Group) specialises in the re-working op soap opera formulae and scripts into localised versions tailored to different cultural and narrative configurations in each European country.[114] New forms of soap opera that have evolved from common artistic ancestors, invented far away in another culture, are emerging across the world. In effect, these are global prototypes, adapted to the tolerances of domestic audiences and successfully flourishing behind national boundaries that are otherwise impervious to the flow of serialised fiction on television.

"REALITY TELEVISION"

The success of this aspect of the globalisation of television, selling programme formulae to different countries and localising the finished version to suit local conditions, can be seen most spectacularly in the recent success of the regenerated genre of "reality TV." This has its roots in American experiments in television in the early 1970s, in the Public Broadcasting Systems cinema verité style series "Family" which gave viewers a serialised "real" experience of living with the Loud family in California for several weeks. The present wave of reality TV is associated with the huge popularity, almost to cult levels, of "Big Brother", originally a Dutch programme produced by Endemol that was copied and adapted in dozens of countries around the world within two years. At the heart of it was a simple formula: nine candidates confined to a house, isolated from the outside world, filmed twenty-four hours a day for one hundred days, encouraged to vent their spleen and reveal their thoughts about other participants in special confessional spaces where the viewer is subjectively positioned as the confessor, subject to a gradual eviction process with voting input from viewers, leading to one contestant winning a substantial prize. It was given multiple slots in television schedules and with massive promotion it commanded huge viewer interest in country after country. In several countries – Netherlands, Germany, Australia and the USA – the public was able to follow the antics of the participants 24 hours a day on the Internet. In the UK, it found a home on the satellite channel E4, which screened the programme 21 hours a day, but terrestrial channels were more restrictive in their editing and scheduling.

Numerous programmes were made about the participants, their lives, families and friends, and documentaries were even made investigating the different versions of the format that were broadcast in different countries around the world.

In the early stages, the programme had no stage-managed features, simply showing the repetitive and often tedious daily routines of nine people, edited in a rudimentary way by the producer. But soon the format changed from cinema verité docusoap voyeurism to offer more sensationalism and something like the carefully managed spectacle of fiction genres. Drama, emotion and intimate revelations were boosted. In the US the obligatory hen-house, which participants had to tend in order to harvest eggs for their table, was replaced by a basketball court. Romantic liaisons between participants were now exploited to the full, although scenes of physical love, often hinted at with bodies moving under the sheets and emphasised with suggestive music, were never shown explicitly on terrestrial channels, though two contestants in Portugal were evicted for having sex. Participants were selected more carefully, to create a more dynamic, homosexual-heterosexual mix or to include people involved in the sex industry. In Germany's third season, the shower door was removed and participants had to bathe naked. In the US, mixed bedrooms were imposed and participants later complained that producers gave them pre-written dialogues. In Australia, an uncut episode sparked outrage over scenes of full frontal nudity, bondage displays and tales of group sex – but it achieved record ratings.

In Paris, hundreds of protestors stormed the location of "Loft Story" France's version of Big Brother and had to be repelled by police tear gas. They were protesting against what they saw as broadcasting standards descending to new lows. One placard read "Trash TV turns people into idiots". Only in Portugal did the broadcasting regulator react firmly to the spiral of ratings competition between competing TV channels which were becoming increasingly controversial. Extracts were being aired in newscasts to stimulate audience interest. TV1 was fined and threatened with a two month suspension of broadcasting order for including depiction of a sex act between two contestants in a nightly newscast. SIC received a similar reprimand for broadcasting a private telephone conversation between one contestant and her parents, reacting with alarm to footage showing contestants handling condoms and a vibrator, and preparing for naked bathing. Before this, TV1 and SIC had been publicly attacking each other for allowing broadcasting standards to drop so low.

Television channels around the world developed other variations on the Big Brother formula that featured "exotic" settings for the game show format, along with more difficult living conditions and a return to more primitive lifestyles. "Survivor" was conceived in the UK by Planet 24 Production Company and tried out first in Sweden, then the US, where it was a huge audience success. This alerted broadcasting managers everywhere to the audience-pulling potential of ordinary people fending for themselves in the wilderness. British TV developed "Castaway" and "The Trench". RTÉ broadcast its version in "Treasure Island" and TG4 produced an Irish-language version of Survivor in "SOS". US viewers were treated to "Fear Factor" featuring contestants being dragged along the ground by horses, leaping across moving trucks and letting snakes and rats crawl all over them. NBC promised something even more spectacular, putting ordinary Americans through their paces at a cosmonaut training centre and blasting the winner into space.

The Big Brother phenomenon which took many parts of the world by storm (from an audience maximising point of view) is based on a fudging of the line between fact and fiction and on an apparent audience reaction away from a taste for carefully scripted programmes and towards television content that seems to offer unscripted spontaneity, where soap opera converges and blends with documentary and game show to produce a new genre. The contradictions in this mix were exploited in 1999 by Television Suisse Romande when it aired "Generation Zero One," a fake reality TV show with a major shock in each episode designed to make audiences reflect, without them realising it initially, on the risks inherent on the current trends in reality TV shows. With intense competition for ratings between channels and "light touch" regulation the norm in most countries, how far will broadcasters go to increase the shock value of what the voyeur sees? Where is the ethical bottom line in a situation where competing media are always tempted to go one step further? We may get the answer when the planned American cable channel Reality Central is launched in 2004, dedicated to a diet of all reality TV. The Big Brother phenomenon, whether judged to be "trash TV" or a very worthwhile new form of entertainment, is undoubtedly a product of the increase in the number of television channels now competing for the relatively fixed amount of viewer time and attention, and of course, the revenue this carries. It is also the result of a more global awareness at managerial level in the television industry generally, supported by a stronger infrastructure of professional conferences and exhibitions and an expanded trade press, which allows managers to become aware very quickly of successful programming developments elsewhere in the world and buy into the franchise of winning formulae. A previous generation of managers would have bought syndicated programmes only, relying usually on successful first runs in the US that have proved their audience-pulling power.

With audiences now showing more interest in locally produced content than in American imports, there are greater incentives to buy the rights to a successful concept or formula and make a local version very quickly. The more flexible infrastructure of small independent production companies makes this easier to achieve outside of the traditional broadcasting organisations, with their fixed overheads – staff and facilities – and longer production planning routines. Localisation of production doesn't always guarantee local audience success, of course, as Eamonn Dunphy's experiment with TV3's Irish version of The Weakest Link demonstrates. But it is a trend in cultural globalisation that is far from exhausted yet.

GLOBALISATION AND ITS IDEOLOGICAL EFFECT

One of the crucial incursions of globalisation is less visible than copycat TV formats but is more profound in its impact: the implantation of a model of broadcasting that has been very successful in the US and is steadily gaining strength in other world regions. Neo-imperial cultural power is not confined to the export to feature films, popular music, magazines, TV programmes, advertisements, news and associated lifestyles, as Herman and McChesney point out.[115] Its crucial impact is ideological, in establishing a common sense about the growth of commercial media systems and their increasing integration into the global system led by the US, the only super-power in cultural, as well as in economic and military matters. The ideological impact of globalisation will vary in intensity of effects by the size and strength of the impacted country, the strength and coherence of its indigenous culture. Although globalisation implies inter-penetration and some degree of feedback from the periphery to the centre (some versions of globalisation theory deny the very existence of a centre any more), a few countries will be net exporters of cultural effects, especially the US, while most will be net importers. Herman and McChesney describe negative effects in four linked areas:

> (a) The ideological effect of commercialised media is to stress consumption as the primary end of life, individualism and the individual right to choose (especially among consumer goods) asserted as the fundamental social condition. The emphasis on individualism can be a progressive force in authoritarian systems where arbitrary rule needs to be threatened, but beyond that, it strengthens materialistic values, weakens concern for the well-being of others and tends to diminish the strength of communal ties. This reduces the power of resistance to market forces and carried to an extreme, may prove dangerous to a democratic order.
> (b) The dominant tendency in commercialised media is to seek large audiences with uncontroversial content, so that news presented in depth, public affairs analyses, political debates, innovative drama and documentaries tend to disappear from prime time viewing. The modalities of entertainment penetrate the public sphere with what is called in the US "happy news",

"infotainment" or "reality news" that stress personalities, conflict and petty exposures of minor crimes. The public sphere is overgrown with entertainment. Even children's television gradually shrivels to proportions appropriate to the lesser command children have over spending. The programmes that remain, beyond the endless repetition of cartoons, stress entertainment over information or education and are closely tied to advertising and the sale of children's toys and other consumables.

(c) The centralising globalising commercial media exercise a conservative political force. Closely linked to the corporate community of which they are members, they support neo-liberal economic policies that serve the general transnational interest at the expense of social democratic options. They foster uncritical support for foreign military excursions to sustain favourable climates for investment for multinational corporations, as was demonstrated most aggressively in Murdoch's Fox Television in its war-drumming for the Anglo-American invasion of Iraq. They are hostile to organised labour and complacent about increasing inequality in income and wealth, out of self interest and linkage with other members of a dominant elite. They press politicians to permit mergers and other corporate strategies that concentrate ownership of media outlets in fewer hands, to relieve themselves of regulatory obligations. They also press politicians to help them weaken and dismantle public broadcasting systems because these not only compete for audiences and financial resources, they also set embarrassingly higher standards in broadcasting, out of concern for the public sphere. The top media moguls in global media corporations tends to be extremely conservative and give especially warm support to conservative politicians (though they can also do business with socialists, as Rupert Murdoch's switch of allegiance from Margaret Thatcher to Tony Blair demonstrates) to assure acceptance of their own plans and needs, making it exceedingly difficult to contain the commercialisation – globalisation process. In many countries, including Ireland, this conservative influence at the level of both national government and EU cultural politics has been manifested in the steady weakening of public broadcasting. It can also be seen in the shift to the right in editorial opinion in newspaper chains.

(d) The impact of globalisation on local cultures varies enormously between dominant and less dominant and subordinate cultures, depending on many factors including indigenous forces of resistance and linguistic barriers. Strong cultures, like Japan, withstand cultural penetration far better than do Latin American cultures, where the elite at least have long since been denationalised by saturation in North American advertising, films, television, news and music and in many cases direct US economic – political – cultural control. The erosion of local cultures is particularly linked to the inability in many parts of the world to continue the resourcing of local television production. This drift is seen in stark relief in many countries in the Caribbean, where scores of television channels from North America are available but almost no TV of any significance is produced locally. It is conceivable in an Ireland of the future that conservative political forces could succeed in ridding the country of any public investment in radio or television, resulting in the Caribbeanisation of Irish broadcasting. This is the dark, pessimistic side to the story of globalisation.

COMPETITION IN TELEVISION

We now turn to a consideration of how public broadcasting in Ireland found itself no longer facing what could be called "passive" competition but having to adjust to what the neo-liberal political forces of de-regulation finally delivered, direct foreign investment in television in Ireland. By passive competition, we mean the conditions that pertained in television until the mid-1990s, where RTÉ had a national monopoly in providing television from an Irish base but viewers could also access British channels in a very open audiovisual space. In 1996, for instance, as plans to launch TV3 were quickening, the following British channels could reach two-thirds of households in the country by terrestrial, cable or MMDS transmission: BBC1, BBC2, Channel 4/S4C and ITV (Ulster TV). Sky1 and Sky News could reach one third of households using satellite. Actual audience share in prime time broke down as follows:

RTÉ ...	...	...	42
Network Two ...		...	18
Total RTÉ	...	...	60
ITV (UTV)	...	...	13
BBC 1	...	...	11
BBC 2	...	...	04
Channel 4/S4C ...			05
Sky One	...	...	03
Sky News	...	...	01
Total non-RTÉ			40

RTÉ has always said, correctly, that it has been operating for a long time in one of the most competitive same-language areas in the world and holding its own very well in terms of audience share, ever mindful of the ammunition supplied to the neo-liberal arguments against public service broadcasting by a dramatic fall in audience share. This fall was precisely the trigger in Portugal twenty years ago for Government turning away from national public service broadcaster RTP and opening a space for former Prime Minister Balsamao's SIC Channel, which then became the beach-head for the entry of Brazilian media giant O Globo into Portuguese television through direct foreign investment. In Ireland, the competition from British channels, some of it the result of terrestrial overspill and some carried on RTÉ's own Relay Cable system, was relatively passive, in the sense that even though it reduced the size of RTÉ's audience, it did not seriously skew the field of potential resources that sustained RTÉ. No other broadcasting interest was attacking the idea of public funding for radio and television and RTÉ had no serious rival for the available television advertising revenue or the licence fee income. Its only limits in advertising revenue were the rate-card charges advertisers were willing to pay and the available minutage for advertising, which was controlled by Ministerial order, a powerful form of political control of RTÉ that rarely receives as much public comment as Government control of the licence fee. In fact, the lack of sufficient advertising capacity on RTÉ television was one of the major factors in impelling business interests to support broadcasting deregulation in the 1980s and lobby for a new national channel to be established.

All this changed in the late 1990s when a number of elements in the Irish broadcasting economy were altered to allow very active competition for broadcasting resources to come into play. Competition intensified in the distribution sector first, especially between NTL (who purchased what had originally been the RTÉ Relay Cable system) and Chorus and BSkyB. More Irish people were able to access more non-Irish television channels and more of their money needed to purchase that access was now going to foreign-based companies. Then some of the British channels – Channel 4 and Sky Television – opened offices in Dublin and began to sell airtime directly to Irish advertising interests for "opt-outs," just as British newspapers were redesigning their Sunday editions with distinctive front pages, supplements and Irish TV listings, and in some cases tweaking their editorial opinion – especially on "the Irish question" – in the editions destined for the Irish market. Finally, in 1998, competition for RTÉ became very active, in the form of the arrival of the Canadian media giant CanWest directly into the Irish broadcasting economy, through its major shareholding and managerial control of TV3. CanWest was later joined by London-based media giant Granada. TV3 was now able to compete very directly with RTÉ for advertising revenue and though its audience share was inevitably smaller than RTÉ's, it was allowed more advertising minutage by the | Minister. This is an indirect but powerful form of public subvention or state aid that TV3 has steadfastly refused to acknowledge as such, but this didn't prevent it from immediately setting about lobbying in Dublin and in Brussels against what it calls the Competition law infringements of the "state aid" going to RTÉ in the form of a licence fee.

All too often, discussions of cultural globalisation move quickly to a level of abstraction and generalisation and fail to find a grounding in the actualities of human behaviour in media industries. Theory and empirical observation frequently diverge rather than come together to illuminate the world, much like the more obtuse and enigmatic pronouncements of some academic comment on globalisation that rely on McLuhanesque versions of technological determinism.[116] Globalisation is about distanciation and time-space compression, yes, but how does this illuminate what we know about the public sphere and the supply of television content in Ireland? In particular, how does it effect two very significant questions: when a large multinational invests in the television infrastructure of small countries, what is the ability of the small country to exert some control over the multinational so that state objectives in broadcasting can be pursued? This problem has already been faced in Portugal, another small country within the EU with strong cultural and linguistic links to a major world economy, when the Brazilian media giant O Globo became directly involved in Portuguese television. And what are the dangers of conglomeration and concentration of ownership at a global level, particularly the corporate pressure to reduce diversity of opinion in news operations across the conglomerate, such that the health of the public sphere in each of the national territories aligned with the conglomerate may be negatively affected?

The launch of TV3 in September 1998 allows us to examine a particular aspect of cultural globalisation: the direct involvement of international capital in broadcasting in Ireland. The origins of TV3 go back to 1989, when the debate about providing an alternative television system to RTÉ – frequently led by an advertising industry eager for more opportunities to reach Irish consumers – culminated by a decision by the Independent Radio and Television Commission (now the Broadcasting Commission of Ireland) to award the franchise for a third national television channel to a consortium of local business men. These included James Morris of Windmill Lane Studios, a leading production house in Dublin, Paul McGuinness, Manager of rock band U2, and Ossie Kilkenny, a show business accountant. The franchise was withdrawn by the IRTC in 1991 for the inability of the TV3 consortium to list all its investors and convince the Commission that it had sufficient financial backing, but later won back after a court battle and after a period in which Windmill Lane Pictures went into examinership after its first abortive attempt to prepare TV3 for launch. An investment by UTV in TV3 in 1995 was welcomed for the links it provided to the British ITV network, keen to establish a presence South of the Border. The Belfast company ran into difficulties with the IRTC the following year, when it pulled out of the TV3 consortium rather than accede to the Regulator's demand that UTV be removed from cable systems in the Republic in order to boost TV3's chances of commercial success. It is ironical that the Canadian media conglomerate CanWest Global replaced UTV as an investor in TV3 but also invested in UTV itself. This double move was seen at the time as a strategy to exploit the linkage with the ITV network in Britain (CanWest had failed in its bid for the UK's Channel 5 franchise) as well as achieve all-Ireland synergies between the Dublin and the Belfast operations. Scottish Media Holdings was also at this time taking a stake in UTV and would soon implement a move to buy into newspapers and radio stations in the Republic.

THE LOVEBOAT NETWORK

Advertising interests received news of the 48 percent CanWest investment with a rapturous welcome. So did the independent production sector. The cost of advertising on RTÉ television had risen sharply from 1991 to 1996. This fact alone fuelled advertisers' passion for "ending the RTÉ monopoly", a goal also advocated by some press commentators, who hoped for "an alternative editorial strategy" from TV3, which would improve the overall provision of television in Ireland. For its part, CanWest was sounding very positive about levels of home-produced programming which would make TV3 stand out against all competition from outside Ireland and give RTÉ a good run for its money. Audiences for Irish television would be "repatriated" from UK channels, thus increasing Irish television audiences overall and thus reducing the inflation of advertising costs. CanWest was not modest about its achievements, indicating that it had a successful history of "start-ups" and "turn-arounds of TV properties."[117] in Canada, Australia and New Zealand and a record of good working relationships with both regulators and local independent producers. Doubts would later be expressed about this, but not in 1997.

Little was known about CanWest in the early stages of its negotiations with the IRTC and eventual involvement in running TV3, under its first CEO, Rick Hetherington. In RTÉ we commissioned a research report within Canada, which confirmed what we were already becoming aware of, that while independent Irish producers were still mesmerised by the promise of a significant increase in worthwhile, indigenous production emanating from TV3, CanWest had a very poor track record in producing Canadian originated television. This earned it the reputation early on as the "bargain basement broadcaster" in Canada. On the RTÉ Authority, we considered sharing this research with the IRTC but decided against it on the basis that such a move would have been seen as self interested, at a time when RTÉ was still being attacked by some hostile press voices for "obstructing" the arrival of private television.

CanWest companies in Canada, Australia and New Zealand were staffed and run at minimum cost and maximum efficiency. Very little programming was made locally. Instead American content was bought in huge volume and shown across the global system, spreading economies of scale and scope in all directions. CanWest was bitterly criticised in the 1990s, particularly in Canada, for making little or no effort to originate television drama and other programming reflecting the society in which they broadcast. When CanWest bought a twenty per cent stake in New Zealand's nearly bankrupt TV3 in 1991, its Chairman, Izzy Asper, according to his own reported account, gathered the employees together in the staff cafeteria and asked them what kind of business they thought they were in. One journalist volunteered an answer. "I'm in the news department and the business we're in is to make sure our audience gets the most carefully researched news and information possible." Asper got similar reasoned responses from other departments. "You're all wrong" Asper said "and that's why you're bankrupt. You're in the business of selling soap." He later told fellow CanWest executives, "they thought they were in the business of making programmes."[118]

Asper's interest in television began with the purchase in 1974 of an ailing local television station in North Dakota, which he relocated across the border into Winnipeg and moved into profit. A series of start-ups or turnarounds followed, all in lucrative urban markets: Winnipeg, Vancouver, Regina, Saskatoon, Ottawa, Halifax, Hamilton, St. John, Victoria and Montreal. Each station showed mostly imported American programmes and began steadily attracting advertising revenues. In the early 1980s, it was known as "The Love Boat" network because of its interest in airing low-cost, low quality American programmes. Ratings were good and press response was bad. The spectacular success of these stations funded the expansion into Australia's Network 10, New Zealand's TV3 and TV4 (as well as several radio stations in New Zealand) and then Ireland's TV3 (a 45 percent stake) and UTV (29.9 percent stake) in its international reach. The internationalisation of CanWest's operations followed a clear logic: limited to a hitherto domestic Canadian population of 28,000,000, it could now spread its programming costs over extra territories from which it earns advertising revenues, yielding an international system that is an extension of CanWest's domestic arrangement. The Hollywood and Australian content it buys can be creatively scheduled with small amounts of local content – much of it inexpensive, studio-based material with local accents, to satisfy local regulatory requirements. Along the way, some unsuccessful ventures included a bid for the UK's franchise for Channel 5 in 1995 (rejected because of its programming plans) and an abortive investment in Latin American television. Its investment in UTV gives it a platform for potentially lucrative British ITV terrestrial activity.

Within Canada, CanWest describes itself not as a network but as a "system". In legal, competitive and regulatory terms, the distinction is crucial. The system is a model for organising groups of television stations with all the benefits of network arrangements but with few of the restrictions. In Canadian law, networks like the public broadcaster CBC or CanWest's great rival CTV, which is owned by its affiliates, are licensed in a different way and must fulfil stringent requirements on content imposed by the regulator, the Canadian Radio, Television and Telecommunications Commission (CRTC). CanWest avoids such stringent requirements by licensing each of its stations as an independent entity, even though it has a national infrastructure for programme acquisition and syndication, as well as advertising sales, which maximise synergies and economies across the corporation. Its obligation for investment in home production is about half of what CTV is required to spend. In 1997, the CBC network spent almost 200 million on French and English programme making in Canada. CanWest spent just 36 million. Without network designation, it is not obliged to pursue universal coverage but can concentrate on the most lucrative population centres, where most of the advertising dollars are spent.

The absence of any significant core of original creative Canadian programming has brought criticisms of creeping Americanisation, especially from independent producers, and of failing to live up to its early promise of defending the Canadian cultural border. This led to defamation action being brought against critics who claimed that CanWest was nothing but a toll collector between Canadian viewers and their access to popular American shows. As one critic put it, "CanWest has ended up moving the border northward and keeping itself on the Southern side,[119] though the CRTC has been trying to put pressure on CanWest to contribute more fully to Canadian broadcasting, with a substantial contribution to original production including Canadian drama. Co-productions with its stations in New Zealand and Australia qualify as indigenous content in each territory and for government incentives in each partner's home country. Co-productions allow for the amortisation of production costs over larger populations spread over two or more countries.

Today, CanWest's holdings include, besides its television interests already mentioned, all the principle metropolitan newspapers in Conrad Black's Hollinger newspaper chain in Canada acquired in 2000, along with Hollinger's leading Canadian Internet portals, its magazine group and most of its community publishing operations. This deal included thirteen large metropolitan English-language dailies, about 136 daily and weekly newspapers in smaller towns and 85 trade publications and directories. In the following year, it bought a group of about eighty magazines from Southam. Like many new broadcasters, it also set about buying film libraries, trying to break into the television distribution business and developing a television – video production presence. These efforts centre on the Endemol film and television library, Toronto-based financier Fireworks Entertainment, Los Angeles-based feature film distributor Fireworks Pictures and television content developer Fireworks TV, as well as London-based distributor Fireworks International. Its new media subsidiary Ten Ventures aims to position the group for involvement in on-line entertainment and CanWest has other investments in Internet content providers. Its Australian investment, Network Ten, besides television, is also involved in outdoor advertising and signage as well as shopping and airport advertising, and is seeking to extend its presence into Malaysia and Indonesia.

In 2002, CanWest's borrowings to pay for this huge expansion into several media amounted to $C 3.9 billion. It was facing debt repayments of $C 127million in 2003 and 2004.[120] It began to consider selling some of its assets to avoid breaching its banking covenants and to service its huge debt. It also announced plans to reduce the debt, beginning with the sale of its New Zealand radio and television holdings, which were beginning to post operating losses, and some of its community newspapers in Canada. This immediately peaked the interest of Granada, which had already acquired a 45 percent stake in TV3. It confirmed late in 2002 that it is interested in doubling its stake in Ireland's commercial television station to 90 percent, though a coy Izzy Asper indicated that TV3 wasn't for sale, not yet. In any case, Granada is currently in the process of merging with Carlton, a deal involving Granada paying one billion pounds sterling for the other ITV giant.

Ireland's TV3 is largely managed today by one of its two major shareholders. Each of these companies is very large in international terms, and one of them, CanWest Global Communications Corporation, is now a major global conglomerate, quoted on the New York stockmarket. It is Canada's largest publisher of daily newspapers. It owns, operates and or holds substantial interests in newspapers, conventional television, new media, outdoor advertising, speciality cable channels, radio networks and Internet portals in Canada, New Zealand, Australia, Ireland and the UK. Its programme production and distribution subsidiary, Fireworks, operates in several countries throughout the world. Its entry into the newspapers business prompted the CRTC, the Canadian federal regulator, when renewing its licence in 2001 for a further seven years, to warn CanWest that it must manage its respective broadcast and print operations separately, though it isn't required to build walls between its news-gathering operations. Over the last year, Canadian politicians, citizen groups and journalistic organisations have voiced strong concerns that concentration of ownership will reduce the number of perspectives Canadians will get in their news and current affairs programming. In Vancouver, for instance, CanWest now owns both daily newspapers and two television stations, raising questions in British Columbia about whether it is appropriate for the four media outlets to share news-gathering at all. Although the CRTC has no power to regulate newspapers, it has authority over how broadcasters conduct their affairs. Its warning about the separation of news operations was aimed at trying to strike a balance between concerns that media concentration would result in fewer voices in the news and the corporate view that merging news operations would create more efficiencies.

CONCENTRATION OF OWNERSHIP

This Canadian debate has direct relevance for the quality of the media infrastructure supporting a healthy public sphere in Ireland. Already fears have been expressed that allowing a large international media company, headquartered outside Ireland, to take over a national television channel, means that very little formal or informal control can be exercised over it by the people its serves. Unlike RTÉ, where many forms of both formal and informal control operate, some of them covert and subtle, others overt and very direct, TV3 is formally regulated in a manner that the Broadcasting Commission of Ireland itself would describe as "light touch," nor is it subject to very many informal controls, especially since major decisions about what it does are controlled from Winnipeg. So it is worth exploring a little more how the intensifying concentration of media ownership is affecting the quality of the information that is fed into Canadian culture. In particular, we will examine the current controversy in Canada about corporate censorship in the news media owned by CanWest Global.

This controversy centres around a national campaign to boycott CanWest launched in the middle of 2002 in response to editorial policies being implemented at newly acquired CanWest newspapers that led to suspensions, blacklistings and the firing of the *Ottawa Citizen*'s publisher. Worries about the Corporation's apparent disregard for journalist freedom alerted Canadians to the dangers of the increasing concentration of media ownership. CanWest controls about 40 percent of the English-language newspaper circulation and as many as 97 percent of Canadians can be reached by CanWest's media outlets in any given day. If cross ownership situations common in the more re-regulated media landscape south of the Canadian border were to be replicated in companies like CanWest, it would mean that the same reporter would now be servicing a number of news outlets at the same time: writing a television story, as well as preparing a newspaper article and editing an on-line version of the same story. Photojournalists would be carrying both still and video cameras on their assignments, meeting continuous rather than daily deadlines and in effect reducing the amount of real news being gathered and disseminated.

The trouble began in Autumn 2001, when CanWest headquarters in Winnipeg instructed their major newspapers to carry, up to three times a week, unsigned editorials written at Head Office, and forbade local staff from contradicting in print these centralised editorial positions. Opposition came to a head when the Ottawa Citizen ran an editorial calling for the resignation of Prime Minister Jean Chretien.[121] It also ran a feature article detailing the track record of the Prime Minister, a close friend of CanWest owner Izzy Asper. The publisher, Russell Mills, was duly dismissed, fuelling criticisms that CanWest's recent entry into the newspaper business, through acquiring Conrad Black's Hollinger Inc. press empire, was aimed at advancing a particular political agenda, which includes lower taxes and less regulation in Canada, unquestioning support for how Israel handles its relation ship with Palestinians and total suppression of news written from a Palestinina point of view. (How the

211

newspapers happened to be for sale is an interesting tale in its own right, centring on the animosity between press baron Conrad Black and Jean Chretien. Some years ago, Chretien urged the British Government not to grant a long-term ambition of Black – to be appointed to the House of Lords. Black renounced his Canadian citizenship, sold his Canadian papers and is today Lord Black of Crossharbour).[122]

News stories that were spiked in 2001/02 included an interview with an internationally recognised Indian activist against genetically modified food, an argument that the US should respond to the terror attacks of September 11th not with howls of revenge but by thoughtful analysis of how US power is used around the world, and a report on Washington's welcome for the recent coup in Venezuela against the elected president Hugo Chavez. The suppression and censorship of news stories, feature columns and reader's letters spread out to include a ban on criticisms of CanWest's editorial policy itself. This intensified a newsroom climate of self censorship. The Newspaper Guild of Canada, the Quebec Federation of Professional Journalists and the Canadian Association of Journalists all denounced CanWest's management style, as did the US National Conference of Editorial Writers, the International Press Institute and the International Federation of Journalists, which compared the level of censorship to Eastern Europe of fifteen years ago. Aidan White, General Secretary of the International Federation of Journalists, noted that "the CanWest corporation is showing the ugly and intolerant face of modern media ... in which the twisted values of the media market always come first and where there is contempt for traditional journalism."[123] The manage ment of CanWest remained defiant. David Asper, Chairman of the Publications Committee, declared "I can say to our critics and to the bleeding hearts in the journalist community that it's the end of the world as they know it, and I feel fine."[124]

The Quebec legislature rebuked CanWest for its policy on centrally controlled editorial positions in a motion supported by both Liberals and Parti Quebecois.[125] A management memo was circulated to all CanWest television newsrooms, informing them of the new policy which now prohibits the company's broadcast journalists from taking part in the same kinds of protests that have occurred in major newspapers like the Montreal Gazette and the Leader-Post in Regina, where reporters were suspended for talking to outside media. What is interesting about this controversy is that the issues of censorship that drive it are continually linked to the relaxation of cross ownership rules and the creation of a conglomerate of unprecedented scope that this relaxation allowed: 120 community papers, 16 television stations, 7 specialty networks, a major news portal, 14 English-language metropolitan dailies, as well as television interests in Ireland, New Zealand and Australia.[126]. One of the benefits of cross media horizontal integration is achieving economies in selling advertising on several platforms – television, radio, newspapers, the Internet – and exploiting cross promotional opportunities, such as directing television viewers to CanWest's Canada.com web site or to its *National Post* newspaper. But this drive towards conglomeration came at a heavy price, a debt burden of C$3.2 billion.

To many Canadians, the CanWest controversy illustrates dangers posed to press freedoms and democratic governance by corporate centralisation of news media, a process that has been accelerating over the last decade throughout North America, steadily freezing out citizens from full participation in the political decision-making process. The key result of centralised editorial control from within the core of the media conglomerate is the negative impact a single company can have on the quality of journalism across a large country, undermining each newspaper's editorial board and giving Canadians a greatly reduced variety of opinion and editorial discussion, especially at regional level, where national issues need analysis in the light of local circumstances. Quebec Communications minister Diane Lemieux called the crisis in the CanWest system "an extremely concrete illustration of the dangers inherent at the heart of corporate media concentration."[127] Other prominent Canadian citizens articulated their worries that CanWest management was threatening freedom of the press in Canada by suppressing local editorial independence and the pluralism of viewpoint that should, in a healthy democracy, be working in the public interest. These included the former president of Southam Newspapers and its former Director, as well as the former publishers of the *Montreal Gazette* and *The Toronto Star*, who published their critique in full page advertisements in non-CanWest newspapers. More general protests and boycott campaigns continued throughout 2002, despite efforts by CanWest lawyers to shut down hostile web sites.

The television wing of the CanWest media empire has not been without controversy either, as the battle to preserve a modicum of Canadian content on television sets North of the US border reached the House of Commons Standing Committee on Canadian Heritage in March 2002.[128] CanWest made a plea to the CRTC for greater access to hitherto restricted revenue, such as advertising for prescription drugs, and for reduced restrictions on foreign investment in Canadian media. It also called for "regulatory flexibility" in relaxing current rules about Canadian content. CanWest would count as Canadian content, if allowed, advertorials or infomercials made in Canada, that is, extended advertisements like those found in television shopping channels. Critics pointed out that unless there is a strict definition of "Canadian content" the very concept will become meaningless, always providing loopholes to allow broadcasters to copycat popular US television programmes and promote these, plus syndicated programmes, at the expense of original Canadian content.

CANWEST AND IRELAND

What is remarkable about the rapid accumulation of media power in CanWest is that it has passed almost unnoticed in Ireland. The sheer size of CanWest now in television and newspapers highlights the danger of media monopoly and in particular the irresistible inclination towards centralised opinion on a range of topics of national and international importance. This tendency arose very quickly at the very heart of the CanWest press empire and led to censorship and the firing of journalists. None of this has generated debate in Irish media, and in fairness to TV3, there is no evidence as yet that it has muzzled opinion, for example on the Middle East, as CanWest has done in Canada. Coverage of the Anglo-American invasion of Iraq in March 2003 will make for an interesting test case, perhaps, to see whether this war is represented in a similar way across all CanWest television channels spread out like a patch-work quilt around the world – Canada, Ireland, New Zealand and Australia – and whether conglomeration has had the same flattening effect on the diversity of viewpoints allowed in news reporting and current affairs analysis as it has had, for example, in Rupert Murdoch's Fox Network and Sky Television in the US and Britain.

The question of local content bedevils CanWest's operations in Canada but it causes tensions in Ireland too. TV3 reported a nett loss of 2.7 million for the year ended August 2002 but then began to move into profit, contributing 2.42 million operating profits to CanWest in the last three months of 2002. CanWest announced this good news in the context of how much better it would be if only RTÉ didn't stand in the way. "TV3 exceeded the market average growth despite concerns over certain practices of RTÉ that we believe have distorted the marketplace," it said, adding that TV3 intended to lodge a complaint under competition law against the national broadcaster.[129] It also expressed grave concerns about the "massive" licence fee increase granted to RTÉ because "this manner of funding perpetuates and exacerbates the preclusion of a meaningful private television sector in Ireland and is essentially guaranteeing future dominance by UK based private broadcasters...Current proposals made by RTÉ...linked to the licence fee increase, failed to improve the prospects for a meaningful increase in Irish-based television choice for Irish consumers."

Given RTÉ's stated policy of using licence fee increases to broadcast more Irish-made programmes, the logic of TV3's claim is strange. But it is consistent with previous TV3 attacks on the current method of funding RTÉ, which argued that a better method would be a mechanism to support production of Irish television programming through direct project-based support to independent Irish producers, funding for which both public and private broadcasters could compete. This mechanism would replicate the TV New Zealand "Arts Council of the Air" funding model in New Zealand, which until recently provided some production funds to CanWest's subsidiary in that country.[130] New Zealand has now abandoned this method of funding, in response to widespread criticism that it has led to serious deterioration in the quality of television in that country.

The Chief Executive of TV3, Rick Hetherington, has made it clear since his arrival in Dublin that the licence fee paid to RTÉ and TG4 made it difficult for TV3 to invest in Irish made programmes and represented "an unfair and unaccountable subsidy, creating massive distortions in the Irish television business."[131] "The distortive effects of the subsidies have made it increasingly difficult for TV3 to invest in home grown television production for Irish viewers and have the inevitable result of reduced opportunities for the Irish creative community, as well as lost inward investment and employment in the Irish economy".

To many people within that "creative community" however, this argument is something of a red herring, after their years of waiting since 1998 for TV3 to live up to its conditions of licensing, which promised a flow of investment to the independent production sector. For the most part, the Irish independent sector is supported by the licence fee and the advertising earnings of RTÉ and TG4. Given the massive failure of the New Zealand funding model to generate a range of high quality content that viewers want to access, it is difficult to see how a similar model could work to improve television in Ireland, even if political difficulties with the idea of investing public money in profit making corporations based in Winnipeg or London could be set aside. It is difficult, furthermore, to see how public funding for RTÉ or TG4 make it more difficult for TV3 to live up to its early promises, made after it had presumably carried out due diligence on the Irish television market in the mid-1990s, and after it had decided to invest in the Irish television production sector. And it goes against all television market logic to assume that were it not for the licence fee, inward investment by non-Irish television interests would increase and expand employment in the Irish independent production sector. A much more likely scenario is that with no licence fee to finance the public service remit of RTÉ or TG4, there would be a huge increase in imports of foreign material, which cost up to one-tenth of what local production would cost, and a dramatic decrease in investment in Irish independent production. The logic of the marketplace would mean that the large proportion of TG4's budget that is currently spent on the production of the highly successful Irish-language serial, "Ros na Rún", for instance, would instead be directed outside the country to buy in a greater volume of cheaper drama from the US, the UK or Australia, where costs of production have already been recouped from a large domestic audience and where the cultural discount on imports is comparatively low. This would deepen an already negative trend that originated with both Channel 4 and Sky Television raising advertising revenue directly from Irish companies for Irish opt-out advertising slots: the revenue paid to them leaves the country, doesn't get taxed in Ireland, creates no Irish jobs and no new programmes in the independent production sector.

Meanwhile in Ireland, tensions between TV3 and RTÉ continue to smoulder, energised not only by TV3's continuous sniping at the very idea of a licence fee supporting RTÉ, but also by the acrimonious dispute over the price RTÉ charges for the use of its transmission network. Despite the fact that TG4 is presently one of the three national television channels operating under the aegis of the RTÉ Authority, supported by RTÉ in a myriad of institutional ways that go beyond programme supply, TV3 claims that RTÉ is guilty of discriminatory pricing and unfair competition because it doesn't charge TG4 anything like the   2.5 million annually that it charges TV3 under the terms of a 1998 contract. Despite signing up to the 1998 deal, TV3 now argues that the transmission charge prevents it from delivering a profit and the BCI has decided to attempt a reconciliation on the charge.

Because of its huge borrowings to purchase Conrad Black's newspaper chain, CanWest found itself in difficulty towards the end of 2002 in meeting its bank obligations. Debt reduction became its priority. A major drive was launched to sell off some local Canadian papers and its television interests in New Zealand. Granada, which took a 45 percent stake in TV3 in 2000 for   48.31 million, expressed an interest in buying out CanWest's interest when it becomes available. If this happened, it would put an end to speculation about CanWest's interest in creating worldwide synergies with Granada and the ITV system in Britain, via both UTV and TV3 in Ireland. It would also put an end to anxieties about CanWest's inclination to tighten editorial control of its news services, though fears about concentration of ownership and a shrinking of diversity of news viewpoints would naturally shift to the role in Ireland's news mix of Granada, now perhaps consolidated with Carlton as the dominating force in the British ITV system. At a minimum, the proposed purchase of Carlton by Granada for 1.58 billion, if approved by British regulators, would open up very cheap access by TV3 to Carlton's most popular programmes, like *Crossroads*, *Peak Practice* and *Inspector Morse*, augmenting the success of Granada programmes on TV3, which include football rights and the popular soaps *Emmerdale* and *Coronation Street*, the latter successfully poached from RTÉ in an auction bidding frenzy that ended with Granada buying equity in TV3.

The departure of CanWest from Ireland would probably be welcomed in Ireland by some of the key sectors involved in television. TV3 is one of the leading anti-trade union employers in the country, according to Seamus Dooley, Secretary of the NUJ, who believes that "just because you decide to be a no frills operator does not mean you have the right to exploit."[132] And the independent producers guild, Film Makers Ireland, would also welcome a stronger Granada role in TV3. Its Director, Tanya Banotti, points out that "culturally, Granada is coming from a place where regulation is quite strict, a place where you have to do more home produced work". TV3 under CanWest is reaching its target of 20 percent home produced material, respecting the letter but not the spirit of the law by including repeats of the Champions League, news and weather. The target is largely meaningless, Banotti believes, because it is based on broadcast time rather than spending, unlike RTÉ's mandated investment in independent production, which is spend based: "We would have much preferred to see TV3 having to commit 20 percent of its budget to home production". TV3 complains in public about regulation, but in comparison with CanWest in Canada, many commentators in Ireland believe TV3 got off very easily from the regulator, the BCI, where there has been, as Humphreys puts it, "no willingness to flex its muscles."

In practice, the dominant tendency in the BCI has been towards "light touch" regulation, including the relaxation of ownership rules in radio as well as television. In October 2001, the BCI dramatically raised its permitted ceiling on ownership of radio stations by one company from 27 percent to 100 percent. It also agreed to allow any one owner to control up to 25 percent of all commercial broadcasting licences. This cleared the way for two companies based outside the state, Scottish Radio Holdings (SRH) and UTV to take over a number of radio stations. SRH then purchased 100 percent and took full control of Ireland's only national radio station, Today FM. SRH now owns both Today FM and Downtown Radio in Belfast, which augment its existing network of stations in Britain, as well as a range of provincial newspapers in the Republic – The Kilkenny People, The Tipperary Star, The Nationalist and Munster Advertiser, The Leitrim Observer and the Longford Leader. UTV has purchased Lite FM in Dublin as well as Live 95 FM in Limerick and the Cork radio group, County Media, which controls 96 FM and 103 FM. It also has a fifty per cent stake in Bocom, a new Dublin company that supplies advertising, news and weather content via satellite to plasma screens in airports, supermarkets and other public areas. UTV's interest in ownership of media companies South of the border hardly qualifies as a major example of globalisation's "influence at a distance," compared to the awesome potential of direct control of Irish news content from Winnipeg, but competition with

UTV is still a significant factor in the Irish media sector, as was illustrated by what bemused British observers called "the soap wars". During the Belfast Agreement talks in 1998, one of the areas of contention, needing direct Ministerial intervention by both London and Dublin, concerned RTÉ's plans to reconfigure its transmitters on the Border so that it could increase its reach into Northern Ireland from 30 percent to 70 percent – the level of reach southwards already enjoyed by Northern Ireland broadcasters. UTV objected that RTÉ could now beam *Coronation Street* Northwards and poach its viewers. The dispute was eventually settled by promising Northern broadcasters new digital wavebands in the Republic.

REVERSE THRUST

One of the central tenets of globalisation theory (often encouraged by corporate discourse) is the notion that once-powerful media centres have lost their position in the new global media structure, which has now become multi-nodal, offering greater opportunities, with the aid of new broadband high capacity distribution systems, for information flows to be diversified in many directions. Does this mean increased opportunities for RTÉ to export television programmes to parts of the huge, wealthy Anglophone world, where Irish content would probably attract very low cultural discount, and work towards a situation where the obvious financial limitations of broadcasting in a small country can be overcome? The BBC broadcasts in English to a domestic population that is almost twenty-five times greater than Ireland's. This allows it to dominate the British broadcasting market not just in final consumption areas but in neighbouring markets further up the supply chain where would-be competitors operate – new digital television channels like The History Channel, Arts World and Digital Classics. Arguably, this capacity means that the BBC is now so powerful it is crowding out actual or potential provision of media content by other suppliers, with a potential adverse impact on competition diversity and pluralism.[133] The relevant point here, of course, is the BBC's ability to globalise its services and find audiences (and revenues) overseas. Like the comparative advantage enjoyed by large American media corporations who can recoup first cover costs in the domestic market before entering foreign markets with low cost products, the BBC is poised to make several of its digital services available overseas and is already doing this successfully in news with BBC Worldwide.

RTÉ too enjoys the comparative advantage of belonging to the Anglophone world, the wealthiest, if not the largest, global language community, and uses this position to attract foreign direct investment by multinational companies keen to operate within the EU. Can this advantage be used to earn extra revenues for domestic production by exporting its television programming to large audiences overseas?

RTÉ became involved in the 1990s in two cable operations overseas, in the US and the UK, aimed at bringing Irish content into media markets where the Irish diaspora was strongest and cultural ties were closest. Celtic Vision was launched in Boston in March 1995 as an "Irish channel" relying mainly on RTÉ programming and relaunched with new partners two years later, aiming for new markets on the East Coast and access to others in a westward roll-out by being available on satellite with a footprint extending right across North America. It was considered to be a high-risk venture, given the maturity of the US cable business and the difficulty in persuading cable operators to make room on their services for another "ethnic" channel. The business plan of Celtic Vision included payments to RTÉ for the supply of programming, but RTÉ was not a shareholder. Given the channel's potential to provide a shop-window for Ireland, serving a variety of political, cultural and commercial purposes, it is surprising that it did not generate more Government attention and support in Ireland. In the final years before it went bankrupt, Celtic was recycling old RTÉ programmes.

Tara Television was launched in the Bristol/ Bath area of England in 1996 as a joint venture between RTÉ (60 percent) and United International Holdings/TCI, affiliated with the Liberty Group that had invested in Chorus Communication (one of the two cable systems in Ireland), and Riordan Communications (10 percent), a company with strong links with to Princes Holdings, the company that had investments in MMDS technology in rural Ireland. Growth in cable in the UK had generally been slow, despite entry into the market of NTL, but subscriber numbers were already climbing considerably, reaching 3.5 million by 2001. RTÉ now had the potential to reach into more homes in Britain than it could in Ireland. Initial feedback suggested that Tara Television had a good "terrestrial feel" to it, since so much of its content, especially news and current affairs programming, was beamed across the Irish Sea by satellite on a daily basis from the Montrose campus in Dublin, drawing heavily on the live or time-shifted output of RTÉ 1 and Network 2. As an investment, Tara's future was likely to parallel that of the immature UK cable market itself, which was struggling to emerge from the shadow of strong competition from BSkyB. RTÉ would receive a share of the gross subscription revenue, which would probably show healthy growth as Tara successfully negotiated delivery direct-to-home by Sky Digital in 2001.

The objective of Tara Television was to provide a high-quality English- language programme service, which would be of particular interest to the Irish community in Britain but also of interest to a wiser audience. About 80 percent of its programming originated in RTÉ, with additional sport and purchased material completing the schedule. Tara had an exclusive option on the bulk of RTÉ programming for use on UK cable services, with additional options in Canada, Australia and New Zealand. Unfortunately, this grand vision was not realised. In March 2002, the business was wound up in the High Court in Dublin, by which time RTÉ had a 20 percent stake. Its liabilities exceeded its assets by 22.8 million, made up of loans advanced to Tara by RTÉ (2.7 million) and United Pan-Europe (18 million). RTÉ had not received any payment in respect of programme costs since Tara started trading in 1997.

As if to underscore the difficulty of generating any reverse thrust in the process of globalisation, and vindicate those theorists who insist that media imperialism has been replaced by a multi-nodal global system, RTÉ's long-wave radio station has also failed in recent times. Operated for many years from studios in Trim, Co. Meath, as the pop station Atlantic 252, it was sold recently to Teamtalk 252, which also went bankrupt. RTÉ has now reacquired the transmission assets and is preparing to re-transmit Radio One on long wave to the UK.

9

CONCLUSION

It is worth pondering, finally, how broadcasting will develop over the next decade, if only to test some of the arguments made in this book and extrapolate from some of the trends identified.

We are now at the dawn of the digital age and since it is unlikely that any newer technology will be deployed in television for several decades to come, we need continual exploration of the social implications specific to both the abundance and the interactive aspects of digital television. Despite the intensive planning in RTÉ for DTT from 1998 on, it is now unlikely that Ireland will have its own DTT system in the near future. The so-called "platform wars" continue, despite earlier predictions that these contests over Internet and television distribution systems would be settled by the start of the new millennium. Take the case of cable television, considered an exciting new distribution system in the 1970s. NTL, one of the global giants with considerable power in the Irish cable television sector, faced huge financial problems in recent years but emerged from bankruptcy protection in January 2003. Its revenue from its Irish operation rose by 28 percent in the first quarter of 2003, due to a price rise and an increase in the digital television subscriber base. It now delivers television to 366,000 customers, but only 45,000 of them accessing digital television, and half of that number expected to be disconnected for non-payment of subscription. Its churn rate of 8 percent is the lowest of all NTL subsidiaries. But there is every reason to believe that the churn rate will soon begin to accelerate rapidly, as a result of a series of recent British Government decisions aimed at poducing a low-cost route towards analogue shut-down across the UK that will yield all the expected benefits of the large amount of elctromagnetic spectrum "saved" from television, made available for farming out to telecommunications. Freeview will reach about 80 percent of UK homes in the main poplation centres and Freesat will complete the coverage in rural areas. There will be no new operating costs for UK broadcasters offering digital services, as the BBC positions the two complementary delivery systems for free-to-air multichannel television and Internet access.

The situation in Ireland is far less predictable but it looks as if the Freesat system will be an overwhelmingly attractive option for many Irish households prepared to pay the once-off charge for a satellite dish, in return for crystal clear reception of UK television and whatever applications of interactivity will emerge. Cable and MMDS services will be immediate losers, as will Sky. Any commercial *raison d'etre* for an Irish DTT service will be removed. There will certainly be an impact on RTÉ's audience share and there may well be an impact on its future ability to acquire broadcasting rights for imported programmes. Thus satellite technology, with its ability to beam signals into a footprint that ignores the boundaries of national territories, brings to a new level the challenges of overspill from Britain that Ireland has had to grapple with since the origins of radio and television.

For how long will Irish public opinion leaders, that network of influential voices sometimes referred to as "the political elite," with favoured access to the media for their views, be interested in tackling the challenges of cultural globalisation and defending television that is distinctively "Irish"? Audience research tells us that if good quality Irish-made programmes are scheduled to maximise exposure, they are more avidly watched than imported content. This was not the case in earlier periods, when American programmes dominated the ratings. In this respect, television differs radically from cinema, where European or Irish-made films enjoy nowhere near the same level of popularity as American imports. This reflects the general European situation, where the huge marketing power of Hollywood has built a century-long momentum to sustain its dominant brand position. Television is quite a different medium with very different audience dynamics, including a thirst for an Irish perspective on world affairs, Irish drama and comedy, and documentaries on subjects close to home. This strong interest in indigenous programming of all kinds doesn't take from our large appetite for global culture; it complements it. The local and the global work in tandem.

In theory, this means that a privately owned television system could meet the audience need for a balanced diet of good local and good global fare. In practice (as we know from studies of television in other countries, especially those where the overall media economy is far more limited in size than people's desire for high quality television) privately owned television, driven by its unique need to produce surplus value for owners, investors and shareholders, can not provide all that is needed by individual citizens and by society generally.

We are sometimes blind to this reality in Ireland because of our access to one of the world's great exceptions to this general rule, the British ITV system, which has always done well in providing a well-balanced output of quality fiction and non-fiction. But the British example cannot be transferred to Ireland, in the form of a fantasy, for example, that TV3 can evolve into something like ITV. The much larger size of the British television economy, the strong regulatory pressure on ITV to address public interest goals in its programming, and the huge standard-setting function of the BBC over many decades, ensures that facile comparisons with ITV don't work. Looking to CanWest is probably a much better way to predict the future programming contribution of TV3 to the Irish public sphere, though the influence Granada, its partner in TV3, has also to be considered.

TELEVISION AS MERIT GOOD

Television has the potential to either restrict or expand the knowledge, emotional experience and imagination of individuals and the stock of cultural capital available in society for general use in everyday interactions in both public and private spheres. The benefits of good television (and radio and newspapers), what economists call "positive externalities," include the sharing of a common stock of information with all members of a national culture, improved social interaction, greater scrutiny of political power, awareness of community needs and values, a greater empathy with "others" in an increasingly multicultural society, an increased sense of social solidarity. Experience in other countries, but predominantly in the US, the most studied of all television systems in the world, has shown that unregulated broadcasting markets with little or no public intervention, will tend to produce more programmes with negative externalities (sensationalised and celebrity-driven news, tabloid values in analysis of current affairs, excessive and unmotivated violence in fiction, cultivation of soft porn in youth programmes, the celebration of showbiz inanity in talk shows, the narrowing of musical taste and so on) than is socially desirable.[134] Broadcasting under such conditions is not at all functioning to service an enriched public culture in which individual liberties can thrive. And just like the polluting chemical plant, the social costs of producing the product are not borne by the broadcaster.

When free markets fail to function optimally, fail to provide sufficient "merit goods," then public intervention is the most efficient way to supply the deficit. If market mechanisms under-supply merit goods that produce external benefits, then public funds are needed to redress this failure. Many of the benefits of public service broadcasting would be completely unprofitable in pure market terms (typically, programmes highly valued by small audiences but having a high cost base) and if there is no revenue from the market to provide those benefits (such as advertising or subscription revenue streams), the private broadcasting sector will produce far less than an optimum quantity of merit goods and there is widespread failure in the culture to provide for citizens cultural rights. The most obvious example of this is RTÉ's consistent support, despite the high cost, of what is broadly called "classical" or "art" music. Pop music, which didn't exist before the twentieth century, has become so pervasive a part of the culture (pumped out not only through the majority of radio stations, but also in public and commercial spaces where it is not possible to avoid it) that is has almost completely crowded classical music out. A very neo-conservative (though deeply anti-artistic) point of view would argue that if something can't hold its place in the market, it doesn't deserve to live. Because of the much larger media economy in Britain, the private radio station Classic FM in London can produce the surplus value from classical music it needs to thrive. In Ireland, support for such music comes not from the private sector, despite opportunities created by the radical deregulation of the radio sector fifteen years ago, but from public subvention in the form of RTÉ's newest radio station, Lyric FM.

Governments must therefore rectify the under-supply of programmes providing external benefits by keeping a flexible hand on the two taps that control most of RTÉ's revenue: the amount of advertising time it can utilise for generating programme production funds, and of course the level of the licence fee. Can we expect politicians in the distant future to recognise the social value of public service broadcasting by attending to those two taps when needed, especially when the broadcaster may be engaged in critical examination of some dark areas of political life that cry out for scrutiny on the mass medium of television? The answer depends not only on the political culture itself (its democratic values, its ability to deal with vested interests in an ethical way, its memory of how good television was produced in the past, its interest in thoroughly researching different broadcasting policy options before major decisions are made) but also on the voices that politicians listen to in the public sphere, either speaking up for the citizen's cultural right to good broadcasting or its opposite, decrying publicly funded television as an anachronism whose burial is long overdue.

We have already examined here the pressures being exerted in Ireland to force broadcasting to conform to a neo-classical market economic model, for example by attacking the concept of the licence fee, in both Dublin and Brussels corridors of power, as a form of unfair "state aid" that distorts the level playing pitch of pure competition. These local battles for advantage are echoed in the public-private tensions that exist at a global level. Take children's television. Note the contrast between, on the one hand, everyday international trade press discourse about globally distributed children's television (the unquestioned assumption that it is all about the ambition to take over all aspects of children's imagination through product-based programming licensed to food chains, toy stores etc.) and, on the other, European sensitivities about programme quotas, advertising minutage, the banning of programme length commercials etc. Cultural rights clash with market liberalisation policies in global arenas like the World Trade Organisation, where West European national demands to enforce obligations of pluralism in film and television are onjected to as "barriers to trade in information services." The current push for global neo-liberal policies reinvigorates similar local initiatives, like the tensions between RTÉ and TV3 in the politics of broadcasting.

As a set of ideas often highly charged with emotional commitment, neo-liberalism is an ideology with a long history that goes back over two hundred years. It developed a critical mass of support in Ireland much later than in other European countries and is now frequently framed by the media as "new" thinking. Calling it an ideology implies two things: that it serves the real interests of a very small sector of society (in the case of broadcasting, those media investors who would materially benefit from the demise of RTÉ) and that it has expanded as a belief system into a full-blown "common sense" for very large numbers of people, whose real interests are not at all served by it. Again, the history of broadcasting in the US provides an example of where this ideology emerged, was challenged, and ultimately triumphed over all its opponents, especially the 200 university-based broadcasters early in the last century, who argued for a public service model for the new medium of radio. Radio schedules, they asserted, should address people's real needs, by highlighting current affairs programming, drama, agricultural news in rural areas, and formal and informal education. It should be aimed at an inclusive audience but especially farmers, the poor, the housebound and the uneducated. Powerful interests rooted in the burgeoning advertising industry, however, were already persuading the US Government by the early 1920s that commercial broadcasting was superior, "innately democratic and American, and that even the consideration of alternatives was absurd if not dangerous."[135]

The rapid emergence of commercial broadcasting, which saw huge potential in advertising, soon eclipsed the impulse towards public funding for socially inclusive purposes. By the late 1920s, advertising was being hailed in Congress as an "inevitable" funding system that was thoroughly "American." The US and the UK models from then on diverged radically, as the British Government adopted a public service model spurred partly by a political culture that was offended by what it saw as the misuse of broadcasting across the Atlantic and partly by its desire to establish radio in the UK as a valuable addition to the existing network of publicly funded institutions set up to provide cultural resources to citizens: libraries, galleries, concert halls and museums. Diffferent social forces on each side of the Atlantic shaped the different struggles over the form broadcasting should take, as different ideologies competed for dominance. In the US the ideological power of unambiguously identifying private enterprise as the most perfect manifestation of American democracy and freedom, gained supremacy. The model of broadcasting it produced held sway even in the face of a significant but doomed Progressive struggle during the Depression to restore public service values to broadcasting.

MEDIA AND IDEOLOGY

In the Ireland of the 1990s, one effect of the increasing opening up of Irish society to global influences is that the ideology of neo-liberalism, so active in the politics of broadcasting in the US eighty years earlier, has begun to assert itself very strongly, especially in the new media that are themselves the product of neo-liberal deregulation. But as the late great French sociologist Pierre Bourdieu pointed out many times, one of the ideological effects of neo-liberal ideology is that it presents itslef as quintessentially a modern way of thinking, concealing and erasing its own lineage. Neo-liberalism is actually a conservative revolution to restore the past, but it drives its project forward in the guise of being progressive. Its opponents are labelled "dynosaurs," and this usually includes those who argue in favour of public service broadcasting. Variants of neo-liberalism embrace the argument that new technology will deal with all social needs by offering such a plethora of television channels that viewers will be able to find anything they want (and pay for just what they consume), without being required to pay for publicly funded free-to-air generalist television channels.

There is a challenge for RTÉ in this technologically determined vision of the media future, especially as youth culture in particular gets quickly bored with television schedules that attempt to cater for all interests (farmers, senior citizens, Irish speakers, children, immigrants and so on) and seek only niche channels that fit within a narrow band of tolerance, providing a flow of large volumes of television content with little variation. RTÉ has demonstrated sensitivity to this problem in its redirecting of its second channel Network Two towards a younger audience, emphasising themed evening schedules. But RTÉ is working within a larger social and ideological context in which we have seen over the last 15 years the idea of the public domain being either undermined or left to wither slowly by many of the dominant voices gaining access to the media. A new "common sense" evolved, which allowed the selling off of public institutions to the private sector, some of it derived from the inflow of political ideas from the European Union, some from neo-liberal projects adopted by Thatcher and New Labour Governments in London. It became more difficult to mobilise social arguments for the desirability of public services, and economic arguments gained supremacy: selling publicly owned institutions woul produce more efficiency or better customer service; downsizing a public company would produce savings to the Exchequer; competition would ensure that everyone would be much happier with the new arrangements being applied to social assets. Arguments centering on the public good, rooted in the principle of public ownership, got marginalised, no longer being heard much in public, or were taken into account only in some tokenistic way, or were dismissed as too idealistic or unacceptably old-fashioned, or even "looney-left." The market place would now decide how value is assigned. Competition would arbitrate fairly and indicate how much something is worth (though as we saw in the saga of the attempt to sell off RTÉ's transmission system, neo-liberal principles could be side-lined when it suited.)

Of course, the media themselves, including RTÉ, play a major role in perpetuating ideologies, that is, strong belief systems that materially benefit a few but are normalised or legitimised as incontrovertible common sense that assumes hegemony over the imagination of the majority. This is where the micro and the macro operation of broadcasting converge, and the devil is in the detail. To seek to understand this is to begin to throw light on the work of producers and researchers who are guardians of the production processes embedded in the organisational routines of RTÉ and other broadcasting organisations, the deadline-driven human environment where content is created before it is sent to the transmission towers. In the talk hohw format, for instance, which is associated with the old broadcasting category of "Light Entertainment," far less attention is paid to questions of balance, impartiality and fairness than would be the case in News and Current Affairs. Yet it is important to analyse guest lists for talk shows and understand empirically how guests are selected from lists of potential contributors, if we find that prominent programmes like"Questions and Answers" or the "Late Late Show" consistently priveledge one particular ideology where alternatives exist. Opponents of "the Stickies" in the 1970s and 1980s, for instance, criticised RTÉ for unfairly promoting guests who favoured a "revisionist" point of view in the very troubled debates bearing on the Irish collective memory of British power in Ireland. We might today question bias in the selection of guests who favour neo-liberal points of view on social issues.

The problem here is the danger of alternative viewpoints disappearing off the agenda of national conversation altogether, a phenomenon sometimes referred to by media researchers as a "spiral of silence". Because of people's fear of social isolation or separation from those around them, they tend to keep their attitudes to themselves when they think they are in a minority. They tend to use the media to scan their environment to see what views seem to be most acceptable. If the dominant media tendency is to favour one side of an issue to the exclusion of others, this further encourages people to keep quiet, which in turn makes it tougher for the media to uncover and register that opposing point of view. "Observations made in one context (the mass media) spread to another and encourage people either to proclaim their views or swallow them and keep quiet until, in a spiralling process, the one view dominates the public scene and the other disappears from public awareness, as its adherents become mute."[136]

Of course, ideology can be spun out consistently but very undramatically through some broadcasting patterns of production. How does one control for balance in attitudes to "the social" where, for instance, the majority of pop stars invited onto Light Entertainment programmes orient themselves to poverty and its alleviation in Ireland, when invited by the presenter to discuss where they apply their wealth and fame, by referring to "my favourite charity" rather than to any political project to redistribute wealth.[137] Editorial processes in broadcasting are ill equipped to monitor biases like this, such is the sheer volume of programming beamed out from transmitters every day. It occasionally happens that groups in civil society organise their own monitoring of RTÉ output, as happened when changing the law on divorce was on the political agenda and even Light Enterainment came under the scrutiny of the stop-watch.

It remains to be seen how changes in the regulation of RTÉ yet to be written into law will have an impact on public service broadcasting in Ireland. It is proposed to give the BCI a more substantial role in regulating RTÉ, but the detail has yet to be determined. In Britain, Ofcom will takes up regulation of the BBC in four areas from December 2003 – harm, offence, fairness and privacy – and the BBC Governors will regulate for impartiality and accuracy. Ofcom has indicated it is not keen to expand its role in the regulation of content, so huge is that job. What needs keen mnitoring in the revamped BCI is not oversight of RTÉ's content but how the regulator will behave in decisions that bear ultimately on dividing up the rather limited pool of resources available for both public and private media. Its instinct to date has been to see broadcasting primarily as a business to be handled with "light touch" regulation, and to respond to business needs for access to audiences rather more than to audience needs for more varied programming. Despite the arrival of a lot of new radio stations since 1988, for instance, complaints are still received about the lack of provision for jazz and world music in new radio station licenses.

The public also needs to be involved in regulation in a broader sense. There is no equivalent in Ireland to the Voice of the Listener and Viewer in Britain, an organisation of citizens who actively monitor radio and television output, research policy options, lobby for change when needed and for the defence of public broadcasting when it is threatened. As mentioned in Chapter Six, the absence of a civil society input into broadcasting is particularly acute when questions about television for children are active. RTÉ is currently organising an Audience Council along BBC lines, which will have a nationwide remit to advise the Authority. It remains to be seen if this will spark further civil society activity, which combined with RTÉ's new commitment to issuing an annual Statement of Commitments to its viewers and listeners, could convince a critical mass of citizens that public service broadcasting is in their own best interest. The trick is getting politicians to listen to their message.

GOVERNMENT AND BROADCASTING

Final considerations in this book must hover over the relationship between public broadcasters and Government. Let's look at two other European countries first.

The Hutton Enquiry was established in London in the second half of 2003 to investigate the role of the BBC and the British Government in conveying to the public information about the level of threat posed by the Saddam regime in Iraq. It brought Government-broadcaster tensions to new levels of intensity. Up to this point, everything had been going very well for the BBC. The New Labour Government had appointed one of Tony Blair's advisors on broadcasting policy (author of the Davies Report on the BBC) to be Chairman and had promised a major role for the BBC in the roll-out of digital television, after the collapse of private sector efforts in DTT. Until Hutton, 2003 had been a very good year for the BBC. Its Freesat digital system will take the Corporation to new heights of success, even beyond the borders of the UK, surpassing its current global expansion as a valued news provider to liberal American audiences via BBC World and its role as main provider of international news to the Public Broadcasting Service in the US Its recent decision to release all its digital archives free to the public sets an impressive example to other public institutions to stress free over premium services, to highlight public more than private value, to foreground social inclusivity rather than exclusion. But all this depends ultimately on the goodwill of the British Government. And now, many in New Labour are asking, is the BBC not biting the hand that feeds it, in a most public and embarrassing way through its news coverage of Iraq, and how will the Hutton revelations impinge on how these two major British institutions relate to each other in the future?

In some countries (including the US and currently much of Eastern Europe that follows its lead), Governments have decided that private television companies can be trusted to be more supine than public broadcasters when it comes to the watchdog role of the media. Hostile newspapers are not to be taken lightly at election time, but hostile television channels are too much to tolerate. In Italy, the Prime Minister Silvio Berlusconi exercises unprecedented power over both the public and the private television systems. He has seen off pressure to put his television conglomerate Mediaset into a blind trust while he is in office, or to yield control of the three terrestrial channels within the Mediaset group. At the same time, his control over the public broadcasting system RAI has tightened, to the point where major broadcasting trade unions are objecting to sinister forms of "manipulation" of RAI news output and documenting it all in a "White Book," while many critics believe RAI news is being deliberately turned into a distraction. Berlusconi's party Forza Italia pushed through Parliament a lifting of restrictions on television advertising and relaxation of cross-ownership rules for newspapers and television. For the first time, RAI's audience share (44 percent) has slipped behind Mediaset and major advertising investment is being diverted to Mediaset from RAI because of the latter's lacklustre performance for advertisers.

In Ireland, the devastating impact of Ray Burke, Minister for Communication in the early 1990s, on public service broadcasting alerted many people to the dangers that can arise when political power is abused. Could RTÉ be damaged in the future by masively negative political influence? Will its structures of regulation and governance always pass the Berlusconi test? In order to ensure that Government will not react aggressively in the future, will RTÉ always be able to follow its editorial, rather than its political instincts, when it is timely to critique Government performance?

In the second half of 2003, TV3 finally mounted a challenge to RTÉ's long-running talk show, the Late Late. Presenter Pat Kenny squared off against TV3's Eamon Dunphy at the same time on the same Friday night in the new television season. This was a major media event. Newspapers and radio stations analysed in detail the relative merits of each programme the following day. RTÉ drew a larger audience with a highly polished production. With Pat Kenny, critisc agreed, the Late Late was in a safe pair of hands. By contrast, Dunphy was less polished and more edgy, but there as a "whiff of danger" off him, as many critics noted. In the early history of the Late Late, with a young Gay Byrne in the presenter's chair, two hours of televised talk on Saturday nights provided compelling viewing for most households across the country, frequently flashing danger signals to Bishops' dominance in the public sphere and administering well-chosen shocks to the residual values of nineteenth-century Catholic piety. But RTÉ television then was the only channel available to most people. In a much more competitive environment, will RTÉ in the future be able to project the "whiff of danger" that audiences increasingly want, particularly when it turns its cameras on the politics of corporate Ireland? Without this, RTÉ will no longer be able to make the vital cultural connections between nation and state that made it such a fundamental engine of development in Ireland for much of the twentieth century.

NOTES

[1] John Horgan (2001) *Irish Media: A Critical History Since 1922*. London: Routledge: 50.

[2] Farrel Corcoran (2002) "The Political Instrumentality of Cultural Memory" *Javnost – The Public*, 9 (3): 49-64.

[3] Philip Elliott (1979) "Media Organisations and Occupations: An Overview," in James Curran, Michael Gurevitch and Janet Woollacott (eds.) *Mass Communication and Society*. London: Sage.

[4] Michael Tracey (1996) "Beyond Governance: The Triumph of Populism and Parochialism in the 21st Century." *Javnost – The Public*, 3: 23-33.

[5] "Rights Monitor Critical of US Media Ownership." *Irish Times*, 30 May 2003.

[6] Report of the Committee on Broadcasting." London, HMSO: 9.

[7] Ray Mac Manais (2003) *Maire Mac Giolla Iosa: Breathaisneis*. Galway: Clo Ian-Chonnachta.

[8] David Miller (1994) *Don't Mention the War*. London: Pluto Press; David Miller (1994) *Rethinking Northern Ireland: Culture, Ideology and Colonialism*. London: Longman; Bill Rolston (1996) *War and Words: The Northern Ireland Media Reader*. Belfast: Beyond the Pale Publications; Liz Curtis (2,000) *Ireland: the Propaganda War*. Belfast: Sasta; Desmond Fennell (1993) *Heresy: the Battle of Ideas in Modern Ireland*. Belfast: Blackstaff Press.

[9] Richard Collins and James Purnell (1996) "The Future of the BBC." *Javnost – The Public*, 3 (2): 71-80.

[10] James Curran (1998) "Crisis of Public Communication." In Tamar Liebes and James Curran (eds.) *Media, Ritual and Identity*. London: Routlege: 192-3.

[11] Robert Savage (1996). *Irish Television: The Political and Social Origins*. Cork: Cork University Press.

[12] John Horgan (1997). *Sean Lemass: The Enigmatic Patriot*. Dublin: Gill & Macmillan: 313.

[13] John Horgan (2001). *Irish Media: A Critical History*. London: Routledge: 152- 153.

[14] *Irish Times*, 18/8/1995.

[15] *Irish Times*, 16/8/1995.

[16] *Active or Passive: Broadcasting in the Future Tense* (1995). Dublin: Stationery Office: 164.

[17] Serge Robilliard (1995). *Television in Europe: Regulatory Bodies*. London: John Libbey: 287.

[18] *Response to the Green Paper on Broadcasting* (1995). Dublin, RTÉ.

[19] Farrel Corcoran (1996). "Arts Council of the Air." *Javnost – The Public*, 3 (2): 9 – 22.

[20] *Clear Focus: the Government's Proposals for Broadcasting Legislation* (1997). Dublin: Stationery Office.

[21] *Clear Focus*: 47.

[22] *IRTC Response to the Green Paper on Broadcasting* (1995). Dublin: IRTC/BCI.

[23] C.S. Andrews (1982), *Man of No Property*. Dublin: Mercier Press: 286.

[24] Robert Savage (1996), *Irish Television: the Political and Social Origins*. Cork: Cork University Press: 109.

[25] John Horgan (1997), *Sean Lemass: the Enigmatic Patriot*. Dublin: Gill and Macmillan: 313.

[26] Horgan (1997): 231.

[27] Lelia Doolan, Jack Dowling and Bob Quinn (1969), *Sit Down and Be Counted: the Cultural Evolution of a Television Station*. Dublin, Wellington publishers: 91.

[28] C.S.Andrews (1982): 106.

[29] C.S.Andrews: 278.

[30] Doolan et al. (1969); 102

[31] T.P.Hardiman (2001): personal communication.

[32] D. Kelley and R. Donway (1990), "Liberalism and Free Speech." In J.Lichtenberg (ed.) *Mass Media and Democracy*, New York: Cambridge University Press.

[33] Centre for Digital Democracy (May, 2003): www.democraticmedia.org

[34] James Curran (1997), "Mass Media and Democracy Revisited." In J. Curran & M. Gurevitch (eds.) *Mass Media and Society*: London: Arnold.

[35] A. Sanchez-Taberno (1993), *Media Concentration in Europe*. Manchester: European Institute for the Media; E. Herman and R. McChesney (1997), *Global Media: the New Missionaries of Global Capitalism*. London: Cassell; J. Tunstall and M. Palmer (91991), *Media Moguls*. London: Routledge; B. Bagdikian (1999), *The Media Monopoly*. Boston, Beacon Press.

[36] P. Chadwick (1989), *Media Mates*. Melbourne: Macmillan.

[37] Curran (1997): 87.

[38] *Irish Times*, 9 November 1995.

[39] *Irish Times*, 9 November 1995.

[40] Horgan (1997): 151.

[41] Horgan (1997): 317.

[42] Francois Godard (2002), "Is There a Second Chance for Cable TV?" *SIS Briefings*: Geneva, EBU.

[43] Bob Quinn (2001), *Maverick: A Dissident View on Broadcasting Today*. Dingle, Brandon.

[44] Quinn (2001): 239.

[45] Quinn (2002): 247.

[46] In 1985, the Fine Gael led Government asked the RTÉ Authority and its Chairman, Fred O'Donovan, to postpone the appointment of a new Director-General, because its selection of John Sorohan was unacceptable. Vincent Finn was then appointed Director-General. Sorohan found himself working in a new capacity with Finn when a new Government appointed him Chairman of RTÉ.

[47] Peter Feeney (2000), "Government and Broadcasting: Maintaining a Balance." In *Government, Elections and Political Communication: A Festschrift for Brian Farrell*. Dublin: RTÉ.

[48] John Horgan (2001) *Irish Media: A Critical History since 1922*. London: Routledge.

[49] Robert Savage (1996) *Irish Television: The Political and Social Origins*. Cork: Cork University Press: 209.

[50] John Sinclair, Elizabeth Jacka and Stuart Cunningham (1996), *New Patterns in Global Television*. Oxford: Oxford University Press; Ali Mohammadi (1997), *International Communication and Globalisation*. London: Sage.

[51] Anthony Giddens (1990). *The Consequences of Modernity*. Cambridge: Polity Press; David Harvey (1989), *The Condition of Postmodernity*. Oxford: Blackwell; Paul Hirst and Gerard Thomson (1996), *Globalisation in Question*. Cambridge: Polity Press; Roland Robertson (1992), *Globalisation: Social Theory and Global Culture*. London: Sage.

[52] *The Impact of Digital Technology on the Transmission of Television Services*. Dublin: RTÉ, 1995.

[53] *Digital Television and the Information Society: An Implementation Strategy*. Dublin: RTÉ, 1997.

[54] *DIGICO Business Plan*. Dublin: BDO Simpson Xavier, 1998.

[55] Síle De Valera, *Dail Debates*, 28th March 2000.

[56] Farrel Corcoran (1999), "Towards Digital Television in Europe." *Javnost – The Public*, 6 (3): 67 – 86.

[57] Richard Collins (2002). " 2002 – Digital Television in the United Kingdom." *Javnost – The Public*, 9 (4): 5 – 18.

[58] *Telecommunications and Broadcasting Services (TBS), BBC 'Freesat' Digital Strategy: the Implications for RTÉ and Ireland Inc.* Dublin: RTÉ.

[59] *Report on Television and Social Behaviour* (1972). Washington DC: US Government Printing Office.

[60] Barrie Gunter and Jill McAleer (1997). *Children and Television*. London: Routledge.

[61] Naomi Klein (2000). *No Logo*. London, Flamingo: 23.

[62] *Broadcasting and Cable*. September 1998.

[63] *Television Europe*, September 1998.

[64] L. K. Wong (1996). "Tobacco Advertising and Children: the Limits of First Amendment Protection," *Journal of Business Ethics*, 15 (2): 1051-1064.

[65] "The Rise and Rise of Pester Power." *Sunday Business Post*, 3 January 1999: 18.

[66] Norma Pecora (1998). *The Business of Children's Entertainment*. New York: Guilford Press.

[67] Pecora: 36.

[68] William Melody (1973). *Children's Television: The Economics of Exploitation*. New Haven, CT: Yale University Press.

[69] Farrel Corcoran (1999). "Towards Digital Television in Europe." *Javnost – The Public*, 6 (3): 67-86.

[70] Colin Hoskins, Stuart McFadyen and Adam Finn (1997). *Global Television and Film*. Oxford: Clarendon Press.

[71] Hoskins, McFadyen abnd Finn: 94.

[72] Jay Blumler and Daniel Biltereyst (1997). *The Integrity and Erosion of Public Television for Children*. Dusseldorf: European Institute for the Media.

[73] Bob Quinn (2001). *Maverick: A Dissident View of Broadcasting Today*. Dingle, Brandon :164.

[74] Robert Savage (1996). *Irish Television: The Political and Social Origins*. Cork: Cork University Press.

[75] Quinn: 189.

[76] E.A. Rubenstrin, G.A.Comstock & J.P.Murray (eds.) (1972). Televison and Social Behaviour, Volume 4: *Television in Day-to-Day Life: Patterns of Use*. Washington DC: US Government Printing Office; F.G.Kline & P. Clarke (eds.) (1972). *New Models for Mass Communication Research*. Beverly Hills, Sage; E.L.Palmer & A.Dorr (eds.) (1980) *Childrean and the Faces of Television*. New York: Accademic Press; D. Greer, R. Potts, W.C.Wright & A.C. Huston (1982). "The Effects of Television Commercial Form and Commercial Placement on Children's Social Behaviour and Attention." *Child Development*, 53: 611-619; D.R.Rolandelli (1989). "Children and Television: the Visual Superiority Effect Reconsidered." *Journal of Broadcasting and Electronic Media*, 33 (1): 69-81.

[77] B.S. Greenberg, S. Fazal and M.Wober (1986). *Children's View on Advertising*. London, Independent Broadcasting Authority.

[78] B.J. Blosser & D.F. Roberts (1984). "Age Differences in Children's Perception of Message Intent." *Communication Research*, 12: 455-484.

[79] D. Kunkel & D. Roberts (1991). "Young Minds and Marketplace Values: Issues in Children's Television Advertising." *Journal of Social Issues*, 47: 57-72.

[80] Gunter & McAleer: 146 ff.

[81] Farrel Corcoran (2003). *Cigarette Advertising and Children's Smoking*. Dublin: Department of Health.

[82] George Gerbner et al., (1980). "The 'Mainstreaming' of America." *Journal of Communication*, 30: 10-29.

[83] Gunter & McAleer: 134.

[84] Edward Herman & Robert McChesney (1997). *Global Media: New Missionaries of Global Capitalism*. London, Cassell.

[85] Celia Von Feilitzen & Ulla Carlson (eds.) (2000). *Children in the New Media Landscape: Games, Pornography, Perceptions*. Goteborg: UNESCO International Clearing House on Children and Violance on the Screen.

[86] Alissa Quart (2002). *Branded: The Buying and Selling of Teenagers*. New York, Persens.

[87] Abram de Swaan(1992). "Notes on the Emerging Global Language System: Regional, National and Super-National. " *Media Culture and Society* 13 (1): 309-323.

[88] Padraig O Riagain & Micheal O Gliasain (1993) *National Survey on Languages: Preliminary Report*. Dublin: Instiuid Teangeolaiochta Eireann.

[89] Reg Hindley (1990). *The Death of the Irish Language: A Qualified Obituary*. London: Routledge.

[90] Terence Browne (1985). *Ireland: A Social and Cultural History 1922-1985*. London: Fontana: 55.

[91] Geraldine Moane (2002). "Colonialism and the Celtic Tiger." In P.Kirby, L.Gibbons & M.Cronin (eds.) *Reinventing Ireland: Culture, Society and the Global Economy*. London, Pluto Press: 109-123.

[92] O Riagain & O Gliasain.

[93] Olle Findahl (1989). Language in the Age of Satellite Television." *European Journal of Communication* 4 (2): 133-159.

[94] O Riagain and O Gliasain.

[95] Odhairnet Ni Cheilleachair (1999). *Teilifis na Gaeilge and the Evolution of a Minority Language Television Station*. Dublin City University: MA Thesis: 17.

[96] *Irish Times*, 13 January 1996.

[97] John Sorohan (1994). Chairman's Introduction. *RTÉ Annual Report 1994*. Dublin: RTÉ.

[98] John Pilger (1998).. *Hidden Agendas*. London, Vintage.

[99] Not for the first, time I found that judicious use of the pages of the *Irish Times* provided a public message board for information that needed to be heard in Government or broadly within RTÉ. The launch of the classical music station Lyric FM benefited from this also. A request for approval for the launch of Lyric FM was sent to the Department early in 1995 and it sank without trace. When we became convinced that it was now or never for the establishment of a dedicated classical music station, I mentioned the Departmental delay to Michael Foley, Media Correspondent of the *Irish Times*, who promptly asked me for enough background information on the project for a full-length article. Approval to proceed with the launch of Lyric was issued within a few days of the publication of Foley's article.

[100] Lorna Siggins, *Irish Times* 23 May 2002.

[101] Lorna Siggins, *Irish Times* 19 February 2003.

[102] Sean de Freine (1965). *The Great Silence*. Dublin: Gill & Macmillan.

[103] Declan Kiberd (1996). *Inventing Ireland: The Literature of the Modern Nation*. London, Vintage: 649.

[104] Cliff Taylor, *Irish Times* 8 January 2003.

[105] William K. Tabb (2002). *Unequal Partners: A Primer on Globalisation*. New York: The New Press; Peter Berger & Samuel Huntington (2002). *Cultural Diversity in the Modern World*. Oxford: Oxford University Press.

[106] Herbert Schiler (1976). *Communication and Cultural Domination*. New York: M.E.Sharpe. Ali Mohammadi (1997). *International Communication and Globalisation*. London: Sage. Herbert Schiller (1989) Culture Inc.: *The Corporate Takeover of Public Expression*. New York: Oxford University Press. Herbert Schiller (1991). "Not yet the Post-Imperialist Era." *Critical Studies in Mass Communication*, 8: 13-28.

[107] Daya Kishan Thussu (1998) *Electronic Empires: Global Media and Local Resistance*. London: Arnold. Jaap van Ginneken (1998). *Understanding Global News*. London: Sage. Cees Hamelink (1994) *The Politics of World Communication*. London: Sage. Daya Kiwshan Thussu(2000). International Communication. London: Arnold.

[108] Anthony Giddens (1990). *The Consequences of Modernity.* Cambridge: Polity Press. David Harvey (1989). *The Condition of Postmodernity.* Oxford: Basil Blackwell.

[109] Arjun Appadurai (1996). *Modernity at Large: Cultural Dimensions of Globalisation.* Minneapolis MN: University of Minnesota Press.

[110] John Sinclair, Elizabeth Jacka & Stuart Cunningham (1996). *New Patterns in Global Television.* Oxford: Oxford University Press; John Tomlinson (1991). *Cultural Imperialism.* Baltimore: Johns Hopkins University Press.

[111] William Tabb: 14.

[112] Colin Hoskins, Stuart McFadyen & Adam Finn (1997). *Global Television and Film.* Oxford: Clarendon Press.

[113] Albert Moran (1998). *Copycat TV: Globalisation, Programme Formats and Cultural Identity.* Luton: University of Luton Press.

[114] Hugh O'Donnell (1998). *Good Times, Bad Times: Soap Operas in Western Europe.* London: Cassell.

[115] Edward Herman & Robert McChesney (1997). *Global Media: New Missionaries of Global Capitalism.* London: Cassell.

[116] Alvin Toffler (1990) *The Third Wave.* New York: Bantam; Kevin Kelly (1999) *New Rules for the New Economy: Ten Ways the Network is Changing Everything.* London: Fourth Estate; Nicholas Negroponte (1995) *Being Digital.* London: Hodder and Stoughton.

[117] *Irish Times,* 26 April 1997.

[118] Kevin Dawson, "The TV Empire of Israel Asper," *Sunday Business Post,* 3 January 1999.

[119] Herchel Hardin (1986) *Closed Circuits: The Sell-out of Canadian TV.* Harper Collins.

[120] Conor Lally, "Granada Confirms Interest in 90 percent Share in TV3," *Irish Times,* 17 October 2002.

[121] "Corporate Censorship," *Index on Censorship,* 17 October 2002;

[122] "Canadian Publsher Raises Hackles," *Washington Post Foreign Service,* 27 January 2002.

[123] IFJ Media Release, 14 March 2002.

[124] "Corporate Censorship," *Index on Censorship,* 18 April 2002.

[125] *The Toronto Star,* 19 December 2001.

[126] "Ownership Chill in Canada." *Colombia Journalism Review:* September 2002: www.cjr.org

[127] *The Toronto Star,* 31 December 2001.

[128] *The Manitoban,* 20 March 2002.

[129] *Irish Times,* 23 January 2003.

[130] Farrel Corcoran (1996) "Arts Council of the Air," *Javnost – The Public* 3 (2): 9 – 21.

[131] Ciaran Brennan, *Irish Times* 16 November 2001.

[132] Joe Humphreys, *Irish Times* 19 October 2002.

[133] Richard Collins (2002) "2002 – Digital Television in the United Kingdom." *Javnost – The Public* 9 (4): 5 – 18.

[134] Farrel Corcoran (2001). "Cultural Rights and Media Performance." In Eoin Cassidy and Andrew McGrady (eds.) *Media and the Marketplace: Ethical Perspectives.* Dublin, Institute of Public Administration: 15-32.

[135] Brian Winston (1998) *Media Technology and Society: A History from the Telegraph to the Internet.* London, Routledge: 81.

[136] Elizabeth Noelle-Neumann (1985). *The Spiral of Silence: Our Social Skin.* Chicago: University of Chicago Press: 5.

[137] For a good discussion of ideological aspect of the representation of poverty in RTÉ's output in

the 1990s, see Eoin Devereux (1998). *Devils and Angels: Television, Ideology and the Coverage of Poverty.* Luton: University of Luton Press.

BIBLIOGRAPHY

Allen, Kieran. (2000) *The Celtic Tiger: the Myth of Social Partnership in Ireland*. Manchester: Manchester University Press.

Amitai-Talai, Vered & Wulff, Helena. (1995) (eds) *Youth Cultures*. London: Routledge.

Anderson, Benedict. (1983) *Imagined Communities: Reflections on the Origin and Spread of Nationalism*. London: Verso.

Andrews, C.S. (1982) *Man of No Property*. Cork: Mercier Press.

Bagdikian, Ben. (1999) *The Media Monopoly*. Boston: Beacon Press.

Berger, Peter & Huntington, Samuel. (2002) *Many Globalisations: Cultural Diversity in the Modern World*. Oxford: Oxford University Press.

Berry, Gordon & Asamen, Joy. (1993) (eds) *Children and Television: Images in a Changing Sociocultural World*. London: Sage.

Blain, Neil, Boyle, Raymond & O'Donnell, Hugh. (1993) (eds) *Sport and National Identity in the European Media*. Leicester: Leicester University Press.

Blosser, B.J. & Roberts, D.F. (1984) "Age Differences in Children's Perceptions of Message Intent." *Communication Research* 12: 455-484.

Blumler, Jay & Gurevitch, Michael. (1995) (eds) *The Crisis of Public Communication*. London: Routledge.

Blumler, Jay & Biltereyst, Daniel. (1997) *The Integrity and Erosion of Public Television for Children*. Dusseldorf: European Institute for the Media.

Breen, Richard et al., (1990) (eds) *Understanding Contemporary Ireland: State, Class and Development in the Republic of Ireland*. Dublin: Gill & Macmillan.

Browne, Terence. (1985) *Ireland: A Social and Cultural History 1922-1985*. London: Fontana.

Boyd-Barrett & Rantanen, Terhi. (1998) (eds) *The Globalisation of News*. London: Sage.

Braman, Sandra & Sreberny-Mohammadi, Annabelle. (1996) (eds) *Globalisation, Communication and Transnational Civil Society*. Creskill NJ: Hampton Press.

Buckingham, David. (1996) *Moving Images: Understanding Children's Emotional Responses to Television*. Manchester: Manchester University Press.

Burns, Tom. (1977) *The BBC: Public Institution and Private World*. London: Macmillan.

Butler, David. (1995) *The Trouble with Reporting Northern Ireland*. Aldershot: Avebury Press.

Byrne, Gay. (1972) *To Whom it Concerns: Ten Years of the Late Late Show*. Dublin: Torc Books.

Calhoun, Craig. (1992) (ed) *Habermas the the Public Sphere*. Cambridge: MIT Press.

Carlson, Ulla & von Feilitzen, Celia.(1998) (eds) *Children and Media Violence*. Goteborg: Nordicom/UNESCO.

Chadwick, Peter. (1989) *Media Mates*. Melbourne: Macmillan.

Clancy, Patrick et al,. (1995) (eds) *Irish Society: Sociological Perspectives*. Dublin: Institute of Public Administration.

Cohen, Akiba et al., (1996) (eds) *Global Newsrooms, Local Audiences*. London: John Libbey.

Collins, Richard & Purnell, James. (1996) "The Future of the BBC." *Javnost – The Public* 3 (2): 71-80.

Collins, Richard. (2002) "2002- Digital Television in the United Kingdom." *Javnost- The Public* 9 (4): 5-18.

Corcoran, Farrel. (1996) "Arts Council of the Airwaves." *Javnost – The Public*. 3 (2): 9-22.

Corcoran, Farrel. (1999) "Towards Digital Television in Europe." *Javnost – The Public*. 6 (3): 67-86.

Corcoran, Farrel. (2001) "Cultural Rights and Media Performance." In E.G.Cassidy & A.G.McGrady (eds) *Media and the Marketplace: Ethical Perspectives*. Dublin: Institute of Public Administration.

Corcoran, Farrel. (2002) "The Political Instrumentality of Cultural Memory." *Javnost-The Public*. 9 (3): 49-64.

Corcoran, Farrel. (2002) *Cigarette Advertising and Children's Smoking*. Dublin: Department of Health.

Corcoran, Farrel. (2003) "Historical Roots of the Public Service Concept in Anglo-American Broadcasting." Paper presented in the Foundations of Communication Studies in Pre-20th Century European Thought Euricom Colloquium, Piran.

Corcoran, Farrel & Preston, Paschal. (1995) *Democracy and Communication in the New Europe*. Cresskill, NJ: Hampton Press.

Curran, James & Gurevitch, Michael. (1997) *Mass Media and Society*. London: Arnold.

Curran, James. (2000) (ed) *Media Organisations in Society*. London: Arnold.

Curtis, Liz. (2000) *Ireland: the Propaganda War*. Belfast: Sasta.

Dahlgren, Peter. (1995) *Television and the Public Sphere*. London: Sage.

De Freine, Sean. (1965) *The Great Silence*. Dublin: Gill & Macmillan.

Department of Arts, Culture and the Gaeltacht. (1995) *Active or Passive? Broadcasting in the Future Tense: Green Paper on Broadcasting*. Dublin: Stationery Office.

De Swaan, Abram. (1992) "Notes on the Emerging Global Language System." *Media Culture and Society* 13 (1): 309-323.

Devereux, Eoin. (1998) *Devils and Angels: Television, Ideology and the Coverage of Poverty*. London: University of Luton Press.

Digital Television and the Information Society: An Implementation Strategy. (1997) Dublin: RTÉ.

Doolan, Lelia, Dowling, Bob & Quinn, Bob. (1969) *Sit Down and Be Counted: the Cultural Evolution of a Television Station*. Dublin: Wellington.

Elliott, Philip. (1979) "Media Organisations and Occupations." In J.Curran, M. Gurevitch & J. Woollatott (eds). *Mass Communication and Society*. London: Sage.

Farrell, Brian. (1984) *Communications and Community in Ireland*. Cork: Mercier Press.

Featherstone, Mike. (1990) (ed) *Global Culture: Nationalism, Globalisation and Modernity*. London: Sage.

Fennell, Desmond. *Heresy: the Battle of Ideas in Modern Ireland*. Belfast: Blackstaff Press.

Findahl, Olle. (1989) "Language in the Age of Satellite Television." *European Journal of Communication* 4 (2): 133-159.

Fisher, Desmond. (1978) *Broadcasting in Ireland*. London: Routledge and Kegan Paul.

Fornas, Johan. (1995) *Cultural Theory and Late Modernity*. London: Sage.

Fornas, Johan & Goran, Bolin. (1995) (eds) *Youth Culture in Late Modernity*. London: Sage.

Gellner, Douglas. (1990) *Television and the Crisis of Democracy*. Boulder: Westview.

Gerbner, George at al,. "The Mainstreaming of America." *Journal of Communication* 30 (1): 10-29.

Gibbons, Luke. (1984) "From Kitchen Sink to Soap." In M.McLoone & J.McMahon (eds) *Television and Irish society: 21 Years of Irish Television*. Dublin: RTÉ/IFI, 21-53.

Gibbons, Luke. *Transformations in Irish Culture*. Cork: Cork University Press.

Giddens, Anthony. (1990) *The Consequences of Modernity*. Cambridge: Polity Press.

Gorham, Maurice. (1967) *Forty Years of Irish Broadcasting*. Dublin: Talbot Press.

Greenberg, Bradley et al,. (1986) *Children's View on Advertising*. London: Independent Broadcasting Authority.

Glasgow University Media Group. (1982) *Really Bad News*. London: Routledge.

Greer, D. et al., (1982) "The Effects of Television Commercial Form and Commercial Placement on Children's Social Behaviour and Attention." *Child Development* 53: 611-619.

Gripsrud, Jostein. (2002) *Understanding Media Cultures*. London: Arnold.

Gunter, Barrie & McAleer, Jill. (1997) *Children and Television*. London: Routledge.

Habermas, Jurgen. (1991) *The Structural Transformation of the Public Sphere*. Cambridge: MIT Press.

Hamelink, Cees. (1994) *The Politics of World Communication*. London: Sage.

Hamilton, James. (1998) *Chaneling Violence: The Economic Market for Violent Television Programming*. Princeton: Princeton University Press.

Harvey, David. (1989) *The Condition of Postmodernity*. Oxford: Blackwell.

Hazelkorn, Ellen. (1996) "New Technologies and Changing Work Practices in the Media." *Irish Communications Review* 6 : 28-39.

Herman, Edward & McChesney, Robert. (1997) *Global Media: New Missionaries of Global Capitalism*. London: Cassell.

Heichel, Hardin. (1986) *Closed Circuits: the Sell-out of Canadian Television*. London: Harper Collins.

Hindley, Reg. (1990) *The Death of the Irish Language: A Qualified Obituary*. London: Routledge.

Holt, Eddie & Sheehan, Helena. (1997) "Television in Ireland." In J. Coleman & B. Rollett (eds) *Television in Europe*. Exeter: Intellect Books.

Horgan, John. (1987) *Sean Lemass: Enigmatic Patriot*. Dublin: Gill & Macmillan.

Horgan, John. (2001) *Irish Media: A Critical History*. London: Routledge.

Hoskins, Colin, McFadyen, Stuart & Finn, Adam. (1997) *Global Television and Film*. Oxford: Clarendon Press.

Humphreys, Peter. (1996) *Mass Media and Media Policy in Western Europe*. Manchester: Manchester University Press.

Hutton, Sean & Stewart, Paul. (1991) (eds) *Ireland's Histories: Aspects of State, Society and Ideology*. London: Routledge.

Ishikawa, Sakae. (1996) *Quality Assessment of Television*. Luton: University of Luton Press.

Kelly, Kevin. (1999) *New Rules for the New Economy*. London: Fourth Estate.

Kelly, Mary & Rolston, Bill. (1995) "Broadcasting in Ireland: Issues of National Identity and Censorship." In P.Clancy et al. (eds) *Irish Society: Sociological Perspectives*. Dublin: Institute of Public Administration.

Kelly, Mary & O'Connor, Barbara. (1997) (eds) *Media Audiences in Ireland*. Dublin: University College Dublin Press.

Kenny, Colum. (1997) "TV3 and the Regulation of Competition in Broadcasting." In M.

McGonagle (ed) *Media: the Views of Journalists and Lawyers*. Dublin: Round Hall- Sweet & Maxwell.

Kiberd, Damian. (1999) (ed) *Media in Ireland: The Search for Ethical Journalism*. Dublin: Open Air.

Kiberd, Declan. (1996) *Inventing Ireland: The Literature of the Modern Nation*. London: Vintage.

Kirby, Peadar, Gibbons, Luke & Cronin, Michael. (2002) *Reinventing Ireland: Culture, Society and the Global Economy*. London: Pluto.

Klein, Naomi. (2000) *No Logo*. London: Verso.

Kline, F.G. & Clarke, P. (1972) (eds) *New Models for Mass Communication Research*. Beverly Hills: Sage.

Kunkel, D. & Roberts, D. (1991) "Young Minds and Marketplace Values: Issues in Children's Television Advertising." *Journal of Social Issues* 47: 57-72.

Lee, Joseph. (1997) "Democracy and Public Service Broadcasting in Ireland." In D. Kiberd (ed) *Media in Ireland: The Search for Diversity*. Dublin: Open Air.

Lichtenberg, James. (1990) *Mass Media and Democracy*. New York: Cambridge University Press.

Liebes, Tamar & Curran, James. (1998) *Media, Ritual and Identity*. London: Routledge.

MacBeth, Tanis. (1996) *Tuning in to Young Viewers: Social Science Perspectives on Television*. London: Sage.

MacManais, Ray. (2003) *Maire Mac Giolla Iosa: Breathaisneis*. Galway: Clo Iar-Channachta.

MacRedmond, Louis. (1976) (ed) *Written on the Wind: Personal Memories of Irish Radio 1926-1976*. Dublin: RTÉ.

Madge, Tim. (1989) *Beyond the BBC: Broadcasters and the Public in the 1980s*. London: Macmillan.

McLoone, Martin. (1991) (ed) *Culture, Identity and Broadcasting in Ireland: Local Issues, Global Perspectives*. Belfast: Institute of Irish Studies.

McLoone, Martin. (1996) (ed) *Broadcasting in a Divided Community*. Belfast: Institute of Irish Studies.

McLoone, Martin & MacMahon, John. (1984) *Television and Irish Society: 21 Years of Irish Television*. Dublin: RTÉ/IFI.

McPhail, Thomas. (2002) *Global Communication: Theories, Stakeholders and Trends*. Boston: Allyn & Bacon.

McQuail, Denis. (1992) *Media Performance: Mass Communication and the Public Interest*. London: Sage.

McQuail, Denis & Siune, Karen. (1998) (eds) *Media Policy: Convergence, Concentration and Commerce*. London: Sage.

Melody, William. (1973) *Children's Television: The Economics of Exploitation*. New Haven: Yale University Press.

Miller, David. (1994) *Don't Mention the War: Northern Ireland, Propaganda and the Media*. London: Verso.

Miler, David (1994) *Rethinking Northern Ireland: Culture, Ideology and Colonialism*. London: Bergman.

Mohammadi, Ali. (1997) *International Communication and Globalisation*. London: Sage.

Nordenstreng, Kaarle & Schiller, Herbert. (1993) (eds) *Beyond National Sovereignty: International Communication in the 1990s*. Norwood NJ: Ablex.

Negroponte, Nicholas. (1995) *Being Digital*. London: Hodder & Stoughton.

Ni Cheilleachair, Ornaith. (1999) *Teilifis na Gaeilge and the Evolution of a Minority Language Television Station*. Dublin City University: Unpublished MA Thesis.

Ni Dhonnchadha, Mairin & Dorgan, Theo. (1991) (eds) *Revising the Rising*. Derry: Field Day.

Noelle-Neumann, Elisabeth. (1985) *The Spiral of Silence*. Chicago: University of Chicago Press.

O'Donnell, Hugh. (1998) *Good Times, Bad Times: Soap Operas in Western Europe*. London: Cassell.

O Riagain, Padraig & O Gliasain, Michael. (1993) *National Survey on Languages*. Dublin: Instituid Teangeolaiochta Eireann.

Ostergaard, Bernt. (1997) (ed) *The Media in Western Europe*. London: Sage.

Palmer, E.L. & Dorr, A. (1980) (eds) *Children and the Faces of Television*. New York: Academic Press.

Pecora, Norma. (1998) *The Business of Children's Entertainment*. New York: Guilford Press.

Philo, Greg. (1990). *Seeing and Believing: The Influence of Television*. London: Routledge.

Pilger, John. (1998) *Hidden Agendas*. London: Vintage.

Pilkington Committee. (1962) *Report of the Committee on Broadcasting*. London: HMSO.

Quinn, Bob. (2001) *Maverick: A Dissident View of Broadcasting Today*. Dingle: Brandon.

Quart, Alissa. (2002) *Branded: The Buying and Selling of Teenagers*. New York: Persens.

Raftery, Mary & O'Sullivan, Eoin. (1999) *Suffer the Little Children: the Inside Story of Ireland's Industrial Schools*. Dublin: New Island.

Report on Television and Social Behaviour. (1972) Washington D.C.: Government Printing Office.

Robbins, Derek. (2000) *Bourdieu and Culture*. London: Sage.

Robertson, Roland. (1992) *Globalisation: Social Theory and Global Culture*. London: Sage.

Robilliard, Serge. (1995) *Television in Europe: Regulatory Bodies – Status, Functions and Powers in 35 European Countries*. London: John Libbey.

Rolandelli, D.R. (1989) "Children and Television: the Visual Superiority Effect Reconsidered." *Journal of Broadcasting and Electronic Media* 33 (1): 69-81.

Rubenstein, Eli, Comstock, George & Murray, John. (1972) (eds) *Television and Social Behaviour*. Washington: Government Printing Office.

Sanchez-Taberno, Alfonso. (1993) *Media Concentration in Europe*. Manchester: European Institute for the Media.

Savage, Robert. (1996) *Irish Television: Political and Social Origins*. Cork: Cork University Press.

Scannell, Paddy & Cardiff, David. (1991) *A Social History of British Broadcasting*. Oxford: Blackwell.

Schiller, Herbert. (1976) *Communication and Cultural Domination*. New York: M.E.Sharpe.

Schiller, Herbert. (1989) *Culture Inc.: The Corporate Takeover of Public Expression*. New York: Oxford University Press.

Schlesinger, Philip. (1991) *Media, State and Nation*. London: Sage.

Sheehan, Helena. (1987) *Irish Television Drama: A Society and Its Stories*. Dublin: RTÉ.

Sinclair, John, Jacka, Elizabeth & Cunningham, Stuart. (1996) *New Patterns in Global Television*. Oxford: Oxford University Press.

Sreberny-Mohammadi, Annabelle et al,. (1997) (eds) *Media in a Global Context*. London: Arnold.

Tabb, William. (2002) *Unequal Partners: A Primer on Globalisation*. New York: New Press.

Taylor, Philip. (1997) *Global Communications, International Affairs and the Media Since 1945*. London: Routledge.

The Impact of Digital Technology on the Transmission of Television Services. (1995) Dublin: RTÉ.

Thussu, Daya. (1998) *Electronic Empires: Global Media and Local Resistance*. London: Arnold.

Thussu, Daya. (2000) *International Communication*. London: Arnold.

Tomlinson, John. (1991) *Cultural Imperialism*. Baltimore: Johns Hopkins Press.

Toffler, Alvin. (1990) *The Third Wave*. New York: Bantam.

Tracey, Michael. (1996) "Beyond Governance: The Triumph of Populism and Parochialism in the 21st Century." *Javnost – The Public* 3 (1): 23-33.

Tulloch, John & Alvarado, Manuel. (1983) *Doctor Who: the Unfolding Text*. New York: St. Martin's Press.

Tulloch, John & Jenkins, Henry. (1995) *Science Fiction Audiences: Watching Doctor Who and Star Trek*. London: Routledge.

Tunstall, Jeremy & Palmer, Michael. (1991) *Media Moguls*. London: Routledge.

Van Ginneken, Jaap. (1998) *Understanding Global News*. London; Sage.

Van Dijk, Teun. (1998) *Ideology: A Multidisciplinary Approach*. London: Sage.

Von Feilitzen, Celia & Carlson, Ulla. (1999) (eds) *Children and Media: Image, Education, Participation*. Goteborg: Nordicom/UNESCO.

Von Feilitzen, Celia & Carlson, Ulla. (2000) (eds) *Children in the New Media Environment: Games, Pornography, Perception*. Goteborg: Nordicom/ UNESCO.

Winston, Brian. (1998) *Media Technology and Society: A History from the Telegraph to the Internet*. London: Routledge.

Wong, L.K. (1996) "Tobacco Advertising and Children: Limits to First Amendment Protection." *Journal of Business Ethics* 15 (2): 1051-1064.

LIST OF ABBREVIATIONS

AIB	Allied Irish Banks
AOL	America On Line
BCI	Broadcasting Commission of Ireland
CBC	Canadian Broadcasting Corporation
CIE	Coras Iompair Eireann
CRTC	Canadian Radio and Television Commission
EBU	European Broadcasting Union
EU	European Commission
FCC	Federal Communications Commission
FMI	Film Makers Ireland
FOI	Freedom of Information
GATT	General Agreement on Tariffs and Trade
IAPI	Institute of Advertising Practitioners of Ireland
IBEC	Irish Business and Employers Confederation
IBI	Independent Broadcasters of Ireland
IMF	International Monetary Fund
IPPR	Institute for Public Policy Research
IRTC	Independent Radio and Television Commission
IRA	Irish Republican Army
ITV	Independent Television
IPU	Independent Production Unit
JNLR	Joint National Listenership Research
NAFTA	North American Free Trade Agreement
NUJ	National Union of Journalists
NWICO	New Information and Communication Order
NZOA	New Zealand On Air
ODTR	Office of the Director of Telecommunications Regulation
OECD	Organisation for Economic Co-operation and Development
OSCE	Organisation for Security and Co-operation in Europe
RTE	Radio Telefis Eireann
SKC	Stokes Kennedy Crowley
TnaG	Teilifis na Gaeilge
UNESCO	United Nations Education, Scientific and Cultural Organisation
UTV	Ulster Television
VLV	Voice of the Listener and Viewer
WIPO	World Intellectual Property Organisation

INDEX